STRATEGIC INTELLIGENCE

STRATEGIC
INTELLIGENCE

2

THE INTELLIGENCE CYCLE: THE FLOW OF SECRET
INFORMATION FROM OVERSEAS TO THE HIGHEST
COUNCILS OF GOVERNMENT

Edited by
Loch K. Johnson

Intelligence and the Quest for Security

PRAEGER SECURITY INTERNATIONAL
Westport, Connecticut • London

Library of Congress Cataloging-in-Publication Data

Strategic intelligence / edited by Loch K. Johnson.
      p. cm.—(Intelligence and the quest for security, ISSN 1932-3492)
  Includes bibliographical references and index.
  ISBN 0-275-98942-9 (set : alk. paper)—ISBN 0-275-98943-7 (vol. 1 : alk. paper)—
ISBN 0-275-98944-5 (vol. 2 : alk. paper)—ISBN 0-275-98945-3 (vol. 3 : alk. paper)—
ISBN 0-275-98946-1 (vol. 4 : alk. paper)—ISBN 0-275-98947-X (vol. 5 : alk. paper)
1. Military intelligence.   2. Intelligence service—Government policy. I. Johnson,
Loch K., 1942–

UB250.S6385 2007
327.12—dc22   2006031165

British Library Cataloguing in Publication Data is available.

Library of Congress Catalog Card Number: 2006031165
ISBN: 0-275-98942-9 (set)
     0-275-98943-7 (vol. 1)
     0-275-98944-5 (vol. 2)
     0-275-98945-3 (vol. 3)
     0-275-98946-1 (vol. 4)
     0-275-98947-X (vol. 5)
ISSN: 1932-3492

First published in 2007

Praeger Security International, 88 Post Road West, Westport, CT 06881
An imprint of Greenwood Publishing Group, Inc.
www.praeger.com

Printed in the Untied States of America

The paper used in this book complies with the
Permanent Paper Standard issued by the National
Information Standards Organization (Z39.48-1984).

10 9 8 7 6 5 4 3 2 1

CONTENTS

PREFACE

THIS FIVE-VOLUME SERIES IN INTELLIGENCE IS SOMETHING of a landmark in the study of intelligence. Thirty years ago, one would have been hard-pressed to find enough good articles on the subject to fill two volumes, let alone five. In those three decades since 1975, however, the study of intelligence has grown considerably. Today there are several solid professional journals in the field, including the premier publications *Intelligence and National Security* (published in the United Kingdom), *International Journal of Intelligence and Counterintelligence* (the United States), and *Studies in Intelligence* (from the Central Intelligence Agency, in both classified and unclassified form). In just the past two years, bulging anthologies on the general topic "strategic intelligence," as well as a "handbook" on intelligence and a collection of chapters within the more specialized niche of "intelligence and ethics" have appeared, along with a tidal wave of books and articles on one aspect or another of this subject (see the bibliographic essay in volume 1).

Except in times of scandal (Watergate in 1973, CIA domestic spying in 1974, the Iran-*contra* affair in 1987), one could find in this earlier era little newspaper coverage of intelligence activities, so tightly held were these operations by the government. Now, fueled by the events of the September 11, 2001, terrorist attacks and the erroneous prediction in 2002 that weapons of mass destruction (WMDs) were being developed and stockpiled by Iraq, hardly a week goes by without reports on intelligence in the *New York Times* and other leading newspapers. These days, the *Atlantic Monthly* and the *New Yorker*, America's top literary magazines, visit the subject with some regularity, too. The latter has hired Seymour M. Hersh, the nation's most well-known investigative reporter with an intelligence beat.

Intelligence studies has come of age.

Certainly the chapters in these volumes display a breadth of inquiry that suggests an admirable vibrancy in this relatively new field of study. Presented here are empirical inquiries, historical treatments, theoretical frameworks, memoirs, case studies, interviews, legal analyses, comparative essays, and ethical assessments. The authors come from the ranks of academe (twenty-five); the intelligence agencies (thirteen); think tanks (seven); Congress, the State Department, and the National Security Council (three); and the legal world (three).[1] Over a quarter of the contributors are from other nations, including Canada, England, Germany, Israel, Scotland, Switzerland, and Wales. The American writers come from every region of the United States. As a collective, the authors represent a wide range of scholarly disciplines, including computer science, history, international affairs, law, sociology, political science, public administration, public policy studies, and strategic studies. Many of the contributors are from the ranks of the top intelligence scholars in the world; a few young ones stand at the gateway to their academic careers.

Notable, too, is the number of women who have entered this field of study. Thirty years ago, it would have been rare to find one or two women writing on this subject. Seven have contributed chapters to these pages, and another two wrote documents that appear in the appendixes. This is still fewer than one would like, especially in light of the major contribution women have made as intelligence officers. One thinks of the heroic efforts of British women in code breaking and in the Special Operations Executive during World War II, and the American women who contributed so much to the analytic efforts of the Office of Strategic Studies (OSS) during that same war. At least, though, the number attracted to the scholar study of intelligence appears to be rapidly expanding.

The end result of this mix is a landscape illuminated by a variety of methods and appreciations—a rich research trove that examines all the key aspects of intelligence. In addition, each of the volumes contains backup materials in the appendixes. These documents provide the reader with access to significant primary and secondary sources referred to in the chapters.

The volumes are organized according to the major topics of studies in the field. The first volume, titled *Understanding the Hidden Side of Government*, introduces the reader to methods commonly used in the study of intelligence. It imparts, as well, a sense of the "state of the discipline," beginning with a bibliographic essay (by the editor) and continuing with an examination of specific approaches scholars have adopted in their inquiries into this especially difficult discipline, where doors are often shut against outsiders.

In the bibliographic essay that opens the volume, I argue that the literature on intelligence has mushroomed over the past thirty years. Some of this literature is unreliable, but much of it is of high quality. Amy B. Zegart follows my chapter with an important caveat: the literature may be more voluminous these days, but intelligence studies as an academic field has yet to be accepted as a vital part of national security scholarship. The mainstream journals of history, international affairs, and political science have still regarded the study of intelligence as a marginal pursuit. In this regard, Zegart points out, there is a major disconnect between academic scholarship and those who make decisions in Washington, London, and other capitals around the world.

Following this introduction, Len Scott and Timothy Gibbs look at methods that have been used to study intelligence in the United Kingdom; Stuart Farson and Reg Whitaker in Canada; and Michael Warner in the United States. The volume then turns to a more specific inquiry into the central question of how intelligence is interpreted by professionals—the issue of analysis—explored by John Hollister Hedley. An overview of the sometimes turbulent relationship between intelligence officers and the policy makers they serve is explored by James J. Wirtz; and British scholar Peter Gill recalls the failures associated with the 9/11 attacks and the poor judgments about Iraqi WMDs, in hopes of extracting lessons from these intelligence disasters. In the next chapter, the youngest scholar represented in this collection, Harold M. Greenberg, takes us back in time with a remembrance of the legendary CIA officer and Yale history professor Sherman Kent, often known as the dean of CIA analysts. Kristin Lord rounds out the first volume with a look forward into future prospects for a more transparent world—the ultimate goal of intelligence.

As with each of the books, Volume 1 has a set of appendixes designed to supplement the original chapters with supportive materials from government documents and other sources. Appendix A contains the relevant intelligence excerpts from the National Security Act of 1947—the founding charter for the modern American intelligence establishment. Appendix B provides a history of U.S. intelligence since 1947, prepared for the Aspin-Brown Commission in 1995–96 by staff member Phyllis Provost McNeil. These two documents present a contextual backdrop for the Volume 1 chapters. Appendix C provides "wiring diagrams" of the intelligence community, that is, organizational blueprints for the sixteen agencies and related entities. One chart displays the community as it is today, and another displays how it looked in 1985. As the contrast between the two illustrates, the events of September 11, 2001, have led to a larger and more complex intelligence apparatus in the United States. Appendix D shows a photograph of the CIA Headquarters Building, as an example of what one of the secret agencies actually looks like from an aerial perspective. The white dome in the foreground is an assembly hall seating around 600 people and to its left is the main entrance to the original CIA headquarters, built during the Eisenhower years. Behind this older wing is the new green-glass structure erected during the Reagan administration, often known as the Casey addition because William J. Casey was the Director of Central Intelligence (DCI) at the time of its construction during the 1980s.

Appendix E lists the top leadership in the America's intelligence community: the DCIs from 1947–2005 and today's DNI. Included here as well are the leaders in Congress who have been responsible for intelligence accountability in the past, along with the current members of the two congressional Intelligence

Committees: the Senate Select Committee on Intelligence (SSCI, or "sissy" in the unflattering and sometimes true homophone of Capitol Hill vernacular) and the House Permanent Select Committee on Intelligence (HPSCI or "hipsee"). Appendix F presents a 1955 statement from historian and CIA analyst Sherman Kent about the need for a more robust intelligence literature. He would probably be amazed by how much is being written on this subject now. Appendix G offers an overview on the purpose and challenges of intelligence, drawn from the introductory chapters of the Aspin-Brown Commission Report. Finally, Appendix H provides an opening glimpse into the subject of counterintelligence, a world of counterspies and betrayal taken up more fully in Volume 4.

With the second volume, titled *The Intelligence Cycle: The Flow of Secret Information From Overseas to the Highest Councils of Government*, the focus shifts from a broad overview of intelligence to a more detailed examination of its core mission: the collection, analysis, and dissemination of information from around the world. The National Security Act of 1947, which created America's modern intelligence establishment, made it clear that the collection, analysis, and dissemination of information would be the primary duty of the intelligence agencies. As Allen Dulles—the most famous DCI (America's top intelligence official, until this title changed to director of National Intelligence or DNI in 2005)—put it, the intelligence agencies were expected "to weigh facts, and to draw conclusions from those facts, without having either the facts or the conclusions warped by the inevitable and even proper prejudices of the men whose duty it is to determine policy."[2] The collection and interpretation of information, through espionage and from the public record, would be the primary responsibility of America's secret agencies.

At the heart of this mission lies the so-called intelligence cycle. Professional intelligence officers define the cycle as "the process by which information is acquired, converted into intelligence, and made available to policymakers."[3] The cycle has five phases: planning and direction, collection, processing, production and analysis, and dissemination (see Appendix A in Volume 2 for a depiction). As former CIA officer Arthur S. Hulnick notes, however, in the opening chapter, the idea of a "cycle" fails to capture the complexity of how intelligence is collected, assessed, and distributed by intelligence officers.

The next five chapters in Volume 2 take us into the world of the "ints," that is, the specialized "intelligences" (methods) used by intelligence officers to collect information. Patrick Radden Keefe and Matthew M. Aid probe the method of signals intelligence or SIGINT, a generic term used to describe the interception and analysis of communications intelligence and other electronic emissions, from wiretapping telephones to studying the particles emitted by missiles in test flights. Both authors are sensitive to the possible abuse of these techniques, which can be and have been used to spy on Americans without a proper judicial warrant. Jeffrey T. Richelson explores the IMINT domain, that is, imagery intelligence or, in simple terms, photographs taken by surveillance satellites and reconnaissance airplanes (piloted and unpiloted). Telephone conversations can be revealing, but in the old saying, a picture can be worth a thousand words. (Appendix B provides photographic examples of these spy platforms, and Appendix C offers illustrations of the IMINT data they can collect.)

Important, too, is information that can be acquired by human agents ("assets") guided by case officers inside the CIA or the Defense Department, the topic of human intelligence or HUMINT, examined by Frederick P. Hitz. Not all the information needed by policy makers is acquired through SIGINT, IMINT, or HUMINT; indeed, the overwhelming majority—upward of 95 percent—is already in the public domain. This open-source intelligence (OSINT) must be sorted through, organized, and integrated with the secretly gained information. Robert David Steele's chapter looks at OSINT and its ties to the other ints.

In the next chapter, Daniel S. Gressang IV dissects some of the technological challenges faced by intelligence agencies in sorting through the avalanche of data that pours into their headquarters from various intelligence collectors around the world. Here is the Herculean task of sorting out the wheat from the chaff (or the signal from the noise, in another widely used metaphor) in the search for information that may warn the nation of impending peril. Here is the vital task of providing "indicators and warnings" (I&W) to a nation's leaders.

One of the most difficult relationships in the complex process of collection, analysis, and dissemination of information comes at the intersection between intelligence professionals and policy makers—groups of individuals that often have very different training, aspirations, and cultures. Jack Davis sheds light on this often turbulent relationship in the United States, and Michael Herman tackles the same topic in the United Kingdom. Minh A. Luong offers a case study on economic intelligence that underscores some of the difficulties encountered as information travels from the collectors and analysts (the "producers" of intelligence) to the policy makers (the "consumers"). Finally, Max M. Holland takes a look at how intelligence agencies examine their own mistakes ("postmortems") and attempt to make corrections—and how political consideration enter into the process.

By way of supporting documentation, in addition to the appendixes already mentioned, Appendix D outlines the general types of reports prepared by the producers of intelligence, along with a listing of specific examples. Appendixes E and F provide samples of key intelligence products: National Intelligence Estimates (NIEs)—the most important long-range and in-depth forecasting carried out by the U.S. secret agencies ("research intelligence," in contrast to shorter intelligence reports that tend to focus on near-term events, or "current intelligence"); Special National Intelligence Estimates (SNIEs), which concentrate on a narrow, high-priority information requirement (say, the capabilities of the Chinese military); and the *President's Daily Brief* (PDB), the most exclusive current intelligence report prepared by the intelligence agencies for the consumption of the president and a few other high-ranking officials.

In light of the fact that every study of the 9/11 and Iraqi WMD intelligence failures find fault, in part, with America's capacity for human intelligence—

especially in the Middle East and Southwest Asia—Appendix G presents one of the most searing critiques of this int. The critique, by the House Permanent Select Committee on Intelligence, has become all the more significant because the panel's chairman, Representative Porter Goss (R-FL), soon after the completion of the report rose to the position of the DCI. Last, Appendix H provides an excerpt from a key report on the Iraqi WMD mistakes, prepared by the "Roberts Committee": the Senate Select Committee on Intelligence, led by Pat Roberts (R-KS).

The third volume, titled *Covert Action: Behind the Veils of Secret Foreign Policy*, enters an especially controversial compartment of intelligence: the means by which the United States attempts to not just gather and analyze information about the world—hard enough—but to manipulate global events through secret activities in the advancement of America's best interests. An ambiguous passage of the National Security Act of 1947 charged the National Security Council (NSC), the boss over the sixteen U.S. secret agencies, to "perform such other functions and duties related to intelligence [over and beyond collection-and-analysis] affecting the national security as the National Security Council may from time to time direct."[4] The phrase "other functions and duties" left the door open for launching the CIA (and more recently the Pentagon) on a wide range of covert actions around the world.

Covert action (CA), sometimes referred to as the "quiet option," is based on the supposition that this secret approach to foreign affairs is likely to be less noisy and obtrusive than sending in the Marines. Sometimes professional practitioners also refer to covert action as the "third option," between diplomacy and open warfare. As former Secretary of State and National Security Adviser Henry Kissinger once put it: "We need an intelligence community that, in certain complicated situations, can defend the American national interest in the gray areas where military operations are not suitable and diplomacy cannot opera-tion."[5] Still others prefer the euphemism "special activities" to describe covert action. Whatever the variation in terminology, the goal of covert action remains constant: to influence events overseas secretly and in support of American foreign policy.

Covert action operations are often grouped according to four broad cate-gories: propaganda, political, economic, and paramilitary (PM) activities. An example of a propaganda operation was the CIA's use of Radio Free Europe during the Cold War to transmit anti-communist themes into nations behind the Iron Curtain. A political CA during the Cold War was the CIA's clandestine funneling of funds to the anti-communist Christian Democratic Party in Italy. An economic example: the CIA attempted to destroy electric power stations in Nicaragua during the 1980s, as a means of undermining the Marxist-oriented *Sandinista* regime. PM operations can including everything from assassination plots against foreign heads of state to arming and guiding pro-American insurgent armies in one country or another. Little wonder this has been a controversial subject.

Gregory F. Treverton introduces the reader to covert action in the first chapter of Volume 3. He is followed by Kevin A. O'Brien and Ephraim Kahana, who discuss the use of covert action by other nations. The next four chapters illuminate certain aspects of CA, with James M. Scott and Jerel A. Rosati providing an overview of CA tradecraft (that is, the tools used to implement such operations); Michael A. Turner evaluating the merits of CIA covert propaganda operations; William J. Daugherty looking at political and economic examples of covert action; Jennifer D. Kibbe exploring the entry of the Defense Department into this domain; and former diplomat John D. Stempel contrasting the uses of covert action to diplomatic initiatives. Winding up the volume is Judge James E. Baker's legal analysis of covert action.

Supporting documents include excerpts from the Church Committee Report on the evolution of covert action as carried out by the CIA (Appendix A). The supervision of covert action went from an informal to a highly formal process, as a result of a law known as the Hughes-Ryan Act, passed on December 31, 1974. The language of this statute is presented in Appendix B, and the covert action procedures that resulted from the law are outlined in Appendix C. At the center of the covert action decision process since the Hughes-Ryan Act is the *finding*, a term of art that stems from the passage in the law that requires the president to "find" that a particular covert action proposal is important and has the president's approval. Appendix D contains two findings from the Iran-*contra* era in the mid-1980s. Covert actions must have an organizational apparatus to carry them out, and Appendix E displays what that apparatus looked like during the Cold War (and in basic form remains the organizational chart today, with a few name changes in the boxes).

One of the most controversial forms of covert action has been the assassination of foreign leaders. Appendix F presents a case study from the Church Committee on the CIA assassination plot hatched against the leader of the Republic of Congo, Patrice Lumumba, in 1960. The Committee's exposé of this and other plots led President Gerald R. Ford to sign an executive order prohibiting assassination as an instrument of American foreign policy (see Appendix G). The executive order has been waived in times of authorized warfare against other nations, however, leading to failed attempts to assassinate Saddam Hussein in the first and second Persian Gulf Wars (he was eventually captured alive in 2004, hidden away in a hole near his hometown in Iraq) and Al Qaeda leader Osama bin Laden during the Clinton administration. Considerable ambiguity exists regarding the current status of the executive order and under what conditions it might be waived by administrations. Finally, Appendix H—drawing on a presidential commission study and congressional hearings—examines covert action at its lowest state: the Iran-*contra* affair of the 1980s, when this approach to foreign policy subverted the U.S. Constitution and several laws (including the Hughes-Ryan Act).

A third intelligence mission, after collection-and-analysis and covert action, is counterintelligence (CI) and its associated activity, counterterrorism (CT).

Here is the concentration in Volume 4, titled *Counterintelligence and Counter-terrorism: Defending the Nation Against Hostile Forces.* Like covert action, CI went without specific mention in the National Security Act of 1947. By the early 1950s, however, it had similarly achieved a status of considerable importance as an intelligence mission. CI specialists soon waged nothing less than a secret war against antagonistic intelligence services (especially the Soviet KGB); and, after the Cold War, CT specialists would focus on efforts to block terrorists who targeted the United States and its allies. Explaining why the mission of coun-terintelligence/counterterrorism evolved, a CI expert has pointed out that "in the absence of an effective U.S. counterintelligence program, [adversaries of de-mocracy] function in what is largely a benign environment."[6]

The practice of counterintelligence consists of two matching halves: security and counterespionage. Security is the passive or defensive side of CI, involv-ing such devices as background investigations, fences, sentries, alarms, badges, watchdogs, and polygraphs (lie detection machines). Counterespionage (CE) is the offensive or aggressive side of CI. The most effective CE operation is the infiltration of an American agent or "mole" into the enemy camp, whether a hostile intelligence service or a terrorist cell—a ploy called a penetration. Thus, the practice of security is, according to one of America's top counterintelligence experts, "All that concerns perimeter defense, badges, knowing everything you have to know about your own people," whereas the CE side "involves knowing all about intelligence services—hostile intelligence services: their people, their installations, their methods, and their operations."[7]

Stan A. Taylor and Nigel West clarify these issues in the first two chapters of this volume, then in the next two chapters Katherine A. S. Sibley and Athan Theoharis examine the challenges of keeping the United States spy-free. Rhodri Jeffreys-Jones looks at the efforts in Europe to create a counterintelligence capa-bility similar to that practiced by America's Federal Bureau of Investigation (FBI). Glenn Hastedt takes the reader into the counterterrorism thicket in Wash-ington, DC, explaining how politics influences CI and CT operations. Richard L. Russell and Jennifer Sims discuss the ups and downs of trying to establish an effective counterterrorism response in the United States, complicated by the fragmentation of authority and widely differing cultures among the sixteen U.S. intelligence agencies. Finally, Katharina von Knop looks at the rising role of women in terrorist organizations.

The back-of-the-book documents in Volume 4 begin with a look at the Church Committee findings regarding counterintelligence in 1975 (Appendix A), followed by the notorious Huston Plan—a master counterintelligence spy plan drafted by White House aide Tom Charles Huston in 1970, in response to a nation at unrest over the war in Vietnam (Appendix B). The Huston Plan is a classic illustration of overreaction in a time of domestic strife. In Appendix C, the Senate Select Committee on Intelligence summarizes its findings about the Aldrich H. Ames counterintelligence disaster. Next the appendixes include a series of U.S. commission conclusions about how to improve intelligence in the struggle against global terrorism, whether locating and penetrating their cells in advance of a terrorist attack or thwarting the ability of terrorists to acquire WMDs. The panel reports include: the Hart-Rudman Commission of 2001 (Appendix D); the 9/11 or Kean Commission of 2004 (Appendix E); and the Silberman-Robb Commission of 2005 (Appendix F). For purposes of comparison, the final appendix (G) examines the conclusions reached by a British commission that also probed the Iraqi WMD failure: the Butler Report of 2004.

The fifth volume in the series, titled *Intelligence and Accountability: Safeguards Against the Abuse of Secret Power*, stems from a concern that secret power might be misused by those in high office. This danger was underscored in 1975 when Congress found the U.S. intelligence agencies guilty of spying against law-abiding American citizens, and again in 1987 during the Iran-*contra* affair when some elements of the intelligence community violated the public trust by ignoring intelligence laws. The United States has been one of the few nations in the world to conduct an ongoing experiment in bringing democratic accountability to secret government activities. Democracy and spying don't mix well. Secrecy runs counter to democratic openness, while at the same time openness possesses a threat to the success of espionage operations. Democracies need intelligence agencies to acquire information that may protect them, but thoughtful citizens worry about having secret agencies in an open society.

Until 1975, the nation's remedy for the tension between intelligence gathering and democracy was to trust the intelligence agencies and hope for the best. Elected officials treated the secret services as exceptional organizations, immune from the checks and balances envisioned by the framers of the Constitution. Lawmakers were satisfied with this arrangement, because if an operation went awry they could duck responsibility. When James R. Schlesinger, DCI in 1973, attempted to inform John Stennis (D-MS), a key member of the Senate Armed Services Committee, about an approaching operation, the Senator stopped him short: "No, no, my boy, don't tell me. Just go ahead and do it, but I don't want to know."[8]

This attitude on Capitol Hill—overlook rather than oversight—underwent a dramatic turnabout in December 1974, however, when the *New York Times* reported on allegations of CIA spying at home and questionable covert actions in Chile. Congress might have waved aside the revelations about Chile as just another Cold War necessity in the struggle against regimes leaning toward Moscow, but spying on American citizens—voters—was another matter altogether. In January 1975, President Ford created the Commission on CIA Activities Within the United States (the Rockefeller Commission, led by his vice president, Nelson Rockefeller). Later that month the Senate established a select committee to investigate intelligence activities. The committee was headed by Frank Church, D-ID, and became known as the Church Committee (the editor served as Church's assistant). A counterpart House committee, led by Representative Otis Pike (D-NY), began investigations the following month.

These various panels, especially the Church Committee, found many more improprieties than they had expected. Not only had the CIA engaged in domestic spying in violation of its charter, so had the FBI and several military intelligence units. Furthermore, the FBI had carried out secret operations, known collectively as COINTELPRO, against thousands of civil rights activists, members of the Ku Klux Klan, and Vietnam War dissenters. The objective was to make their lives miserable by disrupting their marriages and employment. The Bureau even attempted to blackmail Dr. Martin Luther King Jr. into committing suicide. Church Committee investigators also discovered CIA assassination plots against foreign leaders and efforts to topple President Salvador Allende of Chile, even though he had been democratically elected.

These revelations convinced lawmakers that the time had come to bring accountability into the dark recesses of government. Congress established intelligence oversight committees in both chambers—the Senate in 1976 and the House a year later—and, by 1980, required by law timely reports on all secret intelligence operations. The new Committees pored over intelligence budgets, held regular hearings (mostly in closed session to protect spy sources and methods) and seriously examined the performance of America's intelligence agencies. No other nation has ever so thoroughly applied democratic principles to its secret services, although a number are now beginning to follow the leadership of the United States toward greater intelligence supervision.[9]

Since 1975, this effort has evolved in fits and starts. Sometimes lawmakers have insisted on close accountability, as when they enacted the Intelligence Oversight Act of 1980 with its stringent reporting requirements for covert operations, or when a series of laws in the 1980s sought to end covert actions in Nicaragua. At other times, members of Congress have loosened the reins—for example, repealing in 1985 a prohibition against covert action in Angola. On still other occasions, Congress has concentrated on helping the intelligence agencies improve their security and performance, as with a law in 1982 that prohibited exposing the names of undercover officers. The Iran-*contra* scandal of 1987 was a major setback to this new oversight, as the Reagan administration bypassed most of these rules and statutes in its conduct of a covert war in Nicaragua against the will of Congress. The scandal was an alert to lawmakers. The Intelligence Oversight Act of 1991 further tightened intelligence supervision by clarifying reporting requirements. Lawmakers also set up an Office of Inspector General in the CIA, confirmed by and accountable to Congress.

The pulling and tugging has continued, most recently over whether President George W. Bush violated the Foreign Intelligence Surveillance Act (FISA) of 1978 by conducting warrantless wiretaps as part of the war against terrorism in the aftermath of the 9/11 attacks. The FISA required warrants, but the White House claimed (when the secret operation leaked to the media) the law had become to cumbersome and, besides, the president had inherit authority to conduct the war against terrorism as he saw fit. This debate aside for the moment (several authors address the issue in these volumes), one thing is certain: the intelligence agencies in the United States are now very much a part of the nation's system of checks and balances. Americans want and deserve both civil liberties and a secure defense against threats; so the search continues for an appropriate balance between liberty and security, democracy and effectiveness—precisely the topic of Volume 5.

The set of chapters on intelligence accountability are introduced with a chapter by David M. Barrett, the foremost authority on the history of accountability in the early years of modern U.S. intelligence (1947 to 1963). The chief counsel of the Church Committee, Frederick A. O. Schwarz Jr., then reflects back on the effects of that watershed inquiry. Next, the editor offers a previously unpublished interview with DCI William E. Colby, who stood at the helm of the intelligence community as it weathered the storm of the investigations into domestic spying during 1975. Mark Phythian presents a chapter on the British experience with intelligence accountability; and, comparing British and American oversight, Lawrence J. Lamanna contrasts the responses on both sides of the Atlantic to the faulty Iraqi WMD assessments in 2002.

The next chapter, written by Cynthia M. Nolan, looks at contemporary issues of intelligence oversight in the United States. Hans Born and Ian Leigh follow with a comparative dimension by contrasting intelligence accountability practices in a variety other nations. Finally, A. Denis Clift and Harry Howe Ransom, who have witnessed the unfolding of intelligence accountability over the past four decades, offer their appraisals of where the experiment stands today.

The first supporting document in this volume is a succinct legislative history of intelligence accountability from 1947 to 1993, prepared by the Senate Select Committee on Intelligence (Appendix A). Then come a series of important oversight laws, beginning with FISA in 1978. With this law, members of Congress sought to rein in the open-ended authority of the executive branch to wiretap and otherwise spy on individuals considered risks to the national security—a privilege abused by a number of administrations from the 1930s forward. Henceforth, FISA required a warrant from a special court (the FISA Court, whose members are appointed by the Chief Justice of the Supreme Court) before such intrusive measures could be carried out. This law, a hot topic in 2005–6 when critics charged the second Bush administration with violation of the warrant requirement, can be found in Appendix B.

The Intelligence Oversight Act of 1980 is presented in Appendix C. This is a brief but nonetheless far-reaching law, enacted by Congress as an attempt to become an equal partner with the executive branch when it came to intelligence. The 1991 Intelligence Oversight Act (Appendix D) emerged after the Iran-*contra* scandal and provided a tightening and clarification of the language in its 1980 precursor, especially with respect to the approval and reporting rules for covert action. The political tug-of-war over the drafting of this currently prevailing oversight statute was intense, leading to the first and only presidential veto of an intelligence act. President George H. W. Bush found the proposal's insistence on prior reporting of covert action objectionable in times of emergency. Lawmakers entered into a compromise with the chief executive, settling on a two-day reporting delay in emergencies. The bill passed Congress again, this time without a presidential veto.

In 1995, the House Permanent Select Committee on Intelligence launched an inquiry into a wide assortment of intelligence issues, stimulated initially by counterintelligence concerns (Aldrich Ames's treasonous activities at the CIA had recently been discovered) but turning into an opportunity for a broad review of new challenges that faced the secret agencies now that the Cold War had ended. In Appendix E, an excerpt from the Committee's final report examines the state of intelligence accountability in the mid-1990s. The next document, in Appendix F, carries the examination into the twenty-first century, with the appraisal of the 9/11 Commission on the same subject. The commissioners were unimpressed, referring to intelligence accountability as "dysfunctional."

At the center of any efforts to maintain accountability for the secret agencies lies the question of funding—the mighty power of the pursue, held in the hands of lawmakers. Appendix G draws on the findings of the Aspin-Brown Commission to provide official documentation about how the United States spends money for spying. Finally, in Appendix H, DCI Robert M. Gates (1991–93) offers observations about oversight from the perspective of the intelligence community management team, located at that time on the Seventh Floor of the CIA.

Here, then, is what the reader will find in these five volumes. The editor and the contributors hope the chapters and documents will help educate the public about the importance of intelligence agencies, as well as stimulate scholars around the world to further the blossoming of this vital field of study. I am pleased to acknowledge my gratitude to Praeger's Heather Staines, senior project editor, and Anne Rehill, development editor, each a pleasure to work with and most helpful in their guidance; Julie Maynard at the University of Georgia for her administrative assistance; Lawrence J. Lamanna, my graduate research assistant, for his good counsel and logistical help; Leena S. Johnson for her indispensable encouragement and support; and the contributors to these volumes for their outstanding scholarship and their much appreciated cooperation in keeping the publishing train running on time.

These volumes are enthusiastically dedicated to Harry Howe Ransom, who has done so much in the United States to lead the way toward a serious discipline of intelligence studies.

Loch K. Johnson

NOTES

1. Some of the authors have had multiple careers, so in categorizing them I have counted the place where they have spent most of their professional lives.

2. Quoted by Senator Frank Church (D-ID), in *Congressional Record* (January 27, 1976), p. 1165.

3. *Fact Book on Intelligence* (Washington DC: CIA Office of Public Affairs, April 1983), p. 17.

4. National Security Act of 1947, signed on July 26, 1947 (P.L. 97-222; 50 U.S.C. 403, Sec. 102).

5. Comment, "Evening News," NBC (January 13, 1978).

6. Editor's interview with a FBI counterintelligence specialist, Washington, DC (May 16, 1975).

7. Editor's interview with Raymond Rocca, CIA/CI specialist, Washington, DC (November 23, 1975).

8. Editor's interview with James R. Schlesinger, Washington, DC (June 16, 1994).

9. See Hans Born, Loch K. Johnson, and Ian Leigh, *Who's Watching the Spies? Establishing Intelligence Service Accountability* (Washington, DC: Potomac Books, 2005).

1

WHAT'S WRONG WITH THE INTELLIGENCE CYCLE?

ARTHUR S. HULNICK

NO CONCEPT IS MORE DEEPLY ENSHRINED IN the literature than that of the "intelligence cycle." Readers can see this clearly from the other chapters in this volume. I studied the intelligence cycle as an undergraduate in Sherman Kent's book on strategic intelligence and then later when I attended the U.S. Air Force Intelligence School in 1957.[1] In 1965, in the training courses required by the Central Intelligence Agency (CIA), I studied it yet again. When it came time to start writing about intelligence, a practice I began in my later years in the CIA, I realized that there were serious problems with the intelligence cycle.[2] It is really not a very good description of the ways in which the intelligence process works. Additionally, it ignores two main parts of intelligence work, counterintelligence and covert action. There is an alternative view.

THE FIRST STEP

The intelligence cycle is so nicely described in other chapters that there seems no need to go over it here. So, let us start at the beginning and look at what is wrong. The notion that policy makers, or intelligence consumers, as they are sometimes called, provide guidance to intelligence managers to begin the intelligence process is incorrect. Policy consumers do sometimes indicate their main concerns to intelligence managers, but often they assume that the intelligence system will alert them to problems, or provide judgments about the future. Consumers will sometimes tell intelligence managers what they are worried about, or the direction in which they intend to take policy—but not always.

Still, it is usually not too difficult for intelligence managers to learn what policy makers are up to, but the managers often have to take the initiative to obtain the information. If intelligence managers at various levels are in touch with their policy counterparts, this sharing of information may work quite well. Over the years, intelligence managers have tried to systematize this process by asking policy officials to provide specifics on their concerns. In the Carter administration, for example, a system of National Intelligence Topics (NITs) was created as a way of soliciting guidance for intelligence. Later, they were called Key Intelligence Questions (KIQs). In some cases, when policy consumers failed to submit NITs or KIQs, managers had to resort to sending policy officials a list of topics, asking them to cross out the ones they thought were not necessary, or adding those they wanted to add to the list. Even then, the lists were sometimes ignored.

In the end, intelligence managers have to make decisions about the subjects that ought to be covered. Often, this is driven by world events. But, none of this provides guidance for intelligence collection. The guidance comes from within the system. Secretary of Defense Donald Rumsfeld, in the George W. Bush administration, is reported to have once said that "we don't know what we don't know," but that is usually not the case. Intelligence managers often know what gaps exist in the intelligence data base, derived from intelligence collectors, and analysts. Filling the gaps is what drives the intelligence collection process, not guidance from policy makers. Thus, the first step in the intelligence cycle is incorrect in reality.

THE SECOND STEP

The second step is equally incorrect. Collection managers cannot wait for guidance in regard to gaps in the intelligence data base to begin the collection process. The gaps will be filled once the collection process is under way. For example, in running espionage operations, commonly called HUMINT (for human intelligence), it may take months or years to find a person who has access to the information needed and is willing to be recruited as a spy. The same may be true for technical collection sensors. Satellites in space, which make up many of the sensor platforms, are not nearly as flexible as managers would wish. Thus, anticipating the intended targets cannot be overlooked. For example, during the British confrontation with Argentina over the Falkland Islands, the United States could not help the British with space imagery because the satellite, programmed to observe the Soviet Union at that time, only passed over the Falklands at night.

Of course, with the use of unmanned aerial vehicles, imagery collection has become more easily refocused on targets of opportunity, but the unmanned aircraft may still not be in the right place when they are needed. Even open source intelligence (OSINT), which has been given new life in recent years because of the proliferation of information on the Internet, requires planning to ensure access to needed material. Intelligence managers need sophisticated software to mine the data because there is so much of it.

THE REAL DRIVERS

For all these reasons, intelligence managers, and not policy officials, are the real drivers of the intelligence collection process. Clearly, intelligence moves from collection to analysis, as the intelligence cycle holds, but analysts do not always need new intelligence material to understand world events. The data base is already so large that a competent analyst could write about most events without any more than open sources to spur the process. The incremental addition of new intelligence from human sources or technical sensors may modify the analytic process but rarely drives it.

The job of the analyst is, in part, to evaluate raw material and put it in perspective. The analyst receives intelligence material from a variety of sources, including media reports, official reports from other government agencies, as well as reports from the intelligence collection process. In my experience as a practicing analyst in the military and in the CIA, raw reports from human sources or technical sensors are sometimes fragmentary, biased, contradictory, or just plain wrong. In order to analyze the data, the analyst compares the new material with the existing data base and previous analysis. Hanging a finished product—whether it is current reporting or a longer range estimate—on one source usually does not work well. This is apparently what happened in the case of the estimate on weapons of mass destruction (WMD) in Iraq that helped trigger the invasion of that country. The estimate was based, in part, on the reporting of one rather poor and unreliable source. The estimate turned out to be quite wrong, as we now know.[3]

OPERATING IN PARALLEL

A better way of looking at the relationship of intelligence collection and intelligence analysis is to think of the two processes as operating in parallel rather than sequentially. The two processes are co-equal in terms of utility. It is important to note as well that raw reporting from the collection process, set up into standardized formats, usually goes to policy officials as well as to analysts at about the same time. Though this may not always be true in other intelligence systems, it is certainly true in the United States. Whereas senior policy officials may not see a great deal of the raw reporting, there are usually watch centers at the various policy agencies that screen the raw reporting and send forward the most interesting ones.

Unfortunately, as I have already noted, some of this raw intelligence may be incomplete, contradictory, or just wrong. Policy officials sometimes take the reporting as having been judged and evaluated. Thus, I have heard officials say that the CIA has reported an event, when in fact what the officials have seen is an unevaluated agent report passed along to them by their watch centers. It is not possible to stop this flow of raw reporting. As Bob Gates, the former Director of the CIA once noted to me, once the spigot is opened, it is not possible to close it, even though allowing consumers to have raw reporting at about the same time as the analysts receive them creates some serious problems for the analysts. Collection managers often take a different view. They believe they are doing a great service to the policy community by providing this raw reporting. If the intelligence cycle really worked, the circulation of raw reports to policy officials would not happen.

A MAJOR PROBLEM

Since intelligence collection and intelligence analysis operate in parallel and should be co-equal, one would expect that there would be a great deal of information sharing between the two. Regrettably, this is not always the case. Because of restrictions of information sharing, psychological barriers, fears of compromising sources, and security concerns, the intelligence collection process and the intelligence analytic process not only operate in parallel, they are sometimes quite independent of each other. This is a major problem.

When I first joined the CIA, I was assigned on a temporary basis to an office in the Directorate of Plans (DDP), later renamed the Directorate of Operations (DO), and in 2005, renamed yet again as the National Clandestine Service (NCS). My job was to deal with incoming reports from the field. When an interesting report came in one day, I asked my boss if we should alert the relevant analyst about it. He rejected the idea, saying that our job was to send reports like it to the White House, and not to the Directorate of Intelligence, since analysts were not worth the attention. I was shocked. Later, when I became an analyst, I did my best to establish good relations with my operational colleagues, but there were issues.

BARRIERS TO COMMUNICATION

In those days there were physical barriers, manned by armed guards, to prevent analysts and operations officers from visiting each other's offices. Later, the physical barriers were removed, but the psychological ones remained. Operations people feared that somehow analysts would mishandle reports from the field and reveal the identity of clandestine sources. Analysts mistrusted operations officers because they were thought to be devious and untrustworthy. This mistrust was kindled in part because analysts in those days tended to be introverts who found the extroverted personality of the typical operations officers to be abrasive. Operations people tended to think that the introverted analysts were "wimps."

Over the years these stereotypes have largely been overcome, but recent efforts to increase communication between analysts and operators by colocating them have not always been successful. Agency managers have pushed analysts to take tours overseas with field stations, but it is more difficult for an operations officer to serve a tour as an analyst. Similar issues may not arise in other intelligence agencies unless they have co-equal collection and analysis components.

The Defense Intelligence Agency (DIA), for example, was immune to this sort of "stovepipe" problem because it was mostly an analytic rather than collection agency. As Defense HUMINT grows, perhaps the same problem will arise. The National Security Agency (NSA) and the National Geo-Spatial Intelligence Agencies (NGIA) are devoted mostly to collection, but they tend to be tightly compartmentalized, creating a different kind of "stovepipe" problem. In theory, all the intelligence agencies should share raw data and coordinate analysis, but for a variety of reasons they do not always do so. This was one of the main critiques of both the 9/11 Commission and the commission investigating the intelligence failure surrounding the estimate on WMD.

A MIXED BAG

There is a tendency among intelligence agencies to hold back the most sensitive and exciting reports until the agency's leaders have been able to deliver the reports to senior policy officials, thus highlighting the skill and cleverness of their people and "scoring points" with the officials. One effort to spur interagency communications has been the establishment of centers, where all the agencies have representation and where their representatives can easily talk with their counterparts, even informally, to discuss events and incoming intelligence. The establishment of these centers has been something of a mixed bag. We know from the 9/11 investigations that the then-existing counterterrorism center (CTC) was not a place where all information was shared.[4]

Now, efforts at intelligence reform have "morphed" the CTC into a National Counterterrorism Center (NCTC), controlled by the new Director of National Intelligence (DNI). Will that spur the agencies into more easily sharing their best and most sensitive data? It would be nice to think so, but experience shows that this does not always happen, even at the highest level.

THE FINAL STAGES

In the final stages of the intelligence cycle finished intelligence, broken down into a variety of products, emerges from the analytic process. It is supposed to be delivered to policy officials—the literature refers to this delivery as dissemination—and then policy officials either make decisions or create further requirements and the cycle starts over again. This, too, is a distortion of what really happens. Much of this depends on the kind of intelligence product that is being delivered. These products include warning intelligence, in which consumers are alerted to "breaking news," current intelligence to update consumers on world events on which they already have some knowledge, in-depth studies on particular situations or issues, and forecasts of the future, the estimate. All products are received and used in a different way, but none of them really drive the policy process.

Warning intelligence is supposed to alert policy officials to breaking world situations, especially those for which they may have to take action. Both intelligence managers and policy consumers hate surprise. It is embarrassing for intelligence when the system misses an event about which it should have had information. For example, the CIA failed to detect the fact that the Indian government planned to conduct a nuclear test in 1998. Later investigations revealed that this was both a collection and an analysis failure. The CIA had no assets it could tap in India at that time, and the Indian analyst at the CIA had somehow missed the fact that the Indian prime minister had declared his intention to hold the tests. Despite the fact that there was little the U.S. government could do to stop the tests, policy officials were nonetheless outraged at this failure.[5]

Even greater outrage was directed at the entire intelligence community for its failure to detect the 9/11 terrorist attack on the United States. This has been exhaustively examined and has led to the restructuring of the intelligence system. Yet, there is considerable evidence that there was little that might have been done to avert the disaster. But, it illustrates the point that policy officials expect the intelligence system to be all-knowing, all-seeing, and always correct. As Richard Betts pointed out many years ago, intelligence failure is probably inevitable.[6]

Warning of crisis should come early enough so that policy officials can have time to develop some kind of considered response. Unfortunately, the warning may come so late that it is really an alert that the crisis has already begun. Using a system that is composed of warning centers at major military commands, tied in to warning centers at all the intelligence agencies and in policy departments in Washington, and taking advantage of the proliferation of twenty-four-hour TV and Internet outlets, the warning network rarely misses the start of a crisis, and it is then able to reach out to decision makers quite rapidly. When the decision makers ask intelligence officers how they should respond to the crisis, typically intelligence officers decline to provide advice, thus staying clear of the policy process.

THE MOST USEFUL PRODUCT

Current or daily intelligence is the most ubiquitous of all types of intelligence products, delivered at all levels and usually first thing in the morning. It is designed to supplement the media, based on the assumption that policy officials have already gotten their media inputs from newspapers or television news. It is the most popular of all intelligence products because current intelligence is an "easy read," short, and to the point. For those policy officials who only have ten or fifteen minutes a day to absorb intelligence products—and consumer surveys consistently show that this is about all the time policy officials have for such things—current intelligence is rated as the most useful product from the intelligence community. The idea of this product is to summarize events, explain how they fit into some context, and suggest what might happen next. It is a very journalistic methodology.

Unlike warning intelligence that may lead to policy action, as the intelligence cycle suggests, current intelligence hardly ever leads to policy decisions—and it is not meant to do so. Instead, it gives generalists at senior levels a chance to find out about events outside their main areas of responsibility. Specialists often complain that the daily intelligence flow does not provide the level of detail they would need to make policy, but the current intelligence products are not designed for specialists. In fact, it would be quite likely that specialists would have seen a great deal of the raw intelligence data that lay behind the current intelligence product anyway.

During the 9/11 investigation, much was made of the fact that one daily publication, the *President's Daily Brief* (PDB), had on August 6, 2001, reported the possibility that terrorists might use commercial aircraft as cruise missiles to attack commercial or government buildings within the United States.[7] Critics of the president took this to have been a warning the president and his senior staff had missed, but normally the PDB would not have been the kind of intelligence product used for warning. The warning would have been delivered in a much more specific document devoted entirely to the subject. Intelligence managers have never expected the PDB or similar publications to be more than educational in nature. Certainly, these publications do not drive the intelligence process.

IN-DEPTH STUDIES

The same might be said for the myriad in-depth intelligence studies churned out by the analytic components. These studies have proliferated in recent years, although they were rarely attempted at the beginning of the Cold War. These studies are designed to provide in-depth analysis on specific subjects and are meant more for policy officials at working levels rather than senior decision makers, who rarely have the time to read them. These studies help in forcing analysts to come to grips with a specific subject, provide useful information to consumers within the intelligence system, and support policy makers as they design policy initiatives.

The production of these studies grew over the years as a way of giving analysts a vehicle for attacking a problem in more depth than was possible in a daily or weekly publication, and without the fuss and bureaucracy involved in producing the more formal national estimate. Policy officials sometimes request these in-depth studies, along the lines suggested by some versions of the intelligence cycle, but in many cases, the studies are produced because analysts are directed by intelligence managers to write them, or analysts themselves believe they should be written. When Robert M. Gates took over the Directorate of

Intelligence (DI) at the CIA during the early days of the Reagan administration, he decreed that analysts should produce at least two of these in-depth studies every year. Gates was fond of pointing out that the DI produced about 5,000 of these studies one year. It was not clear, however, how many of them were actually read.

In recent years, these studies have been more carefully tailored to the needs of policy officials. The same might be said for the Defense Intelligence Agency products, which are geared to military needs, or those coming from the State Department's intelligence and research unit, which has always focused its analysis on foreign policy issues. The fourth category of product, the estimate, is the one most likely to drive the policy process, at least in theory. But the reality is often different.

THE REALITY OF ESTIMATES

The estimate is a creature of the Cold War, it but has its roots in World War II. It is supposed to be a forecast of the future that decision makers can use to build policy, just as the intelligence cycle proposes. The estimate is supposed to be drawn by analysts from all the producing agencies, coordinated by the analysts among themselves to reach an agreed forecast, with dissenting views included. Then, it is blessed by the agency leaders; is signed off at the top; is sent to the president, the National Security Council, and staffs; and serves as the basis for policy discussions. There are actually cases where this has happened, where decision makers have waited for the intelligence community's views as embodied in the estimate, but these cases are rare.

The reality is that policy officials often know what they want to do even before they receive the estimate and hope that this product will confirm in some way the wisdom of the path they have already chosen. When the estimate conflicts with their views, policy consumers may dismiss it as uninformed, useless, or even obstructionist. When it agrees with what they think they already know, then they may see it as confirming, irrelevant, or again useless. Although one would think that policy makers would want to know when they were heading in the wrong direction, this is not usually the case. Policy consumers do not welcome intelligence that is nonconfirming, perhaps because the large egos that brought them into positions of power do not permit admissions of ignorance.

THE WMD CASE

There is no better example of what can go wrong in the estimates process than the recent experience with the problems related to Iraq and Saddam Hussein's alleged possession of weapons of mass destruction. We now know how the intelligence system politicized the estimate to meet the needs of the George W. Bush administration. The estimate on WMD was flawed from the beginning. It was based on the reporting of only a few unreliable sources. Then, analysts made several faulty assumptions about the weapons Saddam Hussein had had or used before the first Gulf War. Finally, policy officials used the estimate to convince both Americans and other nations that Saddam was about to develop nuclear weapons. All of this was wrong.[8]

According to James Risen, intelligence officials in both the collection and analysis arms of the CIA, as well as those in other agencies, knew the sources were poor and the conclusions wrong, but they could not fight senior managers who wanted to satisfy the political needs of the White House. Even more corrupting, it appears that Secretary of Defense Rumsfeld, fearing that the estimate would not support the already planned invasion of Iraq, sent his own officials, neither of them intelligence officers, to find the "correct" information.[9] All these steps were perversions of the estimates process. One can only hope that such antics will not take place in the future.

For all the reasons cited, it seems clear to me that trying to learn how intelligence works by using the intelligence cycle model will lead to misunderstandings about what really happens in the intelligence world. Collection and analysis are really parallel processes. The key to their effective functioning lies in the extent to which there is good communication between the two processes. There needs to be, as well, good communication between intelligence managers and policy consumers throughout the intelligence process. At the same time, however, intelligence managers must stand up to policy officials when they seek to make the intelligence judgments conform to political needs.

INTELLIGENCE AND POLICY

In the early days of the Cold War, the founders of the CIA debated the extent to which intelligence should be close to policy. Sherman Kent, a Yale professor who went on to establish the national estimates system in the CIA, and one of the early thinkers about the intelligence process, believed as did "Wild Bill" Donovan and others, that if intelligence became enmeshed in the policy process, it would lose its value. Kent argued that the best way to avoid politicization of intelligence was to remain distant and aloof. Later, Roger Hilsman, one of the intelligence chiefs at the State Department, took a different view. Hilsman thought that intelligence had to be close to policy to remain relevant.[10] The experiences of the Bush era suggest that Kent may have been right all along.

Nonetheless, other studies have shown that there must be good communication between policy consumers and intelligence managers if intelligence is to be on target and meet the needs of decision makers. At the same time, intelligence managers have to stand up to efforts by policy officials to skew intelligence judgments when the conclusions are at variance with the political proclivities of partisan officials. No one said this would be easy. It is a constant challenge to provide "truth to power." Intelligence must deliver the unvarnished bottom line. Policy officials can go elsewhere for politicized information if they wish, but at their own peril.

LOOKING AT COUNTERINTELLIGENCE

Leaving aside the collection and analysis processes in intelligence, one cannot understand the entire intelligence system without looking at counterintelligence. Counterintelligence is largely defensive in nature, and it is not part of the traditional intelligence cycle—although some writers have tried to adapt the cycle into a counterintelligence model.[11] In my view, counterintelligence follows an entirely different and unique path, with a model of its own. It is certainly worth studying because counterintelligence is a major function of intelligence, consists of both active and passive components, and has become as controversial as any aspect of the intelligence function in government.

In its earliest forms, counterintelligence usually meant counterespionage, stopping enemy, adversary, or even friendly spies from stealing a country's own secrets. Of course, the target country might very well be carrying out espionage against the enemies, adversaries, or friends at the same time as it tries to defend against similar sorts of spying. Thus, stealing secrets for one's country is good and necessary; having one's secrets stolen is dangerous and despicable. U.S. intelligence officers, for example, are rewarded for their successes in gathering information from their targets, even though some of what they do may be illegal in the countries they target. At the same time, other U.S. intelligence officers are heralded for their ability to root out foreign spies and are castigated when they fail to do so. After all, espionage is illegal in the United States and must be stopped.

MORE DIVERSE

Today, counterintelligence has become much more diverse than just stopping spies. It now means countering terrorism, narcotics flows, global organized crime, and subversion. Whatever the threat, however, the patterns of intelligence activity in fighting all of them are similar. It has nothing to do with the intelligence cycle. Instead, there is a counterintelligence methodology that is unique.

First, in countering national security threats, counterintelligence units must identify and locate the evil-doers. This might be foreign intelligence operatives working for a hostile intelligence service, a terrorist cell, a unit of a crime "army," or a group of narcotics pushers. There are several proven intelligence methods for identifying the "bad guys," including the use of: penetrations, or "moles," to get on the inside of the groups or services; surveillance, either physical or technical; informants; and intelligence derived from captured or detained individuals. All have both positive and negative aspects.

Based on the Cold War experience, we know that it is possible to recruit officials of a foreign intelligence service to turn coat and betray some of the activities of their operatives. There are several known cases where the United States was able to place a mole inside a foreign service, and there were a number of U.S. intelligence officers—such as Aldrich Ames, John Walker, and Robert Hanssen—who gave away U.S. secrets to the Soviets. The FBI seemed quite capable of recruiting penetrations of crime groups such as the Sicilian Mafia. Penetrating a terrorist cell is far more difficult and dangerous. Terrorist cells are usually made up of a handful of people, all of whom may be bonded by family or religious ties. Even if a terrorist cell member wanted to become a "double agent," the first hint of disloyalty to the cell could result in death.

Physical or electronic surveillance is another proven method of identifying counterintelligence targets. Overseas, this kind of surveillance can be mounted against potential targets as a result of decisions by intelligence managers. In the United States, however, the rules are more strict. Counterintelligence officials would, in most circumstances, be required to go through a legal process and obtain a warrant before employing surveillance against a U.S. citizen, a resident alien, or a U.S. person. This issue became frontpage news early in 2006 when the *New York Times* revealed that President George W. Bush had authorized surveillance of communications without warrant, arguing that Congress had given the president the authority to do so.[12] The issue may not be resolved until a court case is brought, or new legislation is passed defining the parameters of surveillance use domestically.

USING INFORMANTS

Informants can be very useful in identifying counterintelligence targets. Informants are not recruited agents, but rather people who see something amiss and report their suspicions to authorities. In hostage situations, informants may be able to point out where unusual activity is taking place. For example, prior to 9/11, flight school managers reported to the Federal Bureau of Investigation (FBI) their concerns about Middle Eastern men seeking flight training only to steer aircraft, rather than learn to take off and land. Unfortunately, FBI senior officials refused to grant field agents permission to interview the informants, claiming that there was no probable cause to do so.[13]

Informants can also cause a lot of wasted effort. During the sniper crisis in Washington, DC, in 2002, in which two men were able to terrorize the area by random attacks on innocent targets, requests for information resulted in more than 100,000 inputs, of which 40,000 were worth investigating.[14] People who have experience in fielding informant reports note that often the reports are used to denounce spouses, parents, or unpleasant neighbors, and provide no useful intelligence. Nonetheless, informants can prove to be helpful in identifying bad guys.

INTELLIGENCE FROM INTERROGATION

After 9/11 a good deal of controversy arose over the use of intelligence gained from the interrogation of detainees, either overseas or here at home. In the wake of 9/11 some men of Middle Eastern Muslim extraction, who were not U.S. citizens, were required to register with the federal government. Some of these people had irregularities in their visas, had overstayed their stay in the United States, or were in the United States illegally. They were detained in somewhat harsh conditions and in some cases, badly mistreated. It did not appear, however, that much effort was made to find out if any of them had ties to terrorism.

At the same time, as the United States geared up to take down the Taliban government in Afghanistan, some Taliban fighters or people associated with Al Qaeda were captured, turned in by informants, or sold to the United States, by Afghan warlords. These people, dubbed "enemy combatants" by the Bush administration, were shipped to the Guantanamo Naval Base in Cuba, where U.S. authorities said U.S. legal rules did not apply to them. These people were interrogated using what some described as harsh methods, or even torture, according to press reports.

After the United States invaded Iraq in 2003, more detainees were captured on the battlefield. These fighters were imprisoned in Iraq at some of Saddam Hussein's former prisons, including the infamous one at Abu Ghraib. It was at this location that the worst abuses took place. Apparently, unschooled, unscreened, untrained guards were turned loose to abuse the prisoners in the mistaken belief that this would "soften them up" for interrogation. All of these situations involving detainees were handled badly.

Long experience has taught that there are effective ways to interrogate prisoners, using methods that do no harm to the subjects while producing useful intelligence. Unfortunately, those lessons were not applied effectively in the post-9/11 situations. The literature on interrogation methods, on training interrogators, on handling subjects should have been readily available to anyone involved in trying to extract intelligence from detainees. Anyone who has been involved in intelligence style interrogations knows that torture is ineffective and counterproductive, as well as abhorrent and illegal. Since those experiences, the rules have been changed to exclude such behavior by U.S. officials.

A good interrogation may yield only bits and pieces of information, but if intelligence collectors are careful, they may be able to piece together a broader picture from a series of subjects. The main aim, of course, is to try to learn something about the cells, or units, that the subjects have come from, especially about their plans for future operations.

STOPPING THE BAD GUYS

After the "bad guys" have been identified, then a decision has to be made about the kinds of operations that will be mounted to stop whatever kind of plan or activity might be under way against U.S. interests. This creates a dilemma. Usually, intelligence officers will press to extend or broaden the collection effort to make sure that all the bad guys have been identified and located. At the same time, law enforcement officials are eager to bring the bad guys to justice. This creates a serious problem, often described as the "cops and spies" dilemma.[15]

The divisions between law enforcement and intelligence in the United States have deep roots. Unlike many other industrialized countries, the United States does not have a domestic intelligence service, such as the MI-5 in Great Britain, or the DST in France. Instead, the United States has relied for many years on the FBI—which is really a law enforcement organization—to gather counterintelligence and then act to bring lawbreakers to justice. In other countries, the domestic intelligence services collect and analyze counterintelligence in parallel with counterpart foreign intelligence organizations, which work beyond the country's borders. When suspected criminal behavior is uncovered, the domestic intelligence services may turn to national police organizations to carry out law enforcement operations against the suspects.

INTELLIGENCE VERSUS LAW ENFORCEMENT

In the United States, however, where no domestic intelligence service has existed, there have been both legal and procedural barriers between the national intelligence services, whose focus has been almost exclusively abroad, and the FBI, which has always had a role in domestic counterintelligence. Traditionally, counterintelligence collected abroad was passed to the FBI, which then determined, usually in consultation with the Justice Department, whether there was probable cause to open a criminal investigation. This would be used to gather evidence that could be brought if a court case arose. This was different from the gathering and analysis of intelligence data, which traditionally was not treated or handled as evidence.

Because of cover considerations and the need to protect the identity of intelligence officers, intelligence managers did not want their people to have to appear in court, and wanted as well to protect the sources and methods used to collect intelligence. The FBI was under no such strictures, but the evidence they gathered had to be backed by appropriate warrants and protected according to legal standards. The Aldrich Ames case is a perfect example of how this system used to work.

A joint CIA and FBI team was able to track down Ames and identify him as a Soviet mole in the CIA. Then, the FBI obtained a warrant under the Foreign Intelligence Surveillance Act (FISA) to be certain that they had the right target.

Once that was done, a second FBI team, with a criminal warrant, took over the investigation and gathered evidence that might be used to prosecute Ames. In the end, Ames agreed to a plea bargain and the case never came to court, but it illustrates how a firewall was in place to separate the counterintelligence investigation from the criminal one.[16]

TAKING DOWN BARRIERS

Since 9/11 some of the barriers between intelligence and law enforcement have been weakened, but the cops and spies dilemma still exists. Under the new rules, the FBI may levy requirements on the U.S. intelligence services to collect information specific to their domestic needs. It is not yet clear if such intelligence would be used as evidence in court cases. More likely, the FBI would ask that intelligence be gathered to support its newly created National Security Branch, which combines the FBI's older counterterrorism and counterintelligence units with its newer intelligence bureau, created after 9/11.

At the same time, the CIA and the FBI have drawn more closely together with a strong push from Congress. FBI agents have been assigned to the CIA for counterintelligence purposes for many years, and more recently, to fight terrorism. CIA officers are reportedly working closely with FBI field offices where antiterrorism task forces have been created. While this may break down traditional barriers between the two agencies, there is still some resentment among CIA officers about the growing role of FBI attachés serving abroad, and FBI concerns about the reluctance of CIA officers to share information.

THE COUNTERINTELLIGENCE MODEL

So, when one looks at the pattern of counterintelligence functions, it does not look at all like the intelligence cycle. Instead, it may be seen as follows:

IDENTIFICATION
PENETRATION
EXPLOITATION
INTERDICTION
CLAIM SUCCESS

In this pattern, exploitation is the process of learning as much as possible about the bad guys before moving against them. Interdiction means either arresting the law breakers or pre-empting their operations. Though political leaders often talk about bringing the enemy to justice, suggesting that they would be arrested and taken to trial, convicted, and punished in the fight against terrorism, pre-emption may be the preferred course of action, especially overseas. In one case, for example, a U.S. *Predator* with a missile on board was reportedly used to strike a terrorist leader in Yemen, killing him and his associates while they were driving in the desert.[17] One might argue that this was punishment before trial, or alternatively, that this was necessary to prevent the terrorist from leading a strike against the United States.

The downside of pre-emption is that sometimes innocent victims are slain along with the intended targets. That was apparently what happened when the Bush administration launched a missile from a drone aircraft against Ayman al-Zawahiri, Osama bin Laden's deputy, early in 2006. The missile killed 17 people, according to press reports, but not the intended target, who later broadcast an attack on Mr. Bush, equating him with Adolf Hitler. Despite the failure to kill Zawahiri, the Bush administration later said that the attack had indeed killed an important terrorist leader and was worth the cost.[18]

EXPLOITATION BEFORE INTERDICTION

In the counterintelligence model, exploitation comes before interdiction, meaning that as much intelligence should be gathered before the case or operation is turned over to law enforcement. Of course, in cases in which there is pressure to stop the enemy or adversary, exploitation may come before the intelligence is fully gathered. For example, in the case of the "Lackawanna Six," exploitation was cut short because of the need for political leaders to show that they were cracking down on terrorism. The Six were Yemeni immigrants living outside Buffalo, New York, who went to Afghanistan before 9/11 in the misguided belief that training with the Talilban fighters was going to be something of a lark.[19]

When they discovered that the Taliban were really training terrorists, the Yemeni immigrants returned to the United States. After 9/11, they turned themselves in to authorities to explain what they had done. They were quickly arrested, and eventually jailed. No one at the time seemed to realize that at least one or two of them might have been sent back to Afghanistan as double agents to penetrate Al Qaeda. Even an effort to learn more about their experiences was cut short by the pressure to achieve quick convictions to show that the government was moving swiftly against terrorism.

CLAIMING SUCCESS

Finally, in the last step of the counterintelligence process, authorities often make public claims of success, a rare step in intelligence work. Normally, intelligence managers try very hard to keep successes secret so that they might be repeated. An oft-quoted CIA saying is, "The secret of our success is the secret of our success."[20] In cases in which intelligence has been gathered successfully, it is critical to protect sources and methods. In counterintelligence, however, the claim of success, made when the case has ended, could be used to convince the public that the government is ever watchful and actually doing something with the billions of dollars spent on intelligence. During his tenure as FBI director, J. Edgar Hoover made a fine art out of going public with counterintelligence success. His senior agents all received training in public relations and the FBI was made to look good, even when serious mistakes had been made.[21]

Whereas intelligence is usually carefully hidden (except for the counterintelligence cases), intelligence failure quickly becomes public. This is a serious problem for intelligence managers. In the early days of the CIA there was no public affairs function even to deal with the public or the media. When Admiral Turner became director, however, he instituted a Public Affairs Office, much to the chagrin of many old-timers. Since then, the CIA has had to wrestle with the appropriate response when media queries arise. This is especially true when a spy case, such as the capture of Aldrich Ames, becomes public knowledge, or when a covert action surfaces.

More forthcoming CIA directors, such as George Tenet, have had the Public Affairs Office respond generously to media questions. Under the successor regime of Porter Goss as CIA director, however, the CIA seemed to return to a more conservative approach. In such cases, it would not be uncommon for the media to receive the standard answer to questions about intelligence. This says that the CIA "can neither confirm nor deny allegations of intelligence activity," which is little more forthcoming than "no comment." Nonetheless, enterprising reporters, such as Bill Gertz of the *Washington Times* and James Risen of the *New York Times*, seem to be quite successful in learning about inside stories at the CIA and other intelligence agencies.

DEFENSIVE COUNTER INTELLIGENCE

There are defensive measures in counterintelligence that do not fit into either the traditional intelligence cycle or the model just described. These measures are often lumped together as various aspects of security. They include careful background checks on prospective employees, including the use of polygraph interviews to verify the information candidates submit on their applications, and continuing monitoring of employees throughout their careers. Facilities used for intelligence and other governmental functions are extensively guarded and patrolled, monitored with alarm and surveillance devices, and protected by barrier entry devices to keep out unwanted visitors.

Some facilities have protective systems in roadways and parking areas that can be activated to stop suicidal vehicle bombers. Buildings may be shielded electronically to prevent an adversary's use of listening devices or electronic surveillance to intercept and steal secrets. Most important, employees are trained in security awareness, so that they can report anything that seems to be a threat.

They are taught to protect the secrets with which they have been entrusted, and this responsibility lasts even after they leave their employment.

For example, those of us who were once inside the system and signed secrecy agreements are obligated to submit their published materials, including this chapter, to their agencies for review before they are given to their editors and publishers. This is not censorship, but rather a system to ensure that no secret information is inadvertently released. Some CIA authors have taken advantage of this system to include blacked-out passages in their books, demonstrating that they really were prepared to release sensitive information but were stopped by the review process. This tends to sell more books and can be a clever marketing ploy.

THE COVERT ACTION FUNCTION

The last function of intelligence—and again one not included in the intelligence cycle—is that of covert action, or special operations. This activity is not really intelligence in its traditional role of gathering and analyzing information, but rather the use of intelligence resources to carry out the national security policy of the state using surreptitious methods. Intelligence agencies around the globe carry out such operations because they have the necessary secret facilities and personnel. All through the Cold War, it was covert action that drew most of the attention and most of the criticism of American intelligence.

General Jimmy Doolittle, one of the notable heroes of World War II, after taking a hard look at intelligence in the immediate postwar period, concluded that the United States would have to be more clever, more tricky, and more devious than our Communist adversaries if we were to overcome their bid for world domination. He stated that Americans would just have to accept this "repugnant" policy.[22] When the CIA became involved in trying to overthrow governments in Guatemala, Iran, Indonesia, and Cuba, and was severely criticized in some quarters for having done so, it became clear that there were limits to what the American people were prepared to accept.

Much has been written about the nature and limits of covert action, and there seems no need to repeat that here.[23] Though covert action does not fit into the intelligence cycle, there is a pattern to this function worth outlining. This pattern is similar to other aspects of policy development and implementation, except that covert action is supposed to be secret and to disguise the role of the United States.

POLICY FORMULATION

The pattern of policy formulation looks a bit like the intelligence cycle, but in reality it is quite different. In the first step of the policy process policy officials within the national security bureaucracy recognize and identify a problem they must address. Theoretically, the identification of the problem comes from intelligence, but in reality policy officials often see this at about the same time as intelligence officials because both receive the incoming data at about the same time, as explained earlier.

In the next step policy officials begin to seek options for dealing with the problem, assuming some role for the United States is necessary. At this point, one of the options might well be a covert action. We know from long experience with covert action that it only makes sense as an adjunct to policy and should not be the policy itself.[24] Thus, the choice of using covert action remains with decision makers and is not chosen by intelligence. The conventional wisdom in some circles during the Cold War was that intelligence managers decided to mount covert actions independent of policy officials. (This notion that the CIA was a "rogue elephant" running amok was debunked during the famous investigations of intelligence held by Senator Frank Church in the 1970s. Church learned that all CIA covert actions had been directed in some way by the White House and funded in secret by members of Congress.[25])

Finally, decision makers at the top choose the option they desire and direct its implementation. In the case of covert action, this requires that the president issue a written finding that the covert action is needed. Then the appropriate intelligence official must brief the Intelligence Oversight Committees of Congress, in secret, about the policy "on a timely basis." Congress has often pressed presidents to issue the findings before the option is implemented, but presidents have usually chosen to ignore this, claiming that it infringes on their freedom of action.[26]

The pattern looks like this:

> PROBLEM RECOGNITION
> OPTION CREATION
> OPTION SELECTION
> IMPLEMENTATION

Intelligence analysis should feed into the process at all stages, but we know that the options that policy officials choose are driven by many things. Intelligence is not always at the top of the list.

CONSEQUENCES OF COVERT ACTION

Covert action has both short- and long-term consequences. This is true of all kinds of policy choices, but because covert action is kept secret, the normal debate about policy choices takes place among a relatively small group of people. The result is that short-term solutions, which may seem attractive at the time they are chosen, may prove to have unintended consequences in the long run. There are too many examples to cover here, and the literature on covert action is voluminous. It is sufficient to say that U.S. governments rarely think about the long-term consequences of policy choices and, in that regard, covert action is no different from more open kinds of policies.

There is a long tradition in intelligence that intelligence officers do not offer policy recommendations to decision makers. Though this may be true for the delivery of finished intelligence products, it is not so in regard to covert action. As Dr. James Steiner, a former CIA officer, has pointed out, in covert action, especially in the war on terrorism, the attempt to be policy-neutral does not apply.[27] For many years, a senior CIA officer has been assigned to the White House staff to help work out the details of covert action when policy makers decide to have such operations.

This officer's role is to make sure that requested covert actions are feasible and supportable. Thus, the officer is as much a policy maker as an intelligence official.[28]

It is argued elsewhere in this chapter that one way to address the short-term versus the long-term consequences of covert action is to set up a center, much like the other interagency centers in U.S. intelligence. This center, however, should include both intelligence and policy officials. Its goal would be to analyze how a covert action might work and what its impact would be. The intelligence officers assigned to such a center should come from both the analytic and the operational units of the CIA. Traditionally, covert action has been kept compartmentalized within operations units, without the benefit of analytic inputs.

It seems pretty clear that presidents will always want to have the option of using some form of covert action against enemies and adversaries. No presidents in living memory, even those who were suspicious of covert action, have ever said that they would not use it. Therefore, the intelligence agencies that might be involved in such operations—primarily the CIA in the present U.S. intelligence community—must be prepared to be tasked to carry out covert action, and must maintain the capability to do so.

A FLAWED VISION

I suspect that, despite my preaching about alternatives to the traditional intelligence cycle, it will continue to be taught both inside government and elsewhere. Nonetheless, it would be encouraging to think that those so deeply wedded to the flawed concept of the intelligence cycle would, in the course of studying this volume, realize that there is an alternative to the traditional view of how intelligence works. Perhaps they might even consider it for discussion. Yet we know that people tend to look for confirming rather than disconfirming data. They will seek to defend the intelligence cycle, rather than consider the alternatives.

Nonetheless, the intelligence cycle is a flawed vision, and thus poor theory. One need only ask those who have toiled in the fields of intelligence.

NOTES

1. Sherman Kent, *Strategic Intelligence for American World Policy* (Princeton: Princeton University Press, 1966). I studied an earlier version published in 1948.

2. See, for example, Arthur S. Hulnick, "The Intelligence Producer-Policy Consumer Linkage: A Theoretical Approach," *Intelligence and National Security* 1 (May 1986).

3. James Risen, *State of War: The Secret History of the CIA and the Bush Administration* (New York: Free Press, 2006).

4. The 9/11 Commission Report (New York: W.W. Norton, 2003), pp. 339–60.

5. Arthur S. Hulnick, *Fixing the Spy Machine: Preparing American Intelligence for the 21st Century* (Westport, CT: Praeger, 1999), p. 59.

6. Richard K. Betts, "Analysis, War, and Decision: Why Intelligence Failures Are Inevitable," *World Politics* 31 (1978).

7. Arthur S. Hulnick, *Keeping Us Safe: Secret Intelligence and Homeland Security* (Westport, CT: Praeger, 2004), p. 16.

8. Risen, *State of War*.

9. Hulnick, *Keeping Us Safe*, pp. 85–86.

10. Roger Hilsman, *Strategic Intelligence and National Decision* (Glencoe, IL: Free Press, 1956).

11. "CSIS and the Security Intelligence Cycle," available at http://www.csis-scrs .gc.ca (accessed 1 April 2004).

12. Risen, *State of War*, pp. 39–60.

13. 9/11 Report.

14. Arthur S. Hulnick, "Indications and Warning for Homeland Security: Seeking a New Paradigm," *International Journal of Intelligence and CounterIntelligence* 18 (Winter 2005–6).

15. Hulnick, *Keeping Us Safe*, pp. 103–18.

16. See, for example, Pete Earley, *Confessions of a Spy: The Real Story of Aldrich Ames* (New York: G.P. Putnam's Sons, 1997).

17. Hulnick, *Keeping Us Safe*, p. 72.

18. Craig Whitlock and Walter Pincus, "Qaeda Deputy Mocks Bush," *Washington Post*, 31 January 2006.

19. Hulnick, *Keeping Us Safe*, pp. 126–27.

20. Hulnick, *Fixing the Spy Machine*, p. 81.

21. Ronald Kessler, *The Bureau: The Secret History of the FBI* (New York: St. Martin's Press, 2002).

22. Harold M. Greenberg, "The Doolittle Commission of 1954," *Intelligence and National Security* 20 (December 2005), pp. 687–94.

23. See, for example, Abram Shulsky and Gary Schmitt, *Silent Warfare* (Washington, DC: Brassey's, 2002).

24. James E. Steiner, "Restoring the Red Line Between Intelligence and Policy on Covert Action." *International Journal of Intelligence and CounterIntelligence* 19 (Spring, 2006), pp. 156–65.

25. See, for example, Rhodri Jeffreys-Jones, *The CIA and American Democracy*, 3rd ed. (New Haven, CT: Yale University Press, 2003).

26. Christopher Andrew, *For the President's Eyes Only* (New York: Harper Collins, 1995).

27. Steiner, op. cit.

28. Hulnick, *Fixing the Spy Machine*, pp. 82–83.

2

THE CHALLENGE OF
GLOBAL INTELLIGENCE LISTENING

PATRICK RADDEN KEEFE

ON DECEMBER 20, 2005, THE *NEW YORK TIMES* revealed that under a new program initiated after the terrorist attacks of September 11, 2001, America's National Security Agency (NSA) had been conducting warrantless electronic surveillance inside the United States.[1] Though the Foreign Intelligence Surveillance Act (FISA), passed in 1978 in response to widespread abuses by the American intelligence community during the Vietnam years, had established a procedure whereby eavesdroppers must apply to a secret court for a warrant to monitor domestic communications, this new program circumvented that procedure altogether. In fact, the program relied on secret cooperation from major telecommunications companies, which built back doors into the hubs and switches through which phone calls and e-mails are routed, so that the NSA could gain unfiltered access to these communications flows.[2]

The ensuing scandal thrust the NSA into the national spotlight, occasioned a firestorm of public and congressional scrutiny of the very secretive business of signals intelligence, or SIGINT, and marked the first major debate about SIGINT activities since the congressional investigations that led to the passage of the FISA three decades earlier. As it happened, James Risen, the *Times* reporter who broke the story, had learned of the program a year earlier, but under pressure from the White House the newspaper had held off on publishing the piece.[3] That the *Times* should refrain from scrutinizing this most secret field of intelligence gathering was unsurprising; the American media has proved positively allergic to covering the NSA, despite the fact that it is the single largest intelligence agency in the country (and the world), with some 60,000 employees and an estimated budget of $6 billion.[4] Nor should it be surprising that the White House sought to quash the story. A studiously low profile has traditionally been considered a sine qua non of any effective SIGINT operation—because if the enemy knows you are listening in, he will stop talking—and the National Security Agency has excelled throughout its history at making the general public forget that it even exists. ("No Such Agency," the old joke goes.) On those rare occasions when agency heads *have* emerged over the years to make statements in public, they have always intoned the same refrain: we gather foreign intelligence; we do not intercept the communications of Americans citizens. In this respect, the revelations in the *Times* amounted to nothing short of a reversal of everything that the intelligence community had been saying about the National Security Agency for the past thirty years. The episode also highlighted the three critical questions that must be addressed in any examination of this form of intelligence: Why is signals intelligence so secretive? How can SIGINT agencies effectively balance an aggressive pursuit of foreign adversaries with respect for legislative and constitutional constraints, and rigorous protection of personal privacy? And perhaps most important—and least often addressed—how effective *is* SIGINT as an intelligence tool?

SECRECY

During the Cold War, the United States and several of its closest allies developed an extraordinary global infrastructure for listening in. Allied cooperation on code-breaking during World War II was so effective that days after the Japanese surrender in 1945 President Harry Truman signed a top-secret, one-sentence memorandum, "to continue collaboration in the field of communication intelligence between the United States Army and Navy, and the British."[5] Out of that initial suggestion that cooperation on signals intelligence be carried on during peacetime grew a secret document, the UKUSA agreement, which formed the basis for another half century of intimate partnership between the United States, Britain, Canada, Australia, and New Zealand.[6] So longstanding and involved is the relationship established by UKUSA that today the National Security Agency operates and communicates much more closely with its sister eavesdropping agency, Government Communications Headquarters (GCHQ), in the United Kingdom, than it does with America's own CIA.

Throughout the Cold War, the NSA and its partners excelled at monitoring Soviet communications. The Soviets formed a relatively stable and predictable target: their political and military establishments were hierarchically arranged and organizational transition generally unfolded at a glacial pace, so UKUSA analysts had little trouble answering one of the crucial threshold questions in communications intelligence: Whom should we be listening to? Technologically, the actual eavesdropping was fairly easy: communications were bounced off of satellites and relayed between microwave towers. The air was so thick with electromagnetic signals that America's spies could erect aerials at "listening bases" around the planet and obtain a high-fidelity preview of enemy strategies and maneuvers. It was like putting a cup out in the rain. Eventually dozens of these bases sprung up around the world, from Bad Aibling, in Germany, to Pine Gap in the desert of central Australia, to Menwith Hill, one of the largest eavesdropping stations on the planet, which continues to operate amidst the stone walls and pasturing cows of England's North Yorkshire moors. The NSA hired more mathematicians than any other organization on the planet, and its headquarters at Fort Meade, Maryland, housed one of the densest concentrations of computing power in history. Agency scientists prided themselves on being ten years ahead of consumer research and development.[7]

But the keystone on which this global eavesdropping empire was built was secrecy. As far back as the famous decision, by Admiral Sir William Hall, to delay acting on the Zimmermann telegram after British code breakers intercepted it, so as not to reveal Britain's interception capabilities, signals intelligence has been shrouded in secrecy.[8] The contemporary analog to the Zimmermann story involves a satellite phone used by Osama bin Laden during the 1990s, which the NSA was able to listen in on. After a Washington newspaper ran a story in 1998 suggesting that U.S. intelligence could intercept the phone, bin Laden stopped using the phone altogether. Michael Scheuer, who ran the CIA's bin Laden desk during that period, suggests that a direct causal line can be drawn between the publication of that story and the events of September 11.[9]

Cautionary tales of this sort have had a pronounced chilling effect in the willingness of the press—and of Congress—to rigorously examine the activities of America's eavesdropping agency. Though the *Times* was praised for breaking the wiretapping story, it had completely overlooked a major story several years earlier, in which it was revealed that the NSA and GCHQ had collaborated on an operation to monitor delegates to the United Nations Security Council in order to short-circuit any proposals for alternative resolutions that might send weapons inspectors back into Iraq. Despite the fact that the operation in question took place on the east side of Manhattan, the *Times* did not run a single news item on it.[10]

Timidity on the part of the press is in large part explained by the difficulty of securing any confirmation or comment on "sources and methods" from the studiously silent professional tribe of eavesdroppers. For employees at the NSA, an institutional fixation with secrecy represents the defining constraint of a career. After a year-long clearance process, new employees are exposed only to the need-to-know parameters of their own highly compartmentalized professional tasks. It is not unusual for someone working on a team in one room to have no idea whatsoever what precisely people down the hall are up to. An employee handbook describes "the security state of mind," and emphasizes that neighbors, family members, even spouses are not to be trusted with anything but the most generic account ("I work for the government") of what it is an individual does.[11]

At its most effective, the professional obsession with secrecy can transcend not only the ties of family and friendship, but the very instinct for survival. On April 1, 2000, a navy EP-3E reconnaissance plane, stuffed with sensitive listening equipment and two dozen American eavesdroppers, collided with a jet over China. The EP-3E survived the crash intact but began to shake and abruptly dove toward the sea, plummeting 22,000 feet. After several minutes the pilot was able to regain some control and announced that they might be able to engineer a rough landing. As the pilot issued maydays and endeavored to steer the plane toward land, the eavesdroppers did not cry or pray or try to contact loved ones. They opened an air hatch and started madly shoving out stacks of classified documents, technical manuals, and frequency lists. While some crew jettisoned paper, others took an ax and began attacking the banks of sensitive equipment, denting and destroying it, doing anything to keep it from falling into Chinese hands. When the pilot managed to land the plane at Lingshui military airfield on Hainan Island, the dazed crew did not scramble out to the safety of land, but stayed in the plane, hand shredding documents as fast as they could. A Navy report later conceded, "The destruction of classified material was accomplished while the aircrew was probably still in shock from the aircraft collision and the subsequent rapid descent of the aircraft." Yet, remarkably, the report lamented the fact that not enough of the classified material onboard the EP-3E was adequately disposed of before Chinese officials boarded the plane, and called for better emergency destruction procedures in the future.[12]

The crew's disciplined one-track response to a crisis is emblematic of the culture of secrecy the NSA has managed to inculcate over its half-century existence, and it is indisputable that eavesdroppers must maintain a high degree of secrecy if they want to be successful. But there are important respects in which the culture of secrecy has been an impediment to the agency as well. A tendency to distrust not only potential foreign adversaries and the press, but also other elements in the American intelligence community, the academic world, and private-sector research and development organizations, has at times frustrated the NSA's working relationship within the intelligence bureaucracy and shut the agency off from promising recruits and new ideas. As the digital and Internet revolutions swept across the United States and around the world, the NSA had its head in the sand, divorced from the lightning-fast technological advances in Silicon Valley, complacent in its belief that agency scientists still had an edge on consumer research and development. By the time Lieutenant General Michael V. Hayden took over as director in March 1999, the agency looked increasingly like a dinosaur of the analog era.[13]

Hayden would go on to become Deputy Director of National Intelligence in 2005, and from the moment he arrived at NSA he adopted a radical new approach. Early in his tenure he announced "A Hundred Days of Change," aiming to undo the NSA's institutional arrogance and insularity, its attachment to outmoded technologies and procedures, and its refusal to take lessons from the outside world. Hayden talked to reporters and made speeches in public, in which he described the challenges the agency confronted. Some wondered whether this was not part of a considered strategy, in keeping with the fundamental tenets of communications interception, to lull adversaries into a false feeling of security.

But it was hard to argue with the basis of Hayden's assessment. In a 2000 lecture at American University, he pointed out that forty years ago, there were only 5,000 stand-alone computers, no fax machines, and no cell phones.

Today, there are over 180 million computers—most of them networked. There are roughly 14 million fax machines and 40 million cell phones, and those numbers continue to grow. The telecommunications industry is making a $1 trillion investment to encircle the world in millions of miles of high-bandwidth fiber-optic cable. They are aggressively investing in the future. As private enterprise has transitioned from the industrial age to the information age, so must government. So far, the National Security Agency is lagging behind.

Hayden acknowledged that a month earlier a software anomaly had caused the NSA to experience a seventy-two-hour network outage, during which it was unable to process or forward intelligence data, and even to communicate internally.[14]

Hayden envisioned a more open agency that was better able to adapt quickly to technological change. He also seemed to recognize that for an intelligence agency that always runs the risk, merely on the basis of its low profile, technical capabilities, and history of Vietnam-era abuses, of being typecast as an Orwellian menace, a small amount of openness can go a long way. James Bamford, the foremost civilian chronicler of the agency, met with suspicion and resistance while researching his ground-breaking book, *The Puzzle Palace*, in the late seventies and early eighties. But while preparing his follow-up volume, *Body of Secrets*, during Hayden's tenure, he found the agency much more accommodating. Hayden welcomed Bamford to the agency, granting him an extensive one-on-one interview, and arranging for a party on the occasion of the book's publication in 2001, to be thrown at NSA headquarters at Fort Meade.[15]

But the goodwill with which James Bamford thanked Hayden in his acknowledgments for "having the courage to open the agency's door a crack" was short-lived, as it would emerge in 2005 that despite his lip-service to openness and accountability, and the apparent hospitality with which he had welcomed Bamford, Hayden was in fact being less than straightforward. Hayden's decision to open the agency to scrutiny now appears to have been not a genuine commitment to a new culture of openness so much as a calculated and highly effective public relations gambit—an effort to neutralize the opposition. It was an irony, but by no means an accident, that the civilian who was granted the most unfettered access to the highest ranks of the National Security Agency was not in fact the one who broke the story about that agency's controversial warrantless eavesdropping program. And when the story was revealed, Bamford made no secret of his feelings of betrayal.[16] In fact, in a startling reversal, in January 2006, he joined a lawsuit against the Bush administration, alleging that the agency might have eavesdropped on him, and remarking that the secret program represented "a return to the bad old days of the NSA."[17]

In fact there had been signs even before the wiretapping revelations that in the context of the war on terror, the eavesdropping agency was retreating from view once again. Despite its central role in the intelligence community, the agency merited only the briefest of mentions in the final report of the 9/11 Commission.[18] Throughout the debates in the years following the terrorist attacks about the function, dysfunction, and structure of the U.S. intelligence community, and NSA was an elephant in the room—a factor of enormous importance that politicians and pundits studiously avoided. In fact, no outcry or discussion greeted the news in December 2003 that the agency had won the authority to automatically turn down requests by U.S. citizens, pursuant to the Freedom of Information Act, for records on the NSA. The agency argued that this was a "labor saver," because officials were wasting too much time processing various requests for information about NSA's operations, only to reject them all anyway.[19]

PRIVACY

More than other types of spying, SIGINT is unsettling to the general populace and its elected representatives, and gives rise to a range of concerns about the protection of privacy and civil liberties. The veil of secrecy that shrouds this kind of activity from public scrutiny or legislative oversight and the demonstrably intrusive technologies that are now available to the enterprising snoop mean that an agency like the NSA will always have a major challenge when it comes to winning the public's trust. When Henry Lewis Stimson was appointed Secretary of State by President Herbert Hoover in 1929 and learned that American code breakers had been intercepting and reading the communications of British, French, Italian, and Japanese diplomats, he famously declared, "Gentlemen do not read each other's mail." But on the contrary, the history of American SIGINT has involved a tendency not only to monitor diplomats and generals, but the public at large as well.

After the abuses of the 1960s and 1970s, in which the NSA cooperated with private companies to monitor international cables entering and leaving the United States, and intercepted the communications of such civilian antiwar protesters as Jane Fonda and Dr. Benjamin Spock, the Foreign Intelligence Surveillance Act was designed to create a wall between foreign intelligence and domestic law enforcement operations. But having passed this landmark piece of legislation, Congress left the law to do the work on its own, and, discouraged by the NSA's penchant for secrecy and the technical complexity of the activities in question, effectively abdicated its role as an oversight mechanism.

In principle the House and Senate Intelligence Committees are authorized to ensure that the National Security Agency operates effectively and within the letter of the law, but in practice, the members of these committees are not cleared to hear the most secret details of the NSA's most significant operations and they enjoy few prerogatives in determining budgets that the more powerful Armed Services and Appropriations Committees cannot undo. Norman Minetta, who served on the House Intelligence Committee during the Reagan years, famously remarked of the relationship between the committee and the intelligence community, "We are like mushrooms. They keep us in the dark and feed us a lot of manure."[20] More recently, Bob Kerrey, who was the ranking Democrat on the Senate committee in the 1990s, said that many senators only serve on the committee for the travel opportunities.[21]

Though the warrantless eavesdropping program generated a great deal of press and debate, it was hardly the first instance since the 1970s in which the NSA had revealed an institutional tendency to overreach in its duties, play fast-and-loose with legal constraints, and potentially infringe upon the privacy of innocent American citizens. Two years before September 11, then Chair of the House Intelligence Committee Porter Goss asked the NSA's general counsel for the internal legal guidelines that govern when the agency could and could not eavesdrop on the conversations of U.S. citizens. The rationale for Goss's request was straightforward:

> If the NSA General Counsel provided too narrow an interpretation of the agency's authorities, it could hamper the collection of significant national security and intelligence information. If, on the other hand, in its effort to provide timely intelligence to the nation's policy makers, the NSA General Counsel construed the Agency's authorities too permissively, then the privacy interests of the citizens of the United States could be at risk.

The matter was clearly one of line-drawing—precisely the kind of line-drawing between robust intelligence and civil liberties that the committees were created to oversee. The agency stonewalled, however, citing a Procrustean extension of attorney-client privilege, whereby any document that happened to be sitting on the desk of an NSA lawyer did not have to be handed over to Congress.[22]

Shortly after September 11, it became clear that the FISA system, which was widely acknowledged to be a rubber stamp, was nevertheless inviting abuse on the part of those seeking surveillance warrants. In May 2002 the famously circumspect secret court established by the FISA to review applications for wiretapping warrants, took the unprecedented step of publishing a 7-0 decision. The court, which approved about 10,000 warrant applications between the passage of FISA and September 11, rebuked the Justice Department and the FBI for providing wrong information in 75 post-9/11 applications for search warrants and wiretaps. The FISA judges called for stricter policing of FISA's delineation between domestic law enforcement and foreign intelligence operations to "protect the privacy of Americans in these highly intrusive surveillance searches."[23]

More dramatic, but largely overlooked, was the disclosure in the spring of 2005, during the Senate confirmation hearings on John Bolton's candidacy for the position of U.S. Ambassador to the United Nations, that the NSA was giving policy makers and other intelligence agencies information about U.S. citizens. Even as enshrined in the FISA, the prohibition on domestic spying without a warrant has always been something of a legal fiction: the standard practice is to go ahead and eavesdrop on the conversations of foreigners, even if the party on the other end of the line is an American citizen. Summaries of these conversations are then routinely distributed throughout the relevant government agencies. The privacy of the American citizens involved is putatively preserved by replacing their names with the phrase "U.S. person" in the summary. During the Bolton hearings, however, it emerged that when he was at the State Department, Bolton on several occasions received summaries of intercepts between foreigners and "U.S. persons" and requested that the spy agency tell him who those Americans were. Without asking Bolton to show any cause for his request or going through a review process, the agency complied. Following this revelation, *Newsweek* discovered that from January 2004 to May 2005 the National Security Agency had supplied names of some 10,000 American citizens in this informal fashion to policy makers at many departments, other American intelligence services, and law enforcement agencies.[24] Bolton told Congress that he asked the spy agency for the names in order "to better understand" summaries of intercepted conversations: "It's important to find out who is saying what to whom." Stewart Baker, a former General Counsel at the NSA, has essentially conceded that the requests were vetted with a rubber stamp. "We typically would ask why" disclosure of an identity was necessary, he said, "but we wouldn't try to second-guess" the rationale.[25]

But whereas the Bolton revelations did not strike a powerful cord with the American public or the press, the revelations some six months later that the NSA was engaged in a warrantless surveillance program of American citizens did. In some respects, it would have been naive to believe that the wall erected by the FISA between foreign intelligence and domestic law enforcement had any hope of enduring in a conflict with terrorist cells that are able to strike from within the United States. And in the wake of the initial revelations it emerged that during the years since September 11, the NSA had been in the process of quietly turning its electronic ear, which had traditionally been oriented outside America's borders, inward.

According to reports on the program, the NSA adopted a wholesale approach, tapping directly into commercial communications arteries, and implicating thousands of innocent civilians in the process. Officials familiar with the program describe a broad-based operation, involving data mining, link analysis, and pattern recognition technologies, which seeks not to listen in to everybody all the time, but rather to scan communications traffic and correlate that data with records from public and private databases to answer a more difficult question: Whom should we be listening to? "Metadata" is the technical name for the routing information associated with a communication—the initiator, recipient, time, and duration of a phone call, or the header information on an e-mail. The NSA program scanned the metadata of thousands, and possibly millions, of communications, performing a kind of social network analysis. When asked about the program, President George W. Bush replied, "If Al Qaeda is calling you, we want to know why." But it seems that in addition, we want to know who you are calling, and who those people are calling. Russ Tice, a former NSA employee who worked on highly classified Special Access Programs, says that NSA analysts start with a suspect and "spiderweb" outward, looking at everyone he contacts, and everyone those people contact, until the list includes thousands of names.[26]

Leaving aside for a moment the dubious legality of this technique, it does seem that such a mile-wide-and-inch-deep review of communications might in fact be less unsettling to the average American than some more comprehensive form of surveillance. Having a computer monitor the metadata of one's communications will reveal less private truths than having a human analyst actually listening to or reading one's words. If in fact you are not calling Al Qaeda, you might assume, you should be of no interest to intelligence analysts, and you will be discarded by the computers that sort the wheat from the chaff on the first level of review.

The problem with this reassuring scenario is that it fails to take into account the danger of false positives. Most people are connected by two degrees of separation to thousands of people, and by three degrees to hundreds of thousands. Thus, even a terrorist hiding out in some mid-sized American city, with a bare minimum of social interactions and acquaintances, could be linked, however tangentially or coincidentally, to innocent civilians. In fact, reports indicate that the overwhelming majority of the leads generated by the NSA program have been false positives—innocent civilians implicated in an ever-expanding associational web. When the Federal Bureau of Investigation (FBI) received a fresh batch of tips from the NSA program, agents joked that this meant "more calls to Pizza Hut."[27] The National Counterterrorism Center's database of suspected terrorists contains 325,000 names—a number which, logic would suggest, must include at least tens of thousands of innocent false positives; the Congressional Research Service recently found that the NSA is at risk of being "drowned" in information.[28]

EFFICACY

The British intelligence writer James Rusbridger once remarked, "It is frequently said about advertising that half the money spent is wasted but no one knows which half. Much the same could be said about intelligence." The particular matter of false positives raises a vexing and enduring question: Just how effective is signals intelligence?[29]

One oft-repeated lesson of September 11 was that the United States had relied too heavily during the 1990s on intelligence gathered by remote control—listening bases, satellites, and other gadgets that seemed to take the place of old-fashioned human intelligence assets. In the post–Cold War period, the United States had fewer than 5,000 spies, all told, and over 30,000 eavesdroppers.[30] The colossal intelligence failure that led to the events of September 11 might have presented an opportunity to re-examine that ratio, and perhaps recalibrate priorities and allocations within the intelligence community. Yet as of May 2004, thirty-two months after the attacks, the CIA's Directorate of Operations had about 1,100 case officers posted overseas—fewer than the number of FBI agents assigned to the New York City field office alone.[31] The intelligence community was investing enormous amounts of money in various artificial intelligence computer programs that effectively wrote the human analyst out of the equation, by scanning massive volumes of information for telltale patterns or identities and sounding an alarm when something looked amiss. At precisely the juncture when effective human spies, with a strong grasp of local cultures and languages, should have been coming to the fore once again, the intelligence community seemed more bent than ever on devising technological crystal balls that would produce timely, actionable information at the touch of a button.[32]

It went largely unremarked that the single biggest item in the U.S. intelligence budget for 2005 was an enormously expensive "stealth" reconnaissance satellite, built by Lockheed Martin for the National Reconnaissance Office, and code-named Misty. Despite the fact that the Senate Intelligence Committee vetoed Misty two years in a row, and that one senator who was briefed on its details described it as "unnecessary, ineffective, over-budget, and too expensive," and revealed that several independent reviews found that other programs already in existence or development could produce the same intelligence at far less cost and technological risk, Misty was saved by the Appropriations Committee. Photo reconnaissance satellites were ideal tools for monitoring Cold War targets, but their utility in current conflicts is questionable. Monitoring nuclear powers with eyes in the sky is a gamble, because many foreign adversaries know when America's satellites are overhead, and can time their operations accordingly.[33] There is evidence that terrorists have caught on as well—American forces in Afghanistan recovered Al Qaeda manuals describing the orbits of U.S. satellites.[34] And in any event, overhead assets are better suited to monitoring Soviet tank divisions than a convoy in the desert or an arms deal in a village square. Moreover, Misty's price tag—$9.5 billion, amortized over several years—will inevitably put a dent in the intelligence community's ability to invest in other types of training and assets. Budget allocations are fundamentally a zero-sum game, and a windfall for one agency or program means cutbacks for another. A single human analyst or operative costs the government less than $200,000 a year, including salary, benefits, and the computer on the desk. In the words of one official who objected to Misty, "With the amount of money we're talking about here, you could build a whole new CIA."[35]

The Misty controversy—or rather, the lack thereof—is an object lesson in the misguided and mutually contradictory priorities of the intelligence community in the years since 2001, and an indication of the strange refusal to hold various intelligence programs to a results-based bottom line. In a Spring 2002 article called "Time for a Rethink," the *Economist* posed a pithy hypothetical:

Imagine a huge $30-billion conglomerate. It operates in one of the few businesses that might genuinely be described as cut-throat. Its competitors have changed dramatically, and so have its products and technologies. But its structure is the same as when it was founded, in 1947. Nobody leads this colossus (there is just an honorary chairman) and everyone exploits it. Demoralized and bureaucratic, it has just endured its biggest-ever loss. The response: the firm has been given even more money, and nobody has been sacked.[36]

The scenario captures the peculiar paradox of the intelligence agency. The nature of the job is such that some measure of failure is more or less inevitable. But the human stakes involved are so high that failure cannot properly be penalized. On the contrary, given that it is the appearance of weakness that can really move money in Washington, it is often the case that failure is rewarded. The intelligence historian Rhodri Jeffreys-Jones regards this as a cycle, wherein appropriations-hungry intelligence agencies "con" Congress into throwing more funding their way in times of crisis. "A disaster happens," Jeffreys-Jones writes. "The government sets up a preemptive inquiry to deliberate until the fuss dies down; the confidence men now say the disaster happened because they had too little money to spend on intelligence; the President and Congress authorize more intelligence funds." He points out that the CIA and the NSA were born out of the intelligence failure at Pearl Harbor, and that the NSA's technical shortcomings in the 1990s inspired not punitive cuts, but larger appropriations.[37]

Jeffreys-Jones may overstate the case somewhat, and it may be absurd to adopt the corporate model that underlies the *Economist*'s hypothetical, which would hold that you could penalize an organization for failing. The intelligence community is not a corporation, after all. Any penalties levied against it could be felt by the entire country, if it meant that agencies were less vigilant for any period of time. But especially in areas where expensive new technologies play a role, it does seem that there is a tendency to throw good money after bad: the NSA, with its colossal global eavesdropping infrastructure, failed to hear so much as a whisper in advance of the September 11 attacks. But rather than judge this type of intelligence harshly, the tendency is instead to reinvest, assuming that it could only have been a funding shortage that was to blame for the intelligence failure, and not some flaw in the very model of that intelligence capability itself.

Raw interception power is not the primary problem for signals intelligence agencies. The NSA intercepts some 650 million communications worldwide every day.[38] Every three hours its satellites collect enough information to fill the Library of Congress.[39] Russ Tice, the former NSA employee, says that the domestic wiretapping program could end up netting a number of potential suspects that is "in the millions."[40] The real challenge is making sense of all of that information in a timely manner. In fact, where SIGINT is concerned, a paradox seems to be built into the traditional "intelligence cycle," in which the collection of raw intelligence and the production of actionable intelligence are part of a mutually reinforcing process. In SIGINT, the better one becomes at collection, the more difficult it is to do good production. On September 10, 2001, the NSA intercepted two phone calls between Al Qaeda affiliates in Saudi Arabia and Afghanistan. One said, "The match begins tomorrow," and the other, "Tomorrow is the Zero Hour." But no one translated these two intercepts until September 13.[41] This sort of story suggests that the NSA's ability to gather haystacks is far outpacing its ability to locate needles.

Even assuming that the threshold question about whom precisely SIGINT analysts should be tracking is answered—and that is a significant assumption, in light of the number of false positives reportedly generated by the "terrorist surveillance program"—there is still the matter of translating those intercepted communications. Even as the cryptologists at the NSA devise new means of breaking strong encryption algorithms, a foreign language can prove as strong a defense for adversaries as an actual code. As a result of a shortage of linguists— not just in Arabic, but in Farsi, Pashto, and other languages spoken in countries where Al Qaeda recruits—a considerable backlog of intercepted but untranslated calls has developed. As of the summer of 2005, the FBI's cache of untranslated counterterrorism wiretaps was an astonishing 8,000 hours long.[42]

While there has been some effort to train more linguists, the shortage re- mains severe. In 2002 American colleges granted a mere six undergraduate de- grees in Arabic.[43] Moreover, Arabic of the sort taught in American colleges is rather like Shakespearean English, and would not provide much help in listening to the conversations of people who speak contemporary, regional dialects. The best way to prepare to really comprehend these spoken conversations is to spend time in the countries in question, immersing oneself in the local language and culture. But as it happens, a summer vacation spent in Egypt or Syria represents a serious security liability in the NSA recruitment and clearance process.[44] Thus, ironically, the kind of experience that is a precondition to actual fluency in a target language is also grounds for disqualification by our nation's intelligence agencies.

Reverting again to a preference for the technical over the human, the intelli- gence community has sought to get around this problem by investing in a variety of new technologies that might supplant the human translator, and interpret written and spoken foreign language conversations in real time.[45] But although auto- mated translation may represent a research and development holy grail for intel- ligence agencies, an actual realization of that objective, with accuracy rates that approach reliable, remains a long way off, and many linguists argue that a com- puter will never grasp nuances of tone—such as sarcasm, exaggeration, or humor, much less idiom, metaphor, or allusion—that a well-trained human analyst can.

And this points to an even graver challenge for signals intelligence. Assume for a moment that in addition to resolving the threshold question of whom one should be targeting, we could conjure some magic algorithm that would resolve the translation problem as well. We would be left with a real-time stream of literally translated communications between suspected adversaries. But what good would that do? Assume that the two September 10 phone calls had been translated on September 10, and distributed through various intelligence and defense channels in a timely manner. What kind of actionable intelligence would, "Tomorrow is the Zero Hour," and "The match begins tomorrow" provide? Mike Hayden told Congress that during the three months prior to 9/11 the agency intercepted thirty such messages obliquely promising imminent disaster.[46] In fact, some intelligence officials have suggested that those two calls referred not to the terrorist attacks in New York and Washington at all, but to the assassination of Sheikh Masood, the Northern Alliance leader in Afghanistan, which took place the day before the call.[47]

Even promptly intercepted, interpreted, and reported, language is at best an opaque eyeglass through which to deduce the plans and activities of an adversary. Perhaps the most telling instance of the intelligence community's overestimation of the reliability of language was Secretary of State Colin Powell's presentation before the United Nations Security Council on February 5, 2003, in which he laid out America's case for war with Iraq. During the presentation Powell played three communications intercepts. He sought to demonstrate, among other things, that Saddam Hussein's Iraq was producing nerve agents, and played a conversation that had been intercepted just weeks before, between two commanders in Iraq's Second Republican Guard Corps. In the intercept, one commander tells the other to remove the expression "nerve agents" wherever it comes up in a particular communication. In the months preceding Powell's presentation, Mike Hayden had personally ordered that $300 million to $400 million of the NSA's annual budget be redirected to "Iraq unique" operations and targets, and this was the fruit of those efforts.[48] Powell asserted that the conversation confirmed the administration's "conservative estimate" that Iraq had a stockpile of between one and five hundred tons of chemical-weapons agents. "That is enough agent to fill sixteen thousand battlefield rockets," he said. "Even the low end of one hundred tons of agent would enable Saddam Hussein to cause mass casualties across more than one hundred square miles of territory, an area nearly five times the size of Manhattan."[49]

Yet eight months after Powell's presentation David Kay, the weapons inspector appointed by the administration to run the CIA's Iraq Survey Group, told the congressional intelligence committees that he could produce no evidence of nerve agents. In fact, he went so far as to say that to the best of the group's knowledge, there had been no chemical-weapons program in Iraq since 1991.[50] So what, one wonders, were those two Iraqi officials talking about? We may never know the answer, but the episode should at the very least insert a note of serious caution into any discussion of the promise of eavesdropping as an intelligence tool: even without the very real challenges of identifying targets, surreptitiously collecting their communications, and translating and analyzing those communications in a timely manner, SIGINT will offer no panacea to intelligence officials. In the final analysis, any conversation to which you are not a party will be something of a Rorschach blot: The parties might very well be saying what you think they're saying. But then again, they might not be.

CONCLUSION

Whatever its actual, operational shortcomings, signals intelligence offers, in theory, a kind of strategic omniscience, and as such it is unlikely that there will be any diminution in the resources accorded to it, or the freedom from oversight or bottom-line scrutiny it enjoys. After promising an aggressive investigation after the December 2005 revelations about warrantless eavesdropping, Congress essentially conceded defeat, calling no NSA officials to testify, and failing to take any creative measures, such as subpoenaing the CEO's of the cooperating telecommunications companies, in order to establish even the broadest parameters of the program. Though some had predicted another investigation of intelligence abuses like the congressional hearings of the 1970s, it was soon clear that this was not to be.

The relationship between secrecy, privacy, and efficacy in signals intelligence could not have been more clearly on display: the official secrecy surrounding the NSA's activities was so forbidding that Congress could not assure the American people that the program incorporated satisfactory safeguards for civil liberties and individual privacy, much less that so bold a departure from the established FISA system was at least justifiable on the grounds of its effectiveness in detecting and capturing terrorists. Lost in the Judiciary and Intelligence Committee's meek proceedings was the warning, from President Bush's own "secrecy czar," J. William Leonard, that "secrecy comes at a price—sometimes a deadly price."[51]

Behind the veil of classified Washington it is likely that America's SIGINT apparatus will continue to grow. Jihadist terrorist groups may take the form of decentralized, difficult-to-detect networks, but these networks rely for their survival, and for their operations, on the kinds of connective links that can only be provided by modern communications technologies. Telephone calls, e-mails, and wire transfers are what connect a sleeper cell in one country with logistical masterminds in another, and so it is only natural that U.S. intelligence will endeavor to pursue terrorist adversaries by searching for and, when possible, monitoring these connections.

As the white noise of contemporary networked communications broadens and intensifies, however, it will be a major challenge for America's SIGINT analysts to quickly ferret out communications that are of interest. It seems likely that any effort to address this problem with a purely, or predominantly, technological approach will both undermine individual privacy and prove so plagued by false positives that the results will be dangerously inefficient. But unless some accommodation is made between the NSA and Congress such that rigorous, closed-door scrutiny of the agency's work is possible, a significant danger remains that the formidable resources of America's eavesdropping apparatus will fail to safeguard privacy, while at the same time failing to keep the country safe.

NOTES

1. James Risen and Eric Lichtblau, "Bush Lets U.S. Spy on Callers Without Courts," *New York Times*, December 20, 2005.

2. See James Risen, *State of War: The Secret History of the CIA and the Bush Administration* (New York: Free Press, 2006), pp. 42–60; Scott Shane, "Attention in NSA Debate Turns to Telecom Industry," *New York Times*, February 11, 2006.

3. Gabriel Sherman, "Why Times Ran Wiretapping Story, Defying Bush," *New York Observer*, December 26, 2005.

4. On the number of employees, see James Bamford, *Body of Secrets* (New York: Doubleday, 2001), p. 482. On the annual budget, Bob Woodward, *Plan of Attack* (New York: Simon and Schuster, 2004), p. 213.

5. Bradley F. Smith, *The Ultra-Magic Deals and the Most Secret Special Relationship, 1940–1946* (Navato, CA: Presidio, 1982), p. 212.

6. On the UKUSA arrangement generally, see Jeffrey Richelson and Desmond Ball, *The Ties That Bind*, 2nd ed. (Boston: Unwin & Hyman, 1990).

7. For the definitive history of the agency in these years, see James Bamford, *The Puzzle Palace* (New York: Penguin, 1983).

8. Barbara Tuchmann, *The Zimmermann Telegram* (New York: MacMillan, 1996).

9. The original article containing the information was by Ernest Blazar, "Inside the Ring," *Washington Times,* August 24, 1998. Scheuer made the remarks at the first annual National Intelligence Conference, in Arlington, Virginia, on February 8, 2005. When administration officials cited this story in critiquing the *New York Times* for revealing the domestic wiretapping operation, some press accounts questioned whether in fact that *Washington Times* story was what actually prompted bin Laden to stop using the phone, and argued, in effect, that the story of bin Laden's satellite phone has become a kind of old wives' tale. See Glenn Kessler, "File the bin Laden Phone Leak Under 'Urban Myths,' " *Washington Post*, December 22, 2005.

10. See Patrick Radden Keefe, "The Leak Was Me," *New York Review of Books*, June 10, 2004.

11. See "NSA Security Guidelines Handbook," available at http://www.tscm.com/NSAsecmanual1.html (accessed March 1, 2005).

12. "China 'Likely' Saw U.S. Secrets," Associated Press, September 12, 2003; Bill Gertz, "China Blamed in '01 Air Collision," *Washington Times*, September 13, 2003; "Beijing Gets Voice Data From Plane," *Washington Times*, May 15, 2001.

13. See Seymour Hersh, "The Intelligence Gap," *New Yorker*, 1999.

14. Lieutenant General Michael V. Hayden, USAF, Director, National Security Agency, Address to Kennedy Political Union of American University, February 17, 2000.

15. See James Bamford, *Body of Secrets* (New York: Doubleday, 2001), and "Director of NSA Shifts to New Path," *Baltimore Sun*, August 8, 2004.

16. Scott Shane, "Leader Who Worked to Reshape Agency's Image Is on the Defensive," *New York Times*, January 24, 2006.

17. Eric Lichtblau, "Two Groups Plan Lawsuits Over Federal Eavesdropping," *New York Times*, January 17, 2006.

18. National Commission on Terrorist Attacks Upon the United States, *The 9/11 Report: Final Report of the National Commission on Terrorist Attacks Upon the United States* (New York: Norton, 2004).

19. "NSA Can Summarily Reject Requests for Information," *Baltimore Sun*, December 11, 2003.

20. Loch K. Johnson, *A Season of Inquiry: Congress and Intelligence* (Chicago: Dorsey Press, 1998), p. 263.

21. Author's interview with Senator Bob Kerrey, New School for Social Research, New York, February 3, 2004.

22. Additional views of Chairman Porter Goss, Intelligence Authorization Act for Fiscal Year 2000, 106th Congress, 1st Session, Part 1, Report 106-30, May 7, 1999.

23. *In All Matters Submitted to the Foreign Intelligence Surveillance Court*, United States Foreign Intelligence Surveillance Court, May 17, 2002, available at http://www.fas.org/irp/agency/doj/fisa/fisc051702.html (accessed March 1, 2006).

24. Mark Hosenball, "Spying: Giving Out U.S. Names," *Newsweek*, May 2, 2005.

25. Patrick Radden Keefe, "Big Brother and the Bureaucrats," *New York Times*, Op-Ed Page, August 10, 2005.

26. Brian Ross, "NSA Whistleblower Alleges Illegal Spying," ABC News, January 10, 2006.

27. Barton Gellman, Dafna Linzer, and Carol D. Leonnig, "Surveillance Net Yields Few Suspects," *Washington Post*, February 5, 2005; Lowell Bergman, Eric Lichtblau, Scott Shane, and Don Van Natta Jr., "Spy Agency Data After Sept. 11 Led F.B.I. to Dead Ends," *New York Times*, January 17, 2006. See also Patrick Radden Keefe, "The Kevin Bacon Defense," *New York Times Magazine*, March 12, 2006.

28. Walter Pincus and Dan Eggen, "325,000 Names on Terror List," *Washington Post*, February 15, 2006; "Data Mining and Homeland Security: An Overview," Congressional Research Service Report, January 27, 2006.

29. James Rusbridger, *The Intelligence Game* (New York: New Amsterdam, 1989), p. 1.

30. "Time for a Rethink," *Economist*, April 18, 2002.

31. Douglas Jehl, "Abundance of Caution and Years of Budget Cuts Are Seen to Limit CIA," *New York Times*, May 11, 2004.

32. See "Data Mining and Homeland Security: An Overview," Congressional Research Service Report, January 27, 2006.

33. Patrick Radden Keefe, "I Spy," *WIRED*, February 2006.

34. Eli Lake, "Noise Pollution," *New Republic*, November 4, 2002.

35. Dana Priest, "New Spy Satellite Debated on Hill," *Washington Post*, December 11, 2004.

36. "Time for a Rethink," *Economist*, April 18, 2002.

37. Rhodri Jeffreys-Jones, *Cloak and Dollar* (New Haven, CT: Yale University Press, 2002), p. 9.

38. Michael Hirsh, "Wanted: Competern Big Brothers," Newsweek.com, February 8, 2006.

39. Michael Erard, "Translation in the Age of Terror," *Technology Review*, March 2004.

40. Brian Ross, "NSA Whistleblower Alleges Illegal Spying," ABC News, January 10, 2006.

41. "Al-Qaeda Tied to Intercepted Phone Calls," CNN.com, June 20, 2002; Scott Shane, "Coded Warnings Become Clear Only in Light of Sept. 11 Attacks," *Baltimore Sun*, June 21, 2002.

42. Dan Eggen, "FBI Faulted on Unreviewed Wiretap Recordings," *Washington Post*, July 28, 2005.

43. Joint Inquiry Into Intelligence Community Activities Before and After the Terrorist Attacks of September 11, 2001, *Report of the U.S. Senate Select Committee on Intelligence and U.S. House Permanent Select Committee on Intelligence*, 107th Congress, 2nd Session, December 2002.

44. Patrick Radden Keefe, "Spy World," *Boston Globe*, February 13, 2005.

45. See Chip Walter, "The Translation Challenge," *Technology Review*, June 2003.

46. Statement for the Record by Lieutenant General Michael V. Hayden, USAF, Director, National Security Agency/Chief, Central Security Service, Before the Joint Inquiry of the Senate Select Committee on Intelligence and the House Permanent Select Committee on Intelligence, October 17, 2002.

47. "Terror Intercepts on Eve of Sept. 11 Too Vague—NSA," Reuters, October 17, 2002.

48. Bob Woodward, *Plan of Attack* (New York: Simon and Schuster, 2004), p. 217.

49. Colin Powell, Remarks to the United Nations Security Council, February 5, 2003.

50. See Thomas Powers, "The Vanishing Case for War," *New York Review of Books*, December 4, 2003.

51. Formal Statement, J. William Leonard, Director, Information Security Oversight Office, National Archives and Records Administration, Before the Committee on Government Reform, Subcommittee on National Security, Emerging Threats, and International Relations. U.S. House of Representatives, March 2, 2005.

3

PROMETHEUS EMBATTLED

A Post–9/11 Report Card on the National Security Agency

MATTHEW M. AID

THERE IS NO QUESTION THAT THE NATIONAL SECURITY AGENCY (NSA) is today one of the most important components of the U.S. intelligence community, if not the most important and powerful intelligence agency in the United States. Before September 11, 2001, the 32,000-strong NSA was struggling to reform and modernize itself with mixed success. Today, the Agency's manpower is rapidly climbing toward 40,000 people, and its budget has topped the $4 billion mark. Its power, however, is not derived from its massive size and budget. Rather, it stems from the fact that the Agency produces the majority of the actionable intelligence coming out of the U.S. intelligence community today. Prior to the 9/11 disaster, approximately 60 percent of the intelligence information contained in the Top Secret Codeword *President's Daily Brief* (PDB) sent to the president of the United States every morning was based on signals intelligence (SIGINT) coming out of the NSA. Today, this number is even higher as the NSA's access to global telecommunications has expanded dramatically in the five years since the 9/11 tragedy.[1] The NSA's standing with the White House and the Pentagon has been helped by the fact that the Central Intelligence Agency (CIA), formerly the NSA's chief competitor within the U.S. intelligence community, has been in a state of freefall since 9/11, with senior intelligence officials describing the current state of the Agency as being one of "chaos and disintegration."[2]

The slow but steady rise of the NSA to the top of the U.S. intelligence community can be traced back to the end of World War II in 1945, and the subsequent shift within the U.S. intelligence community to monitoring America's new principal global protagonist, the Soviet Union. Most of the NSA's accomplishments during the forty-year-long Cold War, of which there were many, remain classified, but two decades of research by the author indicates that during the Cold War, the NSA and its foreign SIGINT partners provided more reliable intelligence on the Soviet Union and its allies than the rest of the U.S. intelligence community combined, with perhaps the exception of the spy satellites of the National Reconnaissance Office.[3]

And yet, despite its many accomplishments during the Cold War, it is now clear that the NSA, like the rest of the U.S. intelligence community, lost its way in the decade after the fall of the Berlin Wall and the collapse of the U.S.S.R. in 1991. The ten-year period from 1991 to 2001 inside the NSA was marked by declining fiscal and manpower resources, poor internal management, and a pervasive bureaucratic inertia that effectively stifled demands for change both from within and outside the Agency. Between 1991 and 1996, the NSA lost one-third of its staff, and its budget was slashed by 35 percent from $5.2 billion to less than $3.5 billion.[4] We now know that these cuts, especially the loss of so many of the Agency's most talented managers, had a devastating impact on the NSA's ability to perform its mission. According to a declassified congressional study: "One of the side effects of NSA's downsizing, outsourcing and transformation has been the loss of critical program management expertise, systems engineering, and requirements definition skills."[5] The NSA's Inspector General, Joel F. Brenner, has written that the 1990s for the NSA was "a decade of under-funding and, in the view of some critics, indifferent management" that left the Agency "behind the curve" in terms of staying abreast of the dramatic changes then taking place in the global telecommunications infrastructure."[6] By the end of the 1990s, the Agency found itself swamped by millions of intercepted radio messages, telephone calls, and e-mail messages, as well as millions of terabytes of digital data traffic, such as bank money transfer messages, which NSA overworked analysts just could not keep up with, much less digest.[7] The NSA also failed to adequately address itself to the rapid proliferation of new intelligence targets that it was required to confront in the post–Cold War era, such as international terrorism, narcotics trafficking, global economics and trade issues, and the proliferation of weapons of mass destruction (WMD) technology around the world. This was coupled with the inability on the part of senior Agency officials to come to grips with the dramatically changing nature of the global telecommunications infrastructure. The NSA's intelligence production declined precipitously during the 1990s, and the Agency's customers inside the U.S. government became increasingly unhappy with both the quantity and quality of the NSA's intelligence output. All in all, the NSA was in trouble and desperately needed someone to shake things up and bring much-needed change to an Agency that historically had resisted attempts at reform.[8]

GENERAL HAYDEN'S MODERNIZATION
AND REFORMATION EFFORT

On February 23, 1999, the Pentagon announced that the new Director of the NSA was to be U.S. Air Force Major General Michael V. Hayden, who was finishing a tour of duty in Seoul, South Korea, as the Deputy Chief of Staff of the

United Nations Command and U.S. Forces in Korea. General Hayden, age 52, was a veteran intelligence officer who had previously held a number of high-level intelligence and policy positions, including commanding the Air Intelligence Agency from January 1996 to September 1997. He had also previously served as the Director of Defense Policy and Arms Control in the National Security Council (NSC) from September 1989 to July 1991.[9]

As noted above, General Hayden inherited a deeply troubled organization. James R. Taylor, the Deputy Director for Operations, told Hayden a month after he took office: "We have good people [working] in a flawed system."[10] After considering all of his options, in October 2000 General Hayden publicly unveiled an ambitious plan to completely reform and modernize the Agency.[11]

The price tag for General Hayden's modernization programs was staggering, even by Washington standards. In 2000, NSA planners put a price tag of a whopping $12 billion on the full range of modernization options then being proposed. A review of the program reduced the price tag to $8 billion by the end of 2001, but everyone at the NSA knew that there was no way that Congress would approve this figure, even in the post-9/11 era. By mid-2002 the NSA had reduced the modernization price tag down to approximately $5 billion, with the costs of the program spread out over a ten-year period.[12]

General Hayden moved quickly to implement the outlines of his modernization program. Dramatic changes took place at the NSA before the October 2000 reform plan had to be altered because of the tragic terrorist attacks on New York and Washington on September 11, 2001. General Hayden completely restructured the NSA's senior management staff, fired or transferred a number of senior managers who opposed his reform plans, and cut the number of management committees involved in high-level policy making down to just one. General Hayden brought in a number of senior managers from the business world to help him reshape the Agency's management practices.

In February 2001 there was a dramatic reorganization of the internal operating structure of the NSA, which put "front-end" operations in the hands of just two organizations: the Signals Intelligence Directorate and the Information Assurance Directorate. All other nonoperational supporting functions were transferred to the director's office.[13] Hayden also immediately ordered a reduction in the size of the NSA's bloated workforce. In November 1999, the NSA cut its civilian personnel by 7.5 percent from 18,945 to 16,753 people, and the following year reduced the size of the Agency's military staff by 10 percent. The NSA also deactivated a number of older SIGINT collection sites, consolidated the Agency's plethora of mission support activities, worked more closely with outside commercial companies to develop new equipment and software for use by the NSA, ceased virtually all of its research and development work on obsolete SIGINT collection and processing systems, and overhauled and realigned its strategic funding relationships with its SIGINT partners at home and abroad.[14]

But critics inside and outside the Agency in interviews have described these changes as "superficial" or "window dressing." The critics noted that the reorganization of the NSA's internal structure did not result in greater efficiency or efficaciousness, especially within the Agency's senior management. There are now at the NSA 100 "super-grade" senior civilian managers trying to run an organization the size of an army corps, which the U.S. Army can run with eight to ten generals. The result, critics contend, is that the NSA's management structure remains bloated and top-heavy. More important, perhaps, a number of Agency insiders believe that Hayden's organizational changes did not resolve the central issue of dealing with the NSA's hide-bound bureaucracy. A recently retired NSA official quipped, "He's just shuffled the cards rather than getting a new pack."[15]

There is also considerable evidence that General Hayden failed in his attempt to reform the Agency's faulty fiscal management practices. NSA insiders believe that the approach of the NSA's senior management in the 1999–2001 time period was to get the money from Congress "while the going was good," then build a modernization package around the money they got, rather than the other way around. This inevitably led to serious clashes between the NSA and the congressional oversight committees. In October 2001 the Senate Armed Services Committee indicated that it intended to "put the brakes" on further spending on the NSA's modernization programs until the NSA "adopt[ed] a more comprehensive acquisition strategy." A committee report stated the "NSA appears to have made only modest progress in the area most important to its future: acquiring the technical ability to operate effectively against the emerging global effort." The Senate report also expressed concern that the "NSA is spending large sums of money on hundreds of in-house development activities, yet it cannot say how or whether these aid modernization." The committee concluded that "more money now, without further reform, will not succeed either."[16] Finally, in July 2003, a clearly frustrated Congress stripped the NSA of its ability to sign contracts with outside businesses, and in the process, transferred control of the NSA's hundreds of millions of dollars of modernization contracts to the Department of Defense to administer until the Agency proved that it could manage these programs in a fiscally responsible manner.[17]

The NSA has also experienced considerable difficulty since 2000 in hiring and retaining sufficient numbers of the technologically oriented engineering and computer science personnel that it needs in order to develop, operate, and maintain the new high-tech SIGINT collection and processing systems that are beginning to come online. In particular, the NSA has had significant trouble recruiting personnel with advanced technology degrees to work at Fort Meade, including systems engineers, software engineers, and program managers versed in computer hardware and software issues.[18] A current serving NSA manager stated the problem simply: "We can't afford to pay these kids anywhere near the amount of money they could get in private industry, much less offer them a decent benefits package or the stock options they would normally receive working for any decent high-tech company in California."[19]

Moreover, intelligence production at the NSA remained relatively flat in the two years after General Hayden became director, with the quantity of intelligence reporting actually declining in some key areas as money was diverted to finance research and development work on new high-tech SIGINT collection and processing systems. Available SIGINT collection and analytic resources were gradually shifted away from older "legacy" targets, such as Russia, the former Soviet republics, Cuba, and the Balkans, to new higher priority global intelligence targets, such as international terrorism and nuclear proliferation. General Hayden was forced to admit to a congressional committee looking into the 9/11 intelligence disaster that he felt "handcuffed" in that he was unable to "churn some $200 million into new age signals ... because we were going to erode our coverage of [other intelligence issues] as part of this effort."[20]

More recently, reports have appeared in the press revealing that not everything has gone according to plan with General Hayden's much ballyhooed multiyear, multi-billion-dollar NSA transformation and modernization effort. Two recent articles in the *Baltimore Sun* have revealed that the two key components of the NSA's modernization program, designated Groundbreaker and Trailblazer, as well as many of their supporting systems, are years behind schedule and hundreds of millions of dollars over budget.[21]

Both projects began relatively well. Initiated with much public fanfare in 1999, Project Groundbreaker was a ten-year, $2 billion program to completely rebuild and modernize the NSA's nightmarish internal information technology (IT) infrastructure.[22] One of the many problems the program was supposed to fix was to remedy the fact that the NSA had sixty-eight different e-mail systems, none of which could communicate with each other. This led General Hayden to comment that it took "an act of God" for him to send an e-mail to all of his employees.[23]

But the centerpiece of General Hayden's modernization effort was a massive overhaul of the NSA's deeply troubled SIGINT collection and processing infrastructure. In January 2000 NSA Deputy Director for Operations, Richard Taylor, proposed a massive reorganization of the NSA's huge Operations Directorate that was designed to refocus the organization on its core mission, SIGINT collection, processing, analysis, and reporting. In addition to putting "our customers squarely front and center in our production process," Taylor proposed reorganizing the Operations Directorate into three functional SIGINT organizations: Collection, Exploitation, and Production, as well as the creation of an Advanced Analytic Techniques organization to "develop and spread the art of analysis." Taylor's proposal also called for removing from the directorate all nonmission functions, such as information technology, policy, budget, and logistics, as well as integrating more military support functions into all of the directorate's functional groups.[24]

The result of Taylor's proposal was the initiation of a highly ambitious program called Project Trailblazer. In January 2000 the NSA announced the initiation of the first phase of its SIGINT processing, analysis, and reporting modernization effort, called Project Trailblazer. According to an internal NSA document, the first phase of Trailblazer was supposed to "deliver tomorrow's analytic tools and functions to automate desktop processing and improve COMINT [communications intelligence] production. It will also provide us with the ability to profile customers' needs and requirements, and will modernize the dissemination process."[25] The classified objective of the Trailblazer program was to build an integrated series of state-of-the-art SIGINT collection and processing systems that would give the NSA the ability to eavesdrop on communications traffic being carried by e-mail, fiber-optic cable, and cellular telephone systems around the world.[26]

The core focus of the first phase of Trailblazer was to design and build a system to attack the new global SIGINT target environment, which the NSA designated Digital Network Intelligence (DNI). The NSA defined DNI as "the intelligence from intercepted digital data communications transmitted between, or resident on, networked computers."[27] Trailblazer was to form the foundation for this attack by mapping "detailed Digital Network Exploitation (DNE) mission requirements to our cryptologic architecture and provide implementation focus. . . . Trailblazer 1 will build the SIGINT system we would want to build—if today's system didn't exist—to attack a tough, evolving DNE target." Among the different technologies being developed under Trailblazer were selection and filtering tools for NSA analysts, as well as hardware and software for "improved front-end access, collection, processing, and filtering" using web-based tools and techniques, a process that has become known within the NSA by the moniker "e-SIGINT."[28]

By October 2002, developmental work on the Trailblazer system was sufficiently advanced that the NSA awarded a contractor team headed by San Diego–based Science Applications International Corporation a $282 million contract to build a functional prototype of the system in only twenty-six months. But this was the last the public heard about the system for the next three years, which in retrospect should have been a red flag that things were not progressing as well as they should.[29]

As is usually the case, the warning signs of problems with these two multi-billion-dollar programs were there for all to see. As early as 2000, NSA officials complained both publicly and privately that the Agency's reorganization and modernization plans were developed and constructed within segregated "stove-pipes" rather than in an integrated and cohesive fashion. The Agency also suffered from an all-too-apparent lack of competent program management, which impaired its ability to effectively manage the various multi-billion-dollar modernization programs.[30] This problem was exacerbated by heavy turnover amongst senior management personnel, which resulted in a failure to reform the Agency's much-maligned contracting practices. As a result, today senior Pentagon and congressional officials are currently concerned that these programs, and related modernization efforts at the NSA, have not been well managed and may not yield the desired results when finally completed.[31]

THE NSA IN THE POST–9/11 ERA

Declassified documents, congressional reports, and the published record of the 9/11 Commission all indicate that the NSA did not commit any egregious errors in the days and months leading up to the attacks. A congressional

investigative report concluded: "Prior to 11 September 2001, NSA had no specific information indicating the date, time, place, or participants in an attack on
the United States."[32] There have, however, been recurring indications received
from both retired and current U.S. intelligence officials that substantive problems
with the Agency's performance prior to 9/11 have not yet been completely revealed because it involves highly classified information concerning the NSA's
"sources and methods."[33]

Like the rest of the U.S. intelligence community, the searing events of 9/11
have dramatically changed the NSA, both for better and for worse. The Agency's
budget has been dramatically increased every year since 2001, climbing to about
$5 billion per annum.[34] NSA manpower has also been shooting upwards at a
forty-five-degree angle, with the NSA hiring 3,500 new civilian staff between
2002 and 2004 alone, which raised NSA manpower to about 35,000 military and
civilian personnel. Press reports and interviews indicate the NSA intends to hire
12,000 additional civilian personnel between 2004 and 2011, bringing NSA
manpower up to more than 40,000 military and civilian personnel by the end of
the decade, after retirements and normal personnel attrition are factored in.[35]
Moreover, the size of the entire U.S. Cryptologic System, including SIGINT
personnel assigned to the CIA, the National Reconnaissance Office, and the
military services, has grown to more than 60,000 military and civilian personnel
since 9/11, making it by far the single largest component of the U.S. intelligence
community. The NSA is in the process of opening new operations centers in San
Antonio, Texas, Denver, Colorado, and Salt Lake City, Utah, which when completed will employ several thousand civilian and military staff.[36] In February
2006 Congress passed an emergency supplemental appropriations bill, which
included $35 million to immediately expand the NSA's huge listening post at
Menwith Hill in northern England, as well as another $700 million to construct
new operational facilities at the Agency's large intelligence collection stations at
Kunia, Hawaii, and Fort Gordon, Georgia.[37]

But despite the massive budget increases and unfettered operational discretion granted to the Agency since 9/11, the NSA still is not functioning as
smoothly or efficiently as it should be. Senior U.S. intelligence officials believe
that one of the signature results of the chaos produced by 9/11 is that the NSA, in
its rush to respond to the Al Qaeda terrorist attacks on the United States, literally
threw away its previous management reform plans. Critics of the Agency within
the U.S. intelligence community point to the fact that since 9/11, the size of the
NSA's multilayered bureaucracy has once again begun to mount, with a resulting
decrease in operational efficiency caused by the retrenchment of stifling bureaucratic practices and procedures at the top levels of the Agency's management. The
NSA has also been hurt by the loss of a number of veteran senior officials, who
have either retired or quit the Agency in the past two years to take higher paying
jobs in the business world.[38] The result, according to the officials, is that in the
five years since 9/11 the NSA's relative effectiveness and efficiency have declined noticeably. In fact, interviews with senior intelligence officials suggests

that the NSA's operational performance has declined somewhat in recent years, with officials pointing in particular to the Agency's disappointing performance to date in Afghanistan and Iraq, which is described in greater detail below.[39]

There is also evidence that NSA attempts to balance its spending between maintaining current SIGINT collection operations and at the same time developing new signals collection technologies for the 21st century have not gone well. In some instances since 2001, NSA SIGINT operations have suffered for lack of investment because available fiscal resources were being directed toward research and development on new technologies needed to allow the NSA to intercept and process signals in the new digital environment. But as noted above, the NSA's Groundbreaker and Trailblazer multi-billion-dollar modernization programs have not been effectively managed. Former NSA officials point to the fact that immediately after 9/11 the Agency abandoned a patient, long-term approach to modernization in favor of dubious, short-term "quick-fixes" that have only compounded the host of existing problems with the NSA's various multi-billion-dollar modernization programs.[40] Compounding these internal problems is the massive technological hurdles that the NSA has had to leap through over the past five years trying to develop and build the new high-tech equipment it needs to do its job. Much of the technology that the NSA desperately needs, such as powerful analytic software that is required to help NSA analysts sift through the immense amounts of data being intercepted every day by the Agency's listening posts, just does not exist today on the open market, which has meant that the NSA has had to spend hundreds of millions of dollars developing these systems in-house, and not always successfully.[41]

Moreover, the NSA was forced to make significant changes in its intelligence targeting in order to devote a substantial portion of its intelligence collection resources to the so-called global war on terrorism. This has forced the NSA to give short shrift to many previously important intelligence targets, such as the former Soviet Union, China, North Korea, Bosnia, and the national narcotics interdiction program. The same thing has happened in England. The British Parliament's Intelligence and Security Committee in its June 2003 annual report warned that the shift of precious intelligence collection resources from other targets to counterterrorism was creating a dangerous situation, stating: "These reductions are causing intelligence gaps to develop, which may mean over time unacceptable risks will arise in terms of safeguarding national security and in the prevention and detecting of Serious Organised Crime."[42] Sources note that the NSA's inability to dedicate sufficient resources to monitoring narcotics trafficking in the western hemisphere has forced the Drug Enforcement Administration (DEA)'s small SIGINT organization to largely take over this responsibility.[43] The increasingly important role of the DEA, the CIA, and the military services in the SIGINT field has led, in turn, to the diminishment of NSA control over the national SIGINT effort. The result has been that the NSA has lost somewhat the all-important "centrality of command" that it once enjoyed over the national SIGINT effort.

Interviews with intelligence officials in Washington suggest that the NSA has improved somewhat its customer relations with its consumers in Washington and elsewhere around the globe since 9/11. But apparently not everyone is happy. NSA officials contend that over the past five years its ever-increasing number of customers in Washington have submitted conflicting requirements on the NSA, which has required years of oftentimes contentious negotiations in order to resolve the differing requirements levied on the agency. Interviews with intelligence officials reveal that there are still widespread complaints about the NSA's inability or unwillingness to share information with other government agencies. In particular, FBI officials complain about the lack of cooperation that they have received from the NSA since 9/11. The single largest barrier to the free flow of intelligence information appears to be the compartmentalized nature of the NSA itself, which has prevented an integrated approach to customer relations between the NSA and the rest of the U.S. intelligence community.[44]

THE NEW GLOBAL BATTLEFIELD

The NSA found that its ability to effectively contribute to the global counterterrorism fight and concurrently support U.S. military forces in Afghanistan, which the United States invaded in November 2001, were hampered by the fact that it was not equipped to deal with unconventional intelligence targets operating in the less-developed countries of the world who typically do not use, much less own, computers connected to the Internet, cell phones, personal pagers, and digital assistants, such as the ubiquitous Blackberry, or even an iPod. One recent press report perhaps said it best that SIGINT today "is far less vital against an enemy that sleeps in caves and cellars, and communicates in whispers."[45] Moreover, the NSA's ability to collecting SIGINT in Afghanistan was an extremely difficult proposition given the almost complete lack of linguists at the Agency who could speak the languages spoken in the country.[46] As of fall 2001, the NSA reportedly only had four linguists fluent in the languages spoken in Afghanistan (Pashto, Dari, Uzbek, and Turkmen), including only one who spoke Pashto, the primary language spoken in Pakistan and Afghanistan.[47]

In other words, the Agency's heavy investment in its multi-billion-dollar high-tech modernization efforts of the late 1990s, although badly needed, sadly may have left the NSA prepared to fight the "wrong war" in the 21st century. In fall 2001 chagrined U.S. intelligence officials discovered that the NSA's newly developed high-tech collection systems, which were designed to cover cellular telephones, the Internet, and communications traffic carried on fiber-optic cables, were largely worthless in the low-tech environment of Afghanistan and in northern Pakistan, where the remaining elements of Al Qaeda and their Taliban supporters operated.[48]

The NSA's underwhelming performance on the battlefield led to numerous complaints from the U.S. military services about the Agency's inability to provide adequate tactical SIGINT support to American military commanders in Afghanistan and to Special Operations Forces engaged in trying to hunt down terrorists in Pakistan and elsewhere around the world. Prior to 9/11 the U.S. Army had denuded its tactical SIGINT collection resources to practically nothing in the mistaken belief that such units were no longer needed in the post–Cold War geostrategic environment. The NSA's failure led the military services, especially the U.S. Army, to allocate over the past five years greater resources to building up their own dedicated tactical SIGINT collection resources that are largely independent of the NSA. As a result, U.S. Army SIGINT assets have now replaced the NSA in Afghanistan.

Over the past three years, U.S. military SIGINT assets in Afghanistan have been gradually reconfigured in order to work more efficiently in the extremely difficult Afghan environment, and more mobile and flexible SIGINT collection and processing systems have been added in recent years.[49] On the plus side of the equation, SIGINT has confirmed that former Taliban commanders based in the tribal areas of northern Pakistan have been orchestrating insurgent attacks against U.S. and Afghan forces in southern and southeastern Afghanistan using satellite phones.[50] SIGINT has also been used effectively to counter Taliban rocket and mortar fire against U.S. military bases in southern and southeastern Afghanistan. By intercepting the walkie-talkie communications traffic of insurgent artillery spotters, U.S. forces have on more than one occasion been able to successfully destroy insurgent rocket and mortar pieces inside Afghanistan, and have forced insurgent forces instead to occasionally fire at outlying U.S. outposts and patrols along the Afghan-Pakistani border without the benefit of spotters inside Afghanistan.[51]

But problems continue to abound in the military's SIGINT collection programs in Afghanistan. Inhibiting the effectiveness of SIGINT in Afghanistan is the fact that the insurgent forces based in northern Pakistan have increasingly moved to the use of couriers and other noninterceptible means of communications rather than radio communications.[52] In addition, persistent shortages of trained linguists have severely hampered the effectiveness of SIGINT in Afghanistan. Since 9/11 the U.S. military has trained at great expense a small number of U.S.-born linguists in the Pashto, Dari, and Urdu dialects to process SIGINT intercepts. But reports from the field indicate that the competency levels of these linguists were so low that they only possessed "the ability to tell the difference between a burro and a burrito."[53] This has meant that the U.S. military today still largely relies on contract employees hired by the Department of Defense to provide U.S. intelligence units and combat units with linguistic capabilities in Urdu, Dari, and Pashto. But according to a 2003 U.S. Army report: "This develops into a big problem, because not only do you have to have fluent linguists, but you also have to obtain one that can comprehend military terms and operations. . . . Laugh if you will, but many of the linguists with which I conversed were convenience store workers and cab drivers, most over the age of 40. None had any previous military experience."[54] Among the contract linguists hired on an emergency basis for the Department of Defense by Titan Systems Corp., a San

Diego–based defense contractor, were a partner in a San Diego pharmaceuticals company, a software engineer from Texas, and an accountant from northern Virginia, who twenty years earlier had been a commander in the anti-Soviet *mujahedeen* forces.[55]

In addition, the NSA's accomplishments against international terrorist targets have slowed dramatically in recent years after a string of early successes immediately after 9/11. SIGINT's last notable success in the war on terror took place in February 2003, when intercepted e-mails and satellite telephone communications led U.S. and Pakistani security officials to the hideout in the Pakistani city of Rawalpindi of 9/11 mastermind Khalid Shaikh Mohammed. At 4:00 am on March 1, 2003, heavily armed Pakistani security forces burst into Mohammed's hideout and arrested him and another key Al Qaeda operative, Mohammed Ahmed al-Hawsawi, while they slept.[56] But since 2003, SIGINT's successes against international terrorist targets have become fewer and farther between as the surviving members of Al Qaeda and allied terrorist group have learned not to trust electronic communications for communicating with each other. Spying on terrorist organizations is inherently difficult, and the same holds true for SIGINT. Testifying before Congress in 2002, NSA Director General Michael Hayden admitted that "cracking into these targets is hard—very hard—and SIGINT operations require considerable patience—sometimes over years—before they mature."[57]

SIGINT AND THE WAR IN IRAQ

Reviews by both the House and Senate Intelligence Committees in 2004, followed by the Commission on the Capabilities of the United States Regarding Weapons of Mass Destruction (the Robb-Silberman Commission) in 2005, were all highly critical of the NSA's performance in the events leading up to the U.S. invasion of Iraq in March 2003. The NSA fared better than the CIA and the rest of the U.S. intelligence community in these investigations, but only because so much of the criticism of the Agency's performance was withheld from the public versions of these reports because of classification concerns.[58]

What was made public in these reports clearly shows that NSA SIGINT coverage of Iraq prior to the U.S. invasion in March 2003 was poor, especially on the question of whether Iraq was indeed pursuing weapons of mass destruction (WMD) programs. The reason for the NSA's poor performance was that virtually all high-level Iraqi government and military communications traffic was carried by buried fiber-optic cables and thus impervious to NSA radio interceptors. Then on March 18, 2003, only a few days before the invasion began, the Iraqi government switched off all telephone service across Iraq, and the use of satellite and mobile phones was banned by the Iraqi Ministry of the Interior. This closed off the last low-level source of SIGINT then available to the NSA about what was going on inside Iraq.[59]

These factors led a postwar review panel to conclude that for NSA SIGINT collectors "changes in telecommunications technology have brought new challenges. This was the case in Iraq, where the Intelligence Community lost access to important aspects of Iraqi communications."[60] As a result, the panel concluded that insofar as helping the U.S. intelligence community assess the nature and extent of the alleged Iraqi nuclear, chemical, and biological programs, SIGINT "on the whole was not useful."[61] For example, the panel concluded that "Signals Intelligence collection against Iraq's chemical activities was minimal, and much was of questionable value."[62]

What makes these revelations about the NSA's performance so disturbing was the fact that the U.S. government, in attempting to sell its vision of the danger posed by Saddam Hussein's Iraq in Secretary of State Colin Powell's presentation to the UN Security Council on February 5, 2003, depended to a very high degree on evidence obtained from SIGINT provided by the NSA. Powell used three communications intercepts during his February 5, 2003, presentation to the UN Security Council, which unfortunately did not provide tangible "smoking gun" proof for the Bush administration's case that Iraq possessed forbidden weapons of mass destruction.

Adding fuel to concern about the NSA's poor performance in Iraq were the revelations in the press that the NSA had been used by the Bush administration to intensively monitor the communications traffic of those countries or international bodies who opposed the Bush administration's Iraq policies. In January 2003, two months before the U.S.-led invasion of Iraq began, the NSA and GCHQ mounted an intensive effort to monitor the communications traffic of the foreign representatives to the UN Security Council, especially those members of the Security Council who publicly had expressed misgivings about the U.S. government's intentions to invade Iraq. This information was leaked to the press in early March 2003 by a GCHQ employee, who was fired from her job.[63] The NSA was also tasked with monitoring the telephone calls and e-mail communications of Mohamed El Baradei, the head of the United Nation's International Atomic Energy Agency (IAEA), because of the White House's intense dislike of his agency's policies with regard to Iraq, which oftentimes ran counter to what Washington wanted.[64]

Since the invasion of Iraq, NSA performance has been described as being disappointing by senior military commanders who have served there. Military and intelligence officials have confirmed that SIGINT has not been as helpful as it was hoped it would be in tracking down members of the insurgency movement in Iraq. Despite this fact, SIGINT is still the number one source of actionable intelligence on insurgent activities.

Sources confirm that SIGINT has been extremely useful in monitoring the activities of the Iranian and Syrian governments in Iraq. This effort, however, was badly hurt in 2004 by the compromise of these SIGINT efforts by Ahmed Chalabi.[65] Among the major complaints heard from many military officials returning from Iraq is that the NSA has emphasized SIGINT collection coverage against Iraq's neighbors, Iran and Syria, as well as the internal machinations of the Washington-backed Iraqi government. But SIGINT has not proven to be a meaningful or viable tool for helping root out Iraqi insurgents, who continue to bedevil U.S. and UN Coalition forces in Iraq despite the best efforts of the U.S. intelligence community.

THE NSA DOMESTIC EAVESDROPPING SCANDAL

The NSA currently finds itself at the center of a politically explosive domestic spying scandal that may very well have serious negative consequences for the Agency and the U.S. intelligence community as a whole. In December 2005 the *New York Times* revealed the outlines of the secret NSA eavesdropping program, the purpose of which was to locate Al Qaeda terrorist cells believed to be operating in the United States without referring the matter to the super-secret Foreign Intelligence Surveillance Activity Court for approval.[66]

The controversy over the legality and propriety of this still highly classified program rages on, exacerbated by the fact that neither the House nor the Senate Intelligence Committee has shown much inclination to examine the legal underpinnings of the program, much less ascertain the details of just how the program has been conducted.[67]

The controversy has proven to be particularly embarrassing to the NSA because former NSA Director Lieutenant General Michael V. Hayden told the House Intelligence Committee in April 2000 in no uncertain terms that the Agency did not engage in spying on U.S. citizens, describing this recurring area of concern an "urban myth." He assured the Committee that the NSA would assiduously abide by the legal strictures on such activities as contained in the 1978 Foreign Intelligence Surveillance Act (FISA).[68] In a March 2005 report to President George W. Bush on the U.S. intelligence community's performance against the Iraqi WMD programs, the NSA reported that FISA "ha[d] not posed a serious obstacle to effective intelligence gathering." It should be noted that at the time the NSA made this statement to the review panel the Agency's secret domestic eavesdropping program, which deliberately bypassed the FISA Court, had been ongoing for almost three and a half years.[69] Since the *New York Times* broke the story of the NSA domestic eavesdropping program in December 2005, General Hayden has become the Bush administration's most prominent defender of the legality and probity of the increasingly controversial program, while at the same time declaring publicly that the NSA had strictly abided by the terms of the law barring government spying on Americans. As he stated in a speech at the National Press Club in January 2006: "I've taken an oath to protect and defend the Constitution of the United States. I would never violate that Constitution, nor would I abuse the rights of the American people."[70]

As with all previous scandals involving the NSA, there were portents of what the NSA was up to. In April 2005 a political controversy erupted in Washington when it was learned that the Bush administration's nominee to be the ambassador to the United Nations, John R. Bolton, had requested from the NSA transcripts of intercepted conversations involving or pertaining to other U.S. government officials. The NSA admitted that it made copies of these transcripts, including the names of the American officials involved, available to Mr. Bolton.[71] A few weeks later, *Newsweek* revealed that since January 2004 the NSA had received between 3,000 and 3,500 requests for transcripts of intercepted communications involving American citizens from various U.S. government departments, 400 of which came from the State Department. The NSA had complied with all of these requests. The report indicated that the names of as many as 10,000 Americans were contained in the transcripts of the intercepts turned over to the various U.S. government agencies who had requested them.[72] It was later learned that Bolton personally had originated ten requests since January 2004 for unredacted NSA intercept transcripts that mentioned the names of U.S. government officials or American citizens.[73]

Since the first article about the domestic eavesdropping program appeared in the *New York Times* in December 2005 further information about the nature and extent of the NSA domestic surveillance program has been slow in coming, but what has been revealed to date suggests that the program may have been far larger and more pervasive than initially indicated in the first press reports. In April 2006, an AT&T technician revealed that the telecommunications giant he worked for had allowed the NSA to place eavesdropping equipment inside its network switching centers in San Francisco and Atlanta, through which much of America and the world's e-mail traffic passes. This may, in fact, be the tip of the iceberg because a number of key American telecommunications companies other than AT&T have plaintively refused to answer questions from reporters about whether they too cooperated with the NSA's domestic eavesdropping effort.[74] These reports, taken together, all clearly indicated that the NSA had crossed the rubicon and was engaged in doing something that it had not done since the days of Henry Kissinger in the late 1960s—give Bush administration officials intelligence products involving intercepted conversations involving U.S. citizens. Unfortunately, the Bush administration refused to turn over to Congress any details concerning these NSA operations, and Mr. Bolton was subsequently confirmed as the U.S. ambassador to the United Nations.

The fear among recently retired and active-serving NSA officers is that the Agency's domestic eavesdropping program, in addition to generating much unwanted negative publicity for the Agency, almost certainly diverted much-needed manpower and fiscal resources from the NSA's foreign intelligence gathering mission to what the Agency officers generally believe to have been a poorly considered and legally questionable domestic monitoring operation that apparently has produced little in the way of tangible results, despite claims to the contrary from the White House. The program has also only served to further exacerbate the NSA's already poor relations with the FBI, which for reasons passing easy comprehension, was deliberately excluded from participation in the domestic eavesdropping program by the White House.

THE SUM OF ALL ITS PARTS

Today, the NSA remains a conundrum. It is by far the largest and most powerful intelligence agency within the U.S. intelligence community. It is today the principal intelligence collector for the entire U.S. intelligence community, accounting for the majority of the highest-level intelligence information going to the president of the United States.

And yet, like the community of which it is an integral part, it remains deeply troubled by a host of problems, many of its own making. NSA intelligence production, while rising in absolute numbers, has been declining in real terms in key areas, such as its ability to find insurgents in Afghanistan and Iraq. General Hayden's internal reform measures at the NSA were left unfinished, in part because all reform measures were largely abandoned after 9/11. All of the NSA's major technical modernization programs are hundreds of millions of dollars over budget and years behind schedule. It has been left to General Hayden's successor at the helm of the NSA, Lieutenant General Keith Alexander, to try to put the NSA's various internal reform and modernization programs back on track while at the same time increase its productivity and good standing within the U.S. intelligence community.

NOTES

1. NSA/CSS, *Transition 2001*, December 2000, p. 33. The author is grateful to Dr. Jeffrey T. Richelson for making a copy of this document available.

2. David Ignatius, "The CIA at Rock Bottom," *Washington Post*, May 7, 2006, p. B7.

3. A detailed examination of the NSA's Cold War accomplishments and failures against the Soviet Union can be found in Matthew M. Aid, "The National Security Agency and the Cold War," in *Secrets of Signals Intelligence During the Cold War and Beyond,* eds. Matthew M. Aid and Cees Wiebes (London: Frank Cass, 2001), pp. 27–66.

4. Matthew M. Aid, "The Time of Troubles: The U.S. National Security Agency in the Twenty-First Century," *Intelligence and National Security* 15 (Autumn 2000), p. 6. See also *Statement for the Record by Lt. General Michael V. Hayden, USAF, Director NSA/CSS Before the Joint Inquiry of the Senate Select Committee on Intelligence and the House Permanent Select Committee on Intelligence*, October 17, 2002, p. 6.

5. Senate Report No. 107-351 and House Report No. 107-792, Report of the U.S. Senate Select Committee and U.S. House Permanent Select Committee on Intelligence, *Joint Inquiry Into Intelligence Community Activities Before and After the Terrorist Attacks of September 11, 2001*, 107th Congress, 2nd Session, December 2002 (declassified and released in July 2003), p. 76.

6. Heritage Lecture #851, Joel F. Brenner, *Information Oversight: Practical Lessons From Foreign Intelligence*, September 30, 2004, the Heritage Foundation, available at http://www.heritage.org/Research/NationalSecurity/hl851.cfm.

7. Michael Hirsh, "The NSA's Overt Problem," *Washington Post*, January 1, 2006, p. B1.

8. This troubled period in the NSA's history is covered in detail in Matthew M. Aid, "The Time of Troubles: The U.S. National Security Agency in the Twenty-First Century," *Intelligence and National Security* 15 (Autumn 2000), pp. 1–32.

9. Vernon Loeb, "General Named to Head NSA," *Washington Post*, February 25, 1999, p. A21; "Agency Welcomes New Director Lieutenant General Michael V. Hayden," *National Security Agency Newsletter*, May 1999, p. 4.

10. Memorandum, Taylor to DIRNSA, *Thoughts on Strategic Issues for the Institution*, April 9, 1999, p. 2, NSA FOIA.

11. Richard Lardner, "NSA Chief Pushes Ahead With Overhaul of Agency's Culture, Operations," *Inside Defense*, October 16, 2000; Vernon Loeb, "NSA's Chief Unveils Restructuring," *Washington Post*, October 17, 2000, p. A31; Laura Sullivan, "Chief of NSA Begins Reforms," *Baltimore Sun*, October 17, 2000.

12. Confidential interview.

13. Vernon Loeb, "NSA Reorganization," *Washington Post*, December 19, 2000, p. A37.

14. NSA/CSS, *Transition 2001*, December 2000, p. 19.

15. Confidential interview.

16. Frank Tiboni, "Bill Calls for Pentagon to Monitor Spy Shop's Spending," *Defense News*, October 1–7, 2001, p. 6.

17. Ariel Sabar, "Congress Curbs NSA's Power to Contract With Suppliers," *Baltimore Sun*, July 20, 2003, p. A1.

18. Thomas R. Temin, "Defense Coders Are Fading Away," *Government Computer News*, May 6, 2002.

19. Confidential interview.

20. Senate Report No. 107-351 and House Report No. 107-792, Report of the U.S. Senate Select Committee and U.S. House Permanent Select Committee on Intelligence, *Joint Inquiry Into Intelligence Community Activities Before and After the Terrorist Attacks of September 11, 2001*, 107th Congress, 2nd Session, December 2002 (declassified and released in July 2003), p. 381.

21. Siobhan Gorman, "System Error," *Baltimore Sun*, January 29, 2006, p. A1; Siobhan Gorman, "Computer Ills Hinder NSA," *Baltimore Sun*, February 26, 2006, p. A1.

22. DIRgram-31: "Fixing NSA's IT Infrastructure," January 6, 2000, NSA FOIA.

23. Neil King Jr., "Big Technology Players Vie to Upgrade NSA Computers," *Wall Street Journal*, March 13, 2001.

24. DIRgram-42, "DO Realignment and Transformation," January 24, 2000, NSA FOIA.

25. DIRgram-37: "Transformation Begins With TRAILBLAZER," January 14, 2000, NSA FOIA.

26. Confidential interview.

27. NSA Scientific Advisory Board, Panel on Digital Network Intelligence (DNI), *Report to Director*, June 28, 1999, p. 20/61. The author is grateful to Dr. Jeffrey T. Richelson for making a copy of this document available.

28. DIRgram-45: "TRAILBLAZER I—A Progress report," February 3, 2000, NSA FOIA.

29. SAIC Press Release, *SAIC Team Wins National Security Agency TRAILBLAZER Contract*, October 21, 2002; Frank Tiboni, "NSA to Boost Range of Cryptologic Capabilities; Earmarks $282 Million for Eavesdropping Network," *Defense News*, January 20, 2003.

30. Senate Report No. 107-351 and House Report No. 107-792, Report of the U.S. Senate Select Committee and U.S. House Permanent Select Committee on Intelligence, *Joint Inquiry Into Intelligence Community Activities Before and After the Terrorist Attacks of September 11, 2001*, 107th Congress, 2nd Session, December 2002 (declassified and released in July 2003), p. 76.

31. Confidential interviews.

32. Senate Report No. 107-351 and House Report No. 107-792, Report of the U.S. Senate Select Committee and U.S. House Permanent Select Committee on Intelligence, *Joint Inquiry Into Intelligence Community Activities Before and After the Terrorist Attacks of September 11, 2001*, 107th Congress, 2nd Session, December 2002 (declassified and released in July 2003), p. 374.

33. For an assessment of NSA's performance prior to 9/11, see Matthew M. Aid, "All Glory Is Fleeting: Sigint and the Fight Against International Terrorism," *Intelligence and National Security* 18 (Winter 2003), pp. 72–120.

34. Confidential interview.

35. Ariel Sabar, "Want to Be a Spy? NSA Is Hiring," *Baltimore Sun*, April 10, 2004; Stephen Barr, "NSA Makes No Secret of Stepped-Up Recruitment Effort," *Washington Post*, April 22, 2004, p. B2; "A Good Spy Is Hard to Fund," *U.S. News & World Report*, November 22, 2004.

36. Sheila Hotchkin, "NSA Will Let Its Dollars Do the Talking," *San Antonio Express-News*, April 16, 2005; Mike Soraghan and Aldo Svaldi, "NSA Moving Some Workers, Operations to Denver Area," *Denver Post*, January 24, 2006; Robert Gehrke, "Key Spy Agency Expands to Utah," *Salt Lake Tribune*, February 2, 2006; Amy Choate, "NSA Seeks Linguists at BYU to Staff Utah Center," *Deseret Morning News*, February 24, 2006.

37. "Emergency War Supplemental Hides Millions," *UPI*, February 20, 2006.

38. Confidential interview.

39. Confidential interviews.

40. Michael A. Wertheimer, "Crippling Innovation—and Intelligence," *Washington Post*, July 21, 2004, p. A19.

41. Joab Jackson, "NSA Seeks Better Analysis Technologies," *Washington Technology*, November 11, 2004, available at http://www.wtonline.com.

42. CM 5837, Intelligence and Security Committee, *Annual Report 2002–2003*, June 2003, p. 20.

43. Confidential interview.

44. Memorandum, Zenker to Joint Tactical SIGINT Architecture (JTSA) Working Group, *Quarterly Meeting Minutes—December 2001*, December 31, 2001. This document has since been reclassified and removed from the Internet site where the author originally found it.

45. Robert Little, "NSA Methods Lag in Age of Terror," *Baltimore Sun*, December 9, 2004.

46. Senate Report No. 107-351 and House Report No. 107-792, Report of the U.S. Senate Select Committee and U.S. House Permanent Select Committee on Intelligence, *Joint Inquiry Into Intelligence Community Activities Before and After the Terrorist Attacks of September 11, 2001*, 107th Congress, 2nd Session, December 2002 (declassified and released in July 2003), p. 336.

47. Ian Bruce, "Mistake in Translation Almost Proves Deadly," *Scotland Herald*, April 24, 2002.

48. Confidential interviews.

49. John L. Girardeau, "TSM Notes—Changes in Tactical Signals Intelligence and Electronic Warfare Forces During Operation Enduring Freedom," *Military Intelligence Professional Bulletin*, October–December 2003.

50. Paul Haven, "Taliban Plans Attacks From Pakistan," *Associated Press*, September 23, 2003.

51. Department of the Army, Center for Army Lessons Learned (CALL), *Newsletter No. 03-27: Project OUTREACH: Tactics, Techniques, and Procedures*, October 2003, p. 19.

52. B. Raman, "Sons' Killings Change Little in Iraq,"*Asia Times Online*, July 31, 2003, available at http://www.atimes.com/atimes/Middle_East/EG31Ak03.html.

53. Department of the Army, Center for Army Lessons Learned (CALL), *Newsletter No. 03-27: Project OUTREACH: Tactics, Techniques, and Procedures*, October 2003, p. 12.

54. Department of the Army, Center for Army Lessons Learned (CALL), *Newsletter No. 03-27: Project OUTREACH: Tactics, Techniques, and Procedures*, October 2003, p. 12.

55. Greg Miller, "Shortage of Linguists Initially Hampered U.S. Intelligence Mission," *Los Angeles Times*, July 28, 2002.

56. Kevin Johnson and Jack Kelly, "Terror Arrest Triggers Mad Scrammble," *USA Today*, March 2, 2003; Rory McCarthy and Jason Burke, "Endgame in the Desert of Death for the World's Most Wanted Man," *Observer*, March 9, 2003; Kevin Whitelaw, "A Tightening Noose," *U.S. News & World Report*, March 17, 2003.

57. Senate Report No. 107-351 and House Report No. 107-792, Report of the U.S. Senate Select Committee and U.S. House Permanent Select Committee on Intelligence, *Joint Inquiry Into Intelligence Community Activities Before and After the Terrorist Attacks of September 11, 2001*, 107th Congress, 2nd Session, December 2002 (declassified and released in July 2003), p. 380.

58. All information concerning the NSA's performance in the Iraqi WMD scandal was deleted from the report of the Senate Intelligence Committee on the U.S. intelligence community's performance prior to the invasion of Iraq, for which see: U.S. Senate, Select Committee on Intelligence, *Report on the U.S. Intelligence Community's Prewar Intelligence Assessments on Iraq*, 108th Congress, July 7, 2004, pp. 264–65.

59. "Iraq Shuts Down Phone Network to Thwart CIA Eavesdropping," *Associated Press*, March 19, 2003.

60. The Commission on the Intelligence Capabilities of the United States Regarding Weapons of Mass Destruction, *Report to the President of the United States*, March 31, 2005, pp. 15, 163–64.

61. Ibid., p. 65.

62. Ibid., p. 130.

63. Martin Bright, Ed Vulliamy, and Peter Beaumont, "Revealed: U.S. Dirty Tricks to Win Vote on Iraq War," *Observer*, March 2, 2003, p. 1.

64. Dafna Linzer, "IAEA Leader's Phone Tapped," *Washington Post*, December 12, 2004, p. A1.

65. Rupert Cornwell, "Chalabi Falls From Grace as U.S. Spy Row Erupts," *Independent*, June 3, 2004, p. A1.

66. James Risen and Eric Lichtblau, "Bush Lets U.S. Spy on Callers Without Courts," *New York Times*, December 16, 2005, p. A1; Eric Lichtblau and James Risen, "Eavesdropping Effort Began Soon After Sept. 11 Attacks," *New York Times*, December 18, 2005, p. A1.

67. See, for example, the heated words exchanged between Republican and Democratic members of the House Intelligence Committee about the NSA's domestic eavesdropping program contained in U.S. House of Representatives, Report 109-411, *Intelligence Authorization Act for Fiscal Year 2007*, 109th Congress, 2nd Session, April 6, 2006.

68. *Statement for the Record of NSA Director Lt. General Michael V. Hayden, USAF Before the House Permanent Select Committee on Intelligence*, April 12, 2000. General Hayden's "urban myth" comment is contained in Neil King Jr., "U.S. Security Agency Defends Eavesdrop Use," *Wall Street Journal*, April 13, 2000.

69. The Commission on the Intelligence Capabilities of the United States Regarding Weapons of Mass Destruction, *Report to the President of the United States*, March 31, 2005, p. 375.

70. Scott Shane and Mark Mazzetti, "Top C.I.A. Pick Has Credentials and Skeptics," *New York Times*, May 6, 2006, p. A1.

71. Douglas Jehl, "Senator Asks U.N. Nominee to Explain His Security Requests," *New York Times*, April 14, 2005, p. A1.

72. Mark Hosenball, "Periscope: Spying—Giving Out U.S. Names," *Newsweek*, May 2, 2005.

73. Katherine Shrader, "Bolton Requested 10 Names in Spy Reports," *Associated Press*, June 27, 2005.

74. John Markoff and Scott Shane, "Documents Show Link Between AT&T and Agency in Eavesdropping Case," *New York Times*, April 13, 2006, p. A1.

4

INTELLIGENCE

The Imagery Dimension

JEFFREY T. RICHELSON

THE USE OF OVERHEAD PLATFORMS TO OBSERVE events on the earth has a long history. According to Chinese and Japanese folklore, spotters ascended in baskets suspended from giant kites or were strapped directly onto them. In April 1794, in the midst of the French Revolution, France organized a company of *aerostiers*, or balloonists. One balloon is said to have been kept in the air for nine hours while the group's commander made continuous observations during the Battle of Fleurus in Belgium.[1]

The United States made similar use of balloons during the Civil War, although little intelligence of value was obtained. By the latter part of the 19th century, Britain was conducting experiments using balloons as platforms from which to obtain "overhead photography."

As a result of Wilbur and Orville Wright's invention of the airplane in 1903, a faster moving reconnaissance platform became available. In January 1911 the San Diego waterfront became the first target of cameras carried aboard an airplane. Between 1913 and 1915 visual and photographic reconnaissance missions were flown by the U.S. Army in the Philippines and along the Mexican border. During World War II the United States made extensive use of airplane photography using remodeled B-17 (*Flying Fortress*) and B-24 (*Liberator*) aircraft. The remodeled B-24, known as the F-7, carried six cameras internally—all triggered via remote control by an operator over the sealed rear bomb-bay doors.[2]

The United States was far from the only nation, in the first half of the 20th century, conducting extensive photographic reconnaissance using airplanes. During World War I British and German aircraft spied on developments on the battlefield. Aerial photography played a significant role in July 1916 in alerting German forces of the impending British attack that launched the Battle of the

Somme. In the interwar years, Britain conducted covert overflights of Germany by hiding cameras on what appeared to be a civilian aircraft, while German aircraft brought back photographs of Soviet territory prior to the German invasion of the Soviet Union in June 1941. Once war arrived, British and American planes photographed German military and industrial installations and areas on a regular basis—to aid in targeting and damage assessment.[3]

The end of World War II was quickly followed by the Cold War and overhead reconnaissance retained, and even increased, its importance—particularly for the United States and its allies, as they sought to pierce the veil of secrecy wrapped around almost every aspect of Soviet life, particularly its military capabilities. At first Cold War aerial reconnaissance was conducted with aircraft, and occasionally with balloons. The possibility that a satellite could be outfitted with a camera to take pictures of any target on earth was noted by the RAND Corporation as early as 1946. In August 1960 that vision was realized when the United States successfully orbited a camera-carrying satellite code-named CORONA.

During the Cold War era, while a multitude of countries used aircraft to obtain overhead images, only the United States, the Soviet Union, and (occasionally) China operated satellites capable of returning the high-quality images needed to extract significant intelligence. Today, though there are still a multitude of nations operating reconnaissance aircraft, there has been a significant proliferation in the nations who also rely on space reconnaissance to provide intelligence. In addition, over the years there has also been an evolution with regard to the different means by which images could be obtained and transmitted.

IMAGERY: VARIETIES AND QUALITY

At one time, the only means of producing an image of a target was through photography. But today, the visible-light portion of the electromagnetic spectrum is not the only segment of the spectrum that is employed to obtain an image. And there are alternative means for converting the signals from portions of the spectrum into images.

Equipment used to produce photographs can be film-based or electro-optical. A conventional camera captures a scene on film by recording the varying light levels reflected from all of the separate objects in the scene. In contrast, an electro-optical camera converts the varying light levels into electrical signals. A numerical value, from 1 to 256, is assigned to each of the signals, which are called picture elements, or pixels. The process transforms a picture (analog) image to a digital image that can be transmitted electronically to distant points. The signal can then be reconstructed from the digital to the analog format. The analog signal can be displayed on a video screen or made into a photograph.

In addition to the visible-light portion of the electromagnetic spectrum, the near-infrared portion of the spectrum, which is invisible to the human eye, can be employed to produce images. At the same time, near-infrared, like visible-light imagery, depends on objects reflecting solar radiation rather than on their emission of radiation. As a result, such imagery can be produced only in daylight and in the absence of substantial cloud cover.

Thermal infrared imagery, obtained from the mid- and far-infrared portions of the electromagnetic spectrum, provides imagery purely by detecting the heat emitted by objects. Thus, a thermal infrared system can detect buried structures, such as missile silos or underground construction, as a result of the heat they generate. Since thermal infrared imagery does not require visible light, it can be obtained under conditions of darkness—if the sky is free of cloud cover.

Imagery can be obtained during day or night in the presence of cloud cover by employing an imaging radar (an acronym for *ra*dio *d*etection *a*nd *r*anging). Radar imagery is produced by bouncing radio waves off an area or an object and using the reflected returns to produce an image of the target. Because radio waves are not attenuated by the water vapor in the atmosphere, they are able to penetrate cloud cover.

The ultimate utility of any imaging system is a function of several factors—the most important being spatial resolution. A simple measure of resolution is the minimum size an object must be in order to be measurable and detectable by imagery interpreters. The higher the resolution (the smaller the size an object can be and be detected), the greater the detail that can be extracted from an image. It should also be noted that resolution is the product of a number of factors—including the quality of the imaging system itself, atmospheric conditions, contrast, and orbital parameters. Thus, the quality of images from the same imaging system will vary depending on whether the image is obtained on a crisp, clear day or a hazy one, on whether a dark (light) target is being imaged against a light (dark) background, and whether the target is imaged from a lower or higher altitude.

The degree of resolution required depends on the specificity of the intelligence desired. Five different interpretation tasks have been differentiated. *Detection* involves locating a class of units or objects or an activity of interest. *General identification* involves determining a general target type, and *precise identification* involves discrimination within target types. *Description* involves specifying the size-dimension, configuration-layout, components-construction, and number of units. Technical intelligence involves determining the specific characteristics and performance capabilities of weapons and equipment.

SATELLITE IMAGERY

The United States pioneered, in a number of ways, the use of satellites to obtain images to satisfy intelligence requirements. It orbited the first satellite to return images—the previously mentioned CORONA. It also pioneered the use of infrared and radar imagery in spy satellites, as well as dramatically altering the means of transmitting the imagery back to earth. The present U.S. constellation of imagery satellites is a reflection of those developments.

On December 19, 1976, the first of a new generation of U.S. imagery satellites was launched from Vandenberg Air Force Base into an orbit that took it as close as 164 miles to the earth and as far as 329 miles away. Another seven would be launched successfully, before they would begin being replaced by a significantly upgraded version in 1988. By that time, that group of satellites was capable of producing images with 6-inch resolution or better.[4]

The KH-11 represented a quantum leap in imagery capabilities because, in contrast to its film return predecessors, it could return its imagery in "near real-time." Its electro-optical system, employing light-sensitive silicone diodes and charged couple devices, converted images into electronic signals that were transmitted to relay satellites and back to a ground station in northern Virginia for near-instantaneous reconstruction.

The satellites flew lengthwise, with the axis of the optical system parallel to the earth. The inclination of the satellites, approximately 97 degrees, meant they flew in a sun-synchronous orbit, so that the sun angle was the same each time the satellite was over a target. In the front was a downward-looking mirror that could be flipped from side to side, allowing the area under observation to be changed from moment to moment. Two benefits resulted from that capability. One was that the menu of targets included not only areas under the spacecraft but areas to the sides and for hundreds of miles in front. In addition to expanding the intelligence community's ability to monitor a given target, it complicated foreign denial and deception activities. In addition, it permitted the production of stereoscopic images.

The advanced KH-11 can carry more fuel than the original model, perhaps 10,000 to 15,000 pounds. This permits a longer lifetime for the new model— possibly up to eight years. A greater fuel supply also allows a greater ability to maneuver. Thus, an advanced KH-11 can operate at times in higher orbits to produce images covering a larger territory than is possible at lower altitudes— and then maneuver to lower orbits to produce higher resolution imagery. The maneuvering capability could be employed in attempts to evade anti-satellite (ASAT) weapons or to defeat denial and deception activities.

In addition to the ability to operate in higher orbits these satellites have other capabilities. They contain an infrared imagery capability, including a thermal infrared imagery capability, thus permitting imagery during darkness. The satellites also carry a system that places the necessary markings on returned imagery to permit its full exploitation for mapping purposes. At the present, three advanced KH-11 satellites constitute a full constellation.

As might be expected, those satellites have imaged a wide variety of targets, including a nuclear reactor in Algeria, intermediate-range ballistic missile complexes in China, a Russian signals intelligence facility in Cuba, the Pokhran nuclear test site in India, suspected weapons of mass destruction facilities in Iraq, tunnel construction in North Korea, an underground command bunker in Russia, refugee movements in Rwanda, and an aircraft carrier in the Ukraine.

A second component of the U.S. space imaging fleet is satellites developed and deployed under a program first known as Indigo, then as Lacrosse, and more recently as Onyx. Rather than employing an electro-optical system, they carry an imaging radar. Though the United States had launched a single radar-imagery satellite in 1964, designated Quill, it had not followed that launch with others—despite the mission's success. Thus, the next radar-imagery satellite would be the first Lacrosse, launched on December 2, 1988, from the space shuttle orbiter *Atlantis*. The satellites closed a major gap in U.S. capabilities by allowing the U.S. intelligence community to obtain imagery even when targets were covered by clouds. Further launches have allowed the United States to maintain two radar-imagery satellites in orbit. The satellites have operated in orbits of approximately 400 miles and have a resolution of 3 to 5 feet, reportedly sufficient to allow discrimination between tanks and armored personnel carriers and identification of bomb craters of 6 to 10 feet in diameter.[5]

When conceived, the primary purpose envisioned for the satellite was monitoring Soviet and Warsaw Pact armor. Recent missions have included providing imagery for bomb damage assessments of the consequences of Navy Tomahawk missile attacks on Iraqi air defense installations in September 1996; monitoring Iraqi weapons storage sites; and tracking Iraqi troop movements, such as the dispersal of the Republican Guard when the Guard was threatened with U.S. attack in early 1998. The satellites may also have been used to determine if submarines operating underwater could be located and tracked via radar imagery.

The United States also operates a stealth satellite, originally known at Misty, which returns electro-optical imagery. Designed to be less detectable than other U.S. satellites by space surveillance systems—due to its design and being operated in an unusual orbit for an imaging satellite—the first version was launched in 1990 and another in 1999.

The Soviet Union trailed the United States in the development of reconnaissance satellites but they still represented a key part of Soviet intelligence capabilities until the collapse of the regime. The first Soviet experimental photographic reconnaissance satellite was launched in April 1962, and the first fully operational satellite in 1964. By the end of 1983 the number of days each year in which a Soviet photo reconnaissance satellite was in orbit was approaching 365. Then in 1984, about seven years after the United States accomplished the feat, the Soviets orbited their first real-time imagery satellite.

As did the United States, the Soviet Union employed its satellites for more than monitoring its main adversary's homeland. Its satellites photographed developments in the 1967 Arab-Israeli war, the Indo-Pakistani war of 1971, the 1973 Yom Kippur War, South Africa's apparent preparations for a nuclear test in 1977, the Iran-Iraq war, the 1983 U.S. invasion of Grenada, and, almost surely, the UN invasion of Iraq in 1991. Since then Russian satellites have undoubtedly monitored terrorist activities in Chechnya, nuclear developments in Iran, as well as U.S. military operations in Iraq.

In the Cold War era space reconnaissance was almost exclusively an activity conducted by the superpowers. Aside from China, whose spy satellite program for a number of years consisted of a single, brief, yearly mission, the only other nations to operate such satellites were the United States and the Soviet Union. But the end of the Cold War has seen a proliferation in satellite reconnaissance operations in countries that previously had to rely on aerial reconnaissance, commercial observation satellites, or the willingness of the United States to share either imagery or intelligence derived from the imagery.

Though such systems represent a significant commitment in terms of technical resources, manpower, and money, several nations have clearly been attracted by both the technical advantages (discussed below) as well as the political advantages. Such nations can reduce their dependency on the United States, be certain of being able to obtain imagery when they deem it important, and have an asset they can trade—because their satellites would be able to supplement U.S. coverage in a crisis.

Israel was the first nation to join the post–Cold War space reconnaissance club, when its third Ofeq (Horizon) satellite was launched in early April 1995. In contrast to other nation's reconnaissance satellites, which operated in polar orbits that allowed them to photograph almost any point on the earth, Ofeq-3 operated in an orbit that limited its view to targets between 37 degrees north latitude and 37 degrees south latitude—which meant that the satellite would spend more time over important Middle East targets. The most recent version of Ofeq, launched in 2002, is reported to have a resolution of between 1.6 and 2.6 feet.[6]

Within months France followed Israel. As early as 1965, France had contemplated building such a spacecraft, but it was not until an Ariane booster lifted off from a launch site in French Guiana in July 1995 and placed Helios 1A in orbit that France actually attained such a capability. Though the reported resolution of the electro-optical satellite was about 3.25 feet—significantly inferior to that produced by U.S. and Russian satellites—it was a considerable improvement over what could be obtained, at that time, from a commercial observation satellite.

Over the next decade France continued to launch Helios satellites. In December 1999 it orbited Helios 1B, and in December 2004, Helios 2A was launched into a 400-mile orbit. The new satellite, partially funded by Spain and Belgium, was a significantly improved version of the earlier generation in several ways. Its imaging quality is estimated to be less than 1.6 feet. In addition, it carries an infrared sensor. It can also deliver about a hundred images a day, in contrast to the dozens that were returned by Helios 1A.

France's commitment to develop Helios, after a number of false starts in earlier decades, was a product of the 1991 Gulf War—which demonstrated the nation's extreme dependence on U.S. satellite imagery. In the case of Japan, it was the August 31, 1998, launch of a North Korean Taepodong missile that convinced Japanese leaders that Japan needed its own spy satellite rather than continuing to debate whether Japan should develop such a system—for warning of the launch came from the United States and not as quickly as the Japanese leadership would have liked. Less than five years after the North Korean launch, in March 2003, Japan orbited two spy satellites, whose names—Optical-1 and Radar-1—also revealed the sensors on board.

All the nations currently operating imaging satellites plan to continue the practice and improve their capabilities. Japan is planning to increase the size of its reconnaissance constellation as well as to improve the resolution of the satellites. Israel's Ofeq-7 is expected to represent a "quantum leap" over earlier models. In addition, Israel plans to launch a radar imagery demonstration satellite in 2006. And other nations, such as Germany and Italy, plan to join the space reconnaissance club.

The continued commitment to space reconnaissance by the nations currently operating such systems and the intent of others to join the space reconnaissance fraternity is a reflection of the benefits attached to such capabilities. Although operating a small fleet of reconnaissance aircraft is far cheaper, and less challenging technically, it cannot provide the benefits of a space reconnaissance capability.

Possibly the most significant impact of satellite reconnaissance is the access it permits to intelligence targets. The U-2 represented a major improvement over the modified bombers employed for photographic reconnaissance that generally operated on the Soviet periphery and very occasionally overflew Soviet territory. But the entire U-2 aerial reconnaissance program (discussed below) involved only twenty-three successful overflights over a period of almost four years. Further, each of those overflights covered a very small portion of the Soviet Union. Their number and extent were a recognition of the limitations on the U-2's range as well as the perilous nature of overflying Soviet territory. Thus, a July 1960 CIA report noted that "7.5% of [the] total land area of USSR is covered by useable [U-2] photography."[7]

In contrast, even the earliest CORONA missions, with one-day lifetimes, would pass over substantial portions of the U.S.S.R. from the western part of the country to Siberia. Of course, while the shoot-down terminated U-2 access to targets in the Soviet interior, all facilities or activities of interest anywhere in the Soviet Union could, assuming favorable weather conditions, be photographed by satellite. Two potential manmade impediments to access did not materialize in any serious way. The Soviet leadership, although authorizing an extensive antisatellite research and development program, never authorized use of such weapons to impede U.S. reconnaissance satellites. And while the Soviets had a significant denial and deception program, managed by a chief directorate of the Soviet General Staff, U.S. imagery satellites were able to produce vast quantities of hard intelligence.

Imaging satellites also gave the United States an ability to access targets in other denied territories such as China (U-2 overflights of which were halted in 1968) as well as allied or friendly countries, such as Israel, where repeated overflights would represent a significant political problem. Similarly, the nuclear programs of Taiwan and France (particularly its southern Pacific testing facility) could be monitored without resorting to intrusive overhead missions. Thus, the CIA conducted one U-2 overflight of the French testing facility and then decided not to repeat such an activity.[8]

Two other major consequences of satellite reconnaissance were the increased frequency with which targets could be imaged as well as the number of targets that could be covered in a given time span. U-2, SR-71, or other overflight missions, if they could be conducted at all over particular targets, could be conducted only sporadically and for very limited durations due to a wide range of reasons, some interrelated. Cost, the availability of pilots and aircraft, the range of the aircraft, and the risks involved in the missions were all factors. In contrast, satellite imagery systems could stay in orbit for a longer period of time—at first by hours, then by days, then by months, then by years, and maybe now by a decade.

In addition, satellites flew at a far greater speed than aircraft as the spinning earth presented a global array of targets beneath them. As a result, targets could be revisited on a regular basis if there was any requirement to do so and the number of targets that could be imaged in any significant time span by a satellite was far greater than possible for an aircraft. This advantage became even more pronounced as the size of the standard imagery constellation grew. In late 1995, with three electro-optical and two radar imagery satellites in orbit, the United States was able to obtain four images a day of the Indian nuclear test site at a time when it was suspected (correctly) that India was preparing to detonate a nuclear device.

Satellites also provided a higher vantage point than aircraft. As a result, a single image taken from a satellite, with its higher vantage point, can encompass far more territory than that taken from an aircraft. As a result of a superior vantage point, the speed of the satellite and rotation of the earth, its ability to operate for longer periods of time than aircraft, and its unimpeded access to targets, the first CORONA (which completed seventeen orbits of the earth and seven passes over the Soviet Union) mission produced 1,432 photos and covered more territory than all twenty-three U-2 overflights of the Soviet Union combined.[9]

The same considerations, technical and political, hold true today—not only for the United States, but for all other nations operating or planning to operate satellite imagery systems. Thus, Japan can obtain satellite images of North Korea with impunity. Conducting aerial reconnaissance missions would involve violations of international law and eventual major domestic and foreign crises. North Korean protests and attempts (which would eventually succeed) to shoot down a Japanese spy plane would certainly trigger both a political crisis within Japan, and a crisis with North Korea. As a result, such missions would never even be proposed, much less authorized.

Further, even if Japan could fly over North Korean territory with impunity, the cost of obtaining the same level of coverage and maintaining the same probability of detecting North Korean activities of interest (e.g., preparations for a missile launch or a nuclear test) would be far greater than employing satellites. The costs would involve a very large fleet of aircraft, personnel, spare parts, and fuel. And, the same satellites that cover North Korea also photograph Chinese targets.

The same considerations apply to Israel, which can avoid the crises that would result from an aerial reconnaissance mission if the plane was shot down and the pilot captured on a mission over Syria or Iran, by employing satellite coverage. In the case of France, it would need, among other things, a series of bases around the world to launch reconnaissance aircraft if it wanted to match the reach of its Helios satellites. With Helios, it only needs its base in French Guiana and a ground station.

AERIAL SYSTEMS

Aerial reconnaissance comes in two basic varieties: manned and unmanned. Nations, even those who have developed advanced space reconnaissance capabilities, have also continued to operate aerial reconnaissance systems.

Providing a hedge against the unexpected failure of one of its limited number of satellites is one reason for a nation to continue to operate such systems. But there are others. They can supplement satellite coverage—a single plane costs far less than an additional satellite. They can provide a quick reaction capability because an aircraft can head directly for a target whereas a satellite cannot photograph a target until its orbit and the rotation of the earth place the target in view—a process which can take several days. Those same constraints mean that a satellite cannot arbitrarily cover any stretch of territory desired, but aircraft can cover the territory between any two points—for example, the movement of an invading army toward its objective or the movement of refugees toward a border.

The initial development and improving capabilities of imagery satellites has not made other forms of overhead imagery collection obsolete. During the early days of the Cold War, U.S. Air Force pilots flew modified bombers, equipped with cameras, along the periphery of the Soviet Union and China to obtain imagery of airfields, ports, and other facilities that could be photographed from outside those nations' borders. Occasionally, those modified bombers were sent into Soviet airspace to obtain imagery of targets farther inland.

Then in 1956 the CIA pilots began flying deep into the Soviet territory, employing the specially designed U-2, which flew at over 65,000 feet and which the CIA believed, incorrectly, would not be detected by Soviet radar. It carried a special, long, focal-length camera capable of photographing objects as small as a man, and brought back images of roads, railroads, industrial plants, nuclear facilities, aircraft, and missile sites within a strip 200 miles wide by 2,500 miles long.[10]

Overflights of the Soviet Union ceased after Francis Gary Powers and his U-2 were shot down on May 1, 1960. But the United States still continues to operate U-2s, and has employed a variety of additional spy planes, particularly the Mach 3 SR-71, in the decades after the United States mastered the art of conducting reconnaissance from space—even after the quality of satellite photos equaled or surpassed that of the lower flying aircraft. U-2s and/or SR-71s were used to photograph installations, military facilities, and military developments in

Cuba, Nicaragua, Libya, and Bosnia. The U-2 has also been used to monitor compliance with cease-fire agreements such as the 1973 agreement between Israel and Egypt and the 1991 agreement between Iraq and coalition forces.

Other nations employed their own reconnaissance aircraft—usually modified fighters or bombers. France has used specially configured Mirage fighters, equipped with a variety of sensors, whereas Britain has relied on modified Canberra bombers, which were employed during the 1982 war over the Falklands.

Another type of overhead imagery system has some of the virtues of satellites and aircraft, and some of its own advantages. Unmanned aerial vehicles (UAVs) equipped with electro-optical systems or infrared sensors are operated without a pilot by remote control—thus the political risks and risk to life involved in manned reconnaissance operations are eliminated. Like aircraft they can move in a straight line—following troops, refugees, or a group of mobile missiles in transit. Unlike satellites or aircraft, UAVs can remain over a target, at high altitudes, for extended periods of time (e.g., twenty hours), keeping watch on a particular target or area, such as a terrorist training camp or nuclear test site.

Whereas the United States began operating *drones* (pilotless aircraft that could not be maneuvered) and UAVs during the Cold War, it is in the post–Cold War that UAVs have become a more significant component of U.S. reconnaissance activities. The CIA began flying Predator UAVs over Bosnia in 1994. After the initiation of military operations in Afghanistan the United States began equipping Predators with Hellfire missiles so that immediate action could be taken if imagery indicated the presence of a terrorist target. Even more recently, the United States has been deploying the Global Hawk UAV—capable of operating at over 60,000 feet for twenty hours and carrying electro-optical, infrared, or radar imaging sensors.

BENEFITS AND LIMITATIONS

That imagery collection can produce intelligence of enormous value has been demonstrated throughout the 20th century. During World War I photographic reconnaissance provided intelligence on enemy troop movements. In World War II all sides conducted extensive photographic reconnaissance operations to identify targets and assess the impact of bombing runs—particularly important in an era in which precision bombing was only a dream.

During the Cold War satellite imagery (along with monitoring of the telemetry from Soviet missile tests) was of primary importance for the United States in assessing the capabilities of Soviet strategic forces. Imagery was vital in determining the numbers of intercontinental ballistic missiles (ICBMs) and submarine-launched ballistic missiles and the locations of ICBM fields. Today it permits monitoring (albeit not perfect monitoring) of Iranian and North Korean nuclear activities, Chinese intermediate missile deployments in regions near Taiwan, and the construction of terrorist training camps.

Soviet photographic reconnaissance satellites allowed the Kremlin's rulers to be confident that they had a good understanding of U.S. strategic capabilities. Collectively, the existence of overhead reconnaissance and other technical collection capabilities allowed the negotiation of arms control agreements—particularly the Strategic Arms Limitation Treaty (SALT) and the Strategic Arms Reduction Treaty (START)—because each side had an independent means of monitoring compliance, and provided reassurance that the other side was not in the process of preparing for a surprise attack.

Today the international environment is significantly different from what it was two decades ago—with the collapse of the Soviet Union, the concern over rogue state acquisition of nuclear weapons, the threat from fundamentalist Islamic forces, and the global reach of international terrorist organizations such as Al Qaeda.

Despite those developments, imagery capabilities remain a significant factor in the ability to gather intelligence. Imagery can still identify the dispersal of strategic and conventional military forces, from missile silos to airbases, the presence of above-ground nuclear facilities, and suspicious construction activities. It remains important to treaty verification, and it can provide warning of events that a nation's senior officials and diplomats would seek to forestall with advance knowledge—as when, in 1995, the United States was able to persuade India to forgo conducting a planned nuclear test after imagery indicated that preparations were under way.

It also remains vital in providing support to military planners and combat commanders when diplomacy fails. Imagery continues to help identify potential targets as well as particular points in such targets to attack, and to assess the damage done from such attacks. And with real-time capabilities, properly equipped commanders in the field have the ability to look over the horizon and see the enemy—his numbers, deployments, and movements—without delay.

Of course, the fact that imagery collection systems can produce significant intelligence does not necessarily imply that they are not without their limitations or that they are, in relative terms, as valuable as they were in an earlier era. Thus, key documents that may shed light on diplomatic or military intentions or capabilities cannot be photographed remotely. At times, such documents can be obtained via a human source.

Imagery systems can be subject to denial and deception. A nation that knows or suspects that some activity—for example, preparations for a nuclear test or WMD production—would be of interest to another nation's reconnaissance satellites may take care to eliminate or minimize the chance that those satellites will detect the preparations. Denial measures that might be taken include operating at night, not operating when a foreign reconnaissance satellite is estimated to be in range, and conducting test preparations under cover of another, more innocuous activity. A significant factor in India's ability to surprise the United States with its 1998 nuclear test was the precautions taken to avoid detection by U.S. spy satellites—including operating at night.

Deception involves more than preventing a foreign satellite or aircraft from obtaining an image of a target. It involves actively trying to induce another nation's imagery interpreters to draw false conclusions. Dummy military equipment, such as fake aircraft, can be deployed at an airbase to produce erroneous conclusions concerning the number and location of aircraft. Or a building might be made to appear as if it had been damaged by fire—as Libya unsuccessfully attempted to do with a chemical weapons facility. Alternatively, a nation may cover up signs of a certain activity to create the impression that no activity is under way. Thus, not only did India hide its preparations for a nuclear test in 1998, it made sure that when U.S. satellites were overhead they saw the same reassuring scene every time—including the same vehicles parked in the same spaces they would be in when no preparations were under way.

The inability of imaging sensors to penetrate through buildings provides a natural protection for targets. Assessing what is going on inside a building may depend on combining the hard data images with assumptions, and even speculation. Thus, in 1979 a U.S. satellite photographed the Severmorsk Weapons Storage Facility. The imagery allowed U.S. interpreters to identify a new arched roof bunker, a weapons-handling and maintenance facility, storage and support facilities, and a weapons assembly facility. But determining exactly what was inside the facility was more difficult. A Defense Intelligence Agency document noted that:

> this bunker, now almost completed, measures approximately 45 meters × 12 meters and will *probably* be used to store SS-N-14 missiles. A second, similar bunker is in the early stages of construction. . . . Taking into account the measurements of the almost completed bunker and *assuming* only one-level stacking with a central aisle for maneuvering will be utilized, about 60 SS-N-14 missiles may be stored. Further, *assuming* the second bunker to be constructed will be the same size, a similar number of stored missiles would bring the total capacity to 120.[11] [Emphasis added.]

A far more recent example of the limits of imagery is the faulty intelligence associated with the 2003 invasion of Iraq. UN inspectors left Iraq in December 1998 after Saddam Hussein's regime policy of obstruction made it impossible for them to carry out their mission. Over the next five years U.S. reconnaissance satellites produced images of reconstruction activities at sites that had been associated with each component of Iraq's weapons of mass destruction program—a nuclear weapons-related site at Al Furat, a chemical weapons site at Fallujah, a biological weapons facility at Abu Ghurayb, and a missile facility at Al Mamoun.[12] Satellite imagery also revealed the presence of vehicles around the facilities and the movement of vehicles to and from the facilities. But the imagery itself did not provide conclusive evidence of what was going on inside those facilities. Thus, interpreters were forced to draw conclusions based not only on the images in front of them, but on assumptions based on past Iraqi activities—assumptions that turned out to be incorrect.

Thus, imagery, like all other forms of intelligence collection, can produce significant intelligence in support of a nation's diplomatic or military endeavors. But there may also be situations when the information it produces is not truly conclusive and one must obtain additional ("collateral") data from another source—sometimes communications intercepts, sometimes a spy—to reach the correct conclusions.

NOTES

1. William E. Burrows, *Deep Black: Space Espionage and National Security* (New York: Random House, 1986), p. 28.

2. Ibid., p. 32.

3. Jeffrey T. Richelson, *A Century of Spies: Intelligence in the Twentieth Century* (New York: Oxford University Press, 1995), pp. 33, 96–100, 157–72.

4. Jeffrey T. Richelson, *The U.S. Intelligence Community* (Boulder, CO: Westview, 1999), pp. 153–54

5. Ibid., p. 155.

6. On developments with respect to reconnaissance satellite proliferation see, Jeffrey T. Richelson, "The Whole World Is Watching," *Bulletin of Atomic Scientists* (January–February 2006), pp. 26–35.

7. Office of Research and Reports, CIA, *Visual-Talent Coverage of the U.S.S.R. in Relation to Soviet ICBM Deployment, January 1959–June 1960,* July 11, 1960, pp. 101–13, in *CORONA: America's First Satellite Program,* ed. Kevin Ruffner (Washington, DC: Central Intelligence Agency, 1995).

8. Norman Polmar, *Spyplane: The U-2 History Declassified* (Osceola, WI: MBI, 2001), p. 208.

9. J. Michael Selander, "Image Coverage Models for Declassified Corona, Argon, and Lanyard Satellite Photography: A Technical Explanation," in *CORONA: Between the Sun and the Earth,* ed. Robert A. McDonald (Baltimore: ASPRS, 1997), p. 177; Photographic Interpretation Center, Central Intelligence Agency, *Joint Mission Coverage Index, Mission 9009, 18 August 1960,* September 1960, pp. 115–25 in Ruffner, ed., *CORONA.*

10. On the history of the U-2, see: Chris Pocock, *The U-2 Spyplane: Toward the Unknown* (Atglen, PA: Schiffer Military History, 2000).

11. *Documents From the Espionage Den (52): U.S.S.R.: The Aggressive East, Section 3-2* (Teheran: Muslim Students Following the Line of the Imam, n.d.), pp. 40–41.

12. National Security Archive Electronic Briefing Book No. 88, *Eyes on Saddam,* April 30, 2002, available at http://www.nsarchive.org.

5

THE IMPORTANCE AND FUTURE
OF ESPIONAGE

FREDERICK P. HITZ

WHEN PRESIDENT TRUMAN SIGNED THE NATIONAL SECURITY ACT of 1947 into law, creating the Central Intelligence Agency (CIA), he believed not that he was creating a new espionage organization for the United States, but rather that he was greatly improving the manner in which important national intelligence would find its way to his desk. Earlier he had disestablished the Office of Strategic Services (OSS), the wartime foreign intelligence collection and analytical entity, declaring that he did not want an American Gestapo in peacetime. By 1947, he had changed his mind on the need for a civilian intelligence organization for three principal reasons. First, and most important, the lessons of the 1941 Pearl Harbor attack strongly suggested the need for greater early warning of a future surprise attack on the United States. Second, he needed a centralizing intelligence organization that would gather and analyze all the intelligence reports headed for the Oval Office and attempt to make something coherent out of them so he would not have to do it himself. It is not clear that he wanted the new organization to go out and collect intelligence information on its own, as this had been tasked primarily to the Armed Services and to the Federal Bureau of Investigation (FBI). Third, he was convinced by Secretary of the Navy James Forrestal and others in his Cabinet that the U.S.S.R. would become a problem now that the Nazis were defeated, and that he needed a window into Stalin's thinking and imperial ambitions, especially in Western Europe. The Cold War was beginning.

The CIA got off to a slow start. Its early directors were military men who had a limited idea of the coordinating role the CIA was intended to play and were aware of the bureaucratic sharks circling them, representing the parochial interests of the military departments, the FBI, and the State Department, all of which wanted to maintain their direct access to the president on intelligence matters.

Two events conspired to change this modest approach. George F. Kennan penned his famous "Long Telegram" from Moscow, alerting Washington in 1946 to Stalin's imperialist designs on that part of Europe not already under Soviet control, and recommending a policy of "containment" by the United States. At the very least, this would require affirmative action by the United States in funding democratic political parties, labor unions, student groups, and cultural organizations in Italy, France, and Western Germany to oppose the Communist elements seeking to dominate these entities. In addition, to be most effective, the hand of the United States should remain hidden. The military were not the appropriate weapon to oppose clandestine Soviet infiltration and the State Department rejected the assignment, so the fledgling CIA got the job. Luckily, there was language in the 1947 Act creating the CIA that directed it to perform, with the authorization of the president, vice-president, and secretaries of defense and state acting as the National Security Council, "such other functions and duties related to intelligence affecting the national security as the National Security Council may from time to time direct." Thus was created the covert action responsibility of the CIA that grew enormously from 1948 to 1952 under the leadership of Frank Wisner. Wisner's so-called Office of Policy Coordination (OPC) was lodged ostensibly in the Department of State, but in reality it was an operational element of the CIA.

The second major development was the arrival on the scene of two savvy Directors of Central Intelligence (DCI). Air Force Lieutenant General Hoyt S. Vandenberg and retired Army General Walter Bedell Smith (who had been Eisenhower's wartime chief of staff) knew what the organization required to move up to the big leagues and were prepared to fight for it. Vandenberg was responsible for securing for future DCIs the requisites to do their job. The National Security Acts of 1947 and 1949 that he had lobbied for (and that had also shown the handiwork of an outside commission appointed by President Truman in 1949 that included Allen Dulles) gave the DCI unparalleled authority in Washington. They gave Vandenberg and his successors as DCI the power to: hire and fire his subordinates; spend money on their own say-so without further justification; short-circuit the federal government's cumbersome procurement authorities in order to perform the intelligence mission; and act across the range of intelligence collection, analysis, and dissemination responsibilities. The scope of authority was to include activities from classic espionage, to special operations (covert action), to all-source analysis, to briefing the president's National Security Council. In short, Vandenberg got the CIA, and the DCI especially, off to a running start before he returned to the Air Force. Bedell Smith took the new organization the rest of the way.

Bedell resuscitated the CIA's estimative intelligence, a function that had earned its stripes during the wartime OSS period but had lain dormant upon the OSS's demise. Estimative intelligence looks out to the future, attempting to foresee problems of concern to the president that may be coming down the line. With Truman's go-ahead, Bedell created a Board of National Estimate reporting to the

DCI, led by the same Harvard history professor, William Langer, who had put it together for General Donovan during World War II. Professor Langer managed to convince a number of wise men from the nation's best universities to work for him and Bedell, tasking them with tracking the future course of the Cold War rivalry with the U.S.S.R.

DCI Smith also made it clear that covert action and special operations existed in a chain of command extending from the DCI, and in coordination with the other espionage capability that the DCI oversaw for the president, the Office of Special Operations (OSO). He thus contrived to bring Wisner's OPC into the CIA in fact.

The OSO's responsibility was to gather foreign intelligence information by secret means (i.e., classic espionage). It was often stumbling over or wandering into operations conducted by the OPC, because the foreign actors who stole the secrets were often the same ones who could manage the propaganda or organize the political meetings for the OPC. This is an important historical point. If the CIA did not take the field to secretly oppose Soviet propaganda, backdoor electioneering, and subversion in Western Europe, several of the United States' most important allies might have been in jeopardy. Furthermore, intelligence activity that connoted "action" was very much in the American character. It drew many adherents in the early CIA both because there was a perceived need (as the constant stream of national security directives from the president and National Security Council attested) and because, if successful, you could see the results. At the same time, the slow, painstaking process of recruiting spies to report on happenings behind the Iron Curtain and in the Soviet Union itself had to be undertaken. In the late 1940s and 1950s this was difficult and dangerous work, new to Americans of whom very few spoke the relevant languages, Russian, Polish, Czech, and Hungarian. It required a patience and professionalism in terms of tradecraft that the OPCers sometimes overlooked or made fun of. The spy recruiters and handlers (of whom DCI-to-be Richard Helms was a prominent representative) were dubbed "the prudent professionals" and were not as esteemed or promoted as quickly as the OPC "action" types. Bedell tried to end all that by making of the OSO and OPC one clandestine service, directed by one chief, Allen Dulles, who reported to him. Over time it worked. The two skill sets became a little more interchangeable, although DCI Smith noted in his farewell remarks to President Truman that he thought the CIA was expending far too little effort with too meager results in acquiring intelligence penetrations of the Soviet Union.

Bedell was, of course, succeeded by DCI Allen Dulles, who jumped on the Eisenhower administration's desire to contain the Soviet Union by mounting covert action programs rather than confronting it with U.S. military force. As Supreme Commander, Allied Forces, Europe, in World War II, General Eisenhower had been a consumer of Britain's ENIGMA German code-breaking successes and knew both the role and the limitations of intelligence. As president, he believed strongly that the Soviet worldwide advance had to be stopped, if not rolled back, and covert action operations seemed a cheap and relatively low-risk way to do it. Enamored of early successes in overthrowing regimes in Iran (1953) and Guatemala (1954), the president and his advisors at the CIA grew accustomed to pushing the envelope in operations, overlooking close shaves and longer term backlash.

However, this extraordinary progress in spying on the U.S.S.R. and containing its influence during the Eisenhower years encountered several highly public setbacks as well. The revelation in May 1960, initially denied by President Eisenhower, that the Soviets had shot down a U-2 surveillance aircraft flying over Soviet territory, disrupted the Paris summit. The plan to secretly train Cuban exiles to land on Cuban soil to overthrow the Castro regime—later adopted by President Kennedy, and put into practice half-heartedly in an indefensible location at the Bay of Pigs—abruptly ended a run of successes by the CIA. Kennan's X article had alerted Washington to the bitter adversities ahead in confronting as politically hardened a foe as the Soviets; so it was naturally only a matter of time before a handful of poorly conceived or blighted operations gave the CIA an enduring notoriety and taint abroad, and dispelled the aura of the Agency's infallibility around Washington. The Bay of Pigs disaster triggered the replacement of Allen Dulles by John McCone, whose signal innovation as DCI was to put the analytical consensus within his own Agency under intense personal scrutiny.

The tattered doctrine of plausible deniability, however, still held an occasionally disproportionate allure for Kennedy and later presidents. After a national wake-up on the shores of Cuba's Bay of Pigs, JFK raised CIA's operational arm from the ashes, only to shoot for the moon all over again in *Operation Mongoose*, which saw the Agency embark on a rash of sometimes frantic missions to overthrow a now-entrenched Fidel Castro.

Despite the evident hazards of the profession, presidents relied substantially on CIA spies in Berlin to counter Soviet pressure there. The Eisenhower-Kennedy years were the beginning of the era of America's greatest technical intelligence successes as well, with spies and electronics working hand-in-glove in Berlin and elsewhere; with the construction of the U-2 high-altitude photo-reconnaissance aircraft; and with the refinement beginning in the 1960s of overhead satellite surveillance, eventually able to communicate images and intercepted electronic signals to Washington in real time. Nonetheless, it was on Cuba, in the October missile crisis in 1962, that U.S. intelligence showed that it had arrived at a position of sufficient maturity in its collection systems to be able to support President Kennedy with intelligence from all three principal collection branches: SIGINT, IMINT, and HUMINT. The U-2 flyovers were the first to supply photographs of Soviet medium- and intermediate-range ballistic missiles being transported to, unloaded, and installed in Cuba. Signals intercepts pointed to a heavy buzz of communications around the part of the island where the missiles were being installed, and human sources witnessed the transfer of mysterious long tubes on highways too small to accommodate them. Although there were many details that human sources were unable to provide, our principal spy,

Oleg Penkovsky, from his vantage point at the pinnacle of Soviet military intelligence, reported on the ranges and characteristics of the IRBMs and MRBMs which were being installed. He also revealed that General Secretary Khrushchev was way out in front of his Politburo in thus challenging the United States so close to its home territory.

The fact that President Kennedy had Penkovsky's insights into Khrushchev's overexposure, confirming the observations of his own former ambassador to the U.S.S.R. Llewelyn Thompson meant that JFK was prepared to give up the strategic advantage of a surprise attack on the installation and, in a masterstroke of statecraft, give General Secretary Khrushchev an opportunity to escape from the corner into which he had painted himself. In my view, this was the apex of U.S. intelligence support to the president during the Cold War.

After October 1962 prosecution of the Vietnam War became the overriding national security concern of Presidents Kennedy, Johnson, and Nixon. The CIA built up its presence in South Vietnam and collected useful human intelligence, from captured Vietcong and North Vietnamese prisoners especially, that permitted it to report consistently that the Government of South Vietnam (GOSVN) was unlikely to prevail in the war unless it took a more active role in the fighting and was able to win over greater support in the Vietnamese countryside. The CIA's rejection of the validity of high body counts that were held by American military intelligence to signal attrition in the North Vietnamese capacity to wage the war is reminiscent of today's intelligence controversy about the import of the nonexistence of weapons of mass destruction (WMD) in Iraq.

In the case of Vietnam, the CIA more or less stuck to its guns that North Vietnam was not being defeated in 1968 despite its loss of manpower, whereas it was "dead wrong" in its assessment of the existence of chemical and biological weapons stores in Iraq in 2003, according to the Silberman-Robb Presidential Commission Report. In both cases the requirement of good, on-the-ground, contemporaneous human source reporting was critical to CIA intelligence judgments. In Vietnam we had it, whereas in Iraq we did not. Silberman-Robb found that the critical National Intelligence Estimate of October 2002 on Iraqi WMD was based on unilateral spy reporting that dated from 1991, and UN weapons inspection reporting that dated to 1998. There was no direct, on-the-ground HUMINT after that before the outbreak of the war. Over the decades, the NIE process had taken on its share of taxing intelligence puzzles, but it was clearly compromised and out of date in this one.

It is ironic that, as today, the great blows to the quality and competence of CIA human source reporting in the 1970s were delivered during a Republican presidency, on the watch of a national security establishment that valued and to some extent depended on good intelligence for its activist foreign and defense policy. Although Richard Nixon privately disparaged the Ivy Leaguers at Langley whom he believed had favored his opponent in the 1960 presidential race against JFK, he needed good intelligence on Vietnam to support the Paris peace talks Secretary of State Henry Kissinger was conducting with the North Vietnamese, and also his overtures to China. Indeed, when it looked as if an unabashed Marxist, Salvador Allende, was poised to win the Chilean presidential election of 1970, it was to the CIA that President Nixon turned, improperly bypassing the rest of his foreign policy establishment and the U.S. Congress to mount a coup against a democratically elected Latin American leader.

Watergate and the Nixon resignation turned the tide against this manifestation of executive imperialism, while the CIA caught a fair measure of popular and congressional backlash. Investigative reporter Seymour Hersh wrote a series of articles in the *New York Times* in December 1974 setting forth the ways in which the CIA (and the FBI) had illegally spied on American anti–Vietnam War protesters, opened people's mail, tested hallucinogenic substances on unwitting subjects, and otherwise acted outside the bounds of an already broadly demarcated charter without the knowledge of Congress or the American people.[1]

Congressional reaction was swift and severe. The U.S. Senate and House of Representatives each convened investigating committees to hold extensive public hearings on CIA abuses. Senator Frank Church, a Democrat from Idaho who was running for president, tried to lock then-DCI William Colby into admissions that the Agency had attempted to assassinate several world leaders such as Fidel Castro, Patrice Lumumba of the Congo, Rafael Trujillo of the Dominican Republic, and Salvador Allende, without a president's authorization, claiming that the CIA was a "Rogue Elephant." In the end, the Church Committee was unable to substantiate these allegations. There was some assassination plotting at the CIA, directed by presidents, but none was shown to have been carried out successfully.

However, the Senate's inquiry caused President Ford to create a blue ribbon panel headed by Vice-President Rockefeller to look into the matter and to preempt Congress's certain desire to legislate restrictions on U.S. intelligence activity. Thus was born the effort to establish greater executive and legislative branch oversight of the intelligence community. President Ford promulgated Executive Order 11905 in February 1976, which banned assassination of foreign political leaders by U.S. intelligence operatives or their surrogates, among other restrictions. The order contained a number of additional dos and don'ts that were binding on the intelligence community, and it was reissued by Ford's successors, Carter and Reagan, in substantially the same form. After several years of trying to pass legislation establishing more comprehensive and binding charters for intelligence community agencies such as the FBI, CIA, NSA, and NRO, real-world dangers posed to the United States by the Soviet Union caused the public and Congress to regain some equilibrium on the subject of further restraining U.S. intelligence gathering capabilities, and the effort was dropped. Congress settled for one paragraph in the Intelligence Authorization Act of 1980. It required the DCI and the president to keep Congress "fully and currently informed" of all intelligence activities, including covert action, consistent with the president's constitutional authorities and the DCI's duty to protect "sources and methods from unauthorized disclosure."

Congress believed it could settle for this paragraph instead of the several-hundred-page charter bill, because it had established in 1975 and 1976 permanent oversight committees of the House and Senate to review intelligence community programs and operations, just as every other department and agency in the executive branch is reviewed.

Some argue that since the creation of the House Permanent Select Committee on Intelligence (HPSCI) and the Senate Select Committee on Intelligence (SSCI), with rotating memberships after seven years service, the CIA has never been the same aggressive collector of human intelligence that it was during the height of the Cold War. I disagree. The world had changed by 1975. Although the Soviets still maintained a nuclear arsenal pointed at America's heartland, it was on the downhill side of the slope economically and politically. It had an aging leadership and an increasing inability to provide for the needs and wants of its people. The United States was receiving more volunteers as spies from the Soviet Union, as its high-ranking cadres became increasingly gloomy about the country's future prospects. In the United States Vietnam had exploded the postwar consensus surrounding U.S. foreign policy, and a stronger demand for oversight and accountability for all of America's overseas activities had emerged.

When this era of intelligence reform ended, the full-time housecleaners who worked at Langley and the FBI had managed to stay out of the headlines for the most part. Spying against private citizens clearly violated the 1947 Act but made for no more than a sideshow when compared to spy-hunting inside the U.S. government. Light almost never shines on this most sensitive area of surveillance, counterespionage, but in this domain of intelligence work especially, tumult has been virtually inseparable from tradecraft. Penetrations and double-crosses can be expected in the competition among major intelligence services, but the integrity of intelligence operations rests on how well very fragmentary and circumstantial clues about possible security breaches can be read. Moles were often uncovered only years after their work got started. Indeed, when the Cold War did end abruptly, counterespionage work was not ready to wind down but was putting itself in high gear, as Americans were making inroads into the former Warsaw Pact services, shedding light on turncoats here at home.

American intelligence contended with a number of notorious penetrations in the Cold War, and most spectacular of these was the early discovery that the Soviets had recruited the top British liaison official in America, Kim Philby. Philby had until then been regarded as one of MI6's best men—a man in line to be its next director, a brilliant and affable character, and a mentor to many of Langley's rising stars. The United States had depended heavily on him personally for many of our early postwar efforts in Europe. Philby had been in a position to alert Moscow to many of the biggest and most sensitive intelligence exploits under way: the development of the atomic bomb and the VENONA project, through which the NSA was attempting to break encrypted communications from the Soviet embassy and the New York consulate during World War II. But he could not prevent the NSA from discovering an old code-name, Homer, referring to a British mole in the U.K. embassy in Washington. Homer was one member of the entire Cambridge Five spy ring, another of whom was quickly tied to Philby, as a friend boarding at Philby's home. In 1951, Philby's official career effectively ended. But it took another decade's worth of revelations for his career as a double-agent to be sufficiently understood to put him in criminal jeopardy, where-upon he defected.

James Jesus Angleton, the CIA's master spy-hunter, was one among many of Philby's former friends on whom his treachery left a lasting impression. Angleton's occupation at the CIA was actually not widely known. He was simply, "the Ghost of Langley," the man who showed up unannounced at the DCI's office for an immediate, private audience with the boss. A classics major and poet at Yale who moved in the same circles as T.S. Eliot and Ezra Pound, Angleton was picked toward the beginning of his career to run the counterin-telligence operation in Rome, during the crucial 1947 elections that kept the Italian Communist Party out of power. Angleton's early career also solidified CIA liaison operations with other services, including those of Britain and Israel. And he worked alongside the Mafia during his Rome posting. The Mafia had operated on behalf of the OSS in wartime Italy, and had helped to perfect some of the more lethal aspects of the CIA's tradecraft.

Angleton's cunning instincts came to the attention of Allen Dulles, who asked him in 1954 to head the CIA's counterspy operations. By 1959, Angleton had unearthed Jack Dunlap as a mole in the NSA who had reached high-level "no inspection" clearances. But in retrospect, though the Philby affair had ignited Angleton's imagination, it had not furnished the CIA with the kind of tradecraft lessons that would shed a much clearer light on future penetration controversies. In 1961 Angleton seemed to be nearing more breakthroughs, having been given personal charge of debriefing a defecting KGB major, Yuri Golitsyn, but Golitsyn became increasing problematic for the CIA over time. In addition to the key information he did betray, he was willing to speculate endlessly about other pen-etrations of U.S. intelligence, and spun out theories that Angleton showed himself ready to embrace. Among the most troubling questions he raised was the identity of the mole Sasha, a code-name that sparked the most tortuous inquisition that the Agency would ever launch: These investigations had such disproportionate im-pact on work at the Agency that their records remain completely restricted to this day. And Golitsyn insisted with some vehemence to CIA officers, after each subsequent defector surfaced, that anyone to follow him would almost certainly be a plant, blunting the CIA Counterintelligence Staff's instincts. The name of one of those subsequent defectors, Yuri Nosenko, was much later cleared of being a Soviet double agent, but Nosenko fell afoul of his own glaring penchant for fabrication, and at first cast the most severe suspicions upon himself. Working on Angleton's behalf, J. Edgar Hoover's FBI went to extremes to try to extract a confession from Nosenko but were ultimately unsuccessful. Meanwhile, No-senko had languished in solitary confinement for three years. In the aftermath,

Hoover judged Angleton poisonously misguided, and the debacle helped to drive a permanent wedge between the FBI and CIA, from which neither agency extricated itself until after September 11.

Angleton put at least fifty intelligence officers under surveillance during his career, and removed at least sixteen from the service. Problems at the CIA became more severe as his views darkened into clinical paranoia over the course of the 1960s. The only personal trust Angleton was ultimately able to sustain was in his closest circle. Meanwhile he elaborated plots with Golitsyn's help. As facts became hunches, and his hunches increasingly bordered on the absurd, he came into permanent conflict with the Agency's leadership. Finally, he could not find a distinction between political loyalty and personal allegiance to his theories. He was barred from direct contact with Golitsyn in 1968 by DCI Dick Helms, and ushered into retirement in 1974 by DCI Bill Colby, while the Hersh revelations of domestic spying were in the headlines. His Counterintelligence Staff was diminished from 300 to 80.

The counterespionage underworld that defends against other powerful foreign intelligence agencies is a reality in which things remain extraordinarily indeterminate. A myriad of conceivable avenues might lead to operational betrayal. Angleton's version of reality was to adopt the premise that the most successful Soviet campaigns were those of knowingly false information—disinformation—that could operate at a great remove from the Agency's headquarters. Penetrations were less important than the false tracks onto which the CIA could be lured. But in truth the kinds of judgment calls are immensely difficult that spy-hunters must make to arrive at breakthroughs in cases of penetration. Major revelations might never come down the road. And surveillance might fail to turn up any mole at all. Moreover, in the life-or-death stakes of the Cold War, there was always the potential that too broad or intrusive a mole-hunt would leave more self-inflicted damage to CIA operations than unearthing a mole would stanch. Nevertheless, crucial countermeasures still had to be taken, and in counterespionage it was often the effort to run down trails of minor lifestyle and procedural misconduct that kept operations secure.

Philby was the result of a relatively spectacular breakthrough, but the Aldrich Ames and Robert Hanssen penetrations during the 1980s and 1990s remained almost entirely invisible for years after the investigations got rolling. Ames and Hanssen did their damage over a period of time when CIA attitudes about lifestyle and procedural misconduct had remained too lax for too long. The Agency lost the distinction between operations in the outside world and the life of discipline required inside. Most espionage operations are carried out in the gray areas of administrative procedure; but over the years, these moles built microcosms of that mission right in the offices that they ran at the CIA and FBI. Like all other skilled professions, intelligence officers have to accept a high level of personal autonomy in those they rely upon; but the basics of tradecraft, on-time reporting, and drug and alcohol-free behavior are important too. Over the long haul, the maintenance of strict operational routine and personal integrity goes a

fair ways toward assuring the success of the intelligence community in its operational mission.

Within the CIA, the chaos that followed Operation CHAOS (the controversial CIA
domestic mail-opening program revealed in 1974) lasted well into the Carter
presidency and the tenure of DCI Stansfield Turner. President Carter put the CIA
back on the offensive in his changing attitude to the Sandinistas in Nicaragua, and
the covert action he instigated to oppose the Soviet takeover of Afghanistan in
1979. Still, it remained for Ronald Reagan to initiate an across-the-board revi-
talization of both U.S. defense and intelligence resources that would reverse the
post–Vietnam War drawdown and counter ongoing outbreaks of Soviet aggression. President Reagan authorized a covert action to train and reinforce the *contra*
resistance to the Marxist Sandinista revolution of 1979 in Nicaragua, and a second
covert program to build up the *mujahedeen* factions opposing the Soviet-
controlled government in Afghanistan. At the same time, he initiated a research
program to intercept incoming missiles in space. The Kremlin began to believe the
United States was trying for a first-strike capability against the U.S.S.R. and
initiated a worldwide intelligence alert called Project Ryan to report on indicators
confirming such an effort. At the same time, old age and sickness were removing
Soviet premiers at a record rate. In March 1985 a completely new figure ascended
to power in the Kremlin, Mikhail Gorbachev, who was focused on curtailing
Soviet commitments to defend communism everywhere (the Brezhnev Doctrine)
and reforming the economy to provide a better response to the needs of the Soviet
people. Meanwhile the Reagan administration was having a difficult time keeping
the U.S. Congress on board for the operation to support the *contra*s. After the
second amendment curtailing CIA support for the *contras* passed Congress—
and was signed into law by the president because it was attached to an omnibus
year-end appropriations bill—some members of the administration on the National
Security staff and in the CIA concocted a scheme to sell embargoed weaponry to Iran in exchange for information about terrorists who had abducted Americans in the Middle East, using the proceeds from the sales to supply weapons
illegally to the *contras*. The Iran-Contra scheme finally blew up in the press in
fall 1986, sending the Reagan White House and William Casey's CIA into a
tailspin.

It took the appointment in 1987 of Judge William Webster as DCI, a former
Director of the FBI and U.S. Court of Appeals judge, to restore legitimacy and
integrity to CIA operations after the Iran-*contra* fiasco. Meanwhile, CIA covert
operators got congressional approval to supply Stinger missiles to the Afghan
mujahedeen, a policy that proved pivotal to driving the Soviets out of Afghanistan. As unintentionally transparent as the Nicaraguan covert action was to the
world, so the cooperation by the CIA with the Pakistani intelligence service to
supply armaments to Afghani and Arab guerillas in Afghanistan was painted as
a state secret within the boundaries of "plausible deniability." The Soviets knew
where the weaponry, especially the Stingers, was coming from, but they were in

no position to do much about it, despite the concerns of Pakistan's nervous chief of state, Mohammed Zia-ul-Haq.

To date, the Afghan covert action has been the last big successful clandestine political operation mounted by the CIA in which the U.S. hand did not show to an impermissible degree. By and large, the CIA officers involved kept their promise to Pakistan's rulers that they would physically stay out of Afghanistan and work through the Pakistani intelligence service, the ISI. The advent of both round-the-clock cable news programming and instant worldwide communications via the Internet have successfully impinged upon the United States's ability to maintain the necessary secrecy of a major covert political operation. This was made manifest in the administration of President George H.W. Bush, when the president, despite his tour of duty as DCI and his appreciation for the role of intelligence, turned instead to the American military to deal with both Manuel Noriega in Panama in 1989 and Saddam Hussein in the first Gulf War in 1991. When President Clinton sought to make use of covert action in overthrowing Saddam in the mid-1990s, he found it was impossible. Congress had gained an appetite for micromanaging an operation that could have high domestic stakes, and the CIA had too few covert assets to bring it off.

By the same token, viewed in retrospect, in the mid-1980s it would turn out that the United States had suffered unprecedented high-level penetrations of its intelligence services, through the handiwork of Aldrich Ames in the CIA and Robert Hanssen in the FBI. Ames began his espionage for Soviet handlers in March 1985 in order to get $50,000 to buy himself out of debt. He was a thirty-year spy in the CIA's operations directorate who had specialized in Soviet matters, arriving at a senior level even though he had a mediocre record—which included numerous episodes of alcohol abuse, security violations, and a chronic inability to get his financial accountings and contact reports about meetings with Soviet officials in on time. In short, Ames probably should never have been permitted to be on the front line, meeting and assessing Soviet officials one-on-one. But he was. And he used his position and his knowledge of how both the Soviet and U.S. intelligence systems operated to betray, over a period of nine years, every agent working for the United States against the U.S.S.R.; details of numerous U.S. operations against the Soviets; and the names of his colleagues who were engaged in the effort. Ames's betrayal led to the certain execution of ten U.S. spies and probably more, along with the compromise of hundreds of U.S. intelligence operations. The arrest of Aldrich Ames in 1994 provoked a wave of disillusionment and dismay in the American public, and among the congressional oversight committees, that such a sloppy and seemingly inept spy could betray so much over such a long period, not only without being caught, but without the CIA having mounted a serious effort to track him. The damage to the Agency's reputation was nothing short of devastating.

For the FBI, no less damaging was the tale of Robert Hanssen, a dour misfit who had used his superior information technology skills to eventually burrow into the deepest corners of the Bureau's counterintelligence operations against the U.S.S.R. Hanssen managed to turn over vast amounts of operational detail and names of U.S. agents to the Soviets in an on again–off again career of espionage that began in the late 1970s and continued until his arrest in February 2001. Hanssen's case was a tougher one to crack than Ames's because Hanssen had been careful never to meet with his Soviet handler, conducting all his business with the Soviets through dead drops in a park near his home in Northern Virginia. Furthermore, Hanssen had compromised many of the same spies named by Ames or by Edward Lee Howard, another CIA turncoat of the period; so it took an analysis of operations that had gone sour that could not have been compromised by Ames or Howard, and also the help of a Soviet source, before Hanssen's own activities could be distinguished and an arrest finally made.

At the same time that these spy wars were taking place between the Soviet and U.S. intelligence services, the CIA was beginning to enjoy real success in running Soviet and Bloc volunteer spies who were supplying vast amounts of useful intelligence information about Soviet and Warsaw Pact war-fighting plans in Europe, and Soviet military research and development (R&D). In the former case, Ryszard Kuklinski, a high-ranking member of the Polish General Staff, passed the CIA all of the Warsaw Pact plans that crossed his desk from 1972 until his defection in 1981; and in the second case, Adolph Tolkachev provided his U.S. case officer with the latest Soviet military R&D on stealth technology and air defense missilery from the late 1970s until 1985, saving the U.S. taxpayer millions of dollars in unnecessary defense expenditure. These successful Soviet spy volunteer recruitments at the end of the Cold War, and others like them, proved the value of a vigorous human source collection program at the time that the Soviet regime was under severe internal stress.

The need for espionage did not disappear with the dismantling of the Berlin Wall in 1989 and the dismemberment of the U.S.S.R. in 1991. The successor Russian government kept its intelligence officers in the field and the West at bay on a number of important issues. Yet, over time, the threats targeted by American intelligence agencies began to shift. As authoritarian regimes calcified or collapsed over the decade of the 1990s—frequently ex–Cold War client governments—the new threats would become proliferating weapons of mass destruction and emerging nonstate terrorist factions, exemplified by Osama bin Laden and Al Qaeda.

In a series of bold and ever more sophisticated attacks, beginning with that on the Khobar Towers, a U.S Air Force billet in Saudi Arabia in 1997; followed by the bombings of U.S. embassies in Dar es Salaam and Nairobi in 1998; and the attack on the *U.S.S. Cole* in 2000, this affluent Saudi veteran of the *mujahedeen* effort against the Soviets in Afghanistan, Osama bin Laden, showed he was capable and desirous of inflicting unacceptable damage on the United States in order to drive it out of the Muslim holy places of the Middle East. His organization, known as Al Qaeda, or the Franchise, had in 1991 volunteered to lead the Islamic effort to force Saddam Hussein to leave Kuwait, but his offer was overlooked by the Saudi royals. Subsequently in exile in the Sudan, and after 1995 in Afghanistan as a guest of the Taliban regime, Osama preached Islamic unity and defiance in opposing the West's continued military basing in the region and the support it was giving to autocratic and selfish rulers in Saudi Arabia, Egypt, and the Gulf who were doing nothing to provide for their populations. The CIA, in particular in the U.S. intelligence community, became alarmed at the growing strength, sophistication, and appeal of Osama's rhetoric against the United States' role in the Middle East, which targeted it as the "far enemy." After President Clinton's weak and ineffective response to the African embassy bombings, the CIA established a task force to track Osama and Al Qaeda, but it was never able to deliver the knockout punch on his compound in Afghanistan or stop his continuing deadly momentum during the Clinton years, even though then-DCI George Tenet "declared war" on Al Qaeda in an attempt to bring focus to American intelligence's counterterrorist strategy.

In 2001 the CIA began receiving heightened liaison reporting from U.S. allies in Europe and the Middle East that Al Qaeda was planning something big. But where—in the region or against a U.S. installation overseas—was unknown. This was becoming Osama's trademark: long months of preparation and then a sudden strike. But just like the U.S. government's previous experience with a massive surprise attack on U.S. territory at Pearl Harbor, we were not prepared nor really expecting an attack in the continental United States. September 11, 2001, was an unforeseen and life-shattering wake-up call on the capacity of nonstate, religious-inspired terrorism to threaten stable societies like the United States and our European allies. It took President George W. Bush minutes to declare that the United States was involved in a war against terror and that all the military and intelligence resources of the United States would be deployed to win it.

What were those intelligence resources? In late 2001, in what condition did the intelligence community find itself to take on Osama bin Laden, Al Qaeda, and the challenge of religious-based international terror? With the passing of the Cold War, the CIA had been downsized and had in addition witnessed the dramatic departure of large numbers of expert spy handlers and analysts whose skills had been shaped by the challenge of the Soviet Union, and who did not have much interest in and familiarity with the milieu of terrorism, drugs, crime, and weapons proliferation, issues which would be the meat and potatoes of Presidential Decision Directive 35 that set the blueprint for intelligence community targeting after the Cold War ended. So they retired, and took with them their knowledge of spy tradecraft and of foreign languages. On top of that, as the 9/11 post-mortems would show, the intelligence agencies had grown into mature bureaucracies without much initiative, imagination, or creativity. They faced a target that operated in the shadows of nation-states but wasn't one; that had low overhead and a tight network of collaborators that it deployed with iron-handed discipline; and that possessed one unassailable attribute: Many of its adherents were willing to commit suicide for the cause, and would strap on a bomb just to take civilian bystanders with them.

Other problems beset the intelligence agencies in 2001 as well. A division between domestic and international spheres of terrorism no longer existed. A plot that could begin in a Hamburg mosque or a Madrid suburb could be planned for immediate execution in New York or Washington. The divided responsibilities between the FBI and CIA that historical accident and concern about domestic civil liberties had spawned in the aftermath of World War II were hindrances in the 21st century to the kind of instant information sharing and teamwork that cell phones and Internet access in the hands of our terrorist attackers demanded. Compartmentalization and "need to know" take on sinister meanings when the effect is to deny intelligence to a sister agency equally charged with the responsibility to pre-empt a terrorist act.

Some of the more egregious barriers to intelligence sharing and teamwork between the intelligence agencies were struck down in the USA-PATRIOT Act passed in October 2002, and in the Intelligence Reform Bill, passed in December 2004. Now, wiretap permissions, when granted, run to the individual who is the target of the surveillance, not the instrument by which he intends to communicate. Grand jury testimony in terrorist cases can be shared among the law enforcement and intelligence entities having an interest in the matter. The Foreign Intelligence Surveillance Act (FISA) has been amended to include among the parties against whom the U.S. government may seek authorization for electronic surveillance from the special Foreign Intelligence Surveillance Court not just spies but terrorists as well; and the standard for authorizing surveillance has been broadened to encompass those as to whom terrorism is "a principal purpose" of their activity and not "the" purpose. There are additional sections in the 2001 Act that beef up the anti–money laundering provisions of federal statute and enhance the "sneak and peek" possibilities open to law enforcement, as well as enable more Internet intrusion of suspected terrorists. It is possible that some of the more aggressive portions of the USA-PATRIOT Act may be modified somewhat to include a greater measure of accountability.

The intended changes included in the Intelligence Reform Act of 2004 date back to the Church Committee era but trespassed on more turf, and would only see the light of day three years after September 11, with some of the most intense bureaucratic lobbying of any intelligence bill. In the Act, there has been a concerted effort to remedy one of the principal perceived deficiencies in the performance of the intelligence agencies prior to 9/11, namely the absence of "an attending physician" who could treat the patient as a whole and be responsible for the work of all the specialists racing around performing tests on the patient on their own. That metaphor, used by the 9/11 Commission to sway Congress and the president, was the premise behind creating the new position of Director of National Intelligence (DNI). The DNI was intended to be the intelligence czar, a Cabinet officer holding both managerial and budgetary authority over the entire intelligence community. He would also be the president's principal intelligence adviser.

When the dust settled after passage of the Act, the DNI's lines of command were not as clear as the Commission hoped for. The Defense Secretary and the Department of Defense (DOD) continue to share many of the DNI's management

and budgetary authorities relating to the intelligence agencies under the command of the DOD. The DOD intelligence agencies—NRO, NSA, DIA, and NGA—
account for 80 percent of the intelligence budget. There is also the matter of
information sharing, which the Act seeks to encourage by requiring the DNI to
have a subordinate responsible for creating an information sharing environment
in the intelligence community.

The 2004 Act also treats the intelligence community's self-inflicted wounds
represented by the failures to warn of the 9/11 attacks and to accurately account
for the weapons of mass destruction stockpiled by Saddam Hussein since 1991—
believed ready for dispersal to terrorists by Saddam at some point if the UN
embargo of Iraq was not lifted. The existence of Iraqi WMD was one of the
principal reasons cited by the Bush administration for preparing to go to war
against Iraq. A seemingly authoritative National Intelligence Estimate (NIE) cir-
culated by the CIA in October 2002 detailed the supposed holdings of chemical
and biological weapons by the Iraqi Ba'athist regime, and the efforts of the regime
to make nuclear weaponry advances. Furthermore, United Nations testimony
drawn from the NIE by Secretary of State Colin Powell in February 2003, on the
eve of the Iraq War, was used to sweep aside Allied opposition to the invasion. It
has become painfully clear since that Saddam suspended his WMD programs
after 1991 to get out from under the UN-sponsored embargo. There were no
WMD stockpiled in Iraq prior to the war, as Saddam had destroyed them.

What made the U.S. intelligence community's views on Iraqi WMD so
objectionable was not that they held such preconceptions (most other knowledgeable intelligence services held identical views—the UK, Russia, Germany,
France, and Israel), but that the NIE sought to justify the weapons' existence on
outdated and unconfirmed reporting. The proprietary data dated from 1991; reports from UN inspectors stopped in 1998; and assessments rested heavily on
unilateral sources like "Curveball" whose credibility was in question. The analytical tradecraft employed by the CIA on the critical NIE was fatally deficient.

At the same time, the president's decision to spread the war from Afghanistan to Iraq sounded alarm bells for quite a few veteran intelligence officers
within the ranks. A number of these in-house critics believed the move into Iraq
would instantly squander goodwill that the American government had gained in
the Islamic world as a result of the September 11 attacks. Some intelligence officers subscribed to the view, later corroborated in the post-invasion Iraq Survey
Group's two reports, that the inspections broken off in 1998 and the sanctions in
place after had already boxed in Saddam.

Moreover, although DCI George Tenet had gained the confidence of the
hawks on the president's war cabinet, both Vice President Cheney and Defense
Secretary Donald Rumsfeld made it known in the press that they harbored deep
distrust of the CIA's analysis of Iraq. The Defense Secretary had steered the 1998
Rumsfeld Commission that took the CIA to task to sharpen its poor nonprolif-
eration reporting, against a backdrop of two missed calls at the Agency in five
years—Saddam Hussein's startling WMD advances up to the 1990 Gulf War, and

India's clandestine nuclear tests in 1996. The vice-president possessed quite the opposite disposition, misappropriating even dubious raw intelligence leads to hype the imminent threat from the Ba'athist regime. Analysts at Langley found themselves frozen out of most White House planning. The war cabinet opened a small ad hoc shop within the Defense Department to cherry-pick intelligence reporting from across the community, to be seeded in the media to reinforce two bogus claims: (1) that Iraq's Ba'athists had entered into an active pact with bin Laden's network, and that (2) the Ba'athists were on the verge of going nuclear. The Secretary was known to scorn the DIA's Iraq analysis as well, and he overruled pointed warnings issued by the Army Chief of Staff that the U.S. military could not occupy the country without a contingent of 300,000 soldiers. Amidst rising tensions and mounting controversy over Saddam's alleged possession of nuclear weaponry, Tenet balked too, sending a formal request to the Department of Justice to begin a criminal investigation to identify the source of a leak of a CIA operative's identity (a career officer who was unwittingly dragged into the dispute over the war's strained *casus belli*) even though it was sufficiently clear that the leaker would have to have been a senior White House official.

As the war wore the military down until it was an occupation in disarray, disgruntlement surfaced publicly. First, Richard Clarke, the former counterterrorism czar at the National Security Council made searing statements against the administration at the 9/11 Commission hearings, and then the departing National Intelligence Officer for the Middle East, Paul Pillar spoke out:

> If the entire body of official intelligence analysis on Iraq had a policy implication, it was to avoid war—or, if war was going to be launched, to prepare for a messy aftermath. What is most remarkable about prewar U.S. intelligence on Iraq is not that it got things wrong and thereby misled policymakers; it is that it played so small a role in one of the most important U.S. policy decisions in recent decades.[2]

The overlord at the DIA for Iraq planning, Spider Marks, told a reporter at the *Times* that prewar misjudgments had been made in many quarters, not just in the Cabinet leadership. "We lost our finger on the pulse of the Iraqi people and built intelligence assessments from a distance."[3] Out in Langley, the CIA has been under a pall.

The blunt consensus in the 9/11 Commission report and on Capitol Hill in the Intelligence Reform Act of 2004 to downgrade the CIA was probably not ill-advised. The Agency now has the leeway to be loyal at arm's length during domestic imbroglios, and in principle it has a new referee in the DNI. This has hardly been an auspicious time, however, to watch the demoralization at the CIA, with constant leaking of sensitive intelligence information and the hemorrhaging of experienced intelligence officers into lucrative private-sector security jobs or retirement. Where does that now leave the CIA and the intelligence community, who bear the preponderant responsibility to inform the president about terrorists and their targets *before* these attacks occur? Future performance alone will provide the answer. The intelligence community has weathered its share of crises in the past. Yet there are some systemic reasons to be concerned.

To start with, the intelligence agencies allowed their capabilities to attenuate markedly during that ten-year period between the disintegration of the Soviet Union and September 11, 2001. There are still too few intelligence officers who have studied and understand Arabic civilizations or who have lived in the Middle East at some point in their careers. Moreover, many of the collection techniques of the Cold War have been rendered obsolete by cell phones, the Internet, and other aspects of changing technology. The CIA cannot continue to operate as it did in the pre-Iraq period, largely excluded from the hard targets that the United States is up against. Where it has no physical presence, the Agency has histori-cally relied for HUMINT primarily on defectors, detainees, legal travelers, oppo-sition groups, and foreign government liaison services, but these sources divulge their secrets at some distance in time and space from the ongoing developments inside the target they are reporting on. Getting inside the adversary's organization is thus a higher priority than it was even in the Cold War. Yet even though the Directorate of Operations budget is now more than double its pre–September 11 levels, an estimated 80–90 percent of intelligence information about Al Qaeda still comes in as SIGINT.[4] The whereabouts, goals, and tactics of terrorists are thus available only imprecisely and intermittently.

In the HUMINT area, American intelligence is still behind other services in having linguists who speak the hard languages of the Middle East, Central Asia, or Southeast Asia. In addition, this assignment is becoming less appealing to spy runners from the standpoint of safety and quality of life. Increasingly, CIA oper-atives will bring back key intelligence only by acting with the flexibility, the skills, and the cover it takes to run operations unlinked with an official installation—under nonofficial cover. Consequently, the problems spies face conducting espio-nage will be more dangerous. Families, too, will be divided, as many overseas tours in areas of prime concern to the intelligence agencies are not safe for young children.

Furthermore, there has been an especially rocky post-Tenet transition for the current Director of the Central Intelligence Agency (DCIA), former Congress-man Porter Goss. Mr. Goss has been criticized for bringing a number of hostile and inexperienced congressional staffers with him to Langley, making for even more precipitous erosion from the ranks among senior officers with substantial field experience. This will hinder the CIA's ability to take full advantage of the uptick in personnel recruitment, because so many experienced officers appear to be leaving. Goss announced that rebuilding the operations directorate would be the overriding priority of his tenure, but an irony thus far has been the number of critics comparing the present impasse to DCI Stansfield Turner's first year, marked by some of the most severe confrontations and mishandled purges the Directorate had ever experienced. By the end of 2005, Goss had lost one

Directorate of Operations head, two deputy directors, and more than a dozen department, division, and station heads.[5]

An equally fundamental point is that Americans are not the "good guys" any more in many areas of the Middle East. This sounds simplistic, yet much of U.S. intelligence success during the mature stages of the Cold War occurred because Soviet and Soviet Bloc officials volunteered to work for the American or British intelligence services as a way to oppose the corruption and misery of their own lives behind the Iron Curtain. That motivation appears less prevalent in the Middle East today. The United States is perceived as a threatening, non-Islamic outside force, only interested in the region's petroleum resources. Perhaps President Bush's hard push for democratic governments in the region will alter this attitude. It will be a hard sell.

The upshot of pervasive suspicions in the region about American aims is that, to be successful, the CIA and the other intelligence community HUMINT collectors will have to work indirectly, and multilaterally, through the good offices of friendly intelligence services, the operational channels called intelligence liaison. Since September 11 the CIA has been doing that in a major way, trading superior resources and technology for on-the-ground intelligence information about terrorist threats. The CIA has built a formalized network of over two dozen liaison offices, and DOD has gotten into the game as well, with less formal and even lower profile liaison and reconnaissance missions for the special forces. These DOD operations do not fill the need for nonofficial cover and penetrations, but they do have a tactical yield.

The difficulty liaison relationships present, however, is that we are no longer in complete control of the spy operation. Our liaison intermediaries will influence both whom we target and how we manage the take. The result is bound in many cases to be a dilution of the product and a diminished timeliness. But the most worrisome deficiency will be a lack of confidence that one is getting the full picture, with the ongoing potential to leave the United States vulnerable and the region unstable. It is worth remembering the lessons of the Pakistani ISI's control over our access to the *mujahedeen* during the 1980s and 1990s in Afghanistan, or the heavily slanted read of the opposition that the Shah's SAVAK presented the CIA in Iran's prerevolutionary decades. Nevertheless, liaison operations account so far for nearly all of the 3,000 suspected terrorists who have been captured or killed outside the Iraq theater.[6]

Disruptions in these liaison relationships comes with the territory, but the CIA's experiences in Latin American counternarcotics operations have provided a number of relatively useful lessons for working with less corruptible, more trustworthy elite units in the more questionable partnerships with foreign services. Porter Goss has rightly pronounced himself wary of leaning too far toward liaison operations. There are, however, elements of liaison operations that cannot be replaced by CIA HUMINT work. The first of these is legal access: To carry out targeted killings in a foreign country, it becomes prudent to give and receive assurances from other sovereign governments. Kidnapping also is best avoided wherever the local service is willing to kick down the door for us. And shutting down nearly endlessly reroutable financing pipelines to terrorists requires a willingness to do so on the part of many sovereign partners simultaneously.

The intelligence community's technical collection programs may not be in much better shape than its HUMINT. Signals intelligence gathering is hindered by inadequate translation capabilities, while a wary target will be more willing to communicate by word of mouth, cleft stick, and carrier pigeon, than by telephone or more modern means. From an operational standpoint, the fallout from the brouhaha over warrantless surveillance by the NSA of communications from potential terrorists abroad with individuals in the United States that arose in early 2006 may further limit the gathering of useful intelligence. Actually, it appears that most Al Qaeda instructions are moving through Arabic websites on the Internet, which intelligence services worldwide are not yet recovering or translating in a comprehensive or timely fashion.

When all is said and done, counterterrorism and counterproliferation intelligence gathering follows a new paradigm. It is less about classic espionage than persistent tracking of terrorists and their potential weapons by good detective work and perceptive mining of reams of open sources. This is no longer back-alley skulking in a trench coat. It is down-and-dirty police investigative work, tracing radicals and their bomb-making materials, and recruiting informants to watch mosques and radical meeting sites. That is why in the United States it is so important for the CIA to work well with the FBI, with Customs, with Immigration and Naturalization, and with local police first responders. Intelligence gathering in the 21st century is now less about James Bond or George Smiley than it is a Frankenstein composite of law enforcement, spies, and forensics.

NOTES

The author wishes to express his gratitude to Princeton Woodrow Wilson School Ph.D. candidate Martin Stein who assisted significantly in the preparation of this chapter.

1. Seymour Hersh, "Huge CIA Operation Reported in U.S. Against Antiwar Forces, Other Dissidents During Nixon Years," *New York Times,* December 22, 1974; Hersh, "President Tells Colby to Speed Report on CIA," *New York Times,* December 24, 1974; Hersh, "3 More Aides Quit in CIA Shake-Up," *New York Times,* December 30, 1974.

2. Paul R. Pillar, "Intelligence, Policy, and the War in Iraq," *Foreign Affairs* 85 (March/April 2006), pp. 15–27, at 16.

3. Michael R. Gordon, "Catastrophic Success: Poor Intelligence Misled Troops About Risk of Drawn-Out War," *New York Times,* October 20, 2004.

4. Dana Priest, "Foreign Network at Front of CIA's Terror Fight," *Washington Post,* November 18, 2005.

5. Dafna Linzer, "A Year Later, Goss's CIA Is Still in Turmoil," *Washington Post,* October 19, 2005.

6. Ibid.

6

OPEN SOURCE INTELLIGENCE

ROBERT DAVID STEELE

OPEN SOURCE INTELLIGENCE (OSINT) IS THE ONLY discipline that is both a necessary foundation for effective classified intelligence collection and analysis and a full multimedia discipline in its own right, combining overt human intelligence from open sources, commercial imagery, foreign broadcast monitoring, and numerous other direct and localized information sources and methods not now properly exploited by the secret intelligence community. OSINT is uniquely important to the development of strategic intelligence not only for the government, but for the military, law enforcement, business, academia, nongovernmental organizations, the media, and civil societies including citizen advocacy groups, labor unions, and religions for the simple reason that its reliance on strictly legal and open sources and methods allows OSINT to be shared with anyone anywhere, and helps create broader communities of interest through structured information sharing.

It can be said that at the strategic level in particular, but at all four levels of analysis (strategic, operational, tactical, and technical) generally, the secret intelligence communities of the world are inside-out and upside-down. They are inside-out because they persist in trying to answer important questions with unilaterally collected secrets, rather than beginning with what they can learn from the outside-in: from the seven tribes[1] and the more than ninety nations that form the coalition. They are upside-down, at least in the case of the United States and selected other major powers, because they rely too much on expensive overhead satellite systems instead of bottom-up ground truth networks of humans with deep historical, cultural, and localized knowledge.

In the long-run, I anticipate that OSINT will displace 80 percent of the current manpower and dollars devoted to secret sources and methods, and that this will offer the taxpayers of the respective nations a return on investment at least one thousand times better than what is obtained now through secret sources and methods. A proper focus on OSINT will alter the definition of "national" intelligence to embrace all that can be known from the seven tribes across both the home nation and the coalition nations, and will dramatically reform intelligence, electoral processes, governance, and the application of the national, state, and local budgets in support of the public interest.

Strategically, OSINT will restore informed engaged democracy and moral capitalism, a new form of communal capitalism, in America and around the world. OSINT is, at root, the foundation for the emergence of the world brain, and the empowerment of the public.

The bulk of this chapter will focus on OSINT and intelligence reform at the strategic level, but it is essential that the reader appreciate the implications of OSINT for electoral, governance, and budgetary reform so as to better realize the enormous implications of the revolution in intelligence affairs[2] for which OSINT is the catalyst.

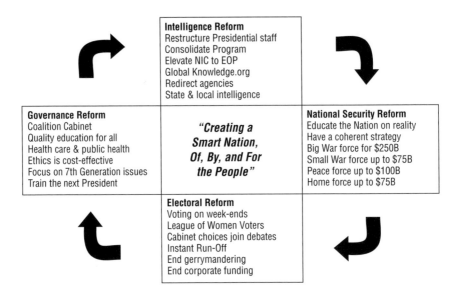

Figure 6-1. Four Strategic Domains for Reform Catalyzed by OSINT

Note: NIC = National Intelligence Council; EOP = Executive Office of the President. It is important to observe that the Global Knowledge organization, now called an Open Source Agency, is intended to be completely independent of both presidential and congressional manipulation. This chart is discussed in more detail in the final section of this chapter on governance reform.

Source: Drawn from "Citizen in Search of a Leader" as prepared 8 January 2003 and posted to http://www.oss.net. Additional detail on each reform domain can be found in that document.

The impetus for reform across all four strategic domains could emerge from within any one of the four. If the economy collapses and the war on Iraq combined with an attack on Iran cause a clear and present danger to emerge in the form of global Islamic counterattacks that are asymmetric and indiscriminate as well as widespread, we can anticipate not just the ejection of the extremist Republicans, but also of the complacent and equally corrupt and ignorant Democrats.[3]

There is a growing awareness within the public, described by some as "smart mobs," or "wisdom of the crowds," or—our preferred term—collective intelligence, that it is now possible for individuals to have better intelligence based on open sources and methods, that is being made available to, or acknowledged by, the president.[4] We will see, within the next four years, a dramatic increase in both historical accountability[5] and current accountability for actions impacting on future generations and other communities.

Electoral reform will be inspired by citizens realizing that both the Republican and Democratic parties have become corrupt as well as inept at representing the public interest.

Governance reform will be inspired by citizens realizing that in today's world, we need a networked model of governance that elevates intelligence to the forefront. Decisions must be made in the public interest and be sustainable by consensus and conformance to reality, not purchased by bribery from special interests who seek to loot the commonwealth and/or abuse their public power to pursue the ideological fantasies of an extremist minority.

Budgetary reform will be inspired by citizens who understand that we still need to be able to defend ourselves, but that waging peace worldwide is a much more cost-effective means of both deterring attacks and of stimulating sustainable indigenous wealth that is inherently stabilizing.

OSINT AND INTELLIGENCE REFORM

Open source intelligence (OSINT) should be, but is not, the foundation for all of the secret collection disciplines, and it could be, but is not, the foundation for a total reformation of both the governmental function of intelligence and the larger concept of national and global intelligence, what some call collective intelligence or the world brain.[6]

Secret intelligence, inclusive of covert action and counterintelligence, has failed in all substantive respects since the end of World War II and through the Cold War. In failing to meet the mandate to inform policy, acquisition, operations, and logistics, secret intelligence has contributed to the "50 Year Wound"[7] and failed to stimulate a redirection of national investments from military capabilities to what General Al Gray, then-Commandant of the Marine Corps, called "peaceful preventive measures."[8]

Secret intelligence became synonymous with clandestine and secret technical collection, with very little funding applied to either sense-making information technologies, or to deep and distributed human expertise. The end result at the strategic level can be described by the following two observations, the first a quote and the second a recollected paraphrase: Daniel Ellsberg speaking to Henry Kissinger: "The danger is, you'll become like a moron. You'll become incapable of learning from most people in the world, no matter how much experience they have in their particular areas that may be much greater than yours" [because of your blind faith in the value of your narrow and often incorrect secret information].[9] Tony Zinni speaking to a senior national security manager: "80% of what I needed to know as CINCENT I got from open sources rather than classified reporting. And within the remaining 20%, if I knew what to look for, I found another 16%. At the end of it all, classified intelligence provided me, at best, with 4% of my command knowledge."[10]

Secret intelligence may legitimately claim some extraordinary successes, and we do not disagree with Richard Helms when he says that some of those successes more than justified the entire secret intelligence budget, for example, in relation to Soviet military capabilities and our countermeasures.[11] However, in the larger scheme of things, secret intelligence failed to render a strategic value to the nation, in part because it failed to establish a domestic constituency, and could be so easily ignored by Democratic presidents and both ignored and manipulated by Republican presidents.[12]

In this first section, we will briefly review both the failings of each aspect of the secret intelligence world, and summarize how OSINT can improve that specific aspect.

History

The history of secret intelligence may be concisely summarized in relation to three periods:

1. *Secret War.* For centuries intelligence, like war, was seen to be the prerogative of kings and states, and it was used as a form of "war by other means," with spies and counterspies, covert actions, and plausible deniability.[13]

2. *Strategic Analysis.* During and following World War II, Sherman Kent led a movement to emphasize strategic analysis. Despite his appreciation for open sources of information, and academic as well as other experts, the clandestine and covert action elements of the Office of Strategic Services (OSS) and the follow-on Central Intelligence Group (CIG) and then Central Intelligence Agency (CIA), grew out of control, well beyond what President Harry Truman had envisioned when he sponsored the National Security Act of 1947.[14]

3. *Smart Nation.* Since 1988 there has been an emergent movement, not yet successful, but increasingly taking on a life of its own in the private sector. Originally conceptualized as an adjunct to secret intelligence, a corrective focus on open sources long neglected, it was soon joined by the collective intelligence movement that has also been referred to as "smart mobs" or "wisdom of the crowds," or "world brain." H. G. Wells conceptualized a world brain in the

1930s. Quincy Wright conceptualized a world intelligence center in the 1950s. Others have written about smart nations, collective intelligence, global brain, and the seven tribes of intelligence.[15]

Although the U.S. intelligence community has individuals that respect the value of open sources of information, and every major commission since the 1940s has in some form or another called for improved access to foreign language information that is openly available, the reality is that today, in 2006, the United States continues to spend between $50 billion and $70 billion a year on secret collection, almost nothing on all-source sense-making or world-class analysis, and just over $250 million a year on OSINT. This is nothing less than institutionalized lunacy.

The future history of secret intelligence is likely to feature its demise, but only after a citizen's intelligence network is able to apply OSINT to achieve electoral, governance, and budgetary reform, with the result that secret intelligence waste and defense acquisition waste will be converted into "waging peace" with peaceful preventive measures and a massive focus on eliminating poverty, disease, and corruption, while enabling clean water, alternative energy, and collaborative behavior across all cultural boundaries.[16]

Requirements

Requirements, or requirements definition, is the single most important aspect of the all-source intelligence cycle, and the most neglected. Today, and going back into history, policy makers and commanders tend to ignore intelligence, ask the wrong questions, or ask questions in such a way as to prejudice the answers. There are three major problems that must be addressed if we are to improve all-source decision support to all relevant clients for intelligence:

1. *Scope.* We must acknowledge that all levels of all organizations need intelligence. We cannot limit ourselves to "secrets for the president." If we fail to acknowledge the needs of lower-level policy makers, including all Cabinet members and their Assistant Secretaries; all acquisition managers; all operational commanders down to civil affairs and military police units; all logisticians; and all allied coalition elements including nongovernmental organizations, then we are not being professional about applying the proven process of intelligence to the decision-support needs of key individuals responsible for national security and national prosperity.

2. *Competition.* We must acknowledge that open sources of information are vastly more influential in the domestic politics of all nations, and that it is not possible to be effective at defining requirements for secret intelligence decision-support in the absence of a complete grasp of what is impacting on the policy makers, managers, and commanders from the open sources world (see Figure 6-2).

3. *Focus.* Third, and finally, we must acknowledge that, at the strategic level, our focus must of necessity be on long-term threats and opportunities that are global, complex, interrelated, and desperately in need of public education, public

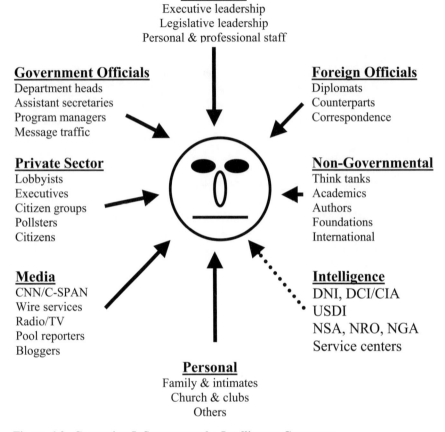

Figure 6-2. Competing Influences on the Intelligence Consumer

recognition, and public policy that is sustainable, which is to say, nonpartisan or bipartisan. Consider, for example, the findings shown in Figure 6-3 from the Report of the High-Level Panel on Threats, Challenges and Change, *A More Secure World: Our Shared Responsibility.*[17]

The average utility and relevance of OSINT to the global threats shown in Figure 6-3 is—on the basis of my informed estimate—82.5 percent, which comes very close to the generic "80-20" rule. We must conclude that any nation that persists in spending 99.9 percent of its intelligence funds on collecting secrets,[18] and less than one half of one percent of its intelligence funds on OSINT, is quite literally clinically insane (or insanely corrupt) at the highest levels.

In all three of the above cases, only OSINT can deliver a solution that is affordable, practical, and infinitely shareable with all stakeholders both in and out of government.

Economic and social threats, including	**95%**
• poverty	99%
• infectious disease	95%
• environmental degradation	90%
Interstate conflict	**75%**
Internal conflict, including	**90%**
• civil war	80%
• genocide	95%
• other large-scale atrocities	95%
Nuclear, radiological, chemical, and biological we	**75%**
Terrorism	**80%**
Transnational organized crime	**80%**

Figure 6-3. OSINT Relevance to Global Security Threats

Collection

Secret collection has made three fundamental mistakes across several generations of management:[19]

1. *Denigrated OSINT.* It chose to ignore open sources of information, assuming that the consumers of intelligence were responsible for their own OSINT, and that OSINT would not impact on secret collection. In fact, OSINT can dramatically reduce the cost and the risk, and increase the return on investment in secret sources and methods, simply by helping with targeting, spotting, assessment, validation, and the overall strategic context of what needs to be collected "by other means." It merits very strong emphasis that this failure to respect open sources of information falls into three distinct forms:

• Complete disrespect for history in all languages. There is no place within the U.S. government where one can "see" all Chinese statements on the Spratley Islands, or all Iranian statements on the competing Caliphate concept, or all Brazilian statements on alternative energy sources. We simply do not compute history, and consequently what little we know about current events and threats is known in isolated ignorance of history.

- Complete abdication of any responsibility for monitoring, understanding, and engaging substate or transnational entities as major factors in international affairs, and as threats or potential allies in domestic security and prosperity.
- Finally, almost complete abdication for more nuanced topics other than standard political-military calculations, with very important sustained failures to collect information on socioeconomic, ideocultural, technodemographic, or natural-geographic matters. This has been compounded by an extraordinary laziness or ignorance in relying almost exclusively on what can be stolen or obtained readily in English—the United States simply does not "do" the key 31 languages,[20] much less the totality of 185 languages necessary to understand the substate threat and the global network of cause and effect.

2. *Official Cover.* We have relied almost exclusively, at least in the United States, on "official cover" for our spies, and known trajectories for our satellites. Non-Official Cover (NOC), which does not offer any form of diplomatic or other official immunity from incarceration or eviction, has been treated as too expensive, too complicated, and not worthy of full development. The result has been the almost total compromise of all U.S. secret agents and case officers overseas, as well as their varied not-so-secret thefts of the codebooks of other nations. We not only don't know what we don't know, we are in denial about the basic fact that what we do know has been compromised.

3. *Failure to Process.* Finally, and this applies to both clandestine human collection and secret technical collection, we have failed, with deliberate ignorance at the management level, to devote any resources of significance to processing—to sense-making. Today, eighteen years after the needed functionalities for an all-source analytic desktop toolkit were published, we still do not have a desktop analytic toolkit. Today, despite major advances in the private sector with respect to machine-speed translation, and machine-speed statistical, pattern, and predictive analysis, the large majority of our classified intelligence analysis is still done the old-fashioned way: reading at human speed, cutting and pasting, attempting to make sense of vast volumes of secret information while lacking equivalent access to vast volumes of open source information (and especially open source information in any language other than English), limited by the physics of the twenty-four-hour day.

OSINT combines the proven process of intelligence with the ability to collect, process, and analyze all information in all languages all the time. We collect, at best, 20 percent of what we need to collect, at 99 percent of the cost, and we spill most of that for lack of processing capabilities. It can be said, as an informed judgment, that Washington is operating on 2 percent of the relevant strategic information necessary to devise, implement, and adjust national strategy.[21] We should not be sending spies where schoolboys can go, nor should we be ignoring scholarship in all languages.

There will still be a need for selected clandestine human operations, especially against organized crime and translation terrorist groups, but they will need to shift toward NOC and multinational task forces. Secret technical collection will need to emphasize commercial collection first, dramatically refocus secret collection, and shift the bulk of the future resources toward processing—making sense of what we do collect—and toward close-in technical collection inclusive of beacons for tracking bad guys and bad things.

Collection management will require draconian reform. Instead of defaulting to the tasking of secret collection capabilities, an enlightened collection manager will first determine if they can *find* the information for free in their existing stores of knowledge; then determine if they can *get* the information for free from an allied government or any of the seven tribes; and then determine if they can *buy* the information from a commercial provider, ideally a localized provider with direct indigenous access, in the time and with the operational security (e.g., cover support plans) appropriate to the need. Only if the first three options are unsuited to the need should the collection manager be tasking secret sources and methods, and even that will have to change to accommodate new possibilities from multinational secret task forces able to leverage the collection capabilities of varied countries, many of them vastly superior to the United States when it comes to both deep-cover clandestine human penetrations, and the related ability to place close-in secret technical collection devises.[22]

OSINT is, without question, the catalyst for a revolution in how we collect intelligence.

Processing

Apart from our failure to actually invest in processing (known within the U.S. intelligence community as Tasking, Processing, Exploitation, and Dissemination, or TPED), we have made three consistent mistakes over time that have made it virtually impossible, and now unaffordable, to actually do automated all-source analysis:

1. *No Standards.* We failed to establish data standards that could be used at the point of entry for both secret and open sources of information. This applies to both information sources and information software. Not only was the intelligence community much too slow to adopt commons standards such as eXtended Markup Language (XML), Resource Description Framework (RDF), Web Ontology Language (OWL), and Simple Object Access Protocol (SOAP), today it is either ignorant of or reluctant to move ahead aggressively with Open Hypertextdocument System (OHS)[23] and eXtended Markup Language Geospatial (XML Geo). The obsession with security, and the pathology of limiting contracts to the established firms in the military-industrial complex who profit from proprietary software and human headcount rather than real-world low-cost answers, can be blamed for the chasm between the secret intelligence world and the real world of open sources and standards.

2. *No Geospatial Attributes.* In fall 1988 it was made known to the U.S. intelligence community and clearly articulated by the author to a meeting of the General Defense Intelligence Program (GDIP), that in the absence of geospatial attributes for every datum entering the all-source processing system (actually an archipelago of private databases), that machine-speed all-source analysis and fusion would be an impossibility. Despite this, the individual secret collection disciplines of clandestine human intelligence (HUMINT), signals intelligence (SIGINT), and imagery intelligence (IMINT) refuse to do anything other than persist with their human analytic reporting that provides date-time-group (DTG) and geographic place names where known, but no standard geospatial attributes for relating information to a map. Today Google Earth is being used in extraordinary ways to visualize relationship databases of real estate, shipping, and other important topics, and the individual citizen is light years ahead of the average "cut-and-paste" analyst at the federal, state, and local levels.

3. *No Integration.* There is no single place where all known information comes together. Despite critical concerns raised by every congressional and presidential commission since the 1940s, the U.S. intelligence community has continued to be "flawed by design"[24] and has persisted in the turf wars between the Central Intelligence Agency (CIA) and the Federal Bureau of Investigation (FBI), between the FBI and the Drug Enforcement Administration (DEA), between the FBI and the Department of Justice (DoJ), and between the Departments of State and Defense. Within the Department of Defense (DoD), the services have not only competed with one another but actively conspired to fabricate and manipulate intelligence to exaggerate the threats relevant to their budget share. A corollary of this abysmal situation is that processing within the stovepipes has been focused on the delivery of documents rather than on making sense of all of the information in the aggregate. With the exception of selected efforts at the National Security Agency, the Army's Intelligence and Security Command, and the U.S. Special Operations Command, virtually all civilian and military analysts are still in cut-and-paste mode, and do not have the tools for pattern or trend analysis or anomaly detection, much less predictive analysis.

In processing, it is machine speed translation and statistical analysis, based on standards and global distributed information integration, that permits early warning, anomaly detection, and structured analysis that can be completed in a timely—that is to say, relevant—manner. OSINT is where the real innovation is occurring, and I anticipate that within ten years the secret world will be sharply restricted to no more than 20 percent of its present cost and size, while the balance of the funding is redirected to a mix of OSINT that can be shared with anyone, with peaceful preventive measures in lieu of a heavy-metal military.

Among the corrective measures required in secret processing, which OSINT will facilitate, are a shift toward the Internet as the common operating environment; the adoption of open source software to provide a generic access and collaborative sharing environment for all seven tribes;[25] the development of 24/7 "plots" at every level of governance in which all information can be seen in time and geospatial context;[26] and the creation of a national skunkworks with an antitrust waiver for the public testing and certification of all open sources, software, and services. Rapid promulgation of free wireless within urban areas and in the Third World will help accelerate both sharing in the North and West, and uploading of useful information from the East and South.

Analysis

In evaluating the failure of analysis, it is important to understand that most U.S. analysts are too young, too inexperienced in the real world, and too isolated from foreign or even U.S. private-sector experts, to realize that the secret information they are receiving is out of context, often wrong, and largely irrelevant to strategic analysis. Their managers are too busy trying to be promoted or to win bonuses or please the White House (or the representative of the White House, the Director of Central Intelligence [DCI]). As a result, the strategic analysis vision of Sherman Kent has been dishonored and largely set aside. There have been three major failures in analysis over time.

1. *Hire Young.* The intelligence management philosophy in both the national civilian hires and at the military theater and service center levels has combined "hire to payroll" with obsessive lazy security parameters that have resulted in an analytic population that is largely young, white, and mostly bereft of overseas experience and especially long-term residency in foreign countries. Budgets have been used to hire low and promote over time, treating analysis as an entry-level hiring challenge rather than a mid-career sabbatical challenge. This has been deeply and pathologically influenced by a low-rent security philosophy that has combined paranoia over foreign contacts (and relatives) with an unwillingness to spend the time and thoughtfulness necessary to clear complicated individuals who have led complicated lives. This personnel management failure stems from the larger philosophical management failure, which confuses secrets with intelligence, and thus demeans expertise from the open source world while assuming that young analysts will succeed because they have access to secrets, rather than because of any application of analytic tradecraft such as might take twenty years to refine.

2. *Hard Target Focus.* In keeping with the military-industrial complex and its desire to profit from the Cold War, the national and military intelligence communities devoted virtually their entire budgets and most of their manpower to the "hard targets" (generally, Russia, China, Iran, India, Pakistan, Libya, and— hard to believe, but true—Cuba). They ignored all of the "lower tier" issues and Third World countries,[27] and also focused only on very big threats, not on very big opportunities for peaceful preventive measures where a few dollars invested in the 1970s might have eradicated Anti-Immune Deficiency Syndrome (AIDS) or dependency on Middle Eastern oil. This was of course in keeping with policy preferences, and even when the CIA did excellent work (for example, accurately forecasting the global AIDS epidemic), it could safely be ignored because its

work was not available to the public or even to most members of Congress. A very important consequence of this narrow focus was the complete failure to ensure that all of the sources of national power—diplomatic, informational, military, economic (DIME)—were funded, acquired, fielded, and applied in a coherent and timely manner. The entire military-industrial-intelligence complex has been skewed toward a heavy-metal military—a few big platforms or big organizations—that are only relevant 10 percent of the time. We are not trained, equipped, or organized for small wars, waging peace, or homeland defense. This is still true—truer that ever—in the aftermath of 9/11 and the invasions and occupations of Afghanistan and Iraq.

3. *Local Now.* Finally, U.S. intelligence (and many foreign intelligence communities) focused on the local now instead of the global future. "Current intelligence" dominated the *President's Daily Brief* (PDB), and over time longer term research fell by the wayside. This problem was aggravated by a draconian editing process in both the national civilian and theater- or service-level military, where a twelve-month research project could be subject to eighteen-month editing cycles, such that the work was out of date or thoroughly corrupted by the time it was finally released to a relatively limited number of policy makers. With most of the intelligence products being released in hard copy, or messages that were printed out and not saved electronically, the overall impact of U.S. intelligence production, and especially Codeword production, must be judged as marginal.[28]

OSINT is "the rival store."[29] Whereas I spent the first eighteen years of my campaign to foster an appreciation on OSINT and focusing on the urgency of integrating OSINT into secret sources toward improved all-source analysis, I plan to spend the next eighteen years burying 80 percent of the classified world. They are too expensive, too irrelevant, and pathologically antithetical to the new and correct Swedish concept of Multinational, Multiagency, Multidisciplinary, Multidomain Information Sharing (M4IS).[30] OSINT analysis will in the future be the benchmark by which classified sources and methods are judged to be relevant and cost-effective, or not. The Director of National Intelligence (DNI) has chosen to remain focused on secrets for the president. So be it. OSINT, from a private-sector and nongovernmental foundation, will capture all the other consumers of intelligence. The day will come when "clearances" are severely devalued and open source access—international open source access in all languages all the time—is ascendant. The DCI must serve all levels of the government, all seven tribes, and must balance between open and closed sources so as to inform decision makers—and their publics—in order to preserve and enhance the long-term national security and prosperity of the United States. Secret sources and methods—and the existing military—have demonstrably failed in both regards.

Analytic tradecraft notes are available online and should be consulted.[31] All-source analysts should not be hired until they have first proven themselves as masters of all open sources in all languages relevant to their domain and not be considered for mid-career hire unless they are one of the top twenty-five cited authorities in the field. They must know how to leverage their historian, their librarian, and the Internet. They must know how to identify and interact with the top 100 people in the world on their topic, regardless of citizenship or clearances. Finally, they must understand that they are—and must be trained to be—managers of customer relations and requirements definition, of open sources, of external experts, and of classified collection management. Analysts must know and practice the "new rules" for the new craft of intelligence, with specific reference to being able to actually do forecasting, establish strategic generalizations, and drill down to the neighborhood and tribal levels, not simply hover at the nation-state level.[32]

Covert Action

Covert action consists of agents of influence, media placement, and paramilitary operations. Covert action assumes two things that may once have been true but are no longer true: that an operation can be carried out without its being traced back to the United States as the sponsor, and that the fruits of the operation will be beneficial to the United States. In each of these three areas, the United States has acted with great disdain for the normal conventions of legitimacy, accountability, morality, and practicality, and today the United States is suffering from what is known as "blowback"—it is reaping the dividends from decades of unethical behavior justified in the name of national security but unfounded upon any substantive grasp of long-term reality.

1. *Agents of influence* are individuals bribed covertly who are charged with getting their governments or organizations to pursue a course of action that the United States deems to be necessary but that may not be in the best interests of the indigenous public or its government. Regardless of what one may think of the local country and its government and public, what this really means is that agents of influence are responsible for disconnecting local policies from local realities, and imposing instead a reality or choice selected by the U.S. government. This is inherently pathological. There are certainly some success stories—support to Solidarity in Poland, for example, but this was a capitalization on the fall of communism, not the cause.
2. *Media placement* uses individuals, generally foreign journalists, who are bribed covertly to create and publish stories that communicate an alternative view of reality, one sanctioned by the U.S. government but generally at odds with the actual facts of the matter. There is a constructive side to media placement, for example the promulgation of information about atrocities committed by dictators or Soviet forces, but generally the U.S. government supports most of the dictators it deals with, and reserves this tool for deposing individuals that dare to oppose predatory immoral capitalism or virtual colonialism. Consequently, most media placement

activities consist of propaganda seeking to manipulate rather than deliver the truth. Media placement by spies should not be confused with public diplomacy by diplomats or strategic communication by the military—the latter two are overt truth-telling missions, although misguided practitioners may occasionally stray into propaganda and the manipulation of the truth.[33]

3. *Paramilitary operations* are not only direct assaults on the sovereignty of other nations, but they tend to bring with them black markets, drug running, money laundering, corruption, and the proliferation of a culture of violence and the small arms with which to do indiscriminate violence. The Phoenix program of assassinations in Vietnam, the support to the *contras* and the mining of the Nicaraguan harbors (an act condemned by the World Court), the arming of the Islamic fundamentalists for jihad in Afghanistan, join the planned overthrows of the governments of Chile, Guatemala, Iran, as causes of long-term and costly "blowback." Of all of these, Iran is the most interesting. Had we allowed the nationalization of the oil in Iran and the fall of the Shah, we might today have both a nonfundamentalist Iran as a bulwark against the radicals from Saudi Arabia, but we might also be less dependent on oil, and less subject to the whims of the extraordinarily corrupt Saudi regime and its U.S. energy company allies.

OSINT is the antithesis of all three forms of covert action. As David Ignatius noted so wisely in the 1980s, overt action rather than covert action delivers the best value in both the short and the long run. Promulgating the tools for truth—cell phones, wireless access, access to the Internet—is a means of fostering informed democracy and responsible opposition. It is also a means of creating stabilizing indigenous wealth. OSINT provides a historical and cultural foundation for achieving multicultural consensus that is sustainable precisely because it is consensual. As Jonathan Schell documents so well in *The Unconquerable World: Power, Nonviolence, and the Will of the People*, there are not enough guns in the world to force our way or protect our borders.[34] Only by fostering legitimacy, morality, charity, and full participation of all can we stabilize the world to the mutual benefit of the United States and the rest of the world.

OSINT, in addition to being vastly superior to covert action as a means for establishing reasonable goals that are sustainable over time, is also very well suited to documenting the extraordinary costs of historical covert actions. Only now is the public beginning to understand the lasting damage caused by the U.S. sponsorship of assassination attempts against Fidel Castro, capabilities that were ultimately turned against the unwitting president, John F. Kennedy, and his brother Robert. We have sacrificed our national values and our international credibility at the alter of covert action, and we are long overdue for a deep "truth and reconciliation" commission that evaluates the true costs of covert action, and that then defines much more narrowly the conditions and protocols for engaging in covert action in the future.

Counterintelligence

Strategic counterintelligence is completely distinct from tactical counterintelligence.[35] In strategic counterintelligence, one is looking for emerging threats at the strategic level, not individual penetrations of specific organizations. This is an area where OSINT should, but does not, shine. The U.S. intelligence community—and consequently the U.S. policy community—have completely missed the end of cheap oil, the end of free water, the rise of bin Laden, and the rise of pandemic disease, even global warming, precisely because national counterintelligence was focused obsessively on penetrating foreign security services, and not on the strategic environment where natural and other threats of omission and commission were to be found. There are three areas in which strategic counterintelligence can benefit considerably from comprehensive OSINT, inclusive of the digitization and statistical analysis of all available historical information.

1. *National Education.* Thomas Jefferson said, "A Nation's best defense is an informed citizenry." This is absolutely correct, and even more so today, when central bureaucracies are no match for agile networked transnational groups. The United States has failed to understand the strategic implications of its lack of border control, its mediocre educational system designed to create docile factory workers, and the trends toward obesity, insularity, and indifference that characterize the bulk of the population today. We have gone hollow for lack of focus.

2. *Environment.* The Singapore military was stunned by the emergence of Severe Acute Respiratory Syndrome (SARS), but unlike the U.S. military they understood it. They realized they were responsible for defending Singapore against all threats, not just manmade or man-guided threats, and added national health and border security against airborne, waterborne, and human- or animal-borne diseases, to their charter. Similarly, the Singapore police have an extraordinarily nuanced and enlightened understanding of their global and regional information needs and responsibilities in relation to deterring and resolving all forms of crime impacting on Singapore. In the United States, and globally with dire consequences for the United States, there are threats associated with the environment and how it changes (including water, energy, and raw material resources) that are simply not understood, not acknowledged, and not being acted upon responsibly by any U.S. administration, be it Democratic or Republican.[36]

3. *Ideology.* There are two ideological threats to U.S. security today, one external, the other internal. The two together are very troubling. Externally, the radical and violent fundamentalist stream of Islam has been armed and energized by jihad in Afghanistan, in Chechnya, and in Iraq. Other small jihads in Indonesia, the Philippines, and southern Thailand, as well as selected locations in Muslim Africa, add to this threat. Internally, U.S. Christian fundamentalists have

assumed a terribly excessive importance in extremist Republican circles, in part because the Texas corporate energy interests chose to make common cause with them. The Middle East, oil, and the almost cultlike extreme religious right have hijacked American democracy. The American left, nominally but not intelligently led by the Democratic Party (which is as corrupt as the Republican Party, but more inept), meanwhile, abandoned faith and God and the sensible calming effect of religion as a foundation for community and ethics.[37] The American ideology of capitalism has also been corrupted. Immoral predatory capitalism, and pathologically inept formulas for "developmental economics" as imposed on failed states by the International Monetary Fund (IMF) and the World Bank have given rise to populism and other forms of indigenous resistance now witting of the collusion between their corrupt elite and immoral foreign capitalism that are in combination looting the commonwealth of many peoples.[38]

In all three of these cases, OSINT has an extraordinary role to play. Under the leadership of Congressman Rob Simmons (CT), a moderate Republican with an extraordinarily deep background in both intelligence and on the Hill, the campaign continues for a national Open Source Agency funded at $3 billion per year, under the auspices of the Department of State (as a sister agency to the Board of Governors that controls the Voice of America and other public diplomacy outlets). However, fully half the budget is intended to fund fifty Community Intelligence Centers and networks across the country (each receiving $30 million at full operating capability). These centers are needed for two reasons: first, to provide 119 and 114 numbers for citizen mobilization (119 alerts all cell phones within a 5 kilometer radius) and citizen neighborhood watch inputs (114 receives cell phone photos, text messages, any form of information, all with geospatial and time tags); and second, to serve as dissemination nodes for transmitting to all schools, chambers of commerce, churches/synagogues/mosques, labor unions, civil advocacy groups, and so on, the wealth of "real world" information to be collected, processed, and shared, free via the Internet, by the Open Source Agency. This will impact very favorably on the environment, as these centers will help citizens at the county, state, and regional levels understand, with precision, where each of them stands with respect to access to clean water, alternative energies and related lifestyle choices, and global threats to their children and grandchildren based on easy access to the actual U.S. federal budget in relation to real world threats and needs. Militarism can be reduced, poverty and disease can be eliminated, and the United States can rejoin the community of nations as a force for good. Finally, all competing ideologies can be subject to scrutiny and understanding, and the majority of Americans who are not part of the right can come together consensually to limit the damage these people can do to the republic, while also holding their political and corporate allies accountable for serving America as a whole rather than a fringe element.

Dramatically redirecting national intelligence toward OSINT will substantially reduce the cost of secrecy, estimated by the Moynihan Commission as being on the order of $6 billion a year (probably closer to $15 billion a year today),[39] and will also eliminate perhaps 70 percent of the costs associated with establishing the trustworthiness of individuals being considered for clearances. The security and clearance system of the U.S. government is broken beyond repair. Not only does it take over two years for most investigations to be completed, but they are generally substandard investigations that go through the motions and generally do not detect basic aberrations, such as a fascination with child pornography and online molestation of children, as was the case recently with a senior manager in the Department of Homeland Security. The fact is that most sheriffs and other state and local officials are not "clearable" for a variety of reasons, and we may as well recognize that not only is OSINT better suited for most national intelligence information sharing, but we really do not need most of the grotesquely expensive and dysfunctional top-secret "compartments" (over 400 of them, half in the civilian world and half in the military world) and all the attendant costs, including the costs of ignorance stemming from compartmentalized information not being shared. At least at the strategic level we need a national intelligence system in which we are less concerned about betrayal from within, and more focused on emerging strategic threats to our long-term security and prosperity, threats that must not be limited to manmade capabilities, but include animal-borne diseases and other environmental conditions that tend to be shut out from national security decision processes.

Accountability, Civil Liberties, and Oversight

As all of the preceding sections should have made clear, OSINT is the essential contributing factor to dramatically improving the accountability and oversight of the U.S. intelligence community and the policy makers, acquisition managers, and operational commanders who respond to White House direction. OSINT is also a means of dramatically enhancing not just civil liberties, but civic engagement in the practice of democracy. By providing citizens at every level with structured OSINT on any issue for any zip code or other geographic grouping, and by making it possible for citizens to immediately connect with other like-minded citizens and with accountable officials, OSINT in practice is an enabler of a new form of constant engaged informed democracy. Civil liberty infractions will be broadcast or podcast, rapidly aggregated, and civil pressure brought to bear. By harnessing citizens as part of the "home guard" and empowering them with immediate and understandable access to indications and warning information, we will dramatically improve the reporting of relevant information, and—through the Community Intelligence Centers—be able to process, make sense of, and act on or discount the "bottom up" dots that I am convinced will comprise at least 50 percent of the relevant dots needed to prevent the next 9/11.

It is also important to emphasize that, at the strategic level, we need to be concerned not just with accountability and oversight of secret intelligence, but with the much larger issue of whether Congress and the Executive are being responsible in representing the public interest. For this reason are included very brief but vital sections at the end of this chapter on OSINT and electoral reform, governance reform, and budgetary reform. OSINT is the ultimate resource for citizens to hold their government accountable, and to protect their civil liberties over time.

Strategic Warning

Although the CIA has done some fine work on global threats, and I particular like the work done under John Gannon as Assistant Director of Central Intelligence for Analysis & Production (*Global Trends 2015*, which led to *Global Trends 2020*),[40] on balance the U.S. intelligence community has failed abysmally at strategic warning because of some fundamental operational and philosophical failures.[41]

Operationally, despite fifty years of extraordinarily generous funding for multi-billion-dollar satellite systems, the U.S. intelligence community still cannot do wide area surveillance, real-time change detection, or "the last mile" inclusive of seeing into an urban area, under jungle canopy, and into the deep ravines of mountainous terrain.

Philosophically U.S. intelligence has been a disaster in strategic terms. The cult of secrecy limited "intelligence" to "secrets for the president" and left everyone else, from Cabinet-level leaders to military acquisition manager and operational commanders, to governors and mayors, completely without "decision-support." Perhaps worse, the U.S. intelligence community has refused to recognize the seven tribes of intelligence, shutting out, for the most part, state and local officials with overseas knowledge, business travelers, academics, nongovernmental observers, journalists, labor union leaders, religious travelers, and so on. The obsession with government secrecy over public sharing has cost this nation fifty years of time—the one strategic factor that can be neither bought nor replaced[42]—and at least 3 billion souls of goodwill. U.S. intelligence is a small part of the overall federal government, and it merits comment that most of our problems today cannot be blamed on U.S. intelligence as much as on a corrupt Congress and Executive all too eager to ignore, for example, the Peak Oil warnings of 1974–79 in order to keep the bribes going and the public docile. This is not, however, to excuse the U.S. intelligence community, in as much a focus on OSINT from 1988 onwards would have done much to illuminate and correct the policy errors that benefited from secrecy, obscurity, and public inattentiveness.

Strategic Sharing

The U.S. intelligence community is incapable today, five years after 9/11, of creating a single consolidated watch list of suspected terrorists. The U.S. government as a whole is incapable of sharing everything that it knows for lack of collaborative mindsets, willing management, interoperable systems, and coherent data sets. There are three primary impediments to the U.S. intelligence community ever being able to share readily:

1. *High Side Security.* The obsession with security is occasioned in part by the fact that the secret intelligence world, even though it has "compartments," has never learned to disaggregate secret from nonsecret information. Everything is stored at the "high side," at the highest possible level of security, meaning that nothing can be shared with anyone who is not cleared for the highest level of security, however unclassified the information might be.

2. *Third Party Rule.* The secret world has for decades operated under a "third party rule" that prohibits the sharing of any information received from one party with another party. This rule is extremely detrimental to multilateral sharing, and imposes enormous time, manpower, and dollar costs when something needs to be shared and the sharing must be coordinated. The default condition of the secret world is "do not share."

3. *Legacy Systems.* As John Perry Barlow noted in an article in *Forbes*,[43] if you want to see the last remnants of the Soviet Empire, go visit the CIA and look at their computer systems. The U.S. intelligence community as a whole is still mired in 1970s technology managed by 1950s mindsets, totally out of touch with 21st-century information networks, both machine and human.

OSINT is going to be the catalyst for M4IS and strategic sharing. OSINT is the only discipline that can easily distribute the collection, processing, and analysis burden across all coalition nations (i.e., the ninety nations comprising the U.S. Central Command coalition), and also the only discipline whose products can easily be shared with nongovernmental organizations as well as state and local authorities all over the world who will never qualify for "clearances." It will be our challenge in the next eighteen years to develop an alternative global intelligence community that relies almost exclusively on "good enough" open sources, and that consequently forces the secret world into proving its "added value" in relation to cost, risk, and time, on every topic, every day.

Emerging Prospects

Apart from increased public access to the Internet—inclusive of electronic mail, the deep web, and the dramatically increased availability of free multimedia communications and information sharing capabilities—several factors are supportive of a displacement of secret sources and methods by open sources and methods:

DIGITIZATION

It is a mistake to believe that all relevant information is being digitized today. Tribal histories (e.g., those from Iraq) and vast quantities of important information are still being produced in Industrial Era media, and Friday sermons by Islamic imans, as well as the sermons by all the other faiths, are not part of the digital revolution. In strategic terms, however, digitization is extremely important for three reasons:

1. Most current information from mainstream and niche media as well as individual publishers and bloggers, in all languages, is now available digitally.
2. Historical information, including policy and financial statements of great importance to specific nations, industries, organizations, and tribes can now be affordably and effectively digitized.
3. Hand-held devices are rapidly becoming a primary means of collecting and sharing information, with imminent prospects of being able to harness, selectively, all that any group of individuals can see and hear and think, and is willing to upload as needed.

VISUALIZATION

Digital information, including historical information, can now be visualized, not only in relation to content analysis and links between paragraphs and among individuals, but in relation to a geospatial foundation such as Google Earth provides in rudimentary but quite compelling terms. This is moving OSINT well beyond secret sources and methods because it can draw on a much greater body of information and expertise in real time, and apply all modern machine analytic tools with fewer security, legal, and policy constraints. The centralized, unilateral, secret bureaucracies are losing ground—rapidly—to distributed, open, multinational networks.

PEER-TO-PEER (P2P)

"Ground truth" is taking on a whole new meaning as individuals exercise the power to share complex information directly with one another, eliminating the intermediary journals, web sites, and government or media offices that in the past have played the role of editor, judge, and broker of meaning and value.

The power of OSINT at the strategic level can neither be exaggerated nor underestimated for the simple reason that it harnesses the distributed intelligence of the whole earth, in real time as well as in historical memory time, across all languages and cultures. There is not a bureaucracy in the world that can match its networked power. To drive that point home, consider the game of baseball. In today's secret environment, government bureaucrats accustomed to unlimited budgets and secret methods continue to try to win the game by bribing a player (clandestine intelligence), putting a "bug" in the dugout (signals intelligence), trying to "sniff " the direction and speed of the ball (measurements and signatures intelligence), or taking a satellite picture of the field every three days (imagery intelligence). The new craft of intelligence integrates the audience. It uses the collective wisdom of all the participants. It encourages the crowd to participate. Open source intelligence harnesses what everyone sees and knows. It changes the rules of the game. Any catch in the stands is an out. That is how we win against asymmetric opponents who know our Achilles' heels all too well.

OSINT AND ELECTORAL REFORM

The United States is a republic. An extraordinary characteristic of republics is that voters have the power to dissolve the government should it become so ineffective or destructive as to warrant its termination. The Constitution, and the voters, are the foundation of the American democracy, not the three branches of government. If the Executive is mendacious, the Congress is corrupt, and the Judiciary is so unrepresentative of the values of the people as to be a mockery of justice, then the public has the power to change the rules of the game for elections. It is OSINT that can be used by citizens to break away from the Republican and Democratic parties, and develop new networked means of demanding minimalist changes such as suggested by Ralph Nader and enhanced by the author: voting on weekends so the poor do not lose work; restoring the League of Women Voters as the arbiters of multiparty debates; demanding that presidential candidates announce their Cabinets in advance of the election, and including at least the Secretaries of Defense and State, and the Attorney General, in Cabinet-level debates; applying the instant runoff concept to ensure a true majority election; and, of course, ending gerrymandering and corporate funding for any elected official.

OSINT AND GOVERNANCE REFORM

Government at the federal level has become incompetent, and is wasteful of the taxpayer dollar for two reasons: special interest corruption both in Congress (bribery) and in the Executive (revolving-door favoritism); and an industrial-era structure that is largely disconnected from reality to the point that ideological fantasy can supplant a reasoned policy process. At a minimum, the republic needs a coalition Cabinet and some means of assuring the citizenry that presidents will not be able to simply appoint cronies from their own party; the Executive needs to be restructured to provide for integrated policy development, not just national security policy development; strategic planning focused out seven generations (over 200 years) must be demanded and be publicly transparent and accountable; and the fundamentals of national power must be mandated: quality education for all, health care for all, and an end to poverty at home. Presidents and their teams must be elected for their ability to govern rather than campaign. OSINT will make all of this possible, sooner than later if a national Open Source Agency is created as a new fourth branch of government, independent of Congress and the Executive, with a lifetime appointment for its Director, and a Board of Directors composed of former presidents, leaders of the Senate and House, and retired Supreme Court justices.

OSINT AND STRATEGIC BUDGETARY REFORM

Finally, we come to budgetary reform. OSINT has already made it clear that we have a Department of Defense costing $500 billion a year (not counting the cost of the war in Iraq) that is relevant to only 10 percent of the threat (state-on-state warfare), that is largely incompetent at small wars and homeland defense, and that we are, as a republic, not investing properly in peaceful preventive measures inclusive of the spread of participatory democracy and moral capitalism. The return on investment on our "big war" military is not only not there, the existence of that big war force leads ignorant presidents and their mendacious vice-presidents to seek out wars as an option for capturing "cheap" oil (never mind the cost in blood, spirit, and treasure). The American republic, specifically, and all other countries are long overdue for what I call "reality-based budgeting." OSINT will restore sanity and sensibility to the public treasury and how it is applied.

There is, in the immortal words of Arnie Donahue[44] in 1992, "plenty of money for OSINT." There is also plenty of money for participatory democracy and moral capitalism. Our problem has been that we have allowed the mandarins of secrecy to pretend to be informing the president, rather narrowly and very expensively, while failing to demand that the republic develop a public intelligence capability suitable for directing public policy and public spending in an intelligent, sustainable manner.

September 11, the Iraq War, and the varied accomplishments—or crimes—of the Bush administration may stand in history as a bright turning point in the history of the republic. One doubts that anything less might have awakened the somnolent public.

NOTES

1. The "seven tribes" is a concept developed by the author and includes government, military, law enforcement, business, academia, the ground-truth tribe (nongovernmental organizations and the media), and the civil-sector tribe (citizen advocacy groups and societies, labor unions, and religions).

2. This term, "Revolution in Intelligence Affairs," is abused by loosely educated individuals who know nothing of revolution and little of all-source intelligence. For a critique of the abuse of the term, and a discussion of the three options for intelligence reform, see the author's "Intelligence Affairs: Evolution, Revolution, or Reactionary Collapse," *International Journal of Intelligence and Counterintelligence* 19 (Spring 2006), pp. 187–189. In a forthcoming issue the author comments on "Intelligence in Denial."

3. This is a practical professional discourse on OSINT, not a political diatribe, but it is essential for those who have the most to gain from OSINT, citizens, to understand that the extremist Republicans have driven out the moderate Republicans (including the author) while the inept Democrats have alienated both the conservative Democrats and the

New Progressives. For an excellent and erudite discussion of why the prevailing mood of the country may well be "a pox on both parties," see Peter Peterson, *Running on Empty: How the Democratic and Republican Parties Are Bankrupting Our Future and What Americans Can Do About It* (New York: Farrar, Straus and Giroux, 2004). Peterson was a Cabinet Secretary under Nixon and Chairman of the Council on Foreign Relations. He joins numerous other moderate Republicans who have published books dismissive of the Republican Party as it has been hijacked by the religious extremists, the neo-conservatives, and corporate war-profiteers. The Democratic leadership is equally corrupt, but so inept as to be incapable of either governing or holding the Republicans accountable.

4. Howard Rheingold, *Smart Mobs: The Next Social Revolution* (New York: Basic Books, 2003); James Surowieki, *The Wisdom of the Crowds* (New York: Anchor, 2005); and Pierre Levy, *Collective Intelligence: Mankind's Emerging World in Cyberspace* (New York: Perseus, 2000). Three other essential references are H. G. Wells, *World Brain* (London: Ayer, 1938); Howard Bloom, *Global Brain: The Evolution of Mass Mind From the Big Bang to the 21st Century* (New York: Wiley, 2001); and Tom Atlee, *The Tao of Democracy: Using Co-Intelligence to Create a World That Works for All* (San Francisco:Writer's Collective, 2003). Robert Steele addresses the concepts and doctrine for actually "doing" collective public intelligence in *The New Craft of Intelligence: Personal, Public, and Political* (Oakton, VA: OSS, 2002).

5. It is now clearly documented that both the White House and the Senate knew that Peak Oil was upon us during varied hearings conducted from 1974–79, and deliberately concealed this fact from the public, and failed to alter energy policy, in order to avoid alarming citizens or angering them over prices, while continuing to reap the rich dividends of bribery from the oil companies. This is a single specific example of where retrospective impeachments would be appropriate as a means of putting all elected officials so that they will be held accountable not just today, but into the future as their treasonous betrayal of the public trust becomes known.

6. There are 20,000 pages on OSINT at http://www.oss.net, and a one-page list of key familiarization links covering history, context, practice, policy, and reference are at http://www.oss.net/BASIC. To this day, the secret intelligence world refers with disdain to OSINT as "Open Sores."

7. The single best book on the cost of the Cold War is Derek Leebaert's *The Fifty-Year Wound: How America's Cold War Victory Has Shaped Our World* (Boston: Back Bay Books, 2003). Chalmers Johnson has written two books in this genre, the first and most recent more methodical than the second: *The Sorrows of Empire: Militarism, Secrecy, and the End of the Republic* (New York: Metropolitan Books, 2004), and *Blowback: The Costs and Consequences of American Empire* (New York: Owl, 2004, reissue). See my partial list of books on blowback at http://tinyurl.com/qrcdu. An entire literature on "why people hate America" has been developing, along with U.S.-based critiques of immoral capitalism and virtual colonialism.

8. General Alfred M. Gray, Commandant of the Marine Corps, "Global Intelligence Challenges in the 1990s," in *American Intelligence Journal* (Winter 1988–89), pp. 37–41. Despite four years of effort by the Marine Corps, the National Foreign Intelligence Board (NFIB) and the Military Intelligence Board (MIB) refused to address General Gray's recommendations that we change our priorities from worst-case least probable to most probable emerging threats, and that we invest in open sources. Had we done so from 1988 to 2000, in those twelve years we would probably have collected enough open sources in

Arabic and other languages to understand the threat represented by bin Laden in terms compelling enough—because they were public—to mandate sustained effective action by all relevant national capabilities.

9. Daniel Ellsberg, *Secrets: A Memoir of Vietnam and the Pentagon Papers* (London:Viking, 2002). This is his recollection of his words to Henry Kissinger, then National Security Advisor to President Richard Nixon. The three pages on the pathological effects of falling prey to the cult of secrecy, on pages 237–39, should be forced rote memorization for all who receive clearances.

10. General Tony Zinni, U.S.M.C. (Retired), former Commander-in-Chief, U.S. Central Command (CINCCENT), as recounted to the author on April 4, 2006, by a very prominent individual close to varied National Security Council and defense personalities, who desires to remain anonymous.

11. As recounted in Richard Helms, *A Look Over My Shoulder: A Life in the Central Intelligence Agency* (New York: Random House, 2003).

12. Cf. Robert Steele, *On Intelligence: Spies and Secrecy in an Open World* (Fairfax, VA: AFCEA, 2000; Oakton, VA: OSS, 2003) with a Foreword by Senator David Boren (D-OK), whose efforts to reform national intelligence in 1992 were undone by a combination of Senator John Warner (R-VA) and Secretary of Defense Dick Cheney. The book remains the single most comprehensive public critique of the shortfalls of the secret world. For a list of other books critical of the past and offering a vision for the future, see my varied lists at Amazon.com.

13. Cf. Walter Laqueur, *A World of Secrets: The Uses and Limits of Intelligence* (New York: Basic Books, 1985). Many other books give accounts of secret warfare going back in time, but culminating in the behind-the-lines operations in World War II, and then the "dirty tricks" of the 20th century.

14. Sherman Kent, *Strategic Intelligence for American World Policy* (Princeton: Princeton University Press, 1948). This is a classic. In reality, Kent did not achieve his vision for two reasons: because the clandestine service took over the Central Intelligence Agency and subordinated the analysts, and because, in so doing, they cut the analysts off from the world of open sources that were the mainstay of Kent's vision in the first place.

15. Robert Steele is the primary author on the concept of "smart nation." Among the early works were "Creating a Smart Nation: Information Strategy, Virtual Intelligence, and Information Warfare," in contributing eds., *Cyberwar: Security, Strategy, and Conflict in the Information Age,* contributing eds. Alan D. Campen, Douglas H. Dearth, and R. Thomas Gooden (Fairfax, VA: AFCEA, 1996), pp. 77–89; "Creating a Smart Nation: Strategy, Policy, Intelligence, and Information," *Government Information Quarterly* 13 (Summer 1996), pp. 159–173; "Reinventing Intelligence: The Vision and the Strategy," *International Defense & Technologies* (December 1995), bilingual in French and English; and "Private Enterprise Intelligence: Its Potential Contribution to National Security," paper presented to the Canadian Intelligence Community Conference on Intelligence Analysis and Assessment, October 29, 1994, reprinted in *Intelligence and National Security* (Special Issue, October 1995), and also in a book by the same name, 1996.

16. The sections that follow deliberately relate OSINT to reform of the secret elements of the intelligence cycle. Complete multimedia lectures, a total of eight, are easily accessed via http://www.oss.net/BASIC.

17. (New York: United Nations, 2004). The endeavor benefited from the participation of The Honorable Lieutenant General Dr. Brent Scowcroft, U.S.A.F. (Retired),

former national security advisor to President George Bush. Terrorism is ninth out of the ten high-level threats. The report, 262 pages in length, can be seen at http://www.un.org/secureworld/report2.pdf.

18. It merits comment that according to the *Report of the Commission on the National Imagery and Mapping Agency*, as published in December 1999, most of the intelligence money is spent on esoteric collection systems, and almost none at all is spent on actually making sense out of the collected information.

19. The author has served in the clandestine service (six tours, three overseas), supported strategic signals intelligence acquisition operations, and been a member of the Advanced Program and Evaluation Staff (APEG) with responsibilities for national-level validation of current and future secret imagery collection programs.

20. The languages that OSS and its partners use to follow terrorism and other topics properly are as follows: Arabic, Aramaic, Berber, Catelan, Chinese, Danish, Dari, Dutch, English, Farsi, Finnish, French, German, Indonesian, Irish, Italian, Japanese, Korean, Kurdish, Kurmanji, Norwegian, Pashto, Polish, Portuguese, Russian, Serbian, Spanish, Swedish, Tamil, Turkish, and Urdu. Arabic variations include Andalusi Arabic (extinct, but important role in literary history); Egyptian Arabic (Egypt), considered the most widely understood and used "second dialect"; Gulf Arabic (Gulf coast from Kuwait to Oman, and minorities on the other side); Hassaniiya (in Mauritania); Hijazi Arabic; Iraqi Arabic; Levantine Arabic (Syrian, Lebanese, Palestinian, and western Jordanian); Maghreb Arabic (Tunisian, Algerian, Moroccan, and western Libyan); Maltese; Najdi Arabic; Sudanese Arabic (with a dialect continuum into Chad); and Yemeni Arabic.

21. This is a very serious indictment of both the policy community and the intelligence community. It is based on direct observation in three embassies overseas (three tours), on a second graduate thesis on strategic and tactical information management for national security, and on eighteen years of advocacy during which over forty governments have been helped to enhance their access to and exploitation of open sources of information.

22. The author spent a tour in the Collection Requirements and Evaluations Staff (CRES) at the CIA, and also consulting in the 2000–1 timeframe to ICMAP, the attempt by the Deputy Director of Central Intelligence for Administration (DDCI/A) to reduce duplicative tasking of the varied classified collection disciplines. Neither the CIA nor the new Open Source Center have a full grasp of how to access all information in all languages all the time, and ICMAP continues to focus on triage among the classified systems, without regard for what can be found, gotten, or bought.

23. This is the only standard that may not be readily apparent when this chapter is published. Invented by Doug Englebart, also the inventor of the mouse and hypertext, this standard enables linkage of related content to take place at the paragraph level, which also allows copyright compliance to be executed at the paragraph level, for pennies instead of dollars.

24. Amy Zegart, *Flawed by Design: The Evolution of the CIA, JCS, and NSC* (Palo Alto: Stanford University Press, 2000).

25. It is a fact that 90 percent of the information that we need to gain access to is controlled or obtainable by nongovernmental, academic, civil, and generally foreign organizations that cannot afford the gold-plated and generally pathologically dysfunctional information technology systems that the beltway bandits have been selling to the secret world for decades. In order to create a global information sharing environment where we

can get much more than we give in the way of content (what we can provide is processing power), it is essential that we establish generic open source software suites of tools, such as the Defense Advanced Research Projects Agency (DARPA) has done with STRONG ANGEL, so that all relevant contributors can join the Open Source Information System (OSIS) via inexpensive collaborative toolkits and access ports.

26. Information technology has not been an obstacle to the creation of 24/7 "plots" but rather mindsets and bureaucratic inertia. For a stimulating and truly enlightening account of both the early mistakes and later successes of the British in World War II in using "plots" to track and anticipate the movements of submarines (a skill applicable to today's terrorists), see Patrick Beesley, *Very Special Intelligence: The Story of the Admiralty's Operational Intelligence Centre, 1939–1945* (London: Greenhill, 2000). As with all books cited, a summative review by Robert Steele, with key points itemized, can be read at Amazon.com.

27. Despite General Gray's concern in 1988, and years of effort by the author that culminated in testimony to the Aspin-Brown Commission resulting in a finding that our access to open sources was "severely deficient" and should be a "top priority" for funding; and despite a report commissioned by DCI George Tenet and delivered by Boyd Sutton in July 1997 on "The Challenge of Global Coverage"—a report recommending that $1.5 billion a year be spent on open sources as an insurance policy, consisting of $10 million a year on each of 150 topics of lower tier countries spawning terrorism, crime, disease, and other ills—Tenet, his predecessors, and his successors have consistently refused to focus on anything other than secrets for the president. The Global Coverage report is easily accessible via http://www.oss.net/BASIC.

28. There are a handful of books that really emphasize the importance of history and the continuing strategy relevance of historical factors including morality and birth control (or not). Among them: Will and Ariel Durant, *The Lessons of History* (New York: Simon & Schuster, 1968); Richard Neustradt and Ernest May, *Thinking in Time: The Uses of History for Decision Makers* (New York: Free Press, 1988); Stewart Brand, *The Clock of the Long Now: Time and Responsibility—The Ideas Behind the World's Slowest Computer* (New York: Basic, 2000); and John Lewis Gaddis, *The Landscape of History: How Historians Map the Past* (New York: Oxford, 2004). Included here are two books on the strategic implications of losing history, and failing to notice fact: Robert Perry, *Lost History: Contras, Cocaine, the Press & "Project Truth"* (San Francisco: Media Consortium, 1999), and Larry Beinhart, *Fog Facts: Searching for Truth in the Land of Spin* (New York: Nation Books, 2005).

29. This term was first used by Alvin Toffler to describe the author, his company, and OSINT. See the chapter on "The Future of the Spy" in which five of the twelve pages are focused on OSINT, in *War and Anti-War: Making Sense of Today's Global Chaos* (New York: Warner, 1995). All of the books by the Tofflers, who now write as a team, are relevant to the information era, but *Powershift: Knowledge, Wealth, and Power at the Edge of the 21st Century* (New York: Bantam, 1991) is rather special.

30. This term (M4IS) was first introduced by the Swedes at the Third Peacekeeping Intelligence Conference held in Stockholm in December 2004. The Swedes have replaced the Canadians as the neutral third party of choice.

31. Googling for "analytic tradecraft" is always useful. The actual notes from Jack Davis can be accessed via http://www.oss.net/BASIC.

32. As with all observations in this chapter, the specifics are easily accessible via http://www.oss.net/BASIC, in this case as "New Rules for the New Craft of Intelligence," under Practice, where other guides to analytic tradecraft may also be found.

33. Cf. Robert Steele, *Information Operations: All Information, All Languages, All the Time* (Oakton, VA: OSS, 2006) and—more focused on the military as well as free— *Information Operations: Putting the I Back Into DIME* (Strategic Studies Institute, February 2006). The latter is easily found by Googling for the title.

34. Jonathan Schell, *The Unconquerable World: Power, Nonviolence, and the Will of the People* (New York: Owl, 2004).

35. The author spent a tour at the national level responsible for offensive counterintelligence against a denied area county, and was also responsible for global oversight of recruitment efforts against all representatives of the same government.

36. In general the reader is referred to the 770+ books reviewed by the author at Amazon.com over the past five years. Dr. Colonel Max Manwaring (Retired) has edited *Environmental Security and Global Stability: Problems and Responses* (Lanham, MD: Lexington, 2002) and there is an entire literature on ecological economics as well as on the health of nations, relating disease, poverty, and the environment.

37. On this vital topic, see on the internal threat, two books: Kevin Philips, *American Theocracy: The Peril and Politics of Radical Religion, Oil, and Borrowed Money in the 21st Century* (New York: Viking, 2006), and Michael Lerner, *The Left Hand of God: Taking Back Our Country From the Religious Right* (New York: Harpers, 2006). On the external threat, though there are numerous books on radical Islam, the best overall discussion of ideology as a means of changing the pecking order among social groups, and grabbing real estate and resources, is offered by Howard Bloom, *The Lucifer Principle: A Scientific Expedition Into the Forces of History* (Boston: Atlantic Monthly, 1997). The book includes a prescient discussion of Sunni versus Shiite, as well as of religion as an ideology used to capture resources.

38. Among the most obvious and hard-hitting current references on immoral capitalism are Clyde Prestowitz, *Rogue Nation: American Unilateralism and the Failure of Good Intentions* (New York: Basic, 2004); John Perkins, *Confessions of an Economic Hit Man* (New York: Plume, 2005); William Greider, *The Soul of Capitalism: Opening Paths to a Moral Economy* (New York: Simon & Schuster, 2004); and, most recently, Jeffrey Sachs, *The End of Poverty: Economic Possibilities for Our Time* (New York: Penguin, 2006). There is a separate literature on "virtual colonialism" and the inner anger that a U.S. military presence inspires, particularly in Muslim countries.

39. *Report of the Commission on Protecting and Reducing Government Secrecy* (GAO, 1997), available at http://www.fas.org/sgp/library/moynihan/.

40. Both are available online.

41. No disrespect is intended in neglecting to address the standard works on strategic warning. The author's concept of strategic warning is much broader than now exists within both the secret intelligence world and the academic world that writes about the secret intelligence world.

42. Colin Gray, *Modern Strategy* (New York: Oxford, 1999). An eight-point summary is at Amazon.com. A superb monograph on strategy (eighty-three pages) by Dr. Colonel Harry (Rich) Yarger (Retired), "Strategic Theory for the 21st Century," is easily found online by Googling the author and title.

43. John Perry Barlow, "Why Spy?" *Forbes* (October 7, 2002), available at http://www.forbes.com/asap/2002/1007/042.html.

44. At the time, Donahue was the ranking director with the Office of Management and Budget (OMB) for all Command and Control, Communications, Computing, and Intelligence (C4I), and one of a handful of individuals with all of the code-word clearances. His boss, Don Gessaman, the ranking civil servant at OMB for National Security inclusive of Programs 50 (International Relations) and 150 (Defense), guided the establishment of Code M320 for defense expenditures on OSINT in 2000. OSINT is seen by the intelligence community as a threat that should not be outsourced, and by OMB as a function that can be accomplished in the private sector and therefore should be outsourced to the fullest extent possible.

7

THE SHORTEST DISTANCE BETWEEN TWO POINTS LIES IN RETHINKING THE QUESTION

Intelligence and the Information Age Technology Challenge

DANIEL S. GRESSANG IV

INTELLIGENCE SERVICES, AND THE PRACTICE OF INTELLIGENCE, are at a threshold. The tremendous changes in the global political, economic, security, and technology environments are radically altering not only the mechanics of intelligence production, but the very roles and purposes of intelligence. The collapse of the Soviet Union and the dissolution of the Warsaw Pact forced Western intelligence services to reconceptualize threats and vulnerabilities as they sought to redefine collection and analysis priorities. The Soviets and their allies are no longer the primary target for intelligence. Instead, the new world of the 21st century offers intelligence a wide variety of potential targets, each of which exhibits a host of unique patterns of activity and capabilities. The world has moved from the bipolar moment of the Cold War, through the unipolar moment of little-questioned American supremacy, to the emerging multipolar moment of an emerging Third World and proliferation of nonstate and substate actors on the global stage. The result for intelligence is a complex array of threats, potential threats, and questions, each of which demands understanding and answers, and a formidable set of challenges intelligence will have to overcome to remain vital and relevant to its customers.

Perhaps the most important challenge faced by the U.S. intelligence community stems from the explosive growth in technology. Improvements in telecommunications, computers, and other high-technology fields have ushered in an era of global connectivity and greater interdependence. Information, the root of all intelligence production, has become the principle commodity in this environment. Indeed, the National Intelligence Council's effort to envision the world of 2020 called the growing connectedness of globalization a "mega-trend" that will "substantially shape all the other major trends" of the future.[1] In politics and governance, technology-driven interconnectedness has fueled the rise of nonstate actors on the world stage, allowing a host of political movements an international status and weight they would not have enjoyed otherwise. In business, technology-driven globalization has broken down trade barriers, allowing both greater flow of goods and services and greater potential for disruption. And in intelligence, it has fostered positive growth and evolution in collection, processing, and analytic capabilities, while also stimulating the capabilities of intelligence collection targets, allowing them new opportunities to prevent or disrupt intelligence collection efforts against themselves. It is, for intelligence, a two-edged sword.

SHIFTING PERSPECTIVES

With the explosive growth in technology and the changes in the international environment, the intelligence community faces very real, and in some ways daunting, challenges. Persistence in conducting the business of intelligence as it always has will quickly prove inadequate, most observers seem to suggest. Gregory Treverton, for example, goes as far as to maintain that "the world as it is now undercuts all the attributes of the old intelligence paradigm, and another decade or more of change would do so even more drastically."[2] Failure to recognize the paradigmatic shift, away from the only one U.S. intelligence has known to an information-dominant one, will result in a diminished capacity for intelligence to serve its core customers of political and military decision makers. As secrets become less and less important and open source information gains greater impact in decision making, the intelligence community must shift focus from state-centric emphasis on secrets to a multifaceted knowledge management approach.

The shift has not been easy, since it engenders a variety of potentially conflicting demands.[3] On the one hand, the intelligence community must overcome technological challenges, deciding in course what is feasible to develop and pursue. Coupled with determinations of technological feasibility are the questions of goals for the community: In what direction does the community need to develop in order to meets its customers' present and future information needs? Both sets of questions, in turn, are wrapped around issues of intent and limitations. There will be, as William Nolte notes, difficult decisions to make concerning the techniques and technologies we may have to leave behind, concerning the risks we are prepared to undertake in pursuit of continued relevance in intelligence production, and in how we choose to envision the future and its needs.[4] In short, one of the most pressing issues for the intelligence community is the way in which it meets the technology challenge of the information age. The way the intelligence community addresses the problems associated with information and technology will ultimately determine the degree to which the community remains an important and relevant contributor in the coming decades.

THE ROLE OF INTELLIGENCE

In some respects, the role of intelligence is quite simple: meet the information needs of its policy-making and war-fighting customers in government. Lieutenant General Michael V. Hayden, U.S.A.F., then-Director of the National Security Agency, outlined the foundational role of intelligence simply and eloquently when he noted that "accurate and timely information about the capabilities, intentions and activities of foreign powers, organizations, or persons and their agents is essential to informed decision making in the areas of national defense and foreign relations."[5] Beyond meeting the immediate information needs of decision makers, however, intelligence must also be forward looking, capable of providing decision makers with an accurate and timely assessment of future threats and possible threats, above and beyond the bounds of the immediate. Intelligence, if it is to fulfill its primary missions, must be able to collaborate within its ranks to produce an understanding of a host of adversaries, from traditional nation-states to emergent substate and nonstate actors.[6]

Indeed, the predictive capacity of the intelligence community is the key to its continued success, because planning and preparation to meet future challenges takes time. Looking to the future, the National Intelligence Council envisions a global landscape that holds both relative certainties and critical uncertainties. Those uncertainties include the spread of new technologies, mainly at the hands of aggressive global businesses, which are expected to result in challenges to governance brought about by greater connectivity and information flow. Though the United States is seen as capable of maintaining its leading position in the economic, technological, and military spheres, emerging nations such as China, India, and Brazil are increasingly capable in technological development, leading to more frequent challenges to U.S. leadership.[7] Meeting those challenges requires a refocused intelligence community, albeit one already in the process of changing. By envisioning an intelligence community transforming to "stay ahead of evolving threats to the United States, exploiting risk while recognizing the impossibility of eliminating it,"[8] the Director of National Intelligence has crafted a series of mission and enterprise objectives designed to keep the intelligence community in a position to "maintain competitive advantages over states and forces that threaten the security of our nation."[9] The key to fulfilling that objective lies in evolving from collection-centric intelligence production to information and knowledge management–driven intelligence production.

Knowledge management, the ability to produce relevant information in context in an appropriate and usable form easily accessible to recipients,[10] is the means by which the intelligence community of the 21st century will remain relevant to government decision makers. Knowledge management, and knowledge production, involve much more than just collection. Collection efforts produce data, often raw, unevaluated observations and facts that typically have little meaning to consumers. Data must be massaged, manipulated, and managed to transform it into information, where it begins to take on the trappings of usable inputs to analysts and decision makers. Information must finally be put into context and usable form, and only then does it become knowledge with lasting relevance and meaning to its recipients.

FINDING DATA: THE IMPACT OF TECHNOLOGY

Finding the data necessary to begin the process of generating knowledge, however, is much easier said than done. Recent advances in technology, particularly communications technology, have meant that the information environment from which data is gathered has exhibited phenomenal growth. The growth of technology means not only that there are more ways to generate information, but that there are also more ways to discover information and more ways to protect and secure information. Technological expansion has been accelerating for a number of years, and can continue to accelerate indefinitely as technological advancements feed off one another and foster new innovations. Technology, then, will become even more of a force multiplier in the information age, available to any and all who have the resources to acquire it and who can grasp the implications of its use.[11]

Forty-five years ago, at the height of the Cold War, for example, communications technology was rather static and predictable in that communications were limited in terms of opportunities and paths of propagation and in terms of available mechanisms for communication. In 1960, for example, there were no facsimile machines and no cell phones, each being at best only an idea. In the 1990s the number of cell phones available and in use rose from 16 million to over 741 million, with an estimated 50,000 new subscribers daily, and by 2000 there were an estimated 14 million facsimile machines in use. Even in the more limited arena of landline telephony, some 630,000 new telephone lines are installed each year, with a growing investment in, and use of, high-capacity fiber-optic lines, one strand of which can carry an equivalent capacity of all existing communications satellites. Investment in fiber-optic cable by the telecommunications industry alone is estimated at $1 trillion or more. Communications traffic on all these systems is reflected in the explosive growth in availability. By one estimate international commercial telephony alone amounted to over 100 billion minutes in 2000, up from 38 billion minutes just ten years earlier. Other estimates suggest there are approximately 35 million voicemail messages left each hour, and the growing use of Voice-over-Internet Protocol (VoIP, in which telephone calls are made using computers) led to the laying of enough fiber-optic cable to transmit the equivalent of one complete Library of Congress every 14 to 15 seconds. Further complicating the picture, the 1990s saw packetized communications, which make computer-to-computer communications over the Internet functional and is widely used in telephony, overtake traditional nonpacketized communications.[12]

The growth and availability of computers mirrors that of telephony yet carries with it even greater implications for intelligence. In 1960 there were roughly 5,000 stand-alone computers worldwide and twenty years later there were still relatively few personal computers in use. By 2000, however, there were estimated to be over 180 million computers in use, most of which are connected to the Internet, with the number of Internet users growing from 4 million in 1990 to over 361 million ten years later. Beyond standard telephone, Digital Subscriber Line (DSL), or cable connections, there are about 100,000 Wireless Fidelity (WiFi) hotspots publicly available, with Europe and North America beginning to catch up to Asia and the Pacific region in availability. In all, some 37 million people log on to the Internet each day, generating 5 million e-mail messages every minute, or some 610 billion messages in 2000 alone, and creating enough digitized content to equal 40 Libraries of Congress. Those same users also generate an estimated 530 billion instant messages a day, with total Internet traffic doubling every 100 days. In static web content alone there were 2.1 billion pages on the Internet in 2000, with 4.2 billion projected by the end of 2001.[13]

The volume of available information is almost incomprehensible, and it continues to grow exponentially. In 2000 the University of California, Berkeley, estimated that all the information created that year totaled 2 exabytes of data, with 1 exabyte equal to 10^{18} bytes. To place that in context, one computer data storage manufacturer estimated that all spoken human communication, since the dawn of time, equaled 5 exabytes.[14] The intelligence community must effectively sift through this vast amount of data to find those bits which are, or have the potential to be, relevant to its customers.[15]

The explosive growth in technology, of which communications and computer technologies are but a part, holds even greater implications for the intelligence community than sheer numbers alone suggest. Fast-growing and dispersing technology empowers those who adopt and apply it, leading to a growing number of state and nonstate actors capable of influencing global politics.[16] Southern Mexico's Zapatistas, for example, emerged from the jungles in January 1994, seized several small villages, and seemed destined to a quick defeat at the hands of the Mexican army. The Zapatistas and their supporters, however, proved adept at leveraging the Internet to gain and rally support from around the world. As a result, the Zapatistas not only survived, but became a relatively potent advocate for Mexico's poor and downtrodden indigenous peoples. In similar fashion, less developed states that adopt emerging technologies not only afford themselves an opportunity to benefit internally through greater command and control capabilities, but also gain the potential for skipping generations of development in ways disproportionate to outlays, investment, and expenditures. By "leapfrogging" stages of development,[17] these states stand to realize significant progress, placing themselves in some respects ahead of developed states. A country such as the Congo, for example, could, with shrewd and intelligent technology investments, effectively shrink its massive size and streamline command and control through effective adoption of satellite- or wireless-based telephony rather than spending billions of dollars and countless years rebuilding a poorly maintained and sometimes nonexistent terrestrial telephony infrastructure. By skipping generations of development, the Congo would effectively multiply the difficulties encountered by any intelligence service seeking to access and exploit an architecture that transitions rapidly from early 20th century to cutting-edge telephony.

MOVING FROM THE INDUSTRIAL AGE
TO THE INFORMATION AGE

Technological advances, as Michael Herman notes, are obscuring boundaries.[18] Internally, they obscure boundaries associated with geographic spread and the necessities of national-level command and control, as the example of the Congo suggests. Internationally, technology is beginning to erase distinctions between the developed and developing worlds, because each is gaining access to the same technologies and proving successful at applying them. Technology is also blurring distinctions, on the global stage, between state and nonstate actors, because technology allows nonstate groups to leverage and benefit from unregulated mass-appeal institutions such as the Internet. But the challenge of evolving into the information age affects not just the global political environment, it affects in fundamental ways the business of intelligence. The challenges for intelligence, which some have labeled a revolution in intelligence affairs, manifest themselves in collection, processing, analysis, and dissemination of intelligence. Not only has technology begun to blur state-to-state distinctions, it dramatically alters the way intelligence must think about its role and its production. Internally to intelligence, technology offers myriad new opportunities to gather and process information for its customers, while also affording intelligence-collection targets greater opportunities to protect information from collection and exploitation. At the same time, the successes enjoyed in intelligence collection carry their own challenges associated with data overload and dissemination.

Technological advances do more than alter the collection process, because the amount of information gathered and the newer means of processing that information help create a significantly greater amount and variety of information available for analysis and dissemination to intelligence customers. Not only is multisensor coordination possible, those advances also allow a much greater volume of direct "sensor-to-shooter" data transmission, making a tremendous volume of raw data immediately available to operational users. To many, these capabilities alone account for some of the most significant capabilities for the intelligence community to maintain and improve.[19]

To some, this revolution in intelligence affairs has been ushered in through technological advances. In this view, technology provides the enabling capabilities necessary to understand and exploit the growing global information network through the development and deployment of sensor-based automated collection systems. Highly developed and finely tuned sensors, available on a global scale, will, in this vision, afford commanders and decision makers with instantaneous or near-instantaneous situational displays of selected targets. It is a grand vision, with technological growth and application leading almost seamlessly to vast increases in data suitable for analysis and exploitation. "A single surveillance satellite on a 15 minute pass," according to Major General W. J. P. Roberts, "produces enough material to occupy 100 analysts with conventional tools for a week."[20]

Yet inherent in such visions stands the potential for critical loss of context. Placing the lion's share of emphasis on automation could easily contribute to contextual tunnel vision, in which one aspect of intelligence production—the tangible—is overstressed at the expense of the other—the intangible. This duality of intelligence,[21] however, demands equal weight be given to understanding the adversary's intent as well as his physical locations and capabilities. Effective intelligence production requires, as Herman notes, movement beyond the mere recitation of physical manifestations of the adversary to incorporate interpretations of intent. Knowing the adversary's order of battle, unfortunately, says little about his goals and willingness to use the resources at his disposal. Whereas physical manifestations can only allude to, at best, possible intent, the more difficult aspects of intelligence—intent—are often the province of human intelligence (HUMINT) and signals intelligence (SIGINT) collection. Yet both sets of knowledge, the tangible and intangible, are necessary for defense and planning purposes.

Intelligence is about things and about intentions. It is about knowing and understanding as much as possible about actual and potential adversaries and competitors. It is also about self-awareness, about understanding one's own capabilities, strengths, and vulnerabilities so that effective counterexploitation measures can be developed and adopted. In short, intelligence is about knowing the information environment from all angles and achieving superiority of the information space. This information superiority lies at the heart of what in the defense community is referred to as dominant battlespace knowledge and information assurance initiatives, as conceptualized in the Defense Department's *Joint Vision 2010*:

> Improvements in information and systems integration technologies will significantly impact future military operations by providing decision makers with accurate information in a timely manner. Information technology will improve the ability to see, prioritize, assign, and assess information. The fusion of all-source intelligence with the fluid integration of sensors, platforms, command organizations, and logistic support centers will allow a greater number of operational tasks to be accomplished faster. Advances in computer processing, precise global positioning, and telecommunications will provide the capability to determine accurate locations of friendly and enemy forces, as well as to collect, process, and distribute relevant data to thousands of locations.
>
> Forces harnessing the capabilities potentially available from this system of systems will gain dominant battlespace awareness, an interactive "picture" which will yield much more accurate assessments of friendly and enemy operations within the area of interest.[22]

Achieving dominant battlespace, or information space, awareness raises critical questions for intelligence planners. How is information superiority to be gained and maintained? Can automated systems effectively manage and filter the tremendous volume of information available and collected? How is the volume of data collected to be managed and used? The questions are daunting, leading William Nolte to point out that the intelligence community "must simultaneously confront how information, information technology and information or knowledge management change the world around us, while adjusting to those developments internally."[23]

THE CHANGING ROLE OF INTELLIGENCE

During the Cold War, access to information was at times limited by technological shortcomings or adversarial security practices. Dissemination, and to a lesser degree collection, depended at times on relatively slow systems that were, in turn, dependent on sometimes unreliable communications circuits. This led to a degree of planned redundancy in order to increase the odds of providing an uninterrupted flow of intelligence information.[24] Reliance on system stability and robustness remains equally important today, but with a greater reliance on technology than in the past comes a greater potential for unwanted disruption when systems fail. One recent example is a software anomaly in the National Security Agency's (NSA) system that resulted in a communication infrastructure failure lasting three days. In that time, the NSA was unable to forward intelligence data, to communicate internally, and to process data. Correcting the causal factors and restoring system operability took roughly $1.5 million and involved thousands of man-hours.[25] Lieutenant General Hayden, then-Director of the NSA, reminded audiences afterward that the episode highlighted his agency's absolute reliance on technology.

Improvements in network speed, availability, and reliability—the NSA's troubles notwithstanding—allow for the more rapid relay of information from collector to processor, to analyst, to consumer. In other venues, improved and expanded connectivity and data transfer capabilities allow for significant increases in direct sensor-to-shooter systems, affording operational elements near real-time access to data suitable for mission success.[26] Yet instantaneous or near-instantaneous availability of massive quantities of raw data, or even processed data, may turn out to be a mixed blessing.

Rather than providing the needed information in a context valuable to specific customer needs,[27] direct sensor-to-shooter capabilities flood recipients with largely unevaluated data. Without sufficient filters capable of sorting through the mass of data on the basis of some predetermined set of criteria and translating the raw collection into a usable form of information, recipients are forced to divert attention from immediate operational concerns to an effort to interpret the incoming flow. Although there are numerous examples of successes in such systems, this approach also holds the potential for disaster, as the example of Beirut illustrates. In 1983 Islamic militants bombed the U.S. Marine barracks in Beirut, Lebanon, with catastrophic results. The Long Commission, tasked with examining the incident to determine and disseminate appropriate lessons learned, concluded on-scene commanders were overwhelmed with data—some relevant, some not; some original, some duplicative—which rendered them ineffective in security planning.[29]

More recently, information overload and the lack of information specificity prevented the intelligence community from developing a clear, comprehensive threat picture prior to the September 11, 2001, attacks on New York and Washington:

> With the huge volume of intelligence reporting that was available prior to September 11, there were various threads and pieces of information that, at least in retrospect, were both relevant and significant. The degree to which the Community was or was not able to build on that information to discern the bigger picture successfully is a critical part of the context for the September 11 attacks.[29]

At the same time, technological evolution and increased technology availability holds the potential for hindering collection and exploitation efforts by enabling adversarial states and groups, thus serving to impose limits on U.S. intelligence production efforts. With each passing day, available technology becomes more standardized as developers and manufacturers embrace the logic and marketability of interoperability. As noted by a panel of experts reviewing technology and business practices at the NSA, "today's information technology is a veritable monoculture. There is very little diversity in the underlying technology and therefore security vulnerabilities found in national security systems as compared with other federal systems [sic]."[30] This developing monoculture provides America's adversaries with significant advantages in that they are better able to network, gain more widespread access to information, and better protect their own communications and information technology systems from exploitation.[31]

Greater interoperability in communication and information technology systems is evident not only in advances in digital telephony and computers, but also in the more widespread use of more effective transmission methods and encryption technologies in the private and public spheres. Digital communications allow more widespread use of *packetization*—the parsing of communication at or near its point of origin, transmission by multiple paths, and reassembly at or near the ultimate destination—and forces intelligence collectors to focus their own efforts in a much narrower range of potential access locations.[32] Digitization also makes simpler the use of a range of encryption and other security practices designed to boost user security. As publicly available encryption algorithms gain in length and complexity, the already difficult task of breaking newer encryption schemes can be expected to get harder over time.

Open source information availability adds to the problems faced by intelligence, sometimes immeasurably so, by giving collection targets access to a range of previously unavailable information and, when security fails, insights into the capabilities and operations of intelligence agencies. Leaks of classified information serve as warnings for those targets, frequently leading to behavioral and technology changes designed to reduce or eliminate vulnerabilities available for exploitation. Press reports in 1998 of American interception of Osama bin Laden's cellular telephone communications, for example, led to bin Laden's abandoning the use of cellular phones and increased significantly America's difficulties in locating and capturing him.[33]

The net result of technological advances is a more complex information environment characterized by increased communications and information systems security, faster and more efficient information transmission practices, and exponential growth in information generation and dissemination. The difficulties caused for the intelligence community are especially acute in the technical disciplines such as signals intelligence. Then-Director Hayden succinctly and eloquently summed up those difficulties in noting:

> The volume, variety, and velocity of human communications make our mission more difficult each day. A SIGINT agency has to look like its targets. We have to master whatever technology the target is using. If we don't, we literally don't hear him; or if we do, we cannot turn the "beeps and squeaks" into something intelligible. We have competed successfully against a resource-poor, oligarchic, technologically inferior, and overly bureaucratic nation-state. Now we [have] to keep pace with a global telecommunications revolution, probably the most dramatic revolution to human communications since Gutenberg's invention of moveable type.[34]

It is, as Hayden acknowledged, a revolution that may be accelerating faster than the intelligence community's ability to keep pace. Government research, development, and procurement practices are often given as reasons for the community's relinquished leading role in technology development and deployment. Explosive growth in the information environment has led, over the past twenty years, to a steady deterioration of the community's ability to access desired data when, where, and how desired. Whereas imagery resources have advanced to the point where much of the world is relatively transparent,[35] the paucity of robust, deeply embedded human collection resources remains a target of intelligence reformers and critics.[36] Despite advances in SIGINT collection and processing capabilities, the percentage of available information actually collected and exploited is smaller today than in the past,[37] due in large part to more rapid commercial development and dissemination.

Though the defense and intelligence communities initiated development of many widespread technologies, the country's position as the world's technology leader is declining. Private industry has moved ahead of government to assume a position at the forefront of technological development and implementation,[38] leaving government—and intelligence in particular—in the unenviable role of playing catch-up. Adding to the intelligence community's difficulty in closing the technology gap with industry are communitywide personnel and resource reductions, often mandated by Congress.[39] The community has, nevertheless, sought to regain much of its lost technological edge by both partnering with private industry and leveraging newer commercial off-the-shelf (COTS) technologies.[40] Yet other factors, such as bureaucratic inertia, resource limitations, and perceptual blinders, limit the community's efforts to overcome the technology challenge.

TRANSFORMATION

In an effort to reverse recent trends, the intelligence community has embarked on a massive effort to transform itself. Many of the organizational and structural changes reach across agency lines, redrawing the community organizational chart to a degree unprecedented since 1947. The technological transformation effort is critical to overall improvement, yet interpretations of the degree of success achieved—and achievable—vary considerably. Some, such as former Director of Central Intelligence Admiral B. R. Inman, note the widening gap between America and the rest of the world in technological development and argue that regaining technological superiority will be possible only with a fundamental shift to private industry leadership. A more optimistic view holds that any future inability to maintain sufficient intelligence production capabilities will not be the result of technological insufficiency.[41] Which of these perspectives will more accurately describe the intelligence community's future is as yet still undetermined. What can be said, however, is that the intelligence community's monopoly on leading-edge technology has been irretrievably broken,[42] forcing the community to rely more on development partnerships and creative leveraging of existing commercial technologies. The intelligence community's targets have seized the advantage, in one respect, in that they are not forced by circumstances to develop unique capabilities; rather, they only need to select, purchase, and use available equipment.[43]

Transformation will not come easy. Efforts to achieve wholesale change in material resource utilization, business practices, organization, and operative perspective are fraught with danger, particularly when change initiatives seek to modify or undo over forty years of institutional inertia. Pressures toward specialization raise the possibility of transforming into an "intelligence boutique" with severe and effectively debilitating limits on production, customer service,[44] and operational flexibility. Resource reductions, particularly funding, increase the likelihood of boutique development as the intelligence community seeks to maximize value by focusing efforts and expertise on a select set of high-value targets. Complex procurement and budget justification practices developed in part to enhance technical superiority and ensure quality control exacerbate this trend,[45] leaving some segments of the community scrambling to reprogram resources.[46]

Technology, in and of itself, however, is not the most pressing problem faced by the intelligence community as it struggles to transition into an effective and efficient information age producer. COTS, and their effective incorporation into the intelligence production process, coupled with robust and mutually beneficial government-private industry partnerships, will likely allow intelligence to keep pace with the technological evolution of its targets.[47] A few speed bumps, most likely of short duration, can be expected along the way, but by and large the intelligence community can be expected to have sufficient foresight into technology evolution, and intelligence needs, to effectively combine the two into a coherent program yielding long-term operational sufficiency. The community's technological evolution efforts will need to remain dynamic and wide-ranging,[48] and whereas research and development efforts are well positioned to meet the technology challenge, static and burdensome bureaucracies characteristic of the community add a slight damper to the transformation effort.[49] The NSA's New Enterprise Team (NETeam), tasked by then-Director Hayden to examine the Agency and its practices to recommend improvements, was rather blunt in noting: "Absent profound change at NSA, the nation will lose a powerful weapon in its arsenal. Stakeholders and customers are resigned to accept diminished NSA capability, not because of insurmountable technological challenges, but because NSA has proven to be a poor steward of the nation's SIGINT and INFOSEC [information security] capabilities."[50] Though systems development capabilities are sufficient to address the technology challenges, oversight and management of the process demand improvements in strategic focus and leadership.[51] Even more pressing, however, is the perspective that informs the lack of management and focus. The changing information environment—the environment in which intelligence technologies and requirements exist—offers a much greater challenge. As Nolte sees it, the problem centers on the inherent adaptability of intelligence:

> The Intelligence Community's response to the information or knowledge management challenges to its internal practices has been almost reduced to three elements: speed, volume, and connectivity. How do we deal with the enormous increase in the amount of information available to us, to our clients, and to our adversaries? How do we meet the information needs of users increasingly demanding support "within the decision cycle" of their immediate and potential adversary?[52]

The information revolution demands a change in practices and in thinking more than it demands a change in technological capabilities. It demands, as Nolte suggests, a change in our understanding of how intelligence is being fundamentally altered by the realities of technological and political evolution. It demands, in short, a change in paradigm.

REINVENTING THE INTELLIGENCE WHEEL

Paradigmatic change is always difficult, for it engenders a wholesale re-evaluation and adjustment of core understandings and beliefs. It is dramatic in its scope and impact. To many, it is unsettling. Yet one who has embraced such a drastic change is Gregory Treverton, who offers a compelling vision of the future of intelligence. Arguing that the intelligence community is structured, and functions, in a way poorly suited to the needs of intelligence consumers in the information age because of purposive centralization, Treverton sees an intelligence community unduly focused on obtaining secrets, with intelligence production and dissemination dictated more by intelligence agencies than by intelligence customers. In the information age, he asserts, secrets are "transitory" and intelligence's greatest value lies in the effective location, processing, packaging, and distribution of largely open source information. It is, he argues, a world in which effective information marketing, of secret and open sources, defines effective intelligence production.[53]

For intelligence to effectively meet the challenges of technology, a shift in paradigm much like Treverton's is necessary, although perhaps not to the same degree. Mere changes in technological capabilities, bureaucratic structure and organization, or business practices offer minor substantive change and do little more than fix intelligence firmly in an operational rut. None of these transformational efforts address the core perceptual needs of effective intelligence production because all are narrowly focused on tangible and explicit manifestations of support structures and practices. The information age, in contrast, is one that requires continual growth, flexibility, and adaptation. In the fluid information environment continued intelligence value will not come from newer and better collection and processing systems, as Nagy asserts,[54] nor will it come from simply reorganizing the intelligence bureaucracy.[55] Whereas future success needs technical innovation, the more lasting and important change will come only to the extent that the community understands and accepts the need to re-envision information, improve data management and data mining capabilities, and redefine its central mission. Nolte perceptively notes: "The first condition we must, therefore, impose on finding our place in the new information environment is to control the tendency to see our needs and our mission as fundamentally exceptional. The corollary is that we must be precise in determining the areas in which those needs and missions do impose unique requirements."[56]

At the same time, the intelligence community needs to take to heart the House Permanent Select Committee on Intelligence's (HPSCI) admonition that perspectives need to change from that of a passive gatherer of information to that of a proactive hunter.[57] While HPSCI specifically addressed the NSA in that critique, the need to shift perspective away from the target and refocus on the customer's information needs is equally applicable to the rest of the intelligence community. Whereas the industrial age offered fairly static, rigidly organized, and behaviorally predictable targets for intelligence collection, the information age is awash with an ever-shifting milieu of actual, potential, and possible targets with little predictability and even less permanent structure. Satisfying customer intelligence needs in that environment means elevating the specifics of the information need to prominence, then determining when, where, and how the best opportunities for gathering the necessary data might be found and exploited. Knowledge management—not at the end point of shifting through collected data, but across the spectrum from initial customer questions to final intelligence product and performance evaluation—is the key to overcoming the technical challenges offered by the present and future.

Simply stated, gone are the days when the intelligence community enjoyed superiority in technical capability and access that, when combined, gave the community the ability to elevate target and collection to prominence. In that rapidly fading world, superiority meant that intelligence agencies could apply the entire spectrum of collection resources against a given target, cast a wide and indiscriminate net for gathering data, then sift through the collection take for those bits and pieces of data that met articulated intelligence requirements. Intelligence collected and processed in this way generally met customer needs when the targets were simpler, more rigidly structured and organized, and technically less sophisticated. U.S. intelligence technical superiority allowed for the large-scale gathering of data against a multitude of targets, leaving analysis to become in some respects little more than the "marketing of collection."[58] Collection, and collection capabilities, drove intelligence operations, with intelligence reporting reflecting more collection priorities and operations than customer needs. Collection capabilities far out-stripped processing and analysis capabilities, leaving a significant portion of the decision making in intelligence to collection managers. Analysis was consequently left not as the driver of intelligence efforts, but the backstage player awaiting the collector's largesse. We produced a lot of hay, to use one telling analogy, and it mattered little because we were good at sifting through it.

The information age, however, fundamentally changes the relationship between collection and analysis. As Director of Central Intelligence Porter Goss noted, in this new era "we need to make tough decisions about which haystacks deserve to be scrutinized for the needles that can hurt us most. And we know in this information age that there are endless haystacks everywhere."[59] Future efficiency and relevance of intelligence, then, lie in a more nuanced, more selective, more focused and appropriate application of collection resources. No longer can collection systems be applied against targets about which they might produce relevant information; instead, likely information-bearing targets, and their vulnerabilities to access, must be more carefully identified in the initial stages of collection strategy development so that the most appropriate collection system(s) can be chosen and thoughtfully applied. Poor results in collection efforts, which were once tolerable given the massive volume of raw intelligence gathered, are no longer acceptable given new limits on resources and access. In the information age such inadequacies also mean failure in efforts to collect and produce timely and relevant intelligence against the highest value targets as well as failure to collect against less well-identified, but potentially important and lucrative targets.

INTO THE FUTURE

To meet the challenges of the information age, few would disagree that the intelligence community must keep pace with technological development. Though certainly not perfect predictors, indicators seem to suggest it can. Changing its perspective, however, is even more important because the way intelligence problems are conceptualized and prosecuted is the ultimate determinant of success. The relationship between collection and analysis has to change in order for the intelligence community to effectively leverage both technologies and opportunities for access available to it. Yet collection will not wither in importance, as some suggest;[60] it will remain vital as the engine that empowers intelligence. Without robust collection capabilities, whether directed against open source or secret information, we surrender the very foundation on which intelligence rests. Information age collection will remain important but will be more driven by specific customer information needs than ever before. The information age forces a reversal of the collection-analysis relationship, placing analysis for the first time as the central driving force that steers collection. The fluidity and rapid growth of the information environment dictates equal parts flexibility and focus in intelligence collection and forces a shift from analyzing what's been collected to analyzing what to collect. The shift is subtle but profound in its impact on intelligence collection and production.

Analyzing what to collect, as a new operative paradigm, brings the analytic and collection disciplines together as never before. The future of intelligence effectiveness requires more than simple cooperation between analysis and collection; it demands a melding of the two into a unitary effort driving both constituent components. The more focused application of collection resources that results increases the potential to gather the most relevant and important data possible against any specified target. Merging collection and analysis, which in many ways engender quite different thought processes, will not be simple, especially where old Cold War perspectives predominate, but the shift is necessary if the community is to fully embrace and exploit information age possibilities.

Effective future intelligence production, built around the perspective of analyzing what to collect, will by definition be customer-defined, -focused, and -driven. Intelligence exists to serve its customers, and the demands of production in an age of greater openness and information availability focus attention on the customer's information and intelligence requirements by highlighting the need to be more selective about target selection, choices in obtaining information access, and collection resource application. There are, as DCI Goss noted, far too many haystacks to search. Information age intelligence needs its customers to define for it the haystacks and the needles they need to understand. Intelligence, in turn, must develop and maintain target knowledge in order to help its customers define and refine requirements and to determine not only the most likely venues through which the most relevant data might be available, but to also determine the best ways to access and exploit target vulnerabilities. Target knowledge, then, includes a thorough understanding of the technologies available to the target, now and as potential acquisitions for the future, as a way of determining target capabilities. Knowledge of target capabilities, defined by the ways the target has chosen to adopt and implement technology, define for intelligence collectors the operational parameters of the targets as well as the target's ability to secure its information from exploitation.

At the same time, target knowledge has to include order-of-battle information, knowledge of target operational capabilities and behaviors, and target tendencies and predilections. From this, the intelligence collector can gain a better understanding of not only target strengths but, more important, of target weaknesses and vulnerabilities. With the identification of actual and potential target vulnerabilities comes the greater opportunity to select the most appropriate collection resource, that which is most capable of exploiting those identified vulnerabilities, from among the available spectrum of collection systems. Collection resource selection requires such knowledge because the most appropriate resource to use often incorporates both the need to exploit vulnerabilities and the ability to gather the sought-after data. One without the other leads to inefficiency and, in times of crises, intelligence failure. A shift to analyzing what to collect opens windows for exploitation that might, given the size and complexity of the information environment, be otherwise overlooked or closed.

Overcoming the challenge of technology and its evolution requires multiple approaches. The U.S. intelligence community can no longer afford to gather and produce intelligence as it did during the Cold War—relying on its superiority in both technology and access. These are monopolies of the past and will do little to allow effective exploitation in the information age. Although the United States may maintain pace with technological advancement, it will probably never again enjoy the overwhelming dominance it once had. Intelligence production will reflect these shifting dynamics in its need to find and adopt appropriate innovations that will allow it to remain vital, relevant, and timely. Improved business practices and streamlined bureaucracies and agencies will almost certainly enable effective adaptation, as will programs either partnering with private industry for technology development or for leveraging COTS technologies as they emerge. Yet it is paradigmatic change, a change in the way we consider information, as well as both analysis and collection, that will afford the intelligence community the ability to make sense of and exploit the information environment. Shifting from the collection resource-centric analyzing what's collected mindset to the newly emergent information needs-centric analyzing what to collect mindset reorients our thinking at a fundamental level and, in doing so, opens up possibilities for effectively addressing the technological challenges of today and tomorrow.

NOTES

The views and opinions expressed in this chapter are those of the author and do not reflect the official policy or position of the Department of Defense or the U.S. government.

1. National Intelligence Council, *Mapping the Global Future: Report on the National Intelligence Council's 2020 Project*, NIC-2004-13, December 2004, p. 10, available at http://www.cia.gov/nic/NIC_globaltrend2020.html. Hereafter cited as NIC-2004-13.

2. Gregory F. Treverton, *Reshaping National Intelligence for an Age of Information* (Cambridge, UK: Cambridge University Press, 2003), p. 220.

3. See William M. Nolte, " 'Information Control Is Dead. What's Next?' The Knowledge Management Challenge for the Intelligence Community in the 21st Century," *Defense Intelligence Journal* 9 (Winter 2000), p. 10.

4. Ibid.

5. Lieutenant General Michael V. Hayden, U.S.A.F., Director, National Security Agency, "Address to Kennedy Political Union of American University, 17 February 2000," available at http://www.nsa.gov/releases/relea00058.pdf. Hereafter cited as Hayden, "Address."

6. Director of National Intelligence, *The National Intelligence Strategy of the United States of America: Transformation through Integration and Innovation* (Washington, DC: Office of the Director of National Intelligence, October 2005), p. 1. Available at http://www.dni.gov/NISOctober2005.pdf. Hereafter cited as *National Intelligence Strategy*.

7. NIC-2004-13, pp. 8, 22.

8. NIC-2004-13, p. 3.

9. *National Intelligence Strategy*, pp. 4–19.

10. Different authors advocate different definitions of knowledge management, but most seem to agree with these core elements. Clinton Brooks, for example, defines knowledge management as "making information available effortlessly, in a useable form, to the people who can apply it in their context, so that it is actionable and, thereby, becomes knowledge. It means getting the right information, to the right people, in the right format, at the right time, so they can derive knowledge, and do their jobs better." Dennis Nagy defines knowledge management as "the ability to sustain the knowledge base and to assemble and communicate only pertinent understanding, uncertainties, relevant facts, and environmental influences to the right commander or decision-maker at the right time to keep it up-to-date in the context of the commander's or decisionmaker's [sic] needs." See Clinton C. Brooks, "Knowledge Management and the Intelligence Community," *Defense Intelligence Journal* 9 (Winter 2000), p. 18, and Dennis M. Nagy, "A Military Intelligence Knowledge Base and Knowledge Management: Cultural Factors," *Defense Intelligence Journal* 9 (Winter 2000), p. 43.

11. See NIC-2004-13, p. 34, for a discussion of technology as a force multiplier in all dimensions of life.

12. See Melanie M. H. Gutjahr, *The Intelligence Archipelago: The Community's Struggle to Reform in the Globalized Era* (Washington, DC: Joint Military Intelligence College, 2005), pp. 114–18; Hayden, "Address"; and Lieutenant General Michael V. Hayden, "Statement for the Record by Lieutenant General Michael V. Hayden, USAF, Director, National Security Agency/Central Security Service Before the Joint Inquiry of the Senate Select Committee on Intelligence and the House Permanent Select Committee on Intelligence, 17 October 2002," p. 6, available at http://www.nsa.gov/releases/relea 00064.pdf. Hereafter cited as Hayden, "Statement for the Record."

13. See Hayden, "Address"; Gutjahr, *Intelligence Archipelago*, pp. 114–18; Michael A. Wertheimer, "Crippling Innovation—and Intelligence," *Washington Post*, July 21, 2004, p. A19; and Hayden, "Statement for the Record."

14. Russ Mitchell, "The Ghosts in the Machine: Can Technology Find Terrorists?" *American Spectator* (November/December 2001), cited in Gutjahr, *Intelligence Archipelago*, pp. 114–15.

15. The National Security Agency, to cite but one example, is said to be falling behind in investments needed to maintain pace with technological growth, according to former Director Hayden. See Hayden, "Address."

16. NIC-2004-13, pp. 34–35 and 75–77.

17. NIC-2004-13, p. 10, 12, and 35. See also Gutjahr, *Intelligence Archipelago*, pp. 115–16.

18. Michael Herman, *Intelligence Services in the Information Age: Theory and Practice* (London: Frank Cass, 2001), p. 52.

19. See, for example, Admiral W. A. Owens, "Intelligence in the 21st Century," *Defense Intelligence Journal* 7 (Spring 1998), p. 28, and Herman, *Intelligence Services,* p. 52.

20. Major General W. J. P. Roberts, "Implications of Information Age Operations," *RUSI Journal* 142 (October 1997), p. 39, quoted in Herman, *Intelligence Services,* p. 53.

21. Herman, *Intelligence Services,* pp. 54–61.

22. Joint Chiefs of Staff, *Joint Vision 2010*, available at http://www.dtic.mil/jv2010/jvpub.htm. See also Nagy, "Military Intelligence," p. 40.

23. Nolte, "Information Control," p. 10. For a more detailed walk through the myriad questions that must be addressed on a daily basis, see Hayden, "Statement for the Record," pp. 4–5.

24. Gutjahr, *Intelligence Archipelago,* pp. 119–20.

25. Hayden, "Address," p. 2.

26. Dennis N. DuBois, "Intelligence Community Information Technology: Driving Architecture to Budget," *Defense Intelligence Journal* 9 (Winter 2000), p. 59.

27. Brooks, "Knowledge Management," p. 17.

28. See Department of Defense, "Report of the DoD Commission on Beirut International Airport Terrorist Attack, October 23, 1983," also known as the Long Commission Report, especially Part Four—Intelligence, pp. 57–66. The report is available at http://www.ibiblio.org/hyperwar/AMH/xx/Mideast/Lebanon-1982-1984/DOD-Report/index.html. See also Nagy, "Military Intelligence," p. 43.

29. U.S. Congress, Report of the Joint Inquiry Into the Terrorist Attacks of September 11, 2001, by the House Permanent Select Committee on Intelligence and the Senate Select Committee on Intelligence, p. 7. Available at http://www.fas.org/irp/congress/2002_rpt/911rept.pdf.

30. National Security Agency, "External Team Report: A Management Review for the Director, NSA," October 22, 1999. Available at http://www.nsa.gov/releases/relea00056.pdf.

31. Central Intelligence Agency, *Global Trends 2015: A Dialogue About the Future With a Nongovernment Expert*, NIC-2000-02, December 2000. Available at http://www.cia.gov/cia/reports/globaltrends2015/index.html.

32. M. C. Libicki, *The Mesh and the Net: Speculations on Armed Conflict in a Time of Free Silicon* (Washington, DC: National Defense University Press, 1995), pp. 140–41. See also Herman, *Intelligence Services,* p. 58.

33. Hayden, "Statement for the Record," p. 2.

34. Ibid, pp. 5–6.

35. See Treverton, *Reshaping National Intelligence*, pp. 217–22, for an interesting discussion of the impact of these changes.

36. See, for example, National Commission on Terrorist Attacks Upon the United States, *The 9/11 Commission Report* (New York: W.W. Norton, 2005), especially pp. 350–52.

37. Hayden, "Address," pp. 5–6, and Hayden, "Statement for the Record," p. 2.

38. Admiral B. R. Inman and Daniel F. Burton Jr., "Technology and U.S. National Security," pp. 117–35, in *Rethinking America's Security: Beyond Cold War to New World Order,* eds. Graham Allison and Gregory F. Treverton (New York: W.W. Norton, 1992), pp. 118–23.

39. As an example, in the 1990s, when telecommunications and information technologies saw some of its most explosive growth, the NSA reduced both its manpower and budget by roughly one-third. Gutjahr, *Intelligence Archipelago,* pp. 116–17.

40. Hayden, "Statement for the Record," pp. 7–8.

41. See Inman and Burton, "Technology," p. 126, and Nagy, "Military Intelligence," p. 41.

42. Bruce D. Berkowitz and Allan E. Goodman, *Best Truth: Intelligence in the Information Age* (New Haven, CT: Yale University Press, 2000), p. 43.

43. See Hayden, "Statement for the Record," pp. 6–7, and Michael Hirsh, "The NSA's Overt Problem," *Washington Post,* January 1, 2006, p. B4.

44. Hayden, "Statement for the Record," p. 6.

45. Inman and Burton, "Technology," p. 124.

46. The NSA, for example, reprogrammed funds from still-productive programs to emerging technologies development and procurement. Despite reprogramming roughly $200 million, the NSA found the amount far below present and future needs. See Hayden, "Statement for the Record," p. 6. By the same token, the NSA's effort to better the SIGINT production process, called Trailblazer, reportedly has consumed over $1 billion while producing less-than-desired outcomes. See Hayden, "Statement for the Record," pp. 7–8, and Siobhan Gorman, "System Error," *Baltimore Sun,* January 29, 2006, p. 1A+.

47. For extensive discussions of this, see Brooks, "Knowledge Management," especially p. 18, as well as Nagy, "Military Intelligence"; Hayden, "Statement for the Record"; Berkowitz and Goodman, *Best Truth*; and Inman and Burton, "Technology."

48. Nagy, "Military Intelligence," p. 42.

49. See Berkowitz and Goodman, *Best Truth*, pp. 45 and 67–73.

50. National Security Agency, "New Enterprise Team (NETeam) Recommendations: A Management Review for the Director, NSA," October 22, 1999, p. 1. Available at http://www.nsa.gov/releases/ relea00056.pdf. Hereafter cited as NETeam Recommendations.

51. Ibid.

52. Nolte, "Information Control," p. 11.

53. Treverton, *Reshaping National Intelligence*, pp. 217–26. Berkowitz and Goodman take a similar approach in advocating virtual intelligence teams, created on an ad hoc basis to focus on specific questions and needs. See Berkowitz and Goodman, *Best Truth*, pp. 78–83.

54. Nagy, "Military Intelligence," pp. 41–42.

55. For an extensive discussion of the importance of, and need for, new systems development, see for example U.S. Congress, Report of the United States Senate Select

Committee on Intelligence and the U.S. House Permanent Select Committee on Intelligence, Joint Inquiry Into Intelligence Community Activities Before and After the Terrorist Attacks of September 11, 2001, S. Rept. No. 107-351, H. Rept. No. 107-792, 107th Congress, 2nd session, December 2002, especially "Technology Gaps," pp. 368–72; "Technical Collection of Terrorist Communications," pp. 373–85; and "Human Intelligence (HUMINT) Collection," pp. 385–92; or the much shorter U.S. House, Permanent Select Committee on Intelligence, Subcommittee on Terrorism and Homeland Security, "Counterterrorism Intelligence Capabilities and Performance Prior to 9-11, A Report to the Speaker of the House of Representatives and the Minority Leader," July 2002, available at http://www.news.findlaw.com/hdocs/docs/terrorism/hsint/71702thsrpt .pdf. Hereafter cited as U.S. House, "Counterterrorism Intelligence Capabilities."

56. Nolte, "Information Control," p. 9.

57. U.S. House, "Counterterrorism Intelligence Capabilities," p. v.

58. Nolte, "Information Control," p. 12.

59. Porter J. Goss, "Global Intelligence Challenges 2005: Meeting Long-term Challenges With Long-term Strategy. Testimony of the Director of Central Intelligence Porter J. Goss Before the Senate Select Committee on Intelligence, 16 February 2005 (as prepared for delivery)," available at http://www.cia.gov/cia/public_affairs/speeches/2004/ Goss_testimony_02162005.html.

60. See, for example, Treverton, *Reshaping National Intelligence*, pp. 226–27.

8

INTELLIGENCE ANALYSTS AND POLICY MAKERS

Benefits and Dangers of Tensions in the Relationship

JACK DAVIS

THIS CHAPTER IS OCCASIONED BY PUBLIC INTEREST in reported tensions between Central Intelligence Agency (CIA) analysts and policy-making officials of the administration of President George W. Bush regarding the significance of ties between the Saddam Hussein regime and Al Qaeda terrorists, an important factor in the U.S. decision to invade Iraq in 2003. No evaluation of the latter case is provided. The chapter addresses, instead, general patterns of tensions between intelligence analysts and policy officials, in order to provide a context for public assessment of the Iraq-Al Qaeda incident when the public record is more complete as well as provide enhanced understanding of similar future instances of tension.

Over the years, most of the tens of thousands of written and oral assessments produced by CIA analysts in an effort to support the policy-making process have been received by policy officials with either appreciation or silence. Many of the assesssments are in response to policy-maker tasking, usually a sign of expectation of useful insights. Many consist of briefings and exchanges via telephone or teleconferencing, where the fact that policy officials invest the time to elicit and discuss analysts' assessment of an important national security issue is testimony to the value the officials expect to receive. Many assessments, as to be expected considering the volume of production, miss the mark for the targeted officials in terms of relevancy, timing, or fresh insights, and thus evoke no reaction.

That said, tensions in the relationship between CIA intelligence analysts and administration policy makers are a common occurrence—an essentially normal by-product of the two camps' distinctive professional missions. The analyst's professional commitment is to assess national security issues without bias for or against the outcomes sought by the incumbent presidential administration; the policy maker's professional commitment is to articulate, advocate, and advance the administration's national security agenda.

Often, the resultant tension in the relationship helps both camps to deal more effectively with the challenges of analytic and policy-making uncertainty that usually attend complex national security issues. Under policy-maker criticism or questioning of judgments, analysts tend to revisit their initial views of the soundness of assumptions about what drives the issue and the implications of incomplete, ambiguous, and contradictory evidence. In response, policy officials often are moved to recalculate the elements of their own assessments of threats to and opportunities for advancing U.S. interests.

At times, though, tensions take a turn that does not serve well sound analysis, effective policy making, or the national interest; charges of *politicization*, or analytic distortion to support or undermine a policy initiative, issue forth from one or both camps. These cases usually arise when policy officials repeatedly reject the analysts' studied interpretative judgments on the status of or outlook for a complex national security issue, especially when such judgments are seen to complicate policy initiatives that are politically important to an administration.

If tensions are a normal occurrence, and their elimination both impractical and unwise, recommendations of ground rules to enhance benefits and curb dangers would seem called for. But first one should make a closer assessment of the roots and branches of the tensions.

Tensions in analyst–policy maker relations in the United States can be traced back at least to the establishment in 1941, under the auspices of the Office of Strategic Services (OSS), of the first bureaucratically independent cadre of intelligence analysts. Sherman Kent, who later played a major role in setting professional standards for CIA analysis, came away from his World War II experience in the OSS with the conviction that relations between producers and consumers of intelligence assessments are not naturally harmonious, despite the common goal of advancing U.S. national security interests. Kent did not much change his views about inherent strains in the relationship during his years of analytic service with the CIA (1951–67).

Why not harmonious? The character of the policy issue at stake, personalities in both camps, the degree of contention about policy direction among administration leaders, and the role of Congress as a third party to the policy-making process from time to time have contributed to the onset and intensity of analyst–policy maker tensions. The underlying constant, though, is the aforemenioned difference in perspective on professsional mission between the producers of intelligence analysis and their policy-making clients.

THE ANALYST'S PERSPECTIVE

CIA analysts are concentrated in the Directorate of Intelligence (DI), which takes pride in its organizational independence from the President, the Secretaries of State and Defense, and the other policy makers its intelligence assessments are intended to serve. The conceit that DI assessments are free of policy and political influence or bias comes across in the slogans by which the analysts and their leaders usually define their professional mission: *objective analysis, carrying truth to power, telling it like it is.*

Over the decades, on many critical and controversial national security issues—for example, Soviet strategic arms, the Vietnam War, Central American insurgencies—considerable substantive expertise, much sweat equity, and tough-minded assessment of assumptions and evidence have gone into the analysts' interpretation of past and ongoing events. The usual bureaucratic result was and is a readiness among analysts to defend key judgments against criticism, even though they are aware of gaps and other flaws in their information.

Regarding prediction of future developments, where unexpected intermediate events can throw seemingly sound forecasts off course, analysts also have confidence in their expertise and work ethic, and they take pride in their belief in the independence of their judgments from policy and political influences.

Concerted public criticism of flawed analytic performance on major national security issues spawns intervals of analytic humility for the DI as an organization, its leaders, and usually the analysts directly involved. But for the most part, confidence, even overconfidence, in substantive judgments is a staple of the analyst's environment. Especially the more experienced DI analysts tend to see themselves as the best informed on the issues they follow as well as the most objective national security professionals in the U.S. government. Over the decades, on many issues they probably have been.

Analysts vary in their experiences with and attitudes toward policy officials. That said, a common first reaction to criticism of their assessments by policy officials is to suspect that either politics or the critics' lack of requisite substantive expertise is at work. Digging in at the heels in defense of the original assessment at times follows. Probably more often, the analysts undertake a reappraisal of their assumptions, evidence, and argumentation, though a substantial change in judgments does not necessarily result.

THE POLICY MAKER'S PERSPECTIVE

Policy officials, for their part, also vary in their experiences with and attitudes toward CIA analysts. A good number of career policy officials over the decades have considered the DI analysts on their accounts not only the best informed among the governmental community of intelligence analysts, but also the quickest to respond to requests for analytic assistance. This subset of policy officials also appreciates that CIA assessments, unlike those issued by analysts in policy-making departments, are rarely skewed to support a party to the bureaucratic politics that usually colors the policy-analysis process on national security issues.

The tendency among officials closest to the president runs differently. These essentially political appointees, because of their own partisan cast, can be quick to attribute partisan motivation to CIA analysts. Especially when a political party has been out of power for some years, newly appointed Republican officials tend to see the Agency as dominated by holdover liberal Democrats, whereas new Democratic officials tend to see the strong influence of Republican conservatives. Many top-level appointees have served in previous presidential administrations and have requisite confidence in their own analytic skills and substantive knowledge of the issues. Some carry over from previous service critical views of the competence of Agency analysts as well as of their perceived propensity to an anti-administration bias.

Regarding professional mission, both career officials and political appointees see themselves as action officers as well as policy analysts. Their job is to get accomplished their vision of the president's national security agenda—the goals, strategies, and tactics that emerge from policy analysis.

Unlike intelligence professionals, policy officials are little pained by a merger of an administration's interests in domestic U.S. politics and foreign policy goals. As a rule, to policy officials, especially presidential appointees, government is politics as well as policy. The merger of policy and political advocacy at times requires building a "yes case" or a "no case" amidst inconclusive evidence of the soundness of a policy initiative and the uncertain implications for policy success of daily developments involving, for example, U.S. diplomatic or military campaigns.

This does not mean administration officials are ready to ignore CIA assessments that, say, would give political opponents in Congress ammunition to criticize policy. Often policy officials will ask analysts to "unpack" their assessment, revealing what is fact and what is opinion, or they will call for a briefing and an exchange of views either to enlighten or to leverage analysts.

In sum, at root, tensions, when they occur, represent a collision between the analyst's mission-driven belief that policy-maker criticism of carefully crafted assesments reflects politics or limited substantive command of issues and the policy official's mission-driven belief that CIA assessments that complicate a well-deliberated initiative reflect antiadministration bias or poor analysis.

THE ANALYTIC BRANCHES OF TENSION: OPINIONS, FACTS, EVIDENCE

Though difficult to untangle in actual cases of analyst–policy maker tensions, separating the varieties of analytic production into three branches—opinions, facts, and evidence—serves to clarify both the character of strains in the relationship and potential ground rules for managing tensions.

Regarding estimative judgments or opinions on issues of high uncertainty (for example, multiyear projections of political developments in unstable foreign countries, or prediction of the outcome of protracted U.S. military and diplomatic engagements in violence-prone regions), even well-informed policy makers at times gain insights from intelligence analysts' well-argued estimative judgments.

But when analysts' bottom-line judgments are seen as implicit criticism of and potentially harmful to policy agendas, administration officials are prone to dismiss them as "opinions."

Secretary of Defense Donald Rumsfeld, in an October 24, 2002, press briefing, went to great lengths to define the limits of the analysts' opinions in such circumstances: "If you think about it, what comes out of intelligence is not fixed, firm conclusions. What comes out are a speculation, an analysis, probabilities, possibilities, estimates. Best guesses."[1] Further, policy officials claim, often with justification, that the opinions regarding future developments spawned by policy analysis are sounder than analysts' opinions, if only because they are able to take fuller account of the weight of carrots and sticks the United States may be ready to deploy.

More than once, policy officials have let it be known, in particular, that they are little interested in whether analysts think U.S. initiatives will succeed. The analyst's main job, according to critics, is to provide assesssments that enable policy analysts to reach sound judgments about what actions to take to implement policy, despite the uncertainty that fogs complex world events. The analyst's focus should be on strengths and weaknesses of foreign players, their tendencies, motivations, and risk calculations that would help policy officials identify potential dangers and U.S. leverage points.

Regarding facts, tensions are infrequent and usually involve competing methods of determining facts. Here a fact is defined as something concrete and reliably detected and measured: what a foreign adversary said in a recorded speech or intercepted conversation, as opposed to what he or she meant or actually intends to do.

A prominent official once observed, regarding facts, that policy makers are like surgeons. "They don't last long if they ignore what they see once they cut the patient open."[2]

When policy officials are hesitant to accept as fact a condition or development reported by analysts that could complicate political goals or policy implementation, they tend to challenge the sources and methods the analysts relied on in their determination of facts. During military engagements, for example, military officials have preferred to determine battlefield damage to the enemy as recorded in post-flight reports by U.S. pilots, and to dismiss the analyst's usually more modest calculations of damage that were based on, say, overhead imagery.

The most noteworthy tensions between CIA analysts and policy officials usually are over differences about the meaning of available evidence—that is, differences over what to conclude about something knowable but not conclusively known to either intelligence or policy professionals.

On the issues that give rise to major tensions, first, there are gaps in information because of secrecy and collection limitations. Second, the available evidence reflects a body of reporting parts of which are of questionable reliability and are contradictory and ambiguous. Concerning, for example, the dispute between CIA analysts and prominent administration officials over Saddam Hussein regime's connection to the U.S. war on terror: What will history show the burden of the evidence to have been regarding the nature of Iraq's prewar ties to Al Qaeda terrorists—a minor or major threat to U.S. interests?

Regarding the meaning of inconclusive evidence, former CIA Director and Cabinet member William Casey (1981–87), in a dispute with analysts over the Soviet role in International terrorism, set forth his standard for keeping a policy-sensitive issue on the table: "Absence of evidence is not evidence of absence."[3] In effect, if a development or relationship is plausible, analysts cannot prove a negative to the satisfaction of officials with minds and agendas of their own.

In disputes with analysts about the meaning of inconclusive evidence, policy makers can insist on raising as well as lowering the bar of proof regarding judgments that could have a negative impact on their agendas. Once, when an analyst averred that reliable evidence had become available that indicated a suspected development that undermined an administration policy initiative was "almost certainly taking place," a policy critic retorted that the analyst "couldn't get a murder-one conviction in an American court with [his] evidence."[4]

THE CRITIC'S CHALLENGES TO
DI TRADECRAFT

Policy officials have been generous in spelling out the elements of their criticism of Agency analysis. In doing so, the officials at times were motivated principally to improve the quality of support they receive for the demanding task of policy analysis and implementation. At times, the motivation also included an effort to defang or discredit politcally unhelpful assessments. And at times the objective was to shape an intelligence deliverable into a tool that would lend political support to administration policy.

It is worth noting that policy officials who have been generally complimentary of the analyst's performance as well as those long dissatisfied with performance table similar criticisms.

Part of the analyst–policy maker tension in evaluating evidence reflects a difference in professional attitude toward odds. To an analyst, the judgment that the evidence indicates that a development favorable to U.S. interests is unlikely usually means the odds against the existence or emergence of the development at issue are roughly 4 to 1. Given such odds, the busy analyst as a rule is ready to go forward with his or her assessment and move on to the next assignment.

In contrast to a policy maker with an agenda to advance, the same starting odds of roughly 1 in 5 can make it promising as well as politically necessary to stay on the case. Moreover, on politically important issues the official will not overlook the prospect that the analyst's pessimistic judgment could be off base because, first, they are insufficiently informed about the current state and potential fluidity of foreign forces at play, and, second, because they do not appreciate the impact on developments of U.S. carrots and sticks, if a policy initiative gathers backing.

The reluctance of critical policy officials to rely on what they see as unhelpful assessments on issues important to an administration goes beyond professionally necessary "positive thinking" on their part. Critics also point out what they see as systemic weaknesses in the analyst's tradecraft (i.e., analytic methodologies).

First, since cognitive bias is pervasive, analysts, like all observers, tend to see more quickly and vividly what they expect to see and, conversely, tend not to see and properly credit information that would undermine their prior judgments. Critics contend that analysts delude themselves if they think they are exempt from this so-called confirmation bias because of their claims to "objectivity."

Critics have made this point over the decades in defending requests that analysts take another look at their interpretation of the evidence regarding the rate of success of the strategic hamlet program in Vietnam (1960s), the seriousness of Soviet plans for winning a nuclear war (1970s), the battlefield successes of U.S.-backed insurgents in Nicaragua (1980s), and after September 11, 2001, the significance of Iraqi-Al Qaeda connections to the war on terror.

The analyst's phrase "we have no evidence that X exists" is judged particularly unhelpful by those officials dedicated to either blunting the threat or seizing the policy opportunity in question. The critics note that analysts rarely admit they have no evidence that X does not exist. Besides, one critic averred, "policymaking is not [done] in a court of law."[5] A similar criticism is that analysts are too tied to the specific reports that reach their "inbox" and do not take sufficient account of the inherent aggressiveness, ruthlessness, and duplicity of U.S. adversaries.

Policy-making critics also complain that analyst training and incentives place too much emphasis on "straight line, single outcome" analysis on complex and uncertain issues. Critics say this "make the call" approach is both unhelpful to sound decision making and prone to error.

Former Deputy Secretary of Defense Paul Wolfowitz, long a critic of Agency analysts, observed in an interview conducted in 1994 that analysts' assertiveness in the face of uncertainty can turn an Agency assessment on complex issues into a weapon for one policy-making camp to use against another. In contrast, by tabling alternative interpretations, analysts would provide a tool useful to all participants in policy debates and decision making.

Further, the critics aver that, especially when policy stakes are high, analysts should expend much more effort evaluating what they don't know and why they don't know it before issuing estimative judgments downplaying dangers on which policy officials are focused. For example, could gaps in information that lead analysts to discount the likelihood of potentially harmful developments of concern to U.S. officials be caused by denial and deception (D&D) operations, or inadequate U.S. collection, or flawed assumptions about which pathways and relationships an adversary is pursuing to effect the feared development?

The 1999 report of a commission chaired by the current Secretary of Defense Donald Rumsfeld, after noting past intelligence failures on timely detection of foreign ballistic missile developments, cautioned analysts not to be quick to conclude that absence of evidence indicated absence of vigorous weapons programs by potentially hostile countries. The report, instead, charged analysts with pursuing alternative plausible explanations for "particular gaps in a list of [program] indicators."[6]

In truth, policy officials may prize the analyst who can come quickly to a crisp conclusion on issues surrounded by uncertainty that supports their agenda. But policy officials who see CIA judgments as obstacles to their agenda are themselves quick to connect the make-the-call culture to the analyst's record of analytic failures from the Cuban missile crisis to the Iraqi invasion of Kuwait.

Perhaps most important, according to the critics, it is the duty of responsible policy officials to ask probing questions; to insist on critical review of the evidence; to send analysts back to the drawing board for another look; in effect, to pull any loose thread in an unhelpful intelligence assessment.

Secretary of Defense Rumsfeld in his October 24, 2002, press briefing referred to the importance of engagement and criticism: "to the extent there's no feedback coming from . . . a user of intelligence, then one ought not expect that the level of competence . . . on the part of people supplying the intelligence will be as good . . . as if there's an effective interaction."[7] Granted, political overtones often color these criticisms. But in tradecraft terms they represent reasonable standards for policy officials to levy on analysts charged with providing distinctive value added to U.S. policy-making efforts.

DEFINING PROFESSIONAL AND UNPROFESSIONAL ANALYSIS

The doctrinal basis for a response to criticism by administration officials should reflect definitions of professional and unprofessional standards for intelligence analysts as agents both of the national interest and of the policy-making process. Thus, a definition of analytic professionalism should posit as equally important standards both *objectivity* (defined as tough-minded evaluation of evidence and other sound analytic practices) and *utility* (defined as distinctive data and insights policy officials find useful for managing threats to and opportunities for advancing U.S. interests).

Neither objectivity without utility, nor utility without objectivity, would meet the test of the author's following definition: The mission of intelligence analysts is to apply in-depth substantive expertise, all-source information, and tough-minded tradecraft to produce assessments that provide distinctive value-added to policy clients' efforts to protect and advance U.S. security interests. The

analyst's long-held standard of analytic objectivity has helped to promote an
institutional ethic of pursing independence from all biases, including policy and
political influences, in making judgments in the face of substantive uncertainty.
But studies, including those commissioned by the Agency, indicate that *substantive biases* (experience-based mindsets) are all but essential for effectiveness
in an environment of high-volume production and tight deadlines. In such circumstances, the effect on production of an "open mind" is akin to the burden
of an "empty mind." In addition, *cognitive biases* (especially seeking confirmation for experience-based assumptions amidst inconclusive evidence) in effect
are hardwired mental traits.

Pursuit of the defined mission regarding objectivity, then, comes down to an
effort to minimize bias by critical review of the assumptions driving the analyst's
mindset and of the adequacy of the available evidence to draw any meaningful
judgment, and, if so, the content of the judgment.

Also to fulfill the defined professional mission, analytic deliverables must be
seen by policy officials to have utility as they define their professional agenda,
which, as previously indicated, is to posit and enact an administration's politically colored policy agenda. The analysts who would produce an assessment with
high potential for utility to the policy-making process can no more ignore the
political context in which their clients operate than they can ignore where the
latter are on their learning curves (e.g., how much background information is
needed) and decision-making cycles (e.g., planning stage or implementation
stage).

To take account of the politics of policy making is not a license for intelligence professionals, as analysts, to become policy makers, or their speech-
writers or spear carriers. But if an analyst is not close enough to the process to feel
the political pressures affecting policy making, he or she probably is not close
enough to produce professionally crafted deliverables that provide distinctive
value added.

Thus, there will always be a danger that analysts, in constructing their written
assessments and oral commentary, will introduce a policy or political slant—
either deliberately or through disregard of analytic standards. Analysts have done
so in the past, and likely will do so from time to time in the future.

A politicized and therefore unprofessional assessment can be defined as an
analytic deliverable that reflects either (1) the analyst's motivated effort to skew
building-block assumptions, evaluation of the evidence, and bottom-line judgments to support—or oppose—a specific policy, political entity, or general
ideology, or (2) a conspicuous disregard for analytic standards that produces
unmotivated but similarly distorted outputs that could affect the policy-making
process.

From the policy makers' agenda-oriented perspective it makes little difference whether what they see as analytic bias is motivated or unmotivated. One
senior official, for example, complained that every assessment that indicated or
implied that an administration initiative was flawed constituted analytic policy

152 THE INTELLIGENCE CYCLE

making, because it provided ammunition for Congress to oppose funding the initiative.

As long as policy-makers' criticism of the objectivity, soundness, or utility of analysis reflects a legitimate tradecraft concern, they are not necessarily putting pressure on analysts to engage in unprofessional behavior. Policy officials have the license to change the intelligence question in search of insights in addition to those embedded in the analyst's initial assessment, to ask that assumptions and evidence be examined more thoroughly, and to request customized follow-on assessments. That is part of their job description, whether they are seeking fresh insights or analytic support for their established views.

Thus, it is not unprofessional behavior for analysts, on their own or when requested, to provide assessments that set out to make the case for an alternative view to their unit's agreed interpretations of ambiguous evidence of ongoing developments and estimative projections of complex trends. The only professional requirements are that such efforts at, say, devil's advocacy, be clearly labeled and vested with appropriate analytic standards for crafting a challenge to the mainline views on an issue embedded with substantive uncertainty.

Additionally, it is not unprofessional behavior for an analyst, when requested, to address matters clarifying tactical policy options for dealing with specific threats to and opportunities for an established general policy. The key to sound "action" or "implementation" analysis is for the analyst to identify plausible initiatives and evaluate them in cost-benefit terms, and for the policy makers to choose what course to pursue and bear responsibility for their decisions.

Finally, for a manager to tighten tradecraft standards on a politically sensitive policy issue before an analyst's assessment goes forward under a corporate DI seal is not necessarily a signal of unprofessional behavior. Painful to the analyst, yes. Politicization of his assessment, no.

Analysts and their managers and leaders must be vigilant in identifying, deterring, and decrying unprofessional assessments as herein defined; when engaged in analysis, they are and must remain intelligence professionals, not policy or political aides—or critics. If an analytic cadre is to deserve its vaunted organizational independence, it must be ready to hold its ground, in the name of the national interest, against pressures for politicization, no matter the source, the intensity, or the circumstances.

But analysts must also take seriously the "cry wolf" danger of levying charges of politicization whenever their authority to control the key judgments of an assessment is abridged.

More to the point, if ever teamwork must prevail over turf warfare and over the individual analyst's sense of entitlement to determine what "call" to make on a matter of substantive uncertainty, it is when the analytic corps is constructing assessments on politically contentious policy issues. Over the decades, many analysts who have made adjustments to initial assessments that maintained objectivity while enhancing utility have felt the sting of colleagues' unreasonable charges of politicization.

THE ANALYST'S RESPONSE TO POLICY-MAKER
CRITICISM: BEST PRACTICES

The challenge for analysts, then, is to turn tensions to professional advantage by maintaining rigorous analytic tradecraft standards while enhancing the utility of their assessments to policy makers. Despite a popular reputation for flawed performance, CIA analysts regularly meet this demanding standard. To turn on its head an observation on policy success and failure attributed to President Kennedy after the 1961 Bay of Pigs debacle: Analytic failures draw a thousand critics; analytic successes are orphans.[8]

Call them "ground rules," call them "best practices," lessons can be learned from both failures and successes, and recommendations made for how analysts should respond to policy-maker criticism. The underlying concept behind the recommendations that follow is that analysts carry the heavier burden of managing tensions in policy-maker relations in a manner that advances the national interest.

The main reason is that the policy-making camp is the more powerful of the two. Policy officials have many alternative sources to Agency analysts for information and insight, including their own staffs and departmental analytic organizations; the academic, research, and business communities; the media and the Internet. In contrast, Agency analysts have no comparable alternative market that would justify the large size of their cadre and high volume of production of assessments. Congress demands and receives a steady stream of oral briefings from Agency analysts but is rarely seen as an equal to administration officials as a client for written assessments.

The central theme of the recommendations is that analysts are professionally required to take the tradecraft elements of policy-maker criticism seriously, no matter how much they may perceive that the politics of policy advocacy also are at play. Analysts, thus, should respond to criticism with a reassessment not only of the argumentation and judgments of the original assessment but also of whether it provided utility or distinctive value for the policy-making community. The goal is to take tradecraft issues off the table, so to speak, in an effort to isolate and then defuse any politically motivated elements of policy-maker criticism.

First, become expert on the policy maker's world. Analysts should commit to learning as much about the U.S. policy-making process and their key policy-making clients as, say, a national security correspondent for a major newspaper or other media outlet is expected to command. Analysts, starting from year one, have to spend quality time analyzing how Washington works, warts and all, even if this slows down the pace of grasping how Baghdad, Beijing, or Buenos Aires work. In particular, analysts should understand their client's role as action officer as well as policy analyst. This investment will enable analysts to role-play the policy clients who have criticized an assessment, not to mortgage analytic integrity but to evaluate tradecraft performance through a different set of eyes.

Second, become accomplished at understanding and managing substantive uncertainty. Analysts are taught and are generally aware that their judgments on complex issues are based on thoughtful but fallible assumptions that in turn color their evaluation of fragmentary, contradictory, ambiguous, and otherwise inconclusive evidence. They have been cautioned about mindset and confirmation bias. Yet the norm is to rely on these powerful but vulnerable mental processes to get their assessments out under tight deadlines, and with a confident judgment.

Usually the resultant assessment holds up well against both the expectations of policy-making clients and the subsequent course of events. Usually. But what to do when a policy official conveys doubts or outright criticism?

Here, without being too quick to jettison original argumentation and judgment, the analysts should move from passive to active awareness of the limitations of their analytic craft. More active attention to the perils of analysis amidst substantive uncertainty entails taking a more thorough accounting of plausible alternative explanations and outcomes that were discarded or downplayed during the crafting of the assessment that drew criticism.

Casual re-examination of an assessment by its author and production unit to take the measure of alternatives at times is helpful, but the process of "talking about alternatives" is prone toward defense rather than critical evaluation of the original argumentation. More structured and externalized challenges to the assessment hold greater promise of fresh insights that either strengthen confidence in, or point to useful modifications of, the assessment that drew criticism.

Tested approaches to alternative or challenge analysis include devil's advocacy, key assumptions check, quality of information review, and argument mapping. A more experimental technique, known as analysis of competing hypotheses, tests which of several plausible explanations for a complex event or trend stands up best against a battery of relevant information.

Third, become adept at role-playing. At times, as indicated, analysts will be well positioned to prepare a professional response to criticism by undertaking an open-minded assessment of the *policy critic's paradigm* (i.e., mental model) on a contentious issue. However colored by political considerations it may at first seem to the analysts, deconstruction will help identify the critic's assumptions, evaluation of evidence, and calculations of likelihood. Once this information is at hand, the analysts may see a path toward revision of their own assesssment that both protects objectivity and enhances utility.

Fourth, lean forward professionally with action analysis. Analysts should not hesitate to respond to criticism about unhelpful analysis by changing the question from the one they initially believed should be addressed to one policy critics call for—again a posssible path to both objectivity and utility. Often the shift, as previously indicated, is from what is the most likely interpretation of an event or relationship or the most likely future path of development, to depiction of the direct and indirect leverage the United States has to reduce dangers and seize opportunities.

In most cases, analysts can be professionally comforted by assuming savvy administration officials, despite a politically required public optimism, know their policy initiative is facing heavy obstacles, even before the CIA assessment elaborated the point. What is now in demand are intelligence insights for doing something about the obstacles.

An analyst once tabled an assessment that placed emphasis on the general political dynamics in country Z, including both domestic reform tendencies promoted by the United States and a deliberate show of independence from Washington on certain international issues. The word came back that the high-level U.S. official who had asked for the assessment "wanted to leverage the president of country Z, not love him."[9]

Fifth, master techniques for evaluating inconclusive evidence. More deliberate analyst attention to evaluating evidence on contentious policy issues is another promising avenue for stripping tradecraft complaints from policy-maker criticism of analytic performance. Careful consideration of alternative meanings of gaps in information, especially regarding suspected programs to develop weapons of mass destruction (WMD), can help build credibility with critics.

Analysts can organize and asssess what is known and unknown to determine, for existance, whether the gaps in expected indicators more likely represent limited U.S. collection and substantial D&D, an innovative approach to WMD development, or nonexistence of a concerted development effort. The aforementioned analysis of competing hypotheses is well suited to provide an externally structured (that is, minimally subjective) competition to see which explanation is the most and least compatible with available related information.

Sixth, use estimative terminology carefully. Analysts have a professional obligation in maintaining integrity while supporting the policy-making process to avoid compounding substantive uncertainty with linguistic confusion. This is essential to managing tensions on sensitive issues. To deter both misunderstanding and manipulation of judgments, analysts should avoid vague estimative phrases such as "real possibility" and "good chance." Though not without risk of an exaggerated precision, analysts should aim to set boundaries to key judgments (e.g., "we judge the likelihood of *development* Z to be low—on the order of 10 to 20 percent"). On controversial issues analysts should also avoid nonfalsifiable judgments such as "it is possible," "suggests that," and "according to reports." They should provide instead an evaluation of the authenticity, adequacy in terms of completeness and consistency, and significance of the evidence. And when no confident judgment can be made, analysts sould say so directly.

As previously indicated, policy officials tend to stick to initiatives even against long odds. An assessment that calculates an estimated probability of a development at, say, roughly 80 percent is making transparent a roughly 1-in-5 prospect of being wrong. An assessment that develops the longshot case using plausible alternative assumptions and evaluations of the evidence, as well as the analyst's preferred 4-in-5 prospect can serve professionally to provide distinctive value added to policy-maker criticis without sacrifice of analytic integrity.

Seventh, be responsive to criticism but not at the cost of objectivity. As long as an analytic unit believes it has done its homework in evaluating evidence and in considering alternative explanations and projections, it should stand by its estimative judgments even if policy-maker criticism persists or intensifies. But the unit should also work to ensure continued access to and credibility with critical clients by varying the focus and perceived utility of its deliverables. Analysts should consider the following "1-3-1" approach to an issue of critical policy import on which they are engaged in producing nearly daily assessments.

- Once a week, issue an assessment that features a net judgment, whether or not the one favored by policy officials. Include a credible accounting of the impact of recent developments and reports.
- Several times a week, put the net judgment approach aside and employ action analysis to address tactical dangers and policy opportunities on which direct and indirect U.S. leverage could be applied.
- Once a week, change the question via the tradecraft of alternative analysis, in order for both analysts and policy makers to examine the issue from another angle, for example: *what-if analysis* (what policy makers would see, if the likelihood of development X increased), *risk-benefit analysis* (the adversary's estimated calculations affecting its motivation for and ability to engage in development X), and *if-then analysis* (implications of the advent of a high-impact, low-probability development regarding X).

Finally, what of the danger that analysts' efforts to curb their own substantive and cognitive biases will generate deliverables that provide unwarranted support to the clients' biases and political agenda while weakening respect for the production unit's professional judgment?

There may be no win-win answer to the vulnerability of unintended consequences of attempts at professional accommodation of the tensions attending policy-maker criticism of analysis. Policy makers, for example, have been known to tear off the cover page (literally and figuratively) explaining the main view of the analysts and the context for presenting an alternative view—and then citing the latter as the Agency's judgment.

But avoidance of the initiatives recommended above for professional accommodation of criticism and instead countering policy-maker exaggeration of certitude with analyst exaggeration will help neither camp. As a rule, a blending of deliverables that indicates an openness toward alternative interpretations with regular affirmation of what analysts believe to be sound, if vulnerable, judgments will protect analytic professionalism, maintain credibility with and access to the policy clients, and best serve the national interest.

Analysts and production units unsure of how to proceed when confronted with policy-maker criticism with political overtones should engage the Agency's Ombudsman for Politicizaton and other detached veteran practitioners for help in identifying the best professional response. Agency training courses that include case studies on managing tensions would also help prepare analysts and managers for their initial exposure to friction with their policy-maker clients.

Largely as a result of internal as well as external reviews of flawed analytic performance regarding judgments about Iraqi WMD arsenals and programs under the Saddam Hussein regime, many recommendations for dealing with criticism of analysis by policy officials similar to those outlined above have been adopted or reinforced as tradecraft doctrine by CIA's senior leadership. As this chapter was written (March 2006) the difficult tranformation from doctrine to practice was under way.

POLICY MAKER PREROGATIVES—AND THEIR LIMITS

The preceding two sections of the chapter addressed: (1) analysts' professional prerogative to stick to their best judgment after testing it for soundness, no matter the intensity of policy-maker criticism; (2) their obligation to mitigate tensions via alternative means of support to policy clients, such as action analysis; and (3) the breach of professionalism entailed in both deliberate and unintentional politicization of analysis.

What about the rights and wrongs of the admittedly more powerful policy-making camp? The national interest is best served when the two camps work together to combine sound intelligence analysis with sound policy analysis. That said, when the two camps clash, what are the prerogatives of policy officials and what actions should be considered a breach of their professional obligations?

The questions and answers that follow are an attempt by the author, long an observer of the relationship but a member of the analytic camp, to set ground rules for policy officials that would enhance the benefits and temper the dangers of tensions in analyst–policy maker relations.

1. Are policy makers entitled professionally to reach, publicize, and act upon estimative judgments that diverge from intelligence assessments on a national security issue?

Yes. As indicated throughout this chapter, intelligence analysis, especially inherently fallible interpretative and predictive analysis, is an input to and not a substitute for policy analysis. Policy makers as analysts take account of other providers of information and judgment, and also bring their own, often considerable, experience, insights, and biases to the difficult tasks of policy formulation and implementation, for which they must take ultimate responsibility.

2. Are policy officials professionally entitled to ask intelligence analysts to take another look at their estimative judgments (e.g., to review assumptions, evidence, and argumentation)?

Yes. Policy makers are commissioned to devise, promote, and enact the president's national security agenda. They know when a policy consensus is taking shape and the time for action is approaching on issues, despite intelligence assessments that sound a caution. Yet officials, especially those with an appreciation for the distinctive role of intelligence analysis, hesitate to ignore intelligence findings and estimative judgments that call into question the underpinnings for U.S. initiatives. One response in these circumstances is to ask analysts to go back to the drawing board. Furthermore, from the point of view of the national interest, well-articulated criticism of analysis is much preferable to inadequate guidance for the execution of intelligence deliverables and scant attention to the assessments once delivered.

3. Are policy makers professionally entitled to urge analysts to review and revise their confidence levels in analytic judgments?

Yes. For the same, usually healthy, reasons, one analyst or intelligence agency challenges another's conclusions on whether a shrouded current relationship or indeterminate future development is *nearly certain, probable,* or *unlikely,* policy makers may ask analysts to rethink their degree of confidence in a judgment. Once again, the answer assumes estimative judgments are inherently subject to error and that policy makers' criticism of analysis is more useful to sound performance than their ignoring of analysis. Needless to say, intelligence analysts are professionally bound to stick to judgments on probability that survive their critical review; and intelligence professionals must take care not to allow the pressure of a process of repeated requests for revision to move the bottom line further toward one supportive of policy than the analysts' tradecraft would justify.

4. Are policy makers professionally entitled to ask analysts to provide well-argued alternatives to their studied bottom-line judgments (e.g., devil's advocacy)?

Yes. Policy officials are at least as wary of the consequences of policy failure as analysts are of intelligence failure. They are professionally entitled to task analysts to use their skills and resources to present for consideration alternative or multiple views of a complex and uncertain issue. At times a call for, say, devil's advocacy may be a caution against the perils of groupthink, especially in cases in which policy makers agree with the analysts' judgments. At times the policy maker's motive will be to move Agency analysis to closer alignment with his or her own thinking. As long as rigorous analytic tradecraft norms are adhered to for whatever form of alternative analysis is solicited, and the analyst's preferred bottom-line judgment is firmly attached to the deliverable, intelligence professionals should welcome the opportunity for customized service to their policy-making counterparts.

5. Are policy makers professionally entitled to ask analysts to change the question they address (say, from whether a development is likely, to how it might occur)?

Yes. Once an administration adopts an initiative, policy makers tend to move forcefully into their action-officer mode and have limited interest in analysts' views, based on the latter's reading of the evidence, on whether the policy is likely to succeed, much less whether the policy was wise to undertake. Policy officials have a job to do—to make the policy work. They are professionally entitled to ask intelligence analysts to provide action or implementation analysis—that is, expert assessment of opportunities for moving the policy forward and of specific dangers to be avoided, taking account of insights into the adversary's strengths, weaknesses, and "game plan."

6. *Are policy makers professionally entitled to seek analytic judgments from sources other than CIA and other U.S. professional intelligence organizations?*

Yes. No matter how strongly intelligence professionals would prefer otherwise, policy officials, in pursuit of their policy-making and political goals, have a right to rely on whatever sources of information and insight they choose, either to supplement or to substitute for the support they get from intelligence professionals. This includes use of business, academic, and other nongovernmental sources; their own staffs, whether configured as a policy-making or intelligence unit; and also, as has happened, foreign intelligence services. Policy makers, in short, are entitled to reap the benefits of as complete and varied a set of substantive inputs as they can command as they undertake the arduous task of managing an uncertain and often perilous national security issue. If policy makers use different sources of analytic support simply because they want more cordial answers than those provided by intelligence professionals, then the policy officials must bear the burdens of self-deception, policy failure, and political censure when such outcomes prove to be the case.

7. *Are policy makers professionally entitled to attribute to intelligence analysts judgments that overstate or understate analysts' confidence levels?*

No. Once a studied, clear, and (if challenged) revisited statement of likelihood regarding a development, relationship, threat, or opportunity is established by Agency analysts, policy officials can attribute it to intelligence in order to buttress their own views, or reject it in favor of their own alternative statement of likelihood. But they do not have the authority to attribute to intelligence professionals an estimative judgment the latter do not hold.

8. *Are policy makers professionally entitled to force analysts to alter their best estimative judgments?*

No. As already acknowledged, policy officials are entitled professionally to reject intelligence assessments and reach and promote their own estimative judgments (Question 1, above), and are also entitled to urge analysts to rethink and recast Agency intelligence judgments (Question 3, above). That clarified, under no circumstances are policy officials professionally entitled to force intelligence analysts to change estimative judgments. Obviously, there are risks to treating as inviolate intelligence judgments that are contrary to policy preferences. Events may prove the analysts to be wrong. Congressmen may complicate the funding and execution of an administration's strategy and tactics by using intelligence findings and estimative judgments to block or modify policy initiatives. Unauthorized leaks to the media of intelligence positions may create an untimely public debate over policy. These circumstances can cause a run-up in immediate costs ranging from embarrassment of the administration to the thwarting of what history may judge to have been a sound policy initiative. But the long-term costs to the integrity and morale of intelligence professionals of forcing them to change their judgments will likely cause much greater harm to the national interest by weakening a vital arm of the national security establishment.

9. *Are policy officials professionally entitled to use the media to criticize intelligence analysts' competence, in an effort to protect an administration from congressional and public criticism of a policy initiative?*

No. As argued in this chapter, policy officials are entitled, indeed encouraged, to criticize through government channels either a specific body of analysis or intelligence tradecraft generally. Furthermore, as policy professionals, they are entitled to raise publicly their criticism of analysis as long as it is couched in analytic terms and is not, in effect, a politically motivated *ad hominem* attack. That is, as policy professionals, they are not entitled to criticize publicly a careful body of intelligence work and the credentials of the analysts who produced it merely to relieve themselves of the burden of credible defense of their own contrary judgments. In principle, nearly all parties to the uniquely American system for making national security policy proclaim the value of maintaining the integrity of intelligence analysis. A practice of trying to leverage a congressional vote or public debate on a policy initiative by criticizing the credentials of analysts who produce uncongenial analysis undermines the principle.

10. *Are policy officials professionally entitled to apply pressure on Agency leaders to remove from a production unit a manager or analyst responsible for assessments with judgments policy makers see as biased, wrong, or otherwise unhelpful?*

No. Analysts and their managers should be judged by Agency leaders solely in terms of professional credentials and adherence to analytic tradecraft norms, including good-faith efforts to respond to tradecraft criticisms by policy officials through the various means outlined earlier in this chapter (e.g., key assumptions check, devil's advocacy). The challenge of reaching sound analytic judgments amidst the perils generated by substantive complexity and uncertainty should not be compounded by a requirement for "political correctness" or fears about job security.

11. *Are policy officials professionally entitled to request Agency analysts to engage in policy advocacy, for example, to produce a "white paper" that is released as an intelligence product?*

No. Agency analysts may assist by providing information for the production of a white paper, but this and other formats of policy advocacy must be issued under the seal of a policy-making department or staff. The role of Agency analysts is to provide analytic support to policy planning and implementation by administration officials—and not to make, advocate, or criticize policy. Again, the long-term importance to the national interest for Agency analysis to be and be seen as a source of substantive objectivity as well as policy utility far outweighs any short-term political advantage gained from using an adulterated form of intelligence analysis to gain public or congressional support for a policy initiative.

CONCLUDING THOUGHTS

What about enforcement of these or any other set of ground rules aimed at moderating tensions in analyst–policy maker relations? U.S. experience has shown that presidents and their inner circles from time to time will play by their own rules. Agreed prerogatives and constraints and authoritative calls of "foul" might nonetheless serve well over the long haul, if only to evoke second thoughts about ignoring a transparent set of rules for improving both intelligence analysis and national security policy making.

Presidential administrations already have an instrument in place for monitoring the adequacy and quality of intelligence analysis, along with all other intelligence functions. The President's Foreign Intelligence Advisory Board (PFIAB) is well situated, both to help shape the ground rules and to monitor for analyst compliance. Over the decades, PFIAB members—former administration officials, members of Congress, and military and business leaders—collectively have commanded formidable knowledge about analysts and policy makers. And as a rule, PFIAB staff reports on analytic performance have been noted for both independence and insight.

For the Agency, the Ombudsman for Politicization has served since the early 1990s to educate new analysts about professional standards, to monitor for politicization, and to counsel analysts about the concerns they raise on the issue. Over the years, the Ombudsman, selected by and serving at the pleasure of the Director for Intelligence, has been a highly qualified former intelligence manager serving part-time as an independent contractor.

The following recommended changes relating to the Ombudsman are intended to strengthen both the educational and protection functions, including by participation in shaping ground rules and more active monitoring for compliance on the part of policy officials as well as intelligence professionals.

- Change the position name to Ombudsman for Analytic Professionalism (OAP). The professional obligations for analysts in the management of tensions involve more than the avoidance of policy or political bias.
- Provide the OAP with a small staff. The rise in importance to U.S. national security of countering weapons proliferation and terrorism—issues on

which conclusive evidence will be a rarity—is likely to increase tensions over the meaning of available information and thus the demands on the OAP.

- To ensure the independence of and enhance analyst confidence in the OAP, have the newly instituted Director of National Intelligence nominate and Congress confirm the title holder to serve a fixed term of five years.
- To help hold policy makers as well as analysts accountable in their management of tensions, require the OAP to provide the intelligence oversight committees of Congress with periodic reports on the compliance of both camps with agreed ground rules.

This chapter, by design, has mentioned Congress only briefly, although it is the third side of the triangle that constitutes the U.S. system for making and implementing national security policy. Yet for any set of ground rules for governing analyst–policy maker relations to have a lasting impact, Congress, on its own or in response to public demand, must take action to promote and monitor such an initiative. The goal, one last time, would be to ensure that the inevitable tensions between Agency analysts and administration officials are managed to the benefit of the national interest.

NOTES

All statements of fact, opinion, or analysis expressed are those of the author and do not reflect the official positions or views of the CIA or any other U.S. government agency. Nothing in the contents should be construed as asserting or implying U.S. government authentication of information or Agency endorsement of the author's views. The material has been reviewed by the CIA to prevent the disclosure of classified information.

1. Quoted in "Rumsfeld on New DoD Intelligence Team," *Early Bird* (newsletter), Department of Defense (October 25, 2002), available at http://www.defenselink.mil/news/Oct2002/t10242002_t1024sd.htm

2. Author's interview with Paul Wolfowitz, "Paul Wolfowitz on Intelligence-Policy Relations," *Studies in Intelligence* 39 (Langley, VA: Central Intelligence Agency, 1996).

3. Author's interview with CIA analysts present when the remark was made at CIA Headquarters, Langley, VA, in 1982, cited in Jack Davis, *Tensions in Analyst-Policymaker Relations: Opinions, Facts, and Evidence,* Occasional Papers, CIA, Kent Center 2 (2003), p. 3.

4. Comment made to the author in April 1980, CIA Headquarters, Langley, VA, cited in Davis, "Tensions," p. 3.

5. Author's interview with Paul Wolfowitz, "Paul Wolfowitz."

6. Intelligence Side Letter [to Congress and the Director of Central Intelligence], Report of the Commission to Assess the Ballistic Missile Threat to the United States (March 18, 1999).

7. Quoted in "Rumsfeld on New DoD Intelligence Team," *Early Bird.*

8. *Editor's note:* After the Bay of Pigs failure in 1961, President Kennedy observed, "There is an old saying that victory has a hundred fathers and defeat is an orphan," cited in Arthur M. Schlesinger, Jr., *A Thousand Days: John F. Kennedy in the White House* (Boston: Houghton Mifflin, 1965), p. 289.

9. Author's recollection of a 1973 incident, cited in Davis, "Tensions," p. 6.

NOTE ON SOURCES

The views on and of policy officials are based on remarks made at press conferences and in unclassified statements in reports by governmental commissions, media interviews, and discussion forums. Note, for example, the following publications that are available on the CIA website (http://www.cia.gov). Note also, the unclassified source cited for the evaluation of and recommendations for analysts by the Missile Commission, chaired by Donald Rumsfeld.

BIBLIOGRAPHY

Armstrong, Fulton T. "Ways to Make Analysis Relevant But Not Prescriptive," *Studies in Intelligence* 46 (2002).
Davis, Jack. "[Ambassador Robert Blackwill] A Policymaker's Perspective on Intelligence Analysis," *Studies in Intelligence* 38 (1995).
———. "Paul Wolfowitz on Intelligence-Policy Relations," *Studies in Intelligence* 39 (1996).
Report of the Commission to Assess the Ballistic Missile Threat to the United States: Intelligence Side Letter [to Congress and the DCI], March 18, 1999.

The views on and of intelligence analysts and on the analyst–policy maker relationship generally are based on the following unclassified publications that, unless otherwise indicated, are available on the CIA website (http://www.cia.gov).

BIBLIOGRAPHY

Davis, Jack. *Analytic Professionalism and the Policymaking Process: Q&A on a Challenging Relationship*, Occasional Papers, CIA, Kent Center, Volume 2, No. 4 (2003).
———. "Combating Mindset," *Studies in Intelligence* 36 (1992).
———. *Improving CIA Analytic Performance: Analysts and the Policymaking Process*, Occasional Papers, CIA, Kent Center, Volume 1, No. 2 (2002).
———. *Improving CIA Analytic Performance: DI Analytic Priorities*, Occasional Papers, CIA, Kent Center, Volume 1, No. 3 (2002).
———. *Sherman Kent's Final Thoughts on Analyst–Policymaker Relations*, Occasional Papers, CIA, Kent Center, Volume 2, No. 3 (2003).
———. *Tensions in Analyst-Policymaker Relations: Opinions, Facts, and Evidence*, Occasional Papers, CIA, Kent Center, Volume 2, No. 2 (2003).
———. "Facts, Findings, Forecasts, and Fortune-telling." In *Intelligence and the National Security Strategist: Enduring Issues and Challenges*, ed. Roger Z. George and Robert D. Kline (Washington, DC: CIA, 2004).
Heuer, Richards J., *Psychology of Intelligence Analysis.* (Washington, DC: CIA, 1999).

9

"THE CUSTOMER IS KING"

Intelligence Requirements in Britain

MICHAEL HERMAN

INTELLIGENCE HAS TO DO FOUR THINGS TO be useful. It has to provide governments with information, assessments, and forecasts on the right subjects. It has to deliver them at the right times and in the right ways. It needs to be close to government, with a credibility that means that what it says is taken seriously. Most important, what it provides should be correct or, at the very least, better than the information and conclusions government's decision takers could muster without it. The four are interrelated, but this chapter concentrates on the first: covering the right subjects.

The need to do this applies to any of government's information systems. Intelligence is just one of them, along with diplomatic reporting, statistics, and the other official sources that add to what is publicly available. It has its comparative advantages over the others on matters of secrecy and national security, yet compared with them it is secretive, expensive, more politically embarrassing, and difficult to monitor and control. Democratic governments must be satisfied that it is properly directed, not the rogue elephant that the CIA was memorably—and unfairly—said to be in the congressional inquiries of the 1970s. It should provide what government asks for. But how can this be assured?

This is a modern problem. In the centuries before government became specialized and institutionalized there were no intelligence agencies. Spies got their directions from the ministers or commanders they served, and they were paid by results. There was a similar clarity within government service; the British consuls in foreign ports who observed local naval preparations in the late 17th and 18th centuries reported directly to the Admiralty Secretaries who told them what they wanted. The small European "Black Chambers" that intercepted and deciphered foreign dispatches reported directly to their monarchs and chief ministers. Permanent military and naval intelligence staffs were created in the following century, but they still served their own departments or commanders. Intelligence had not begun to serve multiple parts of government, and the problems of directing it had not appeared.

But by the early 20th century its covert collection was becoming a matter for specialist agencies, not subordinate to any single part of government. Around the mid-century these became further recognized in the anglophone countries as a collective entity—an "intelligence community," with its own identity and structure. Intelligence at both levels was apparently freestanding, distinct from mainstream government, and opaque within its ring of secrecy. It existed to meet the needs of multiple government departments, but its relationship with them had become one of equals, instead of a subordinate "service" to a particular boss. The relationship became described in private-enterprise terms, as one between "producers" and "customers." ("Customers" might now be described as "stakeholders," a term of political discourse introduced under the present British government, but the producer-customer analogy is well entrenched and is used here.) Customers no longer ran their own intelligence, so what was going to ensure that under its new management it did what they wanted?

In Britain the question first arose in 1909 when the Secret Service Bureau was created to develop agent-running on behalf of the Admiralty, War Office and Foreign Office. It was then posed for intelligence as a whole when the wartime Joint Intelligence Committee (JIC) became part of the peacetime machinery in 1945. The British response at both levels was the concept of government's "requirements," originally on a small scale to secure the interests of particular customers, but subsequently as a comprehensive intelligence discipline. Requirements became accepted as intelligence's driving force, and a system for managing it.

This still applies today in the United Kingdom, perhaps to some extent in the United States. Requirements as a system presents customers' needs, but they are needs adapted to some formality. They are not just shopping lists of requests or "blue-sky" hopes, but are needs tailored to what intelligence can provide or may be capable of providing. They resemble the "operational requirements" that drive military weapons procurement, with their connotations of "demand by authority,"[1] practicability, and conformity for those on whom they are laid. For intelligence they are to a degree a directive mechanism, and in recent years they have also become a touchstone of legitimacy. No respectable intelligence agency or community is now complete without them.

What follows here outlines how this idea of requirements evolved in Britain in the period up to the end of the Cold War, plus some comments on American practice, and references to what is known of recent British developments. It is based on a mixture of the author's recollections and such published evidence as is available.

PRODUCERS, PRODUCT, AND CUSTOMERS

British intelligence producers were then (as now) of two general kinds, and produced two kinds of product. Some were specialist information collectors, each expert in its own particular *techniques* and a producer of "single-source" output based on its own material. The main agencies were Government Communications Headquarters or GCHQ for signals intelligence (SIGINT), the Secret Intelligence Service (SIS or MI6) for human intelligence (HUMINT), and the Joint Air Reconnaissance Intelligence Centre (JARIC) for imagery intelligence (IMINT).

Others were government's experts on their designated *subjects*, and their output on them was "all-source" analysis of all relevant information. The largest all-source producer was the Defence Intelligence Staff (DIS), and all-source assessments for top government were provided by the JIC and its Assessments Staff in the Cabinet Office.

There were also those that were both collectors and all-source specialists. The Security Service (MI5) was both a collector and all-source assessor on espionage, terrorism, and similar threats, and the DIS also ran some collection and controlled JARIC. This mixture of collection and analysis organizations, and some doing both, was also found in the much larger American community of the time. It still is.

All were producers, but their single-source and all-source product differed in kind. It is tempting to say that the collectors produced "facts" and the all-source organizations produced analysis and judgment: that the collectors collected foreign secrets and the analysts studied them. But this is an oversimplification: analysis ran through the whole intelligence process. Nevertheless, the differing single-source and all-source *responsibilities* were reflected in the two kinds of product. Collectors produced "good facts," as meaningful as they could make them from their own material; the others produced authoritative judgments and "big pictures."

Both kinds of product went to customers, as shown in the diagram of the intelligence process shown in Figure 9-1. Customers outside intelligence—those on the right-hand side of the diagram—received both single-source and all-source product. The proportions of the two varied between different customers and their different situations. On the one hand, military commanders had intelligence staffs who briefed them on an all-source basis, so they had little reason to read single-source material themselves; the same may now be true of those taking operational decisions on counterterrorism. On the other hand, diplomats were usually their own intelligence analysts and needed single-source intelligence to add to the other information they had. The same applied to other civil departments. JIC reports were limited to subjects of importance for top government, usually those of interdepartmental concern. In sheer quantity most of the intelligence reaching customers was single-source material reported in detail; only certain subjects got the more consolidated all-source treatment.

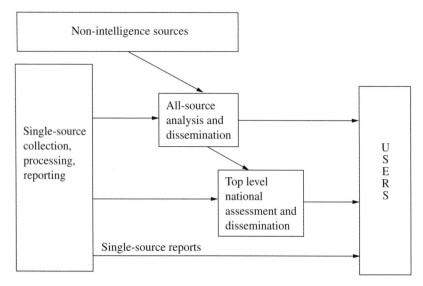

Figure 9-1. Complete Intelligence Process
Source: From Michael Herman, *Intelligence Power in Peace and War* (Cambridge: Cambridge University Press, 1996), p. 103.

That was the pattern of production for which the idea of requirements developed. As the diagram shows, production was geared to three different producer-customer relationships:

- All-source producers and nonintelligence customers
- Single-source producers and nonintelligence customers
- Single-source producers and all-source intelligence customers

Requirements in the third category could have been treated separately as a matter of intraintelligence management, but in practice they were rarely separated from the first two, those of intelligence and the "real" (nonintelligence) customers. A result was that little distinction was often made between the rather different needs of all-source analysts and those who used intelligence for policy or action.

Thus, by the second half of the 20th century intelligence was already a large-scale information system, responding in varied ways to the needs of many different customers and becoming more elaborate. Requirements developed as what seemed a necessary mechanism for coping with the scale and complexity as they increased. How they evolved, and with what effect, can now be considered.

DEPARTMENTAL REQUIREMENTS

Scale and complexity were not the issue when the Secret Service Bureau was created to provide HUMINT for the Foreign Office and Service Ministries. The concern of these departments was to ensure that their individual interests would be met by the new organization. As put by Philip Davies in his work on what later became the SIS, they "were almost exactly as unwilling to delegate responsibility for spying to a separate agency as they were unwilling to go about doing it themselves and risk getting caught." They regarded the Bureau's independence as a matter of cover and convenience, to satisfy the proprieties of the time that respectable departments of state should not engage in spying. The Bureau was a "screen, armature or servant,"[2] unsatisfactory without some way of nailing it down to meeting their individual needs. Hence it was designed so that, while part of it ran agents, the other part had representatives of the Admiralty and War Office intelligence departments (though not the Foreign Office) to direct its targeting and exploit the results. To an undefined extent it was designed to be partly run by its customers. In bits of modern jargon it might be called a matrix organization, operating by customers' "pull" rather than producers' "push," with "embedded" representatives of the "stakeholders" to secure their interests. Requirements from the outset had these suggestions of authority.

British agent-running greatly increased during World War I and was conducted by multiple agencies. Nevertheless, the device of customer representation was preserved when the foreign intelligence part of the 1909 organization was put on a postwar basis in 1919 as the SIS. A separate "Requirements and Circulating" section was established as part of its basic organization. To quote Davies again: "The Requirements side began life as a cluster of consumer-liaison sections. . . . SIS's largest and most powerful consumers—the War Office, Admiralty, Foreign Office and, later, Royal Air Force—seconded sections of their own intelligence branches to SIS to lobby for their partisan interests."[3] This was modified as time went on, notably by filling more of these posts by SIS's own staff. But the doctrine remained that the SIS's production side "mounts operations in response to specific demands laid on it by a tasking, validation and dissemination apparatus referred to as its 'Requirements' side."[4] Whitehall's faith in this idea of customer involvement was illustrated in 1942 when the answer to the armed services' dissatisfaction with SIS's product was for them to appoint more senior representatives as deputy directors, known by their hosts as the "service commissars."[5]

These senior appointments did not continue for long, but the Requirements organization remained important in SIS's postwar structure and retained equal status with Production. Formal, articulated customer requirements became a major part of the service's modus operandi. But as the Cold War developed, with its secrecy, deception, and double-agents, the original Requirements role of reviewing draft reports against customers' needs was extended to validating their quality and reliability by bringing its second opinion to bear on Production's view of its sources. Late in the Cold War this started to change for reasons of economy and efficiency, and in the course of the 1990s Production took over the whole process. The Butler Committee of 2004 that investigated British performance over Iraqi weaponry was advised that this demise of Requirements' validation was responsible for the misleading SIS reports that contributed to the JIC's errors, and it was assured that the earlier arrangements were being restored: a return to the old principle of Production-Requirements duality, though not for the original reason. It is of interest that the CIA's Directorate of Operations has never adopted this British-style duality for managing its HUMINT.

British SIGINT evolved differently. It hardly existed in 1909 and was no part of the Secret Service arrangements of that year. It developed on an extensive scale in World War I as separate efforts under the War Office and Admiralty to meet single-service needs, and the Admiralty also produced diplomatic decrypts for the Foreign Office and joined with the War Trade Department in exploiting cable traffic for continental blockade. In 1919 a national SIGINT organization was created as the Government Code and Cypher School (GC and CS), and two years later was placed under the head of SIS's authority, though with much practical autonomy. On the HUMINT pattern, parties of the three armed forces were included in its organization. The armed forces maintained their own interception efforts, and at least in the 1920s it was expected that much of GC and CS's effort would revert to the individual services in war.

Little has been written about its interwar machinery for handling customers' needs, though it does seem that GC and CS received SIS's customer requirements. As little foreign military traffic was intercepted, military requirements were not a live issue. The main output was decoded diplomatic messages, on which there was productive contact with the Foreign Office, illustrated in a protest from Lord Curzon, the Foreign Secretary, about a plan to move the code-breakers from premises close to Whitehall to a building two miles away. He argued that frequent visits to Foreign Office desks were essential; the code-breakers often needed to draw on Foreign Office information, and the value of their decodes could be time-sensitive: "In many cases the same official visits the F.O. every day, not infrequently several times a day. In cases of difficulty the same official has been known to pass from the School to the F.O. and back 5–6 times a day."[6] This has all the marks of special pleading, but it shows close contact; and it was the producers who visited the customers, not the other way round.

In World War II the situation changed radically. SIGINT became the most important source of intelligence, meeting customer demands throughout the armed forces and government departments. It became a worldwide effort orchestrated by GC and CS at Bletchley Park. Yet it was still complicated by single-service "ownership" of significant parts of the effort, and there was a constant tug between the technical arguments for centralization and the individual armed forces' wishes to exploit "their" SIGINT under their own control.

Wartime Bletchley was indeed a mixed service and civilian organization, and to its service customers there seemed clear analogues with HUMINT. Just as they saw SIS as the expert at running human sources but controlled the results, they conceded GC and CS's expertise in code-breaking but argued that the military parties who were exploiting the decrypts at Bletchley should be under their command. SIGINT could well have developed in that way, but in the course of

1942 it was accepted that the service parties should be controlled by Bletchley. From this the principle was gradually accepted of a single national SIGINT agency with responsibility for the complete SIGINT process: a principle that became a foundation for postwar British SIGINT, and for the American National Security Agency when it was created as its analogue in 1952.

Thus SIGINT requirements never acquired the same salience as for HUMINT. Bletchley's wartime organization evolved around targets and subjects rather than the dyarchy of Production and Requirements. Yet conflicts between competing customer priorities had to be resolved somehow. Bletchley was supervised by a senior interservice Board that might have done this, but in practice it came to be accepted that GC and CS "should carry out without reference to the Board the day-to-day work of reconciling the interests of the services, supervising the programme of the British Sigint centres throughout the world and settling the issues which arose from the ever-expanding collaboration between the British and American Sigint authorities."[7]

How did this come about? It happened from the middle of the war onward, a period of increasing success, when SIGINT abundance had replaced scarcity. Customers had few incentives to rock the boat. Perhaps the young men who juggled daily with Bletchley's resources to break the many German keys had the priestly aura of miracle workers. Perhaps their sports jackets and flannels proclaimed a civilian insulation from parochial single-service interests. It now seems remarkable that Bletchley's authority was accepted with so little controversy, but it happened. "In Whitehall recognition of its [Bletchley's] resourcefulness dissolved the barriers of jealousy and incomprehension which had initially kept the civilians at arm's length and separated the producers of Sigint from those responsible for making the best use of it."[8]

That was the wartime situation. After 1945 GCHQ, the successor of GC and CS, initially adopted a functional organization that included a powerful requirements, reporting, and customer liaison division that may well have been modelled on SIS's "Requirements." Perhaps it seemed that after Bletchley's wartime improvisation the new agency should have a "proper" peacetime structure of that kind. But this reverted after a few years to more target-based arrangements. Customer requirements figured in the professional in-house jargon of the rest of the century, but their most concrete application was in a useful directory: if material on a particular subject became available, which customers should receive it?

There was indeed some peacetime representation of military customers on the 1909 model, but this was at a relatively low level. The armed forces became more pressed for manpower, and more was left to the civilians. Higher level representation made a limited appearance much later, after the end of the Cold War; the first Gulf War and military deployments in the former Yugoslavia had pointed to relearning wartime lessons about support for military operations, and a senior army post was allocated to liaise for this purpose. But this did not lead to wider embedding. Indeed, the trend became to export more SIGINT liaison officers to customers, not the reverse.

For other intelligence producers the problem of choosing between particular customer interests hardly arose. The Security Service succeeded the defensive, domestic part of the original Secret Service Bureau in 1921 with responsibilities that eventually covered counterespionage, countersubversion, and counterterrorism; but it always saw itself as a security service, not an intelligence producer. It often claimed that it was "self-tasking." As for JARIC, it was not regarded as a national agency serving all national customers on the pattern of its American counterpart but was handled as a military institution that did as it was told by the DIS. The DIS itself was equally defense-oriented, and the formal requirements laid on it were in the name of the Chiefs of Staff. The JIC as the top-level producer was regarded as *sui generis*, not covered by the requirements procedure it established for others, to be described shortly.

Thus, securing individual customers' requirements was an issue when British secret intelligence was first institutionalized, but its significance diminished except to some extent for SIS. Coping with competing bids came to be handled on the whole as part of normal day-to-day business. But as requirements settled down at this level, they became important at the new, post-1945 "national" level of the JIC and intelligence as a whole. Intelligence could now be considered as a community. The question became: what was required of it from customers collectively?

THE SHIFT TO COLLECTIVE REQUIREMENTS

Thinking of requirements in this way may have had its origin in the British planning for postwar intelligence that began in 1943. A study of government's future needs was drawn up at that time and may have been the prototype of the subsequent JIC reviews of requirements that were produced after 1945. The titles were varied: At one time they were "intelligence targets," but they were later standardized as "requirements and priorities." They were originally issued at irregular intervals, but in time they came to be produced by the JIC as an annual routine, and subsequently presented for approval by the (official) Permanent Secretaries' Committee on the Intelligence Services (PSIS) that considered intelligence budgets. Subsequently a further layer of approval was added with the creation of a ministerial committee that at least nominally approved requirements along with budgets. Requirements authorized in this way became the main prescription of what the British agencies should do, and by implication not do. They have retained this role: the JIC's latest published responsibilities include the obligation "to submit, at agreed intervals, for approval by Ministers, statements of the requirements and priorities for intelligence gathering and other tasks to be conducted by the intelligence Agencies."[9]

This was a logical complement of a national intelligence community and could be justified on various grounds. Intelligence as a national resource should be orchestrated to meet national needs. Those approving budgets should know what targeting they were endorsing. On major threats there should be an intelligence strategy, as suggested in the memorable British recommendation of 1947 that the intelligence attack on the Soviet target should be mounted as a "campaign."[10] In reality it is doubtful whether any of these justifications was put forward. The long-standing significance of requirements for the SIS probably paved the way for producing them through the JIC, and this probably seemed such a commonsense use of the committee that no particular rationale was needed.

Later, however, the idea of community requirements acquired sharper teeth, as a managerial tool. Establishing intelligence's subjects might provide the framework for better evaluation of its yields, costs and cost-benefits, and more rational management. There were hopes of constructing a logical requirements hierarchy in which national requirements cascaded down to those at departmental and other levels. There were perceptions of a grand intelligence plan in which everything was costed, prioritized, and allocated somewhere to avoid duplication. The community might not be a rogue elephant, but it was a slippery octopus, and attention to requirements seemed one way of getting hold of it. None of this was explicitly articulated, but at the Whitehall center it seemed the way of the future. The intelligence producers for their part supported anything that endorsed their activities and welcomed, at least presentationally, anything that helped them to decide between competing customer requests—though they took every opportunity to ensure that these would not limit their operational flexibility.

It may be that this emphasis on the customer and what he wanted had some subliminal support from the military doctrine that developed in the same period of the "intelligence cycle": the process whereby the customer states his requirement; intelligence responds by collecting, analyzing, and producing; the customer amends his requirement in the light of what he receives; and the iteration continues. The cycle was put forward in many versions, but it tended to be centered on the customer (the military commander): he requested, and intelligence responded.

By the second half of the Cold War this cycle had become the basis of British and American (and North Atlantic Treaty Organization [NATO]) military doctrine for using the increasingly complex collection systems becoming available for the battlefield. It may have made little direct contribution at that time to British thinking about the JIC's requirements; it was then a military concept and the civilians' acquaintance with it was patchy. But it probably had some background influence. It probably also had rather wider currency in the more military-oriented American intelligence community: For many years it featured in the CIA's public factbook, and indeed it still does. The Cold War saw some convergence that, one way or another, intelligence was a requirements-driven process, or should be; and the cycle helped then, and has helped since, to make it the conventional wisdom.

Another prop for requirements' standing came rather later, in the final years of the Cold War and afterwards, when intelligence in Britain moved to a more public and less secretive status. The agencies' roles became defined by legislation, and requirements then fitted as a logical link between them and their translation into practice. They also came to figure in the procedure for ministerial authorization of interception and other sensitive operations, because relevance to JIC priorities demonstrated that operations or proposals were kosher. They also became relevant to the new Intelligence and Security Committee of Parliamentarians and its remit to review the expenditure, administration, and policy of the secret agencies. With these developments it was sensible for requirements' existence and procedure to be described when official accounts of the intelligence community were made public from the mid-1990s onwards. They became part of the British edifice of intelligence legitimacy—a place that they occupy today. The foreigner has the impression that, though they are much used within the American intelligence world, they have perhaps played a rather smaller public part in the U.S. system of democratic oversight than with the British.

So requirements came to stay. But there was no single, perfect scheme for them, and they had a variable record in realizing the hopes vested in them. A complete account is not available, but some recollections can be recorded of the British experience of their development and application.

COLLECTIVE REQUIREMENTS IN PRACTICE

Questions that arose in developing requirements into a system included the following:

- As already explained, the customers for single-source reports were both inside intelligence and outside it: the all-source analysts, on the one hand, and mainstream government, on the other. Should single-source requirements cover the potentially different needs of the two?
- Linked with the first question, were requirements to be set out for both single-source and all-source intelligence, or one or the other? If so, which? Or should there be two sets of requirements and not one?
- Should the same requirements and priorities apply to all collectors, or should each of them be allocated those subjects on which it was best able to contribute?
- What allowance should be made for the availability of extensive American product? Could requirements be met by supplying foreign product, or did they call for a specifically British effort? Conversely, should the American interest in special British contributions (for example, from Hong Kong's special "window" onto China) count as requirements, and with what priority?
- Irrespective of their precise scope, what directive force should requirements and priorities actually have?

For about fifteen years after the end of the Cold War such worries could be kept on a back burner. (A draft JIC report on "Sigint Requirements—1948" issued in May 1948[11] did indeed deal with one source, but as far as can be recalled this was not repeated.) In the author's recollection the norm up to the 1960s was to produce fairly broad lists applying to intelligence as a whole, with relatively simple prioritization. These probably sufficed for airing the pressing question of the 1950s: what priority should be attached to the detailed intelligence on the Soviet armed forces needed for conventional warfare, at a time when thinking was moving toward the impact of missiles and nuclear weapons? As one side of the argument was put by GCHQ's Director in 1955, the time had come for "more intelligence that would help us in the 'cold' war, rather than the 'hot' war."[12] In the event the requirements and priorities reports of the time reflected the compromise that all aspects of the Soviet threat were important, but with some priority for strategic nuclear aspects and intelligence's role of warning.

In fact this debate continued in subdued form through much of the Cold War. Civilians regularly criticized military intelligence for unnecessary "bean counting" of Soviet military *minutiae*, while the military pointed out that it was silly for the United Kingdom to keep large conventional forces to deter the Russians if it then denied them the intelligence that might give them a chance if they actually had to fight them. How was the priority of the big effort on Soviet military targets to be compared with the smaller packets of effort on non-Soviet targets that helped Britain to "punch above its weight" politically in its decades of national economic weakness? Or with the actual conflict with Irish terrorism? The JIC's answers were compromises, as was perhaps inevitable. But its system of requirements and priorities provided some safeguards for military interests and kept everyone reasonably happy. As demanded in 1947, intelligence did wage a coordinated Cold War "campaign," even though not a dramatic one, and the JIC's requirements and priorities played their part in it.

In the 1960s, however, there were hopes of giving them additional teeth. It was a period of British intelligence reform: The three service intelligence directorates and the Joint Intelligence Bureau were combined in 1964 into the new DIS, and successive moves to improve the effectiveness of the JIC's central machinery culminated in its reorganization in 1968. Internationally the Cold War settled into a mood of détente after the Cuban crisis of 1962, and the Soviet threat seemed less pressing. It was also a period of Britain's economic decline, and its withdrawal from its imperial positions in Africa and "east of Suez." The accent everywhere was on financial retrenchment: Reduced commitments should mean intelligence economies. The conviction grew in Whitehall—related to the perception of military bean counting—that customers were getting intelligence they did not really need, or could get from nonintelligence sources. A proper scrutiny of requirements could save money.

These threads came together in serious attempt in the mid-1960s at a comprehensive JIC audit: what parts of government needed "intelligence" as distinct from other information, on what subjects, and for what purposes? Who needed what, from whom? What would emerge as rational priorities? Considerable interdepartmental effort under Cabinet Office chairmanship was devoted to a series of careful area-by-area studies, but the objective of a complete survey leading to evidence-supported, interdepartmentally agreed conclusions remained elusive. Trying to examine everything from A to Z in a committee of differing interests was no way to reach actionable conclusions. Eventually a clever diplomat cut though the complexity to produce a commonsense report that suggested some obvious shifts of emphasis, and everyone was satisfied. This was not quite the last attempt at a review of this kind, because it was followed at the end of the decade by an attempt to audit all the overseas economic information needed by government departments and the consequential requirements for "economic intelligence." But that, too, was not a success.

Nevertheless, the interest in requirements remained, and responsibility for reviewing them was identified as belonging to the new senior post of Intelligence Coordinator, established in the Cabinet Office in 1968. Perhaps to avoid repeating the attempted JIC audit, the Coordinator was initially given some freedom to set out national priorities off his own bat, and for a period in the first half of the 1970s the JIC's annual lists of requirements were discontinued. A short-lived Cabinet Office "Central Monitoring Point" was established to consider requirements again, but it lapsed. After these experiments the system then gradually reverted to the earlier pattern of annual JIC statements. The permanent innovation was that the Coordinator remained the prime mover in the intelligence-customer consultation these entailed.

So there were no more grand investigations, but there were consistent attempts to make requirements more precise and useful. In the last decade of the Cold War, and indeed the 1990s, "value for money" was a catch phrase for governments of both parties, and seeking "better requirements" seemed an appropriate intelligence response. Those seeking value for money in Whitehall inherited the conviction that probes from the center would reveal pots of gold hidden somewhere. It may have been right, but it never found them.

One result was that what in earlier years was guidance for the whole community was focused exclusively on the main collection agencies, SIS and GCHQ, on which most of the money was spent. National requirements for the rest of the community were left in limbo. One consequence was that the requirements presented to the single-source agencies more obviously included those of the all-source analysts; the DIS was involved as a *demandeur* rather than a producer.

A second result was to be more positive about what priorities meant. A distinction was drawn between those subjects that should be targets, and those that should not be targeted but on which material should be reported if it was available as a by-product of other coverage, or from foreign liaisons. The system acquired teeth: the approval of the center was necessary before targeted collection could be initiated against the by-product category. In the last years of the Cold War the idea developed of introducing the discipline of a pseudomarket, whereby customers would bid to "pay" notionally for intelligence to meet their requirements, and intelligence budgets would depend on the bids or results; but it did not get very far.

In these ways JIC requirements remained an accepted part of the scene, as they continue to be. "Better requirements" became a mantra with those outside intelligence who had an interest in it. Considerable effort was put into improving the system. But what difference did it all make?

EFFECTS AND LESSONS

British intelligence had to have a directive of some kind about the subjects it was required to tackle and, by implication, not do so, and about priorities for tackling them. Government had to know what was authorized and demanded in its name, for democratic oversight as well as other reasons. Intelligence had to understand its remit and have community understandings about policy and strategy. The JIC was well suited to formulating requirements and priorities for these purposes, because its membership included the Foreign Office and other principal customer departments along with the intelligence community proper. It was a weakness that when the system was made more sharply focused the DIS ceased to be formally bound by it; and it was a British eccentricity that while JIC requirements applied elsewhere in the community the Committee did not apply them to itself in its role as Britain's top intelligence producer. But these oddities were more apparent than real. The JIC was good at being collegial, and its members were agreed on what they should be doing: not a negligible achievement for a committee of secret organizations.

Yet it is difficult to recall that the requirements procedure ever affected what intelligence actually did. The annual routine was taken seriously, especially after Coordinators came to give their attention to it, but there was an element of ritual about it. Lists of requirements and priorities were drawn up by intelligence and submitted to customers for collective review—the reverse of what strict logic might have suggested. What emerged reflected what intelligence was producing and customers were receiving, subject to some minor annual tweaking. It should be repeated that the JIC dispensed with the whole thing for some time in the 1970s and no one noticed the difference.

Intelligence producers' attitude to the process was mixed. It was valued if it opened new doors for discussion with customers. It might provide excuses for kicking unreasonable customer demands into touch. On the other hand producers regarded good relations with their individual customers as emphatically their own business. Any difficulties with them should be handled one-to-one; nothing good would come of letting the center get into the act. Insofar as the JIC procedure produced benefits, they were in the process and not the product. It was regarded as a necessary routine, to be met with goodwill but without excessive enthusiasm, and with a determination to stop it developing the sharp teeth sought by some.

What lessons should be drawn from this experience? The Cold War was of course a static period compared with what happened afterwards. From 1990 onwards intelligence has had to adapt to new situations and changes of gear far more flexibly than ever before, and customers' requirements might seem to be much more important than before. Nevertheless, the 20th-century weight attached to them should not be the guide for the 21st. This writer's skepticism is explained elsewhere[13] and can only be summarized here. Customers are busy people, not usually given to defining what they don't know. They often have little idea what intelligence might or might not produce. A future American DCI commented that "often the requirement has more to do with the last item that popped into the policy-maker's in-box or some hairbrained idea he concocted while shaving that morning."[14] They tend to be short-termists; intelligence should not stake too much on their forecasts of what their successors will ask for. It has to take longer views, and make investments accordingly.

Intelligence is also like other kinds of knowledge industry—research and development, for example—in not lending itself well to top-down central planning. Its good practitioners are opportunists. What they do against any target should be a multiple of feasibility and potential value—they should not do anything if the answer to either is zero. But operational feasibility looms larger than for more conventional information producers. Intelligence needs customers' ideas about what they want—including the hairbrained and "blue-sky" ones—and should seek every opportunity for dialogue with them, but stimulation usually comes better from developing customers' feedback on the intelligence they receive than from taking requirements as the starting point.

This takes us back to the market analogy with producers and customers. Intelligence's professionalism is grounded in production standards—seeking to be right—but is wider. The intelligence officer is an information entrepreneur, skilled in engaging individual customers, evaluating its product with them, ascertaining what gaps it leaves unfilled, and feeding the conclusions back into the production machine. Market research and selling are part of the core skills. The analogy with the market is a good one, better than a picture of intelligence in a requirements-driven command economy; but the producer-customer market does not have a perfect balance between supply and demand. Customers have more important things to worry about. Intelligence itself has to supply the dynamic and has the most powerful incentive to do so: Ultimately it goes out of business if customers cease to want its product, whereas customers are normally less dependent. The intelligence-customer relationship is much more "producer-push" than the "customer-pull" implied if requirements are seen as the driving force. The requirements-driven approach reviewed here has the danger of being too mechanistic.

The same criticism might be also applied to the command-driven intelligence cycle as developed in the same period; yet on this there is the puzzle that it retains the confidence of the military and indeed is now more widely seen as the intelligence paradigm. It may be that war is unrivaled in making commanders intelligence-conscious and intelligence-educated to degrees not found in peacetime, except perhaps in counterterrorism. Or perhaps the cycle should be revisited as a training metaphor, rather than a description of real life, and its emphasis on the commander revised. Other military doctrine now emphasizes subordinates' initiative through "mission command," and perhaps this should be brought to the cycle's exegesis. The problem here may be that those looking at intelligence as a whole just do not know enough about the cycle in recent military experience. Despite battlefield intelligence's modern importance, we lack published accounts of its dynamics in practice.

So there has to be this qualification. But despite this, the lesson from the period considered here can be suggested with some confidence. Requirements as developed in the Cold War served admirable purposes for broad direction, strategy, and legitimacy. Attempts to develop them further had mixed success. It is fortunate that individual agencies' influence in the collegial British system meant that ideas of developing them in ambitious management systems never got off the ground. In all, they did some good and not much harm.

The regret is that they presented a simple, rather seductive approach to understanding intelligence or controlling it. Those dealing with intelligence from outside saw too much promise in it, in years in which there were already too many other nostrums about effectiveness in the public service. Those brought up on the inside were realistic and cautious, but allowed it to absorb effort that might have been used more profitably.

The British community actually needed more central authority than it had. Throughout the period under review, and until quite recently, the need for some authority of this kind was half-recognized, but there was great uncertainty about its purpose. The result for the community was what the Committee of Parliamentarians described as a hole in the center. Supervision of "Requirements" seemed a comprehensible point of entry, but hindsight suggests that it was too narrow. The community needed something more comprehensive, yet more subtle: bound up with the attributes of leadership, rather than a management system.

The recently retired very senior member of the Cabinet Office who had occupied the revised post of Security and Intelligence Coordinator gave a fresh definition of that role at intelligence's center. It was the conviction of "his personal responsibility for intelligence's professional health": a notable statement. It is to be hoped that attention to customer requirements will be handled as part of this more encompassing view of managing intelligence, and not as a short cut.

NOTES

I am grateful for comments and suggestions to John Morrison and Philip Davies. For requirements in SIS I have drawn extensively on the latter's *MI6 and the Machinery of Spying* and other publications.
1. Dictionary definition, *Longman's,* 1984.

2. Both quotations from Philip H. J. Davies, *MI6 and the Machinery of Spying* (London: Frank Cass, 2004), p. 50.

3. Philip H. J. Davies, "A Critical Look at Britain's Spy Machinery," *Studies in Intelligence* 49 (2005), p. 44.

4. Ibid., p. 43.

5. Davies, *MI6 and the Machinery of Spying*, p. 156.

6. Keith Jeffrey, "The Government Code and Cypher School: A Memorandum by Lord Curzon," *Intelligence and National Security* 1 (September 1986), p. 455.

7. F. H. Hinsley with E. E. Thomas, C. F. G. Ransom, and R. C. Knight, *British Intelligence in the Second World War, Vol. 3* (London: H.M. Stationary Office, 1984), pp. 459–60.

8. F. H. Hinsley, *British Intelligence in the Second World War,* abridged edition (London: H.M. Stationary Office, 1993), p. 117.

9. *National Intelligence Machinery* (Norwich, U.K.: H.M. Stationary Office, 2005), p. 24.

10. Air Chief Marshal Sir Douglas Evill, *Review of Intelligence Organizations, 1947*, Misc/P 4781, November 6, 1947, CAB 163/7, National Archives, United Kingdom.

11. Discussed and reprinted in Richard Aldrich and Michael Coleman, "The Cold War, the JIC and British Intelligence, 1948," *Intelligence and National Security* 4 (July 1989).

12. Michael Herman, *Intelligence Services in the Information Age* (London: Frank Cass, 2001), p. 119.

13. Herman, *Intelligence Power in Peace and War*, pp. 283–96.

14. Quoted in ibid., p. 289.

10

GLOBAL ECONOMIC ESPIONAGE

An Ancient Art, Now a Science

MINH A. LUONG

Imitation is the sincerest form of flattery. Others call it economic espionage.

ONE OF THE BASIC MOTIVATIONS THAT DRIVES innovation is the reward from developing an invention, business process, or product. The steady advancement of technology through the ages has led to the development of a global economic system that has raised the overall standard of living and promises to address some of humankind's greatest challenges. In order for the global economy to continue to thrive and innovation to continue, the challenge of global economic espionage needs to be successfully addressed.

Economic espionage is the use, or facilitation of, illegal clandestine, coercive, or deceptive means by a foreign government or its surrogates to acquire economic intelligence. Economic espionage activities may include collection of information, or acquisition or theft, of a manufactured item through clandestine means with the intent of using reverse engineering to gain proprietary or classified data.[1] Economic espionage also includes the theft of product designs, marketing plans, proprietary information such as manufacturing techniques, and intellectual property such as computer software applications.

If left unabated, economic espionage, practiced on a global scale, threatens to destroy the incentives to innovate and will eventually reduce the quantity and quality of new ideas and inventions brought to the marketplace and for the benefit of humankind.

GLOBAL ECONOMIC ESPIONAGE: AN ANCIENT PRACTICE

One of the earliest recorded cases of economic espionage comes from the 18th century, with the European acquisition of the manufacturing process of ceramic porcelain that was a closely guarded secret of the Chinese.[2] The Chinese started producing white porcelain china and tableware as early as the 7th century, and trade in porcelain wares with European royalty was robust toward the end of the 13th century. For over four hundred years European traders and luxury goods makers desperately sought the manufacturing secrets of this "white gold" that fetched large sums of money for entire serving sets and place settings. Because the Chinese recognized the tremendous economic value of holding a global monopoly in porcelain manufacturing, the Chinese emperor centralized all porcelain production and relocated all porcelain craftspeople in an industrial city called Kin Te-Chen that closely guarded the materials, manufacturing process, and potters who produced the porcelain goods. Porcelain production was banned in all other parts of China. Despite all attempts of foreigners to infiltrate the city, bribe craftspeople who were familiar with the manufacturing process, or otherwise learn the secrets of making porcelain, ironically, it was a Jesuit missionary named d'Entrecolles who turned out to be one of the world's first industrial spies.

Because he was a priest, d'Entrecolles was thought to be trustworthy and was allowed access to Kin Te-Chen, where he observed the entire manufacturing process. He became friends with the potter families who produced various porcelain goods and, despite the extensive security procedures of the royal Chinese guards, managed to obtain and send to his contacts in Europe a sample of kaolin clay, the raw material used to produce the valued white Chinese porcelain. Of even more value, d'Entrecolles wrote numerous letters explaining in great detail the elaborate production procedures he learned from his visits to Kin Te-Chen. With d'Entrecolles's sample of kaolin and step-by-step description of the production details, a Saxon chemist named Johann Friedrich Böttger began working on a formulation to produce European porcelain. His initial efforts yielded a porcelainlike material but due to the clay found in Germany, his first sets of products were colored red. It was only through chance discovery of a powder used to dust white wigs that Böttger discovered the elusive final key ingredient necessary to produce white porcelain. Like the Chinese, Böttger implemented elaborate security measures to protect the formulation and manufacturing process that he spent years to perfect. But unlike the Chinese, who were able to protect their trade secrets for four centuries, Böttger was able to maintain exclusive production of European porcelain for less than a decade. Because of industrial espionage against Böttger's firm, porcelain was produced all across Europe by the end of the 18th century.

The rise of mercantilism provides another illustrative example of economic espionage. England, with few domestic natural resources and a relatively small population, used its comparative advantage in technology and global trade to become one of the world's richest countries and controlled a vast empire. The British either colonized or established British-owned trading companies in many resource-rich areas around the globe that produced spices, teas, whale oil, pelts, silk, cotton, and other valuable raw goods. Through importation of raw materials such as cotton and production of finished goods such as bolts of colorful cloth, articles of clothing, and other textile goods, English textile mill owners and, through trade taxes, the English monarchy, grew rich and powerful.

Two of the premier innovations that kept British industrialists at the forefront of global production and profitability were the cotton spinning process, which automated the process of turning raw cotton into uniform-thickness, high-quality thread, and the famous Cartwright loom, which used the power of falling water from streams and rivers to power massive mechanical looms that weaved cotton thread into large swaths of finished cloth. Thousands of bolts of this unsurpassed cloth were produced by British weaving mills on a weekly basis and because of the uniformity of size and high quality of British textile goods, global demand often outstripped production capacity. Because of the mercantile system and the successful application of spinning and weaving technologies, textile production was as much a goldmine for the British as porcelain production was for the Chinese.

Despite the enormous commercial success of the British textile industry, there were numerous warnings about the longevity of the British monopoly on automated cotton spinning and weaving processes. The impressive feats of British industrial spy Thomas Briand in stealing French industrial secrets on behalf of British interests underscored the importance of protecting industrial and trade secrets. The British realized that their higher standard of living, combined with the costs of transporting raw materials to England and shipping finished goods back to customers around the globe, added significant expense to their final production costs. If their technological and production secrets were ever compromised and lost to manufacturers who could produce those same finished goods in their own countries, many British industrialists would go bankrupt or at the very least be forced to compete with manufacturers that were located closer to their customers and enjoyed much lower overall production costs.

After witnessing repeated failures on the part of firms throughout the European continent to protect their own industrial trade secrets, England adopted a different approach to protecting Britain's mercantile system and industrialists who were pillars of the British economy. In 1765 the English Parliament passed a series of laws prohibiting the transfer of "new machines or plans or models" with the aim of preserving England's technological and manufacturing superiority. The law also forbade tradesmen, repairmen, and others knowledgeable in the workings of protected machines from leaving the country. British industrialists were expected to do what they could to protect their own proprietary information and trade secrets, but the British crown used its network of marshals and constables as well as customs inspectors to investigate suspected industrial spies.

It was not long before an American colonist and engineer named Samuel Slater traveled to England and, through working in various British cotton spinning

mills, learned the entire process of the proprietary British system from preparation of raw cotton bales to winding the finished thread onto large shipping
spools. Slater had the gift of a photographic memory to which he memorized the
blueprints for various spinning machines and their attendant devices. He also
committed to memory the various nuances of cotton spinning learned from working at several of England's best cotton spinning mills. Because Slater worked
at each mill for only a short time, he was able to stay one step ahead of the
British agents who were charged with identifying industrial spies and, through
his work at several mills, was able to learn the advantages and shortcomings of
each mill's process. This surreptitious journey made Samuel Slater one of the
world's foremost experts in cotton spinning as he was able to convince the normally secretive British cotton processors and spinners in succession to hire him
to improve their operations.

Slater was a confident man, and his photographic memory served him well
on many occasions. But Slater was also a careful engineer and knew that once he
left England, there would be no opportunity to return if he forgot a critical detail
or part. So for the most detailed spinning machines, he left nothing to chance and
carefully reproduced mechanical blueprints onto large canvas cloths. Knowing
that he had now come under the suspicion of the British authorities, Slater left
England earlier than he had originally planned but had collected nearly everything that he had set out to discover about the cotton and spinning processes. By
leaving on a small ocean sloop Slater was able to evade most of the British immigration control officers and agents who were awaiting him near the berths of
the larger galleys headed to the New World. His bags were searched, however, by
a customs officer just as he boarded his ship and with nothing that constituted a
violation of the British technology control laws, Slater was allowed to travel
without incident back to the American colonies. Little did the British authorities
know that Slater had arranged to have his canvas mechanical drawings rolled up
and hidden in one of the horizontal masts of the sloop, which the British customs
officer missed during his search of Slater's baggage and the sloop's cargo hold.
Upon his return to New England, Slater quickly raised the funds and built the
first cotton-thread spinning mill in the American colonies, which helped start
the economic rise of the new republic and earned him the title of "Father of
American Manufacture."[3]

Samuel Slater's spinning mills started producing cotton thread in significant
quantity, but without an indigenous automated and high-volume looming and
textile production capability, producing finished textile goods outside of England
remained elusive. The British were furious with Slater's illegal transfer of their
cotton spinning technology and production methods and, as a result, refused any
imports of finished thread from the American colonies. So the hope of producing
cotton thread in America and having that thread woven into cloth by machine in
Britain was quickly extinguished. Thus, American cloth remained loomed by
hand on small, manually operated looms that produced smaller swaths of cloth

that were inferior in quality and quantity to those of the British automated power-loomed cloths.

By the early 1800s the United States had won its independence from England and American textile mills were desperate to successfully compete with their British counterparts. Thus, a renewed effort to learn the secrets of the British power cotton weaving process began in earnest. Previous attempts by other would-be industrial spies who wanted to be the next Samuel Slater failed as the British enhanced their security procedures and enforcement of their technology transfer laws. But the one industrial spy who would succeed where all others had failed previously was also a highly unlikely candidate by the name of Francis Cabot Lowell, a rich and successful Harvard-educated shipping magnate who came from a prominent and cultured Boston family.[4] Because of his extensive business ties with British trading firms and family ties to England that preceded the American Revolutionary War, Lowell was welcomed by the British textile manufacturers not only as a self-made kindred spirit of sorts, but also as a potential customer and business partner with connections all over the globe. He was given extensive tours of the finest weaving mills and any question he asked was answered in great detail by the mill foreman or the owner of the weaving plant himself. For his part, Lowell kept up the ruse by bringing his family with him to England and telling his hosts that he was in poor health and needed an extended vacation that included consultation with England's best physicians. Like Slater, Francis Cabot Lowell possessed a photographic memory but left little to chance: After each visit to a weaving mill, he sketched drawings of the weaving machines he examined and transcribed the conversations that he had with British weaving experts. By the end of Lowell's "health vacation," he had gathered all the information necessary to reproduce a large powered mill and loom back in America. Though the British industrialists never suspected Lowell of stealing their industrial and trade secrets—after all, he was a gentrified, educated global shipping magnate who knew nothing of their business and would never be a threat to them—British customs authorities were far less convinced. Not wanting to risk being discovered as an industrial spy on British soil and endanger his family who was with him, Lowell arranged to have his drawings and notes smuggled out of England separately, although the exact method was never revealed by Lowell. British customs officers searched the Lowell family's bags repeatedly during their journey to the port, but after coming up empty each time, the officers let Lowell and his family depart England with the second and perhaps most important of England's industrial secrets. Upon his return to Massachusetts, Lowell and his brother-in-law started the Boston Manufacturing Company, and after improving on the water-power delivery mechanism and the designs of the weaving looms themselves, Lowell's mills were weaving more than two miles of very high-quality finished cloth per week—a significant improvement in both quality and quantity over the British mills. The American textile industry witnessed steady growth for the next century and was a major engine of the American economy until the rise of steam power overtook textile production a few decades later.

Because of Samuel Slater and Francis Cabot Lodge's economic espionage, the industrial revolution began with a strong start in the United States and, along with protective tariffs that allowed fledgling domestic industries to take hold and grow, witnessed the meteoric rise of the United States as a major world power. The rise of the American economy allowed greater capital investments and advancements in industrial technology, which has been the mainstay of American economic growth and power. Today the United States is the world's economic giant, but with that distinction come the pressures of globalization and competition that have led to increased economic espionage against U.S. companies. In essence, the cycle has come full circle. In response to a sharp rise in economic espionage against American industrial firms and military contractors, the U.S. Congress passed the Economic Espionage Act of 1996 (EEA), which imposes prison terms up to fifteen years and fines up to $10 million for stealing trade secrets for the use or benefit of anyone other than the owner. Even with the EEA and increased enforcement by the Federal Bureau of Investigation (FBI), economic espionage in the United States continues to grow at an alarming rate. The lessons of the British technology protection acts of 1765 will serve today's American industrialists and political leaders well as they protect their technological advantages against industrial spies from rival countries.

ECONOMIC INTELLIGENCE: BENCHMARKING NATIONAL COMPETITIVENESS

National governments, regardless of form or type, are under increasing pressure to satisfy the needs of their domestic populations and maintain economic stability and growth. Growing populations around the globe expect paying jobs in order to feed, house, and clothe their families; and an educated elite, frequently educated in the best universities in Asia, Western Europe, and the United States, have rising expectations for their own prosperity and well-being. In an increasingly global marketplace, the competitiveness of domestic industries often means the difference between national prosperity and security versus poverty and instability. For all countries, making intelligent investments in the right industries at the right time is a critical part of national economic policy. Economic intelligence gathered from competitor nations is an essential component in making the right investment decisions.

These investment decisions affect different countries depending on their present stage of economic development. For developing countries, accurate economic intelligence helps direct scarce investment funds to industries that show the greatest promise for long-term growth. In the case of developed countries, economic intelligence is used to help support established but aging industries that need to improve their competitive standing against rival firms from other nations that frequently operate on a lower cost basis. For all nations, capital investment funds at competitive interest rates are a finite resource and managing those funds effectively requires access to accurate, complete, and timely economic intelligence.

ECONOMIC ESPIONAGE: RESEARCH AND DEVELOPMENT AT LITTLE OR NO COST

Countries collecting economic intelligence use those data to compare how their industries are performing relative to those of other countries. Many countries discover that their national industries require significant capital and technological investments in order to become or stay competitive in the global economy. The policy decisions that result from such findings frequently cross the dividing line between economic intelligence and economic espionage. For countries that can afford to raise capital funds to improve their industries, they certainly engage in economic intelligence but tend to avoid engaging in economic espionage to maintain positive relations with larger trading partners and access to overseas investment funds. Yet for countries that cannot afford to pay to improve their industries, they still face the same demographic, economic, and political pressures of other countries but choose to acquire stolen technology and proprietary information to bolster their uncompetitive industries. These countries maintain legitimate businesses and interact in the global economy but choose to supplement their economic growth with benefits from economic espionage.

The National Counterintelligence Executive (NCIX), the U.S. government agency charged with protecting American industry and trade information, noted that "[i]ndividuals from both the private and public sectors in almost 100 countries attempted to illegally acquire US technologies in FY2004."[5] The report also observed that the United States is not the only country that has experienced losses through economic espionage. The People's Republic of China, Russia, and South Korea all reported cases of foreign economic espionage occurring within their borders.[6] Economic espionage is a global phenomenon that occurs at three levels: National governments engage in economic espionage to benefit their national industries and military forces; companies steal intellectual property and trade secrets from competitors and even joint venture partners; and individual data collectors, also known as industrial spies, gain employment at target firms and steal proprietary information and trade secrets. This information is then sold to competitor firms or foreign governments.

As illustrated in the beginning of this chapter, the benefits of engaging in economic espionage have been demonstrated repeatedly. By stealing completed or near-completed product plans, a competitor can produce and market a copy of the product without incurring the normal research and development costs of bringing that product to market. For industries with high research and development costs—such as pharmaceutics, biotechnology, computer hardware and

software, and military equipment—theft of even a single high-investment product can be enormous. To make matters worse for the original developer, if products derived from stolen proprietary data are manufactured in a country with
lower production costs, the original developers may find themselves in an uncompetitive position, even though they developed the product in the first place.
Firms that manufacture products derived from stolen proprietary data frequently
do not market them in the country or region where the product plans were
acquired. This tactic reduces the likelihood of detection by the firms that originally developed the products.

   Estimating the losses from global economic espionage is very difficult, if not
impossible, due to the fact that some firms do not discover that their product plans
or intellectual property have been compromised for months or even years after
the initial loss. Many companies never learn that they have incurred a loss from
industrial espionage and assume that their reduced market share or lack of success in the market is due to other business factors. Some firms that discover that
they have been victims of industrial espionage make a business decision not to
report the loss to the authorities for fear of negative publicity, loss of customer
confidence, or even a drop in their stock prices.[7] The culture of silence among
firms suffering losses from economic espionage has hampered efforts to uncover
how modern industrial spies operate and how to develop more effective protective measures.

ECONOMIC INTELLIGENCE AND ESPIONAGE
ON THE RISE

   Virtually every national intelligence service gathers some form of economic
intelligence. Some use economic data to keep national leadership updated on
global trends, but most countries with significant economic assets and industrial
capacity use their intelligence services in a more proactive way: Intelligence
services are increasingly tasked with actively helping domestic firms win business overseas and with collecting valuable industrial secrets to help their own
national industries. Some intelligence research firms and think tanks estimate that
some of the world's most active intelligence agencies spend between a quarter to
a third of their entire intelligence budgets on collecting economic data and industrial trade secrets.[8] The phenomenon of globalization, combined with lowering or eliminating protective tariffs, has greatly increased competition among
industrialized nations with rapidly growing developing countries providing even
more pressure with their lower wages and production costs.

   To keep current with an ever-changing global marketplace, the world's
major economic powers have greatly expanded their economic intelligence
capabilities since the 1990s. As competitiveness in European markets heated up
through the 1980s and into the 1990s, the British Parliament passed the British
Intelligence Services Act of 1994, which expanded the scope of its Secret

Intelligence Service (SAS), also known as MI6, to include areas relevant to "the interests of the economic well-being of the United Kingdom."[9] In March 1994 the French government authorized its intelligence services to expand operations into collecting economic and industrial intelligence. Moreover, the following year the French government established the Committee for Economic Competitiveness and Security, which focused on protecting economic secrets and set up an economic intelligence office in the French Foreign Trade office.[10] The People's Republic of China (PRC), also frequently cited as a major collector of economic intelligence and a leading practitioner of economic espionage, operates mainly through the Ministry of State Security (MSS) and the People's Liberation Army, General Staff Department, Second Department (also known as the Military Intelligence Department), coordinating a vast and enhanced overseas collection effort.[11] In the United States the Central Intelligence Agency (CIA) has maintained a large economic intelligence analysis capability since the end of World War II that was enhanced significantly during the Cold War,[12] but that capability was further expanded as the National Security Agency (NSA) upgraded its signals intelligence collection capacity through its ECHELON system, which reportedly is capable of intercepting millions of electronic messages per hour.[13] In the late 1990s, the European Parliament accused the United States, Great Britain, Australia, and New Zealand of using the ECHELON system to gather economic and commercial intelligence against many European countries and their industries.[14] The Science and Technology Options Assessment Panel of the European Parliament (STOA) released several reports on the ECHELON system, culminating in a final report released in 2001. That same year, U.S. Presidential Decision Directive (PDD) 75 on counterintelligence was released, and the directive created a new office, the National Counterintelligence Executive (NCIX), responsible for protecting American economic and industrial interests.[15] In 2003 Japan established the Secretariat of Intellectual Property Strategy Headquarters, tasked with protecting Japan's technological advantages, which is chaired by the prime minister.[16]

Economic espionage has even become a formal academic and professional discipline. France, which has been cited by numerous sources as one of the largest collectors of economic intelligence and foremost practitioners of economic espionage, opened the *Ecole de Guerre Economique* (EGE), or School of Economic Warfare, in 1997.[17] The EGE's mission statement emphasizes "offensive strategy." It trains students in a wide range of intelligence disciplines and awards degrees in economic intelligence, including a doctorate. In the United States there are an increasing number of universities that offer intelligence and national security degrees, some of which specialize in industrial and technological security.

Countries use economic intelligence to assess the state of their own national industries, measure the competitiveness of industries in other countries, and inform policy makers and industry leaders about which domestic industries are in need of further investment or reorganization. Nations that engage in economic espionage do so to improve or maintain the competitiveness of their own national industries by lowering or eliminating associated research and development costs by illegally appropriating advanced technology and other proprietary information to bring products and services to market at lower cost and frequently faster than if they were developed indigenously.

TYPES OF INDUSTRIES TARGETED

Economic espionage collectors have concentrated their efforts against a number of specific industries due to their value in promoting economic growth and global competitiveness. In the commercial sector, these include agriculture, biotechnology, chemical, computer technology, fiber optics, medical devices, pharmaceuticals, robotics, and telecommunications.[18] Commercial sector industries all play a role in fostering economic growth. For countries that cannot afford to purchase large quantities of expensive pharmaceutical therapies for their populations, scientists reverse-engineer or discover through research in U.S. or European patent offices the formulations. With the correct formulas, domestic pharmaceutical manufacturers can produce the same drugs for a mere fraction of the price charged by the patent-holding developer. Because there is a significant up-front research cost in identifying a promising compound and developing it into an effective therapy, the pharmaceutical industry has been particularly vulnerable to economic espionage. Commentators who have justified economic espionage in this area or defend ignoring patents for certain drugs argue that it is unethical to deny people needed medicine simply because they cannot afford to pay the price set by the patent holder. Pharmaceutical companies have countered that they have offered to provide drugs at cost or even for free, but countries have their own interest in protecting their own pharmaceutical companies.

In countries where domestic food production has leveled off or has dropped, purchasing agricultural technology and materials has proven to be a costly endeavor. Through industrial espionage, acquiring countries can obtain agricultural technology and the formulations to produce fertilizers and pesticides at a much lower cost, provided that they have the necessary domestic manufacturing capability and access to required raw materials. An important point to note here is that although copy-cat equipment and chemicals derived from economic espionage may not perform as well as products manufactured from their original makers, that issue is not the primary concern. The key factor is whether the copy-cat products are better than no products at all or are better than antiquated products currently in use. Given the low cost/high payoff of acquiring technology and products through economic espionage, the improvements are worth the expense.

With respect to military technologies, many countries use economic espionage to improve the capabilities of their military forces as well as to improve the competitiveness of their arms industries. Targeted military industries include aeronautics, armaments, energetic materials, chemical and biological systems, guidance and navigation systems, information systems, manufacturing and fabrication, marine systems, sensors and lasers, and space system technologies.[19] Countries that engage in economic espionage to collect military and dual-use technologies are frequently trading partners but are restricted from receiving military-grade technologies due to national security export restrictions. Countries with the most advanced military technology and greatest number of export restrictions include the NATO countries of Western Europe and the United States. The investments required to maintain military advantage of potential enemies are significant, running into the billions of dollars in research, development, and deployment costs. Compromised technology losses through economic espionage put these investments at significant risk.

ECONOMIC INTELLIGENCE AND ESPIONAGE COLLECTION METHODS

With the advent of the Internet, conducting basic economic intelligence research is relatively simple. Many governments make their economic data available on the Internet, and government ministries and agencies regularly make data available to international lenders such as the World Bank, International Monetary Fund, and regional development banks as well as private international lenders. When government-supplied data are neither available nor accurate, estimated data are available from investment firms, university research centers, and organizations that specialize in selling economic research to business and governmental clients.[20]

For collectors of economic intelligence, there is a significant difference in operating between open and closed economic systems.[21] In open economic systems, obtaining economic intelligence is relatively easy and utilizes tools not unfamiliar to a stock investor. Government economic reports and company quarterly and annual disclosures make up the foundation of any country analysis. This information can be supplemented and cross-verified by private data and analysis from research firms and investment companies. On-site visits of companies and manufacturing plants are possible if arranged in advance. Even open source analysis of media reports and academic and trade journals provides rich streams of economic data. In closed economic systems, the economic intelligence collection task becomes more challenging. Harassment from law enforcement officials and state security officers hampers collection activity. Government reports and company disclosures are frequently inaccurate, incomplete, misleading, or simply unavailable.[22] Travel restrictions within the country and the need for special permits encumber collection efforts. When contacted for interviews, company officials grow suspicious of any foreigners or persons asking for company data.

For countries with significant national technical means such as satellites and communications interception capabilities, a new dimension of economic data is available. Satellite imagery and analysis can help produce accurate agricultural yield estimates, projections of industrial output, even mortality rates. Interception of phone calls, Internet messages, fax transmissions, and other communications can be used to verify or confirm intelligence findings. Finally, economic intelligence sources can include businesspeople, academics, and researchers who live in or visit targeted countries. Intelligence services around the world utilize these types of human sources and though some services prefer to debrief citizens who have returned from abroad, others provide a list of targets beforehand so that citizens can exploit any opportunity they encounter.

For economic espionage collectors, the method of operation can vary significantly. Because of their open economic systems, countries engaging in economic espionage frequently establish front companies in Europe and the United States from which to base their operations. These firms operate like domestic companies, and their foreign ownership ties are either not disclosed or are hidden. For the past decade, acquisition of sensitive commercial, military, and dual-use technologies has been at the top of the target list for economic rivals of the European Union and the United States. These front companies attempt to purchase restricted technology and illegally transfer it out of the country. In other instances, these firms form joint venture partnerships with companies who have developed sensitive technologies and the foreign joint venture partner transfers the proprietary information to a third party in violation of the joint venture agreement. Another popular collection method is to arrange an on-site visit where the targeted technology or products are produced. Though the information exchange is supposed to be bidirectional and mutually beneficial, there have been reported incidents of foreign experts entering restricted areas, photographing sensitive areas, and discussing matters and asking questions that are outside the agreed list of topics.[23] Some countries utilize their student and academic connections in targeted countries, recruiting them to serve as intermediaries or even collectors at academic conferences, university laboratories and libraries, industry meetings, and trade shows. One potential area of concern for significant economic espionage losses is through compromised computer systems. An industrial espionage collector, working within a targeted firm with access to the company's computer system, can download and collect computer files containing critical proprietary data. With the advent of high-capacity, low-cost storage devices such as small hard drives and thumb-sized memory sticks, gigabytes of information can be stolen in minutes and detection is virtually impossible.

As companies expand their operations to other countries, computer networks that support overseas operations are vulnerable to attack from a number of sources. If a firm has a presence in a country with an aggressive intelligence agency, that firm is far more vulnerable to penetration because the intelligence agency is more likely to have control of or influence over the local telecommunication system, power grid, even the construction company that built the structure. Intelligence agencies have even planted eavesdropping devices in the facilities of foreign firms.

ECONOMIC ESPIONAGE: DESTROYING INNOVATION AND INVESTMENT

Economic espionage can affect any country's economy regardless of its state of development. In fact, there are countries that benefit from economic espionage and yet are victims of it at the same time. But the dangers to the international trade system from economic espionage are becoming increasingly clear, and this phenomenon affects nearly every level of a nation's economy.

As economic espionage grows in frequency and scale, knowledge that inventions are regularly stolen greatly reduces or even destroys the normal incentives to innovate. Inventors have been deterred from developing products and bringing them to market for fear of having their life's work and investment stolen. Bankers are increasingly leery of making business loans to firms whose products are at risk from industrial espionage. Investors may be discouraged from making investments in companies operating in foreign countries or whose bottom line may be negatively affected by losses from economic espionage. And joint ventures, hailed by many business scholars as a way of linking the developing and developed worlds to create mutually beneficial results, are fraught with dangers of one partner stealing from the other. Officials in countries that engage in economic espionage as national policy defend their practice by saying that their best minds study in highly industrialized nations but never return to help their native country, so stealing technologies and other industrial trade secrets is a way of equalizing for the potential loss of these educated citizens. The "brain drain" effect is difficult to quantify, but it does provide a rationale for engaging in economic espionage.[24]

These types of risks lead to reduced business efficiencies. The risk from economic espionage has deterred companies from entering promising markets due to weak intellectual property protections and risk of economic espionage. The additional expense for enhanced security increases overhead costs and reduces workplace efficiencies as more time is spent on maintaining security measures. Economic espionage has even led to discrimination in the workplace because certain nationalities and ethnicities are associated with industrial espionage.

THE COUNTERINTELLIGENCE CHALLENGE FOR GOVERNMENTS

Some of the largest targets of economic espionage such as the United States have enacted laws punishing economic espionage collectors. For example, in 1996 the United States passed the Economic Espionage Act (EEA), which punishes firms and individuals who steal or transfer trade secrets with prison terms of up to fifteen years and monetary fines up to US$10 million.[25] In 2002 the U.S. Attorney General strengthened the EEA by giving federal prosecutors more latitude in interpreting violations of the Act. In 2005 the United States adopted a new national counterintelligence strategy that signals a change in approach in addressing economic espionage. The new strategy shifts counterintelligence efforts from a reactive to proactive approach with more emphasis on protecting sensitive technologies. Law enforcement agencies such as the Federal Bureau of Investigation will devote more resources to defeat foreign intelligence operations within U.S. borders. The new strategy also promises to "ensure a level economic playing field for US businesses and industry." Whether that means that U.S. intelligence agencies will be tasked to directly assist individual companies or industries is unclear, but so far the official U.S. government position is that the U.S. intelligence community does not offer assistance to specific companies or firms.

Countries can and should take a more aggressive approach in combating industrial espionage. The primary goal should be to create awareness of the dangers of economic espionage in their business communities. Another top priority should be to train police officers, investigators, and prosecutors about industrial and economic espionage and how to interpret those laws. Customs officers and technology export control officers should work closer with the intelligence and law enforcement agencies to coordinate their enforcement efforts, and governments should work harder to convince companies that should they suffer losses from industrial or economic espionage, they should report the loss to law enforcement and assist prosecutors in the case.

Overall, the counterintelligence challenge is to discourage economic espionage activity while maintaining the integrity and health of a robust international trading system. Governments can work together to establish mutually acceptable intellectual property and patent conventions with the agreement to enforce them uniformly regardless if the violator is from their country or another country. One forum could be the World Trade Organization, which has attempted to create and enforce intellectual property conventions.

PROTECTING PRIVATE FIRMS FROM ECONOMIC ESPIONAGE

Companies need to be more aware of the dangers of economic espionage and take active measures to protect their proprietary information and inventions. This includes training all employees and executives about economic espionage and which procedures to follow. Individuals should take responsibility if they encounter acts of industrial espionage in their firms by reporting incidents to their firm's security officer and law enforcement.[26] Most firms do not realize that economic espionage is an enterprise-level threat. Prevention of economic espionage is the best solution for any firm's long-term financial health, but effective responses to industrial spying require that all employees are trained and prepared to challenge anyone who exhibits behaviors of an industrial spy.

Employees who participate in or speak at industry conferences or academic symposia should be aware that foreign governments and rival firms target individual experts for specialized knowledge. Collection methods include asking questions during casual conversations, dinner meetings in which more information can be obtained, and requests for previous articles or conference papers— or even working papers in progress. Invitations to deliver guest lectures and presentations, especially overseas, should be carefully considered for industrial espionage potential.

The company computer network is subject to compromise from within the company and from outside hacker attacks. Companies should perform regular security audits of computer file access logs and store critical information on servers with higher grade security. Remote access should be granted only to employees with a bona fide need, and additional security measures beyond passwords should be required. After an employee leaves the company, that person's company identification card should be returned and all computer access codes should be deactivated.

Executives traveling with laptop computers containing important company documents, marketing or product plans, budgets, client lists, and other information valuable to a competitor or foreign government should be especially careful. Laptop computers are frequently stolen and the information stored on the hard drive compromised. If industrial spies have access to an executive's hotel room, the hard drive can be copied when the owner is out of the room. Wireless Internet connections, while convenient, provide minimal security and industrial spies are able to capture transferred files and access passwords. One of the biggest vulnerabilities is the potential for industrial spies to load a monitoring program onto a firm's or executive's computer that sends screenshots and keystroke logs via the Internet. Data that is displayed on the screen and typed on the keyboard can be sent anywhere in the world that the industrial spy designates.

Companies should consider their security measures the first line of defense against industrial spies and economic espionage collectors. Too often executives rely on patent protections, joint venture partnerships, noncompetition agreements, and the goodwill of employees and business partners to protect the crown jewels of the company. Other executives assume that legal proceedings will provide an adequate remedy should the company fall victim to economic espionage. The unfortunate reality, however, is that most firms never discover that their proprietary data has been compromised and that foreign intelligence agencies and industrial spies are far beyond the reach of their country's law enforcement and legal system. The competitive environment of today's global economy dictates a much more self-reliant, proactive approach to securing intellectual property and proprietary information.

CONCLUSION

Economic espionage is an ancient practice that has evolved into a sophisticated science. Rarely practiced by individuals working alone anymore, economic espionage is now practiced by national governments, multinational firms, and groups of sophisticated industrial espionage professionals. Industrial and economic espionage has been growing in frequency and scope, and there is no current evidence that the current trend will change significantly. Several countries in particular are known for their economic espionage activities and, because of the high stakes in today's global economy, they run the risk of having trading partners and political allies turn against them. History is replete with examples and object lessons of economic espionage, and we would be wise to learn from past experience.

If continued development of new technologies and innovations is part of the future of the global economy, then business people and entrepreneurs will need to work harder to protect their inventions, companies will need to work harder to create secure workplaces and select trusted business partners, governments will need to work harder to protect their own economies and industries, and the global community will need to work harder to address the root causes of economic espionage. The challenges of the new millennia will require an unprecedented level of innovation and creativity. The threat posed by widespread economic espionage undermines the core motivation for turning ideas into innovations: that an inventor, company, or country can be rewarded for their innovations without fear of having that work stolen. If the global community can restore the incentives to innovate and raise the disincentives for engaging in economic espionage, then the global economy has a better chance of fulfilling its promise with innovations that will benefit every region around the world.

NOTES

1. Interagency OPSEC Support Staff, "Economic Intelligence Collection Directed Against the United States," *Operations Security Intelligence Threat Handbook* (1996), available at http://www.fas.org/irp/nsa/ioss/threat96/part05.htm.

2. A brief description of Europe's success in acquiring the secrets of manufacturing Chinese-style porcelain can be found on the NBH (National Security Office of the Republic of Hungary) website at http://www.nbh.hu/english/bmenu94.htm.

3. For a complete history of the theft of ideas and inventions, see Pat Choate, *Hot Property: The Stealing of Ideas in an Age of Globalization* (New York: Knopf, 2005).

4. For a complete treatise on Francis Cabot Lowell's exploits and analysis of current-day economic espionage, see John Fialka, *War by Other Means: Economic Espionage in America* (New York: Norton, 1997).

5. The Key Collectors, National Counterintelligence Executive Annual Report, 2004, p. 3, available at http://www.ncix.gov/publications/reports_speeches/reports/fecie_all/Index_fecie.html.

6. Appendix A, National Counterintelligence Executive Annual Report, 2004, p. 15, available at http://www.ncix.gov/publications/reports_speeches/reports/fecie_all/Index_fecie.html.

7. Ibid., p. x.

8. For example, the Federation of American Scientists (FAS) maintains websites dedicated to the world's intelligence and security agencies, including estimated budgets and their activities. See http://www.fas.org/irp/world/index.html.

9. Controller of the HMSO, the Queen's Printer of Acts of Parliament, Intelligence Services Act of 1994. See http://www.opsi.gov.uk/acts/acts1994/Ukpga_19940013_en _2.htm.

10. B. Raman, "Economic Intelligence," South Asia Analysis Group Papers, February 1999, available at http://www.saag.org/papers/paper50.html.

11. Nicholas Eftimiades, "Chinese Intelligence Operations," statement before the Joint Economic Committee, U.S. Congress, May 20, 1998.

12. By 1951 the National Security Council directed the CIA to determine the overall requirements for the collection and management of "foreign economic intelligence." See Philip Zelikow, "American Economic Intelligence," in *Eternal Vigilance? 50 Years of the CIA,* eds. Rhodri Jeffreys-Jones and Christopher Andrew (London: Frank Cass, 1997), p. 166.

13. The actual capabilities of the NSA's ECHELON system have been subject to intense debate. The Federation of American Scientists (FAS) maintains an ECHELON information website containing various reports on ECHELON, including those of the European Parliament Temporary Committee on the ECHELON Interception System. See http://www.fas.org/irp/program/process/echelon.htm.

14. The Final Report of the European Parliament Temporary Committee on the ECHELON Interception System is no longer available on the European Parliament website, but FAS has a PDF copy available at http://www.fas.org/irp/program/process/ rapport_echelon_en.pdf.

15. National Counterintelligence Executive, History of Counterintelligence, undated. See http://www.ncix.gov/history/CIReaderPlain/Vol4Chap4.pdf.

16. For the English-language version of the Japanese Secretariat of Intellectual Property Strategic Headquarters website, see http://www.ipr.go.jp/e_materials.html.

17. See http://www.ege.fr/.

18. See Minh A. Luong, "Espionage: A Real Threat," *Optimize* (October 2003), available at http://www.optimizemag.com/issue/024/security.htm.

19. Ibid.

20. There has been a steady increase in firms that conduct country-specific and specialized economic research. One of the best known is the Economist Intelligence Unit, which produces reports covering political and economic issues on over 200 countries. See http://eiu.com/.

21. For the purposes of this discussion, an *open economic system* is defined as an economic system that promotes transparent and accurate financial and operations reporting. A *closed economic system* is defined as an economic system in which financial and operations reporting is restricted, secret, or distorted as to become inaccurate. Closed economic systems also tend to be heavily influenced or controlled by the government.

22. Field researchers have discovered that economic reporting in closed economies is heavily influenced by political concerns or to mask inefficiencies or corruption.

23. National Counterintelligence Executive Annual Report, 2004, p. 6, available at http://www.ncix.gov/publications/reports_speeches/reports/fecie_all/Index_fecie.html.

24. This point is discussed briefly in John J. Fialka's *War by Other Means: Economic Espionage in America* (New York: Norton, 1997).

25. For the text of the EEA and other resources, visit the U.S. Department of Justice EEA resource website at http://www.cybercrime.gov/ipmanual/08ipma.htm.

26. Many acts of industrial espionage are caught by administrative assistants and support staff who stop and challenge individuals who search trash and recycling bins, who attempt to access computer equipment outside their normal work area, and who access sensitive company files without authorization.

11

THE POLITICS OF INTELLIGENCE POST-MORTEMS

MAX M. HOLLAND

AT LEAST FOURTEEN SEPARATE INVESTIGATIONS, by one count, have been conducted since 2001 into real and/or alleged failures by the U.S. intelligence community. These inquiries have ranged from quiet, internal probes mounted by inspectors general or consultants, to highly publicized congressional inquiries replete with partisan edges, to semi-public inquests conducted by presidentially sanctioned, bipartisan commissions. By early 2004, so many different bodies had claimed a piece of the post-mortem pie that Senator Pat Roberts (R-Kansas), chairman of the Select Committee on Intelligence, was moved to remark, "Is there anybody left down at [Central Intelligence Agency headquarters in] Langley doing their job? I think the only thing lacking is an independent commission to investigate all the independent commissions and investigations."[1]

Roberts's observation may have been tongue-in-cheek, but he actually suggested an interesting and neglected question: How objective, and useful, are intelligence post-mortems? Such analyses, particularly when produced by Congress or blue-ribbon commissions, are usually accorded an exalted status from the moment they are released. Frequently, they are considered a reliable account of what went wrong and why, if not an authoritative and objective one.

But should post-mortems be embraced so often at face value?[2] Or are they subject to personal/political/institutional pulls and tugs that can easily distort their findings? Admittedly, it can be argued that every congressional post-mortem is congenitally partisan, and that bipartisan special commissions are also not immune from political considerations, although their politics may be much more subtle.[3] In addition, such efforts are invariably confronted with the not insubstantial problem of gaining access to all the relevant information residing in the Executive Branch. Consequently, any baseline examination of this question would seem to require a series of post-mortems about a single episode, all of them conducted outside the public eye to minimize the influence of partisan politics, and with unfettered or at least roughly equal access to the pertinent information. Ideally, each of these post-mortems would also have been conducted by a different individual or panel, and intended for divergent audiences, in order to gauge the influence, if any, of these variables.

A series of post-mortems on the Cuban missile crisis, all conducted at various altitudes of the U.S. government in 1962–63, fits these parameters. The four post-mortems have actually received scant notice despite the vast literature about the October 1962 crisis.[4] The inattention probably stems from the fact that all of the post-mortems were undertaken in secret and were highly classified initially. Three have gradually become available since 1992, although one post-mortem remains inexplicably classified.[5]

What is striking was how the four ex post facto analyses varied in their findings and conclusions regarding the performance of the intelligence community in the run-up to the missile crisis, notwithstanding the sameness of the facts at issue.[6] The post-mortems were subject to extraneous influences that distorted their findings and even their presentation of fact. It mattered greatly who wrote the post-mortem, when, and for whom. The government's seeming inability to be consistently objective in 1962–63, in turn, is a sobering thought during a period when looking backwards is a growth industry.

CRITICAL ISSUES AFTER OCTOBER 1962

The public terms of the settlement all but guaranteed that the missile crisis would be perceived as a manifest success for the Kennedy administration and the intelligence community—one that the CIA sorely needed, still laboring, as it was, under the Bay of Pigs millstone.[7] Yet the Agency's margin of success was actually very narrow. Once all the facts were in, the missile crisis could be fairly called a "near-failure of American intelligence . . . of the first magnitude," as one scholar put it in 1974.[8] All intelligence estimates prepared prior to mid-October predicted that the Soviets were not likely to implant surface-to-surface missiles (SSMs) on Cuban soil. Of equal if not greater moment, the first hard evidence of the deployment was not in hand until October 15, more than a month after the SSMs had arrived and just days before the CIA would deem some of them operational.[9] That meant Soviet Premier Nikita Khrushchev had come surprisingly and uncomfortably close to accomplishing his strategic surprise.

Three shortcomings thus warranted close examination. One was estimative, namely, the months-long miscalculation of Moscow's intentions. Another was analytical, or the seeming failure to grasp indicators that suggested something other than a defensive build-up was taking place. The third shortfall concerned collection, or the seeming delay in acquiring hard evidence of the missile deployment.[10] These intelligence deficits were hinted at in newspaper stories as early as October 31, just after the acute phase of the crisis peaked. One immediate question, as an article in the *New York Times* put it, was whether intelligence "estimates [had been] tailored to fit top policy beliefs," or if administration officials had "reject[ed accurate] estimates as erroneous."[11] Another outstanding question, which would be variously dubbed the "intelligence," "picture," or "photo" gap, concerned why it had taken the administration so long to detect the deployment. "[T]here is general mystification about how the Russians could have built so many missile sites so quickly without warning," the *Times* article observed.

All four post-mortems (and many nonofficial ones) would address these primary questions. There was, however, a dramatic difference in the political consequences attached to these shortcomings. With respect to the misestimates and any analytical deficit, unless it could be shown that the White House had tried to influence the process or ignored evidence presented to it—in particular, the mistaken Special National Intelligence Estimate (SNIE) of September 19, 1962—only the intelligence community, rather than the administration, stood to be criticized.[12] The exact opposite was true with respect to the photo gap. In this case, the administration would surely bear the brunt of criticism, because it was the White House and State Department that had effectively ordered the CIA to attenuate U-2 aerial surveillance in mid-September.[13] Conceivably, the intelligence community might be criticized for acceding too easily to the administration's cautious overflight policy, dictated just as the first surface-to-surface missiles were actually arriving in Cuba. But much of the onus for the fact that "American intelligence . . . went blind for five crucial weeks" was going to fall on policy makers in the Kennedy administration—that is, if all the facts came out.[14]

Although the post-mortems were not exactly unanimous in their findings about the misestimates and analytical shortcomings, those deficits will not be addressed here.[15] For the purposes of this chapter the telling issue—the one that genuinely reveals the limits on and of post-mortems—was the serial treatment of the "photo gap" during the inquests conducted from late 1962 to early 1963. The photo gap represented a genuine political problem for the administration. It left the president vulnerable to the charge that he had been taken in by the Soviets' elaborate campaign of deception, to a point where the administration had even tried to foist a false sense of security onto the country.[16]

THE LEHMAN REPORT

Richard Lehman, a 13-year veteran of the Agency by 1962, held the formal title of assistant for special projects in the Office of Current Intelligence (OCI) at the time of the missile crisis. He had made his mark by successfully developing the President's Intelligence Checklist (PICL, pronounced "pickle") in the spring of 1961, a time when the CIA was particularly anxious to please the president.[17]

Allen Dulles's presentations had been considered somewhat patronizing and shallow, and simultaneously, the White House had felt overwhelmed with redundant and often tedious publications from various arms of the intelligence community.[18] The White House had informed OCI director Huntington Sheldon that his office had to come up with an entirely different way of presenting its information in order to gain the president's confidence.[19] It had fallen to Lehman, working under Sheldon, to write a concise, jargon-free, and reliable summary of everything the intelligence community thought the president should know. To the Agency's great relief, Kennedy responded with enthusiasm to the new document, and the PICL instantly became a CIA fixture, making Lehman's reputation in the process.[20]

On Saturday, October 27, 1962, the very day that would prove to be the turning point in the missile crisis, Russell Jack Smith, Sheldon's successor as OCI director, called Lehman into his office and said John McCone, the director of Central Intelligence (DCI), wanted an analysis of the Agency's performance to date.[21] Although the end of the crisis was seemingly not yet in sight, "McCone wanted to know how we had got[ten] there," Lehman later recalled, "what we [had done] right, what we [had done] wrong, and so on.[22] The timing, in retrospect, was quintessential McCone. With typical foresight, the business tycoon-turned DCI was already anticipating what he might need next. Once the November election passed, McCone fully anticipated the possibility of congressional hearings akin to the Pearl Harbor investigation launched by Congress in 1946.[23]

The DCI "pushed the button" so that Lehman had access to everything he wanted to see, and Lehman's research was aided greatly by the fact that McCone had a habit of "keeping meticulous memoranda for the record" of actions, meetings, and conversations.[24] Within four days Lehman had a manuscript of nearly 100 pages on the events leading up to the missiles' detection, including some long-hand annexes that were "for McCone's eyes only."[25] All told, the OCI officer worked on his report for $2\frac{1}{2}$ weeks, making one revision of his initial draft. The final product was in the same "warm, direct, somewhat Thoreau-like style," that had made the PICL so accessible and successful.[26] The report, like the PICL, was jargon-free and its tone candid.

With respect to the key operational shortcoming, Lehman correctly zeroed in on the events of September 10 as being absolutely "crucial to the record."[27] On that day, an extraordinary meeting had been convened at the White House by McGeorge Bundy, Kennedy's national security adviser, in concert with Secretary of State Dean Rusk. The two men, still smarting over criticism that they had not done enough to protect the president before and during the Bay of Pigs invasion, were anxious to prevent an embarrassing U-2 incident over Cuba now that surface-to-air missiles (SAMs) capable of downing the high-altitude surveillance aircraft were being installed all over the island.[28] Bundy and Rusk were deeply concerned that continuation of intrusive overflights would climax in a fatal incident that would put the president in a double bind: Abroad he would be criticized for violating sovereign airspace, while at home, conservative critics would claim the incident was a *casus belli* that provided the perfect opportunity to "do something" about the unprecedented Soviet military build-up on the Caribbean island.

Consequently, on September 10, Bundy had asked the members of the Committee on Overhead Reconnaissance (COMOR), the U.S. Intelligence Board (USIB) subcommittee that developed U-2 requirements for presidential approval, to attend a special White House meeting at 5:45 pm. In the absence of McCone, who was vacationing on the French Riviera, and under pressure from Bundy and Rusk, the COMOR agreed to attenuate the thorough, bi-monthly overflights of Cuba that had been the routine since early 1962. The next four U-2 flights would either pass quickly over discrete portions of the island or skirt it altogether. In this manner, the Kennedy administration degraded the one intelligence-gathering tool capable of delivering precisely the kind of dispositive information about possible missile deployments that the White House was insisting upon. Together with delays caused by predictably inclement weather, the net result was a dysfunctional intelligence regime in a dynamic situation.[29]

Lehman's blunt recollection of his post-mortem, forty-one years later, was that President Kennedy had "shot himself in the foot" by attenuating U-2 coverage over Cuba.[30] Needless to say, that was not how the OCI officer characterized his findings in 1962. Insofar as Lehman reached conclusions in a report not initially intended for wide circulation, they were careful and understated—more like observations than conclusions. The report was not exhaustive, but it did reflect the gist of what had happened in the weeks leading up to the discovery of the missile sites.[31] One of the senior officials known to have read the report was Dr. Herbert Scoville Jr., the deputy director of research (DD/R). The paper was an "excellent presentation of the facts insofar as [Scoville] knows them," although the DD/R differed regarding one significant aspect.[32]

Lehman noted, with respect to the photo gap, that the U-2 overflights permitted after September 10 were successful, inasmuch as they established new facets of the military build-up, including the complete pattern of SAM deployments throughout the island. Yet the U-2 missions "did not—and since they were designed to avoid SAM-defended areas, could not—detect the ballistic missile deployments then under way."[33] Lehman also observed, and quite correctly, that responsibility for the cautious overflight policy might not appear to be as clear-cut as it in fact was. Coming away from the September 10 meeting at the White House, COMOR members had understood, in no uncertain terms, that intrusive overflights, if proposed, would not be sanctioned by the Special Group Augmented (SGA) for submission to the president for final approval.[34] Still, the record showed that the president authorized everything the SGA had requested, and technically, the SGA had not turned down any written requests from the COMOR for more intrusive overflights. A critical condition imposed on the overflight regime for five weeks had not actually been captured on paper, and this fact would assume ever-larger significance in succeeding post-mortems.

THE IG (OR EARMAN) REPORT

Several days before Richard Lehman completed his report in mid-November, Jack Earman, the CIA's Inspector General (IG) since May, took up virtually the same task. Earman had been an Army lieutenant colonel prior to joining the Central Intelligence Group, forerunner to the Agency, in 1946. For most of his intelligence career, he had enjoyed a view from the top, serving from 1950 until 1962 as a special assistant to the DCI.[35] Analyzing the performance of the intelligence community prior to the discovery of the missiles would easily be the most important assignment he had undertaken since becoming IG six months earlier.

The reason why McCone asked for two internal post-mortems remains unclear, but there is no doubt that he did. Perhaps after his comparatively informal request to Lehman, McCone wanted a more structured or explicit effort. Inexplicably, Earman's report remains classified. Still, there is one extant, albeit redacted, memo that sheds light on Earman's treatment of the photo gap.

Earman finished a draft of his post-mortem on November 20, about one week after Lehman had put the final touches on his report. With respect to the photo gap, Earman's initial account apparently glossed over this operational deficit entirely, or otherwise treated it in a manner that roused McCone, perhaps by placing too much of the onus on the Agency. The DCI instructed Earman to take another look at the factors behind the decision to attenuate U-2 coverage in September.[36] In response, Earman described, in a November 26 memo, how he intended to incorporate McCone's criticism in a revised account.

> We have been told by several Agency officers that there was a widespread understanding in CIA that overflights of known SAM sites were forbidden by the Special Group [Augmented]. I believe this understanding stemmed from the desires which Secretary Rusk expressed at the 10 September 1962 meeting in Mr. Bundy's office which was not in fact a duly constituted meeting of the Special Group. However, the records do not reveal that CIA pressed for additional missions or changes in coverage of overflights approved for September 1962.[37]

Earman then went on, in the same memo, to recount the history of September overflights in some detail, and recited his new conclusion—one that would not be that different from Lehman's, although Earman's point was not as sharp. The net effect of the "extreme caution" after September 10, he wrote McCone, was that "the period of time during which the western part of Cuba was not covered by aerial photography was greatly lengthened."[38] The precise wording of his finding, Earman wrote, would be "[t]hat extreme caution with regard to U-2 flights following the incidents in Sakhalin and China affected the planning of Cuban reconnaissance overflights during [September]."[39]

Thus, McCone essentially put the Lehman and IG reports into consonance with one another on the reasons for the photo gap.[40] Neither of these internal post-mortems attempted to shift the entire responsibility onto the State

Department and/or White House for the deficit in coverage. More than anything, they were simply candid about the fact that estimative and analytical errors, together with the administration's overweening concern about an international incident, had led to a significant degradation of dispositive intelligence-gathering precisely during the period when the first offensive missiles were being maneuvered into place.

THE USIB (OR DCI'S) REPORT

On November 14, the same day Lehman turned in his report to McCone, Dr. James Killian, chairman of the President's Foreign Intelligence Advisory Board (PFIAB), asked the CIA to produce an "all-source, all-agency" review. [41] Killian requested that this survey of the community's performance include all intelligence activities up until the discovery of offensive missiles on October 14, and for the seven days afterwards, ending with President Kennedy's address to the nation on Cuba. Killian further requested that the post-mortem be submitted in time for the PFIAB's next meeting on December 7, 1962.[42]

The PFIAB, an elite, ostensibly nonpartisan panel established by President Eisenhower in 1956, was composed of experienced U.S. officials currently outside the government, augmented by some of the best scientists in the nation.[43] Its purpose was to advise the president directly on all matters concerning U.S. intelligence, from technical collection to counterintelligence. President Kennedy had all but ignored the advisory panel as an unnecessary, bureaucratic impediment very early in his administration, only to revive it hastily after the Bay of Pigs debacle. Thus, PFIAB's standing as one of the few external overseers of the intelligence community, along with its access to the president, guaranteed that the stakes in the third post-mortem would be very high.

Wearing what he called his "DCI hat," McCone transmitted Killian's request to the USIB the very next day.[44] This interagency body, in existence since 1958, represented the pinnacle of the intelligence community at the time, counting among its principal members the CIA, Defense Intelligence Agency (DIA), National Security Agency (NSA), and the State Department's Bureau of Intelligence and Research (INR).[45] The USIB post-mortem would thus not bear the CIA's imprimatur alone, but represent the coordinated judgment of the intelligence community, just as most of the community had been engaged in the intelligence coverage prior to the missiles' discovery.[46] To prepare the report, the USIB immediately appointed a steering committee composed of McCone and several other USIB principals: Roger Hilsman, director of INR; Lieutenant General Marshall "Pat" Carter, deputy director of the CIA; Lieutenant General Joseph Carroll, director of the DIA; and Lieutenant General Gordon Blake, director of the NSA. Simultaneously, a working group was established inside the CIA to do the actual research, analysis, and drafting of the post-mortem, with each of the principal intelligence agencies permitted to assign one officer to this subcommittee.

McCone's choice for chairman of the working group was Jack Earman, the CIA's IG, who was, of course, six days away from wrapping up his own report.[47] In one sense, this third post-mortem would simply be an extension of the analysis Earman was already deeply engaged in. Yet it also differed in two enormous respects. The USIB post-mortem would be conducted with the active participation of intelligence chiefs and officers with direct stakes in the findings, and these same drafters (apart from Earman) would be, in effect, examining their own performance.

Not surprisingly, perhaps, and unlike the first two internal post-mortems, this study instantly evoked wariness among some of the offices that stood to be closely scrutinized. A day before Killian formally submitted the PFIAB request, Dr. Scoville, the head of the CIA directorate that contained the Office of Special Activities (OSA), which actually operated the CIA's U-2s, made the following announcement to his staff, as recorded by an assistant.

> An inquiry would be made into the intelligence coverage and reporting of the missile build-up in Cuba and [Scoville] said that a post-mortem from the standpoint of how more timely and precise intelligence might have been achieved would be a good idea. His fear was that there might be some buckpassing and he wanted OSA to review carefully all factors leading up to the 14 October date (when missiles were actually discovered), taking into account all requirements, COMOR actions, Special Group actions, weather factors, etc.[48]

Scoville's remark about "buckpassing" was almost certainly a reference to the operational deficit in U-2 coverage. The DD/R was apparently anticipating the distinct possibility that some parties represented on the USIB might be inclined to obfuscate the factors that created the photo gap, if not place the onus for the deficit on the CIA in general and his directorate specifically.

Scoville's concern was shared at other levels, including by James Reber, the COMOR chairman. After experiencing two post-mortems already, Reber had considerable doubt about the "validity of people's memories[,] as they unintentionally embroidered the facts."[49] No one, of course, knew better than Reber how the photo gap had come about; he had attended the extraordinary September 10 meeting at the White House when McGeorge Bundy made the president's wishes directly known.[50] Reber also advised Scoville that the CIA representative on COMOR was "exercised because he felt that COMOR performance in the Cuban situation was not being adequately defended."[51] Reber himself was still sanguine about the USIB post-mortem, probably because Jack Earman was in charge of writing up what was by now a supposedly well-established chronology. Reber had read the IG report to the DCI, which he thought was excellent; parts of this earlier post-mortem might even be incorporated in toto, or so Reber believed.

But a problem with establishing the facts soon surfaced. The officers seconded to the working group had been tasked with making sure that their respective agencies provided all relevant information, and accordingly, an eight-page questionnaire had been submitted to every IC entity, with responses and documentation due back by November 23. As the questionnaires started to trickle in, however, it became apparent that not everything of import was fully reflected in the written record.[52] Some significant "happenings...were not recorded except in memory," because few, if any, officials and officers were as diligent as McCone was in jotting down detailed descriptions of key encounters.[53] And nowhere was this lack of documentation more telling than with respect to the photo gap, as Lehman had been the first to point out. The September 10 decision to degrade overflights was imperfectly reflected in the written record, and the documentation that did exist left the implication that the CIA had not been very exercised by this limitation on overflights imposed from the White House.[54] No one in the CIA seemed to have energetically pressed for additional missions or changes in coverage, according to the written record, until the DCI himself made the case on October 4. Consequently, it could easily be made to appear as if the Agency got exactly the operational coverage that it had asked for.[55]

The relative paucity of contemporary documentation might have been less of a problem but for the predispositions INR Director Roger Hilsman brought to the post-mortem. Hilsman had had a difficult relationship with the Agency from the outset of the Kennedy presidency, and he viewed the post-mortem as nothing less than a crucial engagement in his ongoing war with the CIA. Like many liberals in the administration, he had come into the government believing that the CIA had gotten so powerful during the 1950s that "it was running the foreign policy of the United States."[56] Allen Dulles had been a "de facto Secretary of State," and one of the tasks Hilsman had set for himself was "cutting [the Agency] back in power," and "sav[ing] the [State] Department from the CIA" by reducing the latter's alleged policy-making proclivities and overweening influence.[57] Hilsman regarded the CIA as a mortal rival in the intelligence sphere because the Agency wanted "anything that smack[ed] at all of intelligence interpretation to be theirs."[58] Rank-and-file CIA officers who dealt with Hilsman regarded him as "often wrong, but never in doubt," an able person with a marked propensity for the "perpendicular pronoun" who was always seeking to insert himself in the bureaucratic process.[59] Others pegged the INR director as more of an ambitious sycophant than anything else, interested primarily in ingratiating himself with the Kennedy brothers whenever possible.

One illustration of the antagonistic relationship was an incident that allegedly occurred on October 16, the very day President Kennedy learned of the missiles in Cuba. The scuttlebutt around the Agency that day was that as Hilsman was preparing to see Dean Rusk that morning, the INR director remarked that he was going to have to report a "tremendous failure on the part of U.S. intelligence."[60] When DDCI Marshall Carter called Hilsman and asked him about the reported comment, Hilsman averred that he didn't recall saying anything of the kind—only that he, along with almost everyone else in the administration, did not expect the Soviet deployment.[61]

Coming from his perspective, Hilsman was intent on using his position on the steering committee to scrub the USIB post-mortem for anything that seemed like the CIA patting itself on the back at the expense of the State Department, and the administration in general. This goal was all the more urgent, of course, because only McCone, from among all the president's advisers, had anticipated the emplacement of offensive missiles and distinctly warned Kennedy of that possibility. The aftermath of the crisis thus promised to afford McCone an opportunity to "manipulate [the missile crisis] to his advantage," and strengthen the DCI's and CIA's position within the administration—this, at the very time when Hilsman was intent on "cutting them back in power."[62]

Although contemporaneous documentation about the internal wrangling over the USIB post-mortem is not extant, there is little doubt that extended negotiations over its language took place; that Hilsman was at the center of these disputes; and that much of the contention revolved around how to depict the "extreme caution" that degraded U-2 coverage from September 10 until mid-October, and the consequences that flowed from that policy.[63] Much of the evidence for these inferences comes from McCone's reaction to the first draft of the USIB post-mortem as submitted by Earman in mid-December. Typically, the DCI minced no words in his December 17 response. ". . . your brief treatment [of the September 10 decision] gives me the impression that we are obscuring the fact that there were policy decisions based on concern over . . . a U-2 incident," he wrote Earman.[64] Indeed, the DCI felt the draft did not answer many questions he still had about the pivotal September 10 decision that had been reached in his absence. "I do not have an explanation of this and I'd like to know where this change in procedure came from, by whose order, and under what circumstances," McCone wrote.[65]

The USIB working group went through three drafts before a version was even deemed fit for review by the steering committee on December 5. By that time, it was obvious the report would not be submitted to PFIAB by December 7, as requested by Killian, so the steering committee gave PFIAB an oral progress report on December 6 and 7, after which McCone promised to have a final, coordinated draft in no more than two weeks. It then took a flurry of meetings of both the steering committee and working group before a "final" draft—the sixth—was agreed to on December 23—although three days later, Hilsman expressed reservations yet again.[66] By that time, McGeorge Bundy had gotten wind that the post-mortem was nearing completion, and given his role in attenuating the U-2 coverage, he requested that a copy be delivered immediately to him in Boston, where he was spending the Christmas holiday. Bundy also insisted that no copies be distributed outside of the government until he had had an opportunity to read the politically sensitive document, and that included no copies to the PFIAB.[67] The matter would finally come to an end on January 3, 1963, when the USIB steering committee agreed that no further amendments were necessary and McCone was authorized to inform Killian that the seventh draft of the report was, in fact, the final one. The post-mortem was officially submitted to the PFIAB on January 7.

Apart from McCone's initial reaction, and the arduous negotiations that went into the numerous drafts, the best insight into Hilsman's influence on the USIB process is gained by comparing the USIB post-mortem to his controversial 1967 memoir, *To Move a Nation*.[68] Juxtaposing the two, if nothing else, starkly reveals the not-so-hidden agenda Hilsman brought to USIB deliberations over the post-mortem's language. Hilsman's position was that of loyalty to the administration rather than the facts, with the goal of insulating the administration from criticism for having degraded the one intelligence-gathering tool that was indispensable.

In his memoir Hilsman devoted an entire chapter to the aftermath of the missile crisis, which he entitled "The Intelligence Post-Mortem: Who Erred?" Specifically referring to the USIB report, Hilsman termed it one of "two attempts by insiders to allege that policy [had] interfered with intelligence."[69] McCone instituted the study, Hilsman wrote (incorrectly),

immediately after the crisis to determine if the missiles would have been discovered sooner if the Secretary of State had not requested on September 10 that the next [U-2] flight be broken up into four separate flights. For a while there was some uneasiness at the possibility of some real alley fighting developing. But it was not difficult to show, first, that any delay caused by making four flights instead of one was negligible; and, second, that there had never been a turndown of any flight that intelligence had asked to be approved, but that on the contrary both the White House and the State Department had actually pushed for more intelligence all along.[70]

In an adjacent passage Hilsman flatly asserted that there was "no evidence of any attempt by the policy-makers to suppress information or to hamper intelligence-gathering activities. No request from the intelligence community to fly a U-2 over Cuba was ever refused."[71]

It was disingenuous to claim, of course, that the September 10 decision had not markedly interfered with the collection of hard intelligence, not to mention dishonest to pretend as if the extraordinary session at the White House had never happened. At the same time, and despite these denials, Hilsman tacitly admitted that there had been some kind of delay in discovering the missile sites. But that, still, was a nonissue, because it was reasonable to believe that the U-2 flight on October 14 "found the missiles at just about the earliest possible date."[72] Ultimately, Hilsman concluded that the discovery of the missiles had to be "marked down as a victory of a very high order" for American intelligence, though "it had also been—in one sense at least—a little lazy."[73]

As but one member of the steering committee, Hilsman could not dictate the USIB post-mortem, much less unilaterally impose his peculiar views about what had happened. Yet when Hilsman's 1967 account and the USIB report are juxtaposed, it seems clear that his preferred conclusions carried the day. The issue of the photo gap—by any measure the most important operational shortcoming in the run-up to the missile crisis—was not even raised until page 69 of the ninety-page post-mortem, when the September 10 "special meeting" was mentioned for the first time. Jack Earman was apparently able to wring only one concession: that the CIA at least believed the overflight regime had been degraded in mid-September.

> There was a difference of opinion in the 4 October Special Group (Augmented) meeting on whether a restriction had been imposed on overflying known SA-2 sites. Because of the skimpiness of records, it cannot now be discovered whether there was or was not such a restriction. It is clear, however, that the operational elements were under the impression that such a restriction did exist. Evidence of this belief can be found in the reference to such a restriction by the DCI at the 4 October meeting of the Special Group (Augmented).[74]

Besides obfuscating responsibility for attenuation of photo coverage, the USIB post-mortem concluded, almost like Hilsman would four years later, that the photo gap had not mattered even if it existed. "The procedures adopted in September delayed photographic intelligence," stated the USIB report in its con-clusionary chapter, "but this delay was not critical, because photography ob-tained prior to about 17 October would not have been sufficient to warrant action of a type which would require support from Western Hemisphere or NATO allies."[75] In this regard the INR director probably did not have to be so per-suasive, as all the USIB members had a vested interest in propagating this con-clusion, or something close to it, to anyone outside the immediate intelligence community, even the PFIAB. Not uncoincidentally, perhaps, this position was nearly identical to the administration's public posture, which had been roughly hammered out in the midst of the crisis.[76] This finding was in decided contrast to the Lehman and IG reports, which made no such claim and, indeed, suggested the opposite.[77] Presumably, during the deliberations over the USIB report, Earman probably maintained that the post-mortem would be remiss if it did not some-where state that the September 10 change in the surveillance regime resulted in a delay of photo coverage. In turn, Hilsman argued vigorously, in all likelihood, for qualifying language that simultaneously rendered this operational deficit meaningless, if it had to be admitted at all. The bottom line was a compromise finding notable for being acceptable to both sides and the administration's public position, rather than the truth of the matter.[78]

Overall, the USIB report, the only coordinated post-mortem that would be produced, was a carefully structured and detailed description of the intelligence accumulated and evaluated on a communitywide basis in the run-up to the missile crisis.[79] It was much more systematic and workmanlike than Lehman's analysis, the tone of which was informal. Its key conclusion, which it shared with its predecessors—no doubt because it was incontrovertible and not controversial—was that the IC's "analytic effort, using a variety of sources, identified each of the major weapons systems introduced into Cuba before the system reached opera-tional capability."[80] But in contrast to the Lehman and IG reports, the USIB report has to be considered as a negotiated (if not compromised) post-mortem, the product of a hard bargain between competing and conflicted government elements that was, ultimately, not even satisfying to those same elements.[81] The USIB report tried hard to give the appearance of presenting the facts in a plain, unvarnished manner. But whenever a problematic fact reared its head, the language was massaged until the post-mortem was acceptable to vested interests—bureaucratic as well as those of the incumbent administration.

THE PFIAB POST-MORTEM

The USIB report, despite the intense bargaining over the precise language of its findings, was never viewed as an end in itself by PFIAB members, only a starting point. Mindful of their direct access to the Oval Office, a privilege they jealously guarded, the board always intended to gather additional information as necessary and make its own evaluation for submission to the president.[82] From the perspective of PFIAB's nine members, the USIB's coordinated post-mortem was likely to represent a "best foot forward" approach by the intelligence community and its titular head, the DCI, if only because its drafters were examining their own performance.[83] Any and all estimative, analytical, or operational deficits were likely to be downplayed, buried, or rationalized into insignificance.

But PFIAB members were also inclined to be skeptical because relations with John McCone—at least from PFIAB's perspective—were uneasy at best. DCIs, it seemed, tended not to like having an independent board looking over their shoulder, "encroaching on their prerogatives."[84] In this regard, McCone was scarcely different from Allen Dulles. Upon taking over as DCI in November 1961, McCone had allegedly attempted to alter PFIAB's standing so that it reported to him rather than the president. The panel members had not forgotten this alleged "early run" at PFIAB's authority, and relations with the conservative and outspoken DCI were, as a consequence, fairly tense.[85]

McCone's relationships with Dr. Killian and Clark Clifford, the two most important PFIAB members, further complicated matters. A former president of MIT, Killian had had several bruising run-ins with McCone in the late 1950s, while McCone was chairman of the Atomic Energy Commission and Killian was both President Eisenhower's first science advisor and, simultaneously, chairman of both PFIAB and the President's Science Advisory Committee. McCone was of the general opinion that "scientists cause trouble" in the federal government because they tended to inject themselves into political matters rather than sticking to what they knew and were supposed to be do, which was provide the best technical advice.[86] Killian, naturally, took exception to McCone's attitude. After President Kennedy had announced McCone's appointment as the new DCI in September 1961, the *Washington Post* reported that Killian "was so out of sorts over the appointment that he threatened to resign as [PFIAB's] chairman."[87] Although Killian promptly denied the story, it was nonetheless true.[88]

Yet the McCone-Killian relationship wasn't even the most problematic. If McCone could be said to have a true nemesis on the board, it was Clark Clifford, the archetypal Washington lawyer, and a skilled, consummate, and partisan defender of the president's interests, specifically, and the Democratic Party's, in general. Clifford styled himself as having been "present at the creation" of the postwar intelligence community, although he probably exaggerated his role in drafting the legislation that established the CIA.[89] Still, the experience was sufficient for him to consider himself something of an expert on intelligence matters. Moreover, in the wholesale reshuffling of the administration that occurred after the Bay of Pigs debacle, President Kennedy reportedly offered Clifford the DCI's job, only to have Clifford decline the honor of succeeding Allen Dulles.[90] Thus, Clifford operated from a position where he was confident of his expertise and knew he was Kennedy's preferred choice for DCI, and he did not regard the notoriously inflexible McCone as a very good second choice. McCone's standing as a rich Republican businessman who had served Eisenhower and remained close to Richard Nixon, plus McCone's reputation as a "deeply ideological anticommunist," also inclined Clifford to be critical and wary of the DCI.[91] Just as McCone was taking up the reins at the CIA in November 1961, Clifford, at the president's request, had submitted a briefing memo outlining what Clifford thought would be the most important points to keep in mind as Kennedy began the relationship with his new DCI.[92] That only underscored Clifford's sense of having a direct, and perhaps even superior, line of communication with the president.

Clifford apparently agreed to serve on PFIAB after declining the DCI post, once Kennedy reconstituted the board after the Bay of Pigs debacle. Since PFIAB's inception in 1956, its appointees had been selected largely for their scientific knowledge or foreign policy expertise on a bipartisan basis. Clifford, a "veteran of Democratic politics, [who] is one of the capital's most widely sought attorneys, and a trusted private adviser to the President," represented something of a departure.[93] Clifford's appointment was the first time someone known largely for being a "Washington fixer" had ever been appointed to the board; moreover, he was appointed with the additional understanding that he would be Killian's successor as chairman in just a few months.

Besides not appreciating, along with his colleagues, McCone's alleged effort to cut off PFIAB's direct access to the president, Clifford also took exception to McCone's outspokenness as director of Central Intelligence. McCone "did not submerge his strong personal opinions inside official assessments in the manner of most senior intelligence officers," Clifford would later write, not knowing or impervious to the fact that President Kennedy had expressly asked McCone to express his policy views.[94] And the fact that the press, after the missile crisis, was hailing McCone for being the only senior official to predict that the Soviets would implant missiles in Cuba displeased Clifford greatly.[95] The friction between the suave lawyer and blunt, engineer-turned-tycoon would reach, in Clifford's words, a "crescendo" during the missile crisis post-mortem.[96]

Although the record of PFIAB's deliberations is spotty, there are some extant and revealing primary documents, and the one panel member who was almost certainly the most influential in shaping the post-mortem—Clark Clifford— fortunately wrote about the episode in some detail. When PFIAB began contemplating a review of the intelligence aspects of the crisis, "we were faced with a dilemma," according to Clifford. "We did not wish to criticize the President, who had handled the crisis brilliantly once the Soviet missiles had been positively identified by American intelligence," wrote Clifford, "but we felt the length of time it had taken to discover the missiles was dangerously and inexcusably long. We were particularly disturbed that there had been no overflights of Cuba between August 29 and October 14 despite public charges that offensive missiles were being installed."[97] Thus, if Clifford's memoir is taken at face value, it seems that he and the other PFIAB members correctly identified the key operational deficit early on, and instantly recognized its political sensitivity.[98]

PFIAB's own deliberations began in earnest in early December, when McCone appeared to discuss the mechanics of the USIB post-mortem and answer the panel's questions in person. In tow were Lieutenant General Carroll, director of the DIA; Lyman Kirkpatrick, executive director of the CIA (and the DCI's liaison with PFIAB); and Richard Helms, the Agency's deputy director of Plans (DD/P). McCone had voluntarily provided PFIAB with a copy of the Lehman report, and had also mentioned the existence of the IG report.[99] After briefing the panel on the scope and progress of the USIB report, McCone said he thought it would be a good idea for PFIAB to have its own special briefing on clandestine operations in Cuba in order to see precisely how they had contributed to the intelligence mosaic leading to the missiles' discovery. The panel then heard from Richard Helms about the human intelligence that had been provided, particularly by agents recruited under MONGOOSE, one of whom had been instrumental in pinpointing the trapezoid-shaped location where the first SSMs were discovered.[100]

After Helms's presentation ended, and in response to questions, McCone mounted a stout defense of the intelligence community's performance, minimizing the estimative, analytical, and operational deficits. It was akin to an "all's well that ends well" perspective. At one juncture, former diplomat Robert Murphy asked if "any handicaps had been placed on the collection of intelligence about Cuba."[101] Here, if the DCI wanted it, was an opening to apportion responsibility for the degradation of U-2 surveillance in September. But McCone, acting as an administration loyalist, eschewed the opportunity to criticize policy makers for putting blinders on the CIA. "No," answered McCone, before he briefly recounted the establishment of a CIA agent network recruited under MONGOOSE.[102]

At this juncture the questioning became more pointed. Clark Clifford brought up the issue of McCone's personal estimate regarding Soviet offensive missiles, first enunciated in August, and also asked about distribution of the so-called honeymoon cables.[103] "Then these telegrams had not gone anywhere outside

CIA?" asked PFIAB member Gordon Gray. "No," replied McCone, explaining that "it would have been wrong to go over the head" of Marshall Carter, the acting DCI, by disseminating these cables to the principal members of the USIB.[104] Frank Pace, another PFIAB member, then asked point-blank the critical question: How much earlier than mid-October might the U-2 have discovered offensive missiles? McCone responded that uncovering the missiles was conceivable from about September 20 onwards but claimed that nothing clinching the case was likely until mid-October. Besides demonstrating his loyalty in private to the administration's public position, the DCI was foreshadowing the negotiated finding of the USIB post-mortem.

Throughout the grilling, McCone replied in a very measured way and recited the facts mostly without characterizing them. He referred briefly to the "timidity" and "attitude of caution" that existed in September but the relaxed attitude about the consequences that existed now—a posture at considerable odds with his actual position in late September/early October.[105] "There was nothing convincing" until the intelligence community conducted the mid-October aerial surveillance, McCone asserted.[106] But that perspective was not very persuasive to the PFIAB members. They probably regarded it as evidence of McCone's belief that any post-mortem conducted by PFIAB (if not the board itself) was more of a hindrance than a help. McCone's appearance primarily served to harden PFIAB's inclination to take a close look at the USIB's post-mortem.

Even before the final draft arrived, PFIAB began drawing up its own lessons learned, with Clark Clifford acting as the prosecuting attorney. Clifford argued, with apparent persuasiveness, that not only had the CIA been remiss in its photo coverage, but McCone had been derelict for failing to push the intelligence community into "making a more intensive effort to corroborate his [own] beliefs" about the likelihood of a Soviet deployment.[107] Clifford intimated, moreover, that McCone had put his personal life before his official duties by being absent from Washington during a crucial period. "From France [McCone] sent strongly worded personal messages—the so-called honeymoon cables . . . but he still did nothing to speed up the pace of air reconnaissance," as Clifford later put it.[108] This was a tendentious rendering of the situation that prevailed in Washington in late August. At that time McCone's hunch was based primarily on intuition and was otherwise unsupported except by refugee reports that had proven to be uniformly mistaken.[109]

Once the PFIAB received the USIB report on December 26, weeks later than originally promised, the board met immediately to discuss the coordinated findings. McCone personally presented the USIB post-mortem, but after the DCI left, Clifford declared himself profoundly unimpressed. As he later wrote, Clifford bluntly labeled the report a "snow job" because of the way it depicted the photo gap, and criticized the excessive "delicacy" with which the issue of U-2 overflights had been addressed.[110] "Everyone was pointing the finger at someone else," Clifford wrote, although presumably, sorting out who did what, when, and why, was precisely the point of any post-mortem.[111] To a degree, of course, the urbane Washington lawyer was right. The USIB report was a "snow job," attributable to the fact that it was a coordinated history drafted by the same offices that had collected and evaluated the intelligence. Still, the direction in which the post-mortem was bent insulated the Kennedy administration from criticism, at least as much, if not more than, it benefited the intelligence community.

Clifford then posed a direct question to his colleagues: If a similar situation were to be encountered again, would anyone on PFIAB argue that the president had been well served by the intelligence community? There was silence—until Clifford answered his own question. The successful outcome of the missile crisis should not "lull us into a false sense of comfort," he argued.[112] And then Clifford openly inserted a political consideration into PFIAB's deliberations. The Republican National Committee had leveled a "preposterous" allegation against President Kennedy, namely, that he had deliberately withheld and/or manipulated information about the missiles in order to gain a political advantage.[113] The facts proved otherwise, said Clifford, and had to be brought out in PFIAB's own report because the intelligence community was obviously unwilling to face up to its own shortcomings. "The delays had been caused by decisions made *within the intelligence community* for internal reasons," declared Clifford (emphasis added).[114] The outstanding deficit was "the state of mind within the intelligence community . . . which rejected the possibility of offensive missiles in Cuba." And he was concerned that the president "would be hurt by the CIA's efforts to protect itself."[115] In sum, Clifford was aiming to shift the entire onus for the photo gap onto the CIA, if not a Republican DCI.

Despite the sharp questions from PFIAB members, McCone had left the meeting on December 28 apparently unaware of the depth of their dissatisfaction with the USIB report. When he met with the president on January 7, the subject of the PFIAB study came up, an interim version of which had been submitted to the White House on December 28.[116] McCone thought it was good insofar as it went, though it was mostly prescriptive. PFIAB's findings about the community's pre-October performance had yet to be incorporated. McCone nonetheless used the occasion to express his own unvarnished beliefs to Kennedy directly for perhaps the first time. The IC had done a good job but "could have done better," observed McCone.[117] The principal errors were, in order, the photo gap; the estimative deficit; and last, the failure to analyze correctly some indicators that might, in retrospect, have challenged the estimate. With respect to the photo gap, McCone was careful to spread responsibility around, noting that it was due to "timidity throughout the government."[118] In response, the president said little but did express sympathy for the estimators' plight. In effect, Kennedy adopted what would be Sherman Kent's formulation: that the Soviets' estimate (if there in fact was one) of the U.S. reaction to the missile deployment was the most flawed estimate of them all.[119]

PFIAB, meanwhile, pressed ahead with its study. According to Clifford's memoir, this involved gaining access to material and information that went beyond the post-mortems and briefings McCone had made available. When

McCone allegedly refused to provide more materials, Clifford declared the DCI's obstructionism intolerable. "If McCone was going to set himself up as a censor of what the PFIAB could and could not see," Clifford later wrote, "then [PFIAB's] functions and rationale would be destroyed."[120] Clifford threatened to resign, and when President Kennedy heard about the dispute he reportedly instructed McCone to be forthcoming. Even so, from Clifford's perspective "a breach had been opened with McCone" that would remain until the end of his tenure.[121]

On February 4, 1963, PFIAB submitted its final report to the White House, and little more than a month later the findings were presented directly to President Kennedy during a seventy-nine-minute meeting on March 9.[122] The PFIAB post-mortem read more like a lawyer's brief than a disinterested analysis, something the president could use to rebut the Republicans' uphill efforts to attack his handling of the crisis. PFIAB concluded that the intelligence community achieved a very high level of performance between October 14 and 22, 1962, but the same could not be said of the pre-October 14 period. The "Soviet move came dangerously close to success," noted the report, primarily because there was not, within the intelligence community, a "focused sense of urgency or alarm which might well have stimulated a greater effort."[123] Specifically, PFIAB found the community's effort deficient in two areas: the acquisition of intelligence via human assets in Cuba and the failure to make "full use" of aerial surveillance, particularly during September and October.[124] Responsibility for the photo gap was put squarely in the lap of the intelligence community, which failed "as a whole to propose to the Special Group U-2 reconnaissance missions on a scale commensurate with the nature and intensity of the Soviet activity in Cuba.... [especially] in view of the inadequacy of clandestine agent resources."[125]

PFIAB's analysis, markedly influenced by Clifford, was almost transparent in its effort to absolve policy makers from any responsibility for the photo gap. The longest paragraph in PFIAB's ten-page post-mortem pertained to the September 10 meeting. Owing to the paucity of records, the board claimed it was "impossible to determine whether or not there was a restriction" that prevented intrusive overflights of Cuba, although PFIAB did allow that the CIA was clearly under the "impression" that such an injunction was imposed.[126] But rather than apportion the consequences of the photo gap in a fair manner, PFIAB only found fault with the intelligence community. In what was becoming a familiar litany, the president "granted authorization for all U-2 flights which were recommended to him by ... the Special Group [Augmented]."[127] The SGA "was not made fully aware of the delaying effects on the acquisition of aerial intelligence" that stemmed from the September 10 decision, and the SGA "should have been informed of the factors operating to delay the four-flight coverage, and given an opportunity to reconsider the advisability of a mission over the critical target areas urgently requiring surveillance."[128] Such a judgment betrayed definite bias and one-sided critique. As everyone involved in the U-2 program knew, one of the fundamental ways the Special Group and the president imposed managerial discipline on the overflight regime was to insist upon completion of approved flights before they would entertain new requests.[129]

McCone was not one to let PFIAB's post-mortem go unchallenged; in fact, he was seething about the criticism, which he apparently considered akin to Monday-morning quarterbacking.[130] In a February 28 memorandum to President Kennedy he defended the performance of the intelligence community, especially with regard to the photo gap. Somewhat ironically, doing so put McCone in the position of at least partly defending the timid overflight policy he had so vigorously lobbied against the previous fall. The "reluctance or timidity" to direct U-2 flights over Cuba was understandable in context, McCone now contended, given the severe international criticism of such flights dating back to the Francis Gary Powers incident in May 1960.[131] Admittedly, the intelligence community had failed to communicate adequately the consequences that flowed from the September 10 decision and the urgency of resuming more intrusive overflights, noted McCone.[132] Anyone reaching such a conclusion, however, "must first carefully weigh the serious considerations that enter into a decision to overfly denied territory," the DCI observed.[133] McCone reminded the president that he was not an intelligence careerist determined to defend the community's performance against any and all criticism, and that his own estimate had differed from that of all the experts. Still, after examining the community's performance with a "critical eye," he believed the coordinated USIB post-mortem "reflect[ed] a more reasonable judgment of the performance of the intelligence community in the six months' period prior to the October crisis" than PFIAB's findings.[134] The USIB post-mortem was certainly more congruent with the administration's public position than the PFIAB report, though McCone left this unsaid.

The dispute over whose post-mortem was more accurate did not end there. PFIAB responded to McCone's rejoinder, and the board's deliberations continued into March 1963, according to Clifford's memoir. In what was apparently the last meeting on the subject, former Ambassador Robert Murphy, speaking for the panel, told McCone that PFIAB "had reached the conclusion that there had been a significant intelligence failure," and that it was their duty to report as much to the president. McCone, according to Clifford, responded angrily, and stated that Murphy was "misstating the facts."[135]

PFIAB's "important" post-mortem cast a jaundiced eye on the intelligence community's performance.[136] That was fair enough, especially in light of the coordinated USIB report, which tended to explain (and implicitly excuse) all the deficits.[137] Yet it is impossible to separate out the harshness of PFIAB's findings from the fact that many board members were "averse" to John McCone, as Robert Kennedy would put it in 1964.[138] McCone "had made a lot of enemies," several of whom were on PFIAB, and this was an opportunity to strike back—or, at least, dim the luster of the Agency's achievement under McCone's stewardship.[139] Consequently, in its eagerness to tarnish the CIA's performance, and cut down McCone's newly won reputation for prescience, PFIAB erred in the other direction, taking the deficits out of the context in which they had occurred, as if the intelligence community operated in a vacuum, immune from the pressures or concerns of policy makers.[140] Such a perspective diminished the accuracy and usefulness of PFIAB's post-mortem, because when all was said and done, discovery of the missiles before they became operational was vital to a peaceful resolution of the crisis, and thus, represented the CIA's "finest hour" of the Cold War—according to almost everyone but PFIAB. In place of an objective and dispassionate report, the president's board produced a handy tool for rebutting Republican charges about the administration's performance, which certainly served what was Clifford's primary interest.[141]

About a month after PFIAB finished work on its post-mortem, Clifford was elevated, as planned, to chairmanship of the board.[142] The august *New York Times* thought so ill of Clifford's ascension in intelligence matters that it ran an editorial criticizing the appointment.[143] Clifford "has a brilliant mind," observed the *Times,* "but, as a long-time trouble-shooter for the Democratic party, he is inextricably associated with partisan politics. The selection is at best unfortunate. It is bound to give the impression that our intelligence activities will now be monitored—not by a chairman who is an expert in the field—but by one who is essentially a politician."[144] It is not known whether the *Times'* editorial writer knew about the raging internal dispute over PFIAB's critical post-mortem. If not, he was as prescient about Clifford's influence on PFIAB as McCone had been about the emplacement of Soviet missiles.[145]

CONCLUSION

Weeks after the missile crisis subsided, DD/I Ray Cline asked both McGeorge Bundy and Robert Kennedy how much the CIA's photo surveillance of October 14 was worth to the nation. Both responded that it fully justified all the CIA had cost the country since its inception in 1947.[146] None of the four classified post-mortems made this precise point, although they were certainly unanimous in believing that the CIA's discovery of the first missiles in mid-October was critical.

A close analysis of each post-mortem shows at least three of the four differed substantially on another crucial point: why the missiles' discovery was delayed, and who or what was responsible for that tardiness. The Lehman and IG reports, insofar as they are known, were in close agreement over the plain facts and their meaning. But as responsibility for an ex post facto analysis moved outside the confines of the CIA, both facts and their meaning became increasingly contested. The first result was a post-mortem that deliberately muddled the narrative of what had happened and why (the USIB account) and then a PFIAB report to the president that turned the story nearly upside down. Put another way, the analyses careened from one that simply recounted the somewhat messy, nontextbook manner in which the missiles had actually been discovered, to one that asserted the nation had in fact experienced a nearly catastrophic intelligence failure, owing solely to the CIA's dereliction of its responsibilities. The four post-mortems bring to mind Akira Kurosawa's film masterpiece *Rashômon*. When each one is examined closely, it cannot be separated from the person(s) who wrote it and the external or extraneous circumstances involved in its production.

What makes this finding all the more sobering is that this intense struggle over assessments, if not history itself, occurred completely behind the scenes, and over a crisis that was widely considered an unmitigated triumph for the incumbent administration. If there was so much disagreement and difficult bargaining over an intelligence success, it must be incomparably more difficult to reconcile competing interests when an intelligence failure is the subject of the inquiry. And conducting a post-mortem outside the intelligence community seems only to compound the problems inherent in producing objective history, as evinced by the contemporaneous findings of the Senate Preparedness Subcommittee, the only congressional panel to mount an investigation into intelligence aspects of the missile crisis. The subcommittee's 1963 report "examined this question [of an alleged photo gap] as thoroughly as possible and . . . found the allegations with respect to it to be *unfounded*" (emphasis added).[147]

For all their problems, post-mortem exercises would seem clearly desirable under controlled conditions. In fact, the argument could be made that one of the chief failings of the intelligence community as it existed until 2004 was that post-mortems occurred too irregularly, and on an ad hoc basis when they occurred at all. There was only one sustained effort to institutionalize a rigorous and systematic post-mortem program, and that occurred in the 1970s. For roughly two years, from late 1973 to late 1975, the DCI, together with the USIB, mounted a program that resulted in the production of seven post-mortems on a variety of topics. But the effort was soon abandoned after the unfortunate confluence of internal and external factors. Inside the community many officers opposed post-mortems on the grounds that "candid critical reviews" offered "at best, an unbalanced look at the condition of the profession and, at worst, [were] an unnecessary exercise in self-flagellation."[148] Externally, the House Select Committee on Intelligence (a.k.a. the Pike Committee) all but sounded the death knell for the program when it attempted to wield the post-mortems against the very community that had produced them.

In the absence of demanding standards and objective procedures for conducting post-mortems, the lesson from 1962–63 would seem to be that all such inquests should be viewed critically, and with the utmost caution. They can easily be as flawed as the intelligence product and process they purport to judge, if not more so. After all, not knowing the future at least imposes a certain degree of honesty. With the benefit of hindsight, everyone knows what side to be on.

NOTES

This article is adapted from one originally prepared for the *International Journal of Intelligence and CounterIntelligence*, and appears with gracious agreement of that journal's editor.

1. Chris Strohm, "Intelligence Chiefs Cite Advancements, Challenges," *Government Executive*, March 9, 2004.

2. Some post-mortems have been subject to immediate discount, most often when they were competing with a contemporaneous congressional probe. See, for example, public reaction to the *Report to the President by the Commission on CIA Activities Within the United States* (Washington, DC: U.S. Government Printing Office, 1975), a.k.a. the Rockefeller Commission, or the *Report of the President's Special Review Board* (Washington, DC: U.S. Government Printing Office, 1987), a.k.a. the Tower Commission.

3. For a recent work that explores the nature of several blue-ribbon panels, see Kenneth Kitts, *Presidential Commissions & National Security: The Politics of Damage Control* (Boulder, CO: Lynne Rienner, 2006).

4. A fifth, semi-public post-mortem was conducted by the Senate Armed Services' Subcommittee on Preparedness, chaired by Senator John Stennis (D-MS). This interim report was published in 1963, but the hearings were conducted in secret. It is not included in this chapter, though it well might be, because it involved two variables not present in the other inquiries: political partisanship over a post-mortem intended for public consumption, and limited access to the necessary information. The subcommittee relied primarily on testimony from administration officials taken in executive session. U.S. Senate, Committee on Armed Services, Preparedness Investigating Subcommittee, "Investigation of the Preparedness Program: Interim Report on the Cuban Military Buildup" (Washington, DC: U.S. Government Printing Office, 1963).

5. In chronological order, the post-mortems were: Memorandum for the Director of Central Intelligence, "CIA Handling of the Soviet Build-up in Cuba, 1 July–16 October 1962," November 14, 1962 (hereafter Lehman Report); Memorandum for DCI McCone from J. S. Earman, Inspector General, "Handling of Raw Intelligence Information During the Cuban Arms Buildup," November 20, 1962 (hereafter IG Report); "Report to the President's Foreign Intelligence Advisory Board on Intelligence Community Activities Relating to the Cuban Arms Build-up (April 14 through October 14, 1962) by the Director of Central Intelligence," December 26, 1963 (hereafter USIB Report); and "Report of the President's Foreign Intelligence Advisory Board on the Soviet Military Build-up in Cuba," February 4, 1963 (hereafter PFIAB Report). In 1992 four pages of the Lehman Report, and the entire PFIAB Report, were excerpted in Mary McAuliffe, ed., *CIA Documents on the Cuban Missile Crisis* (Washington, DC: Central Intelligence Agency, October 1992), pp. 99–102, 361–71. A sanitized version of the USIB Report first became available in 1998 under provisions of the John F. Kennedy Assassination Records Collection Act; in 2004 more complete versions of the USIB and Lehman Reports were released via the CIA Records Electronic Research Tool (CREST) at the National Archives in College Park, Maryland (hereafter NARA). The Earman post-mortem is cited in an official history of the U-2 (Gregory Pedlow and Donald Welzenbach, *The CIA and the U-2 Program,* Washington, DC: Central Intelligence Agency, 1998), p. 206. At this writing, however, this document has not been released via CREST, and in response to a 2003 Freedom of Information Act request, the CIA wrote that it was unable to locate the report. Letter, CIA Information and Privacy Coordinator to the author, December 22, 2005.

6. The four post-mortems were essentially unanimous in their praise of the intelligence community's work after the discovery of Soviet missiles on October 15, 1962.

7. As the *New Yorker*'s Washington correspondent observed, "the handling of the October crisis was, of course, superb (an easy *ex-post-facto* judgment, based wholly

upon success)." Richard Rovere, "Letter from Washington," *New Yorker,* March 2, 1963.

8. "The Cuban Missile Crisis, 1962," in *Deterrence in American Foreign Policy: Theory and Practice,* eds. Alexander George and Richard Smoke (New York: Columbia University Press, 1974), p. 473. Decades later, another scholar would label the pre-October 14 intelligence product "deficient due to *operational,* as much as *analytical,* reasons" (emphasis in the original). Gil Merom, "The 1962 Cuban Intelligence Estimate: A Methodological Perspective," *Intelligence and National Security* (hereafter *I&NS*) 14 (Autumn 1999), p. 52.

9. September 17–18 was subsequently fixed as the earliest date after which SSMs might have been detected, had there been constant and intrusive aerial surveillance. CIA/ Office of Research and Reports, "Cuba 1962: Khrushchev's Miscalculated Risk," February 13, 1964, National Security File, Country File: Cuba, Box 35, Lyndon B. Johnson Library (hereafter LBJL), pp. 2–3.

10. As one respected scholar of the intelligence process later wrote, it really should not have mattered "what intelligence 'thought' " about the likelihood of missiles being deployed in Cuba. "But it did matter, imperatively, that intelligence collect the data which would permit a firm judgment whether or not the missiles were there." Cynthia Grabo, *Anticipating Surprise: Analysis for Strategic Warning* (Lanham, MD: University Press of America, 2004), p. 140.

11. Hanson Baldwin, "An Intelligence Gap: Experts Ask If Reports on Cuba Were Poor or Adapted to Policy," *New York Times,* October 31, 1962. If the estimates had been tailored, the article suggested that an alleged overcentralization of intelligence was likely the cause, because it might have created an IC "unduly influenced by the knowledge of what current policy was."

12. "The Military Build-up in Cuba," SNIE 85-3-62, in *CIA Documents,* ed. McAuliffe, pp. 91–93.

13. Max Holland, "Politics and Intelligence: The 'Photo Gap' That Delayed Discovery of Missiles in Cuba," *Studies in Intelligence* (hereafter *SII*) 49 (2005), pp. 15–30.

14. Max Frankel, *High Noon in the Cold War: Kennedy, Khrushchev, and the Cuban Missile Crisis* (New York: Ballantine, 2004), p. 27. In his history/memoir, McGeorge Bundy hinted at the significance of the photo gap, which otherwise received short shrift in his book. "The photographs of October 14 were taken in good time, but they had been delayed, first by our own caution in overflying Cuba. . . . If our primary interest here were in the intelligence process, these matters would deserve further attention." McGeorge Bundy, *Danger and Survival: Choices About the Bomb in the First Fifty Years* (New York: Random House, 1988), p. 687. That the crucial October 14 overflight induced great anxiety in the administration, and only received approval by a slim margin, was evinced by a remark made during a conversation on October 12 between DDCI Marshall Carter and U.S.A.F. General William McKee, vice chief of staff under General Curtis LeMay. "This is the most overcontrolled operation I've ever been in," McKee observed to Carter. Second conversation between General Carter and General McKee, October 12, 1962, released to the author under the Freedom of Information Act (hereafter FOIA), December 2005.

15. Besides being a primary topic of the official post-mortems, the misestimates and analytical shortcomings have been extensively written about in the intelligence-related literature about the crisis. See Sherman Kent, "A Crucial Estimate Relived," *SII,* Spring 1964; George and Smoke, *Deterrence,* pp. 477–81, 488–91; Raymond Garthoff,

"US Intelligence in the Cuban Missile Crisis," *I&NS* 13 (Autumn 1998), pp. 20–26; and Merom, "1962 Cuban Intelligence Estimate," pp. 48–80.

16. In his posthumously published memoir of the crisis, Robert Kennedy would admit, "We had been deceived by Khrushchev, but we had also fooled ourselves." Yet Kennedy was far from specific about how close his brother's administration had come to being surprised by the deployment of operational missiles. Robert Kennedy, *Thirteen Days: A Memoir of the Cuban Missile Crisis* (New York: W.W. Norton, 1969), pp. 27–28, and Holland, "Photo Gap," pp. 27–28. Not all students of the crisis agree that the photo gap was an exceptionally sensitive issue. See James Blight and David Welch, "What Can Intelligence Tell Us About the Cuban Missile Crisis, and What Can the Cuban Missile Crisis Tell Us About Intelligence?" *I&NS* 13 (Autumn 1998), p. 6. According to these scholars, it was "for the most part a red herring—less interesting to students of intelligence than to followers of sordid Camelot sub-plots."

17. John Helgerson, *CIA Briefings of Presidential Candidates, 1952–1992* (Washington, DC: Center for the Study of Intelligence, 1996), p. 69.

18. Ibid., p. 66.

19. Richard Kovar, "Mr. Current Intelligence: An Interview With Richard Lehman," *SII* 9 (Summer 2000), p. 57; Helgerson, *CIA Briefings*, p. 67.

20. "For current intelligence people, [the President's engagement with the PICL] was heaven on earth!" Russell Jack Smith, *The Unknown CIA: My Three Decades With the Agency* (Washington, DC: Pergamon-Brassey's, 1989), p. 149.

21. Strictly speaking Marshall Carter, Deputy Director of Central Intelligence (DDCI), was the first high official to ask for a post-mortem; Carter probably anticipated that criticism for the photo gap would be directed at him because he had been acting DCI when the coverage was degraded. James Reber, Chairman of the Committee on Overhead Reconnaissance (COMOR), submitted a memorandum to Carter on October 24, 1962, in response to the DDCI's request. Reber concluded, in the midst of the crisis, that nothing had indicated "that any other approach would have served us better." Of course, Reber had some reason to be defensive also, as the White House might claim that the COMOR, charged with developing overflight requirements, failed to keep the president fully apprised of the dysfunctionality of the surveillance regime after September 10. Memorandum for DDCI, "Historical Analysis of U-2 Overflights of Cuba," October 24, 1962, released under FOIA, December 2005.

22. Kovar, "Mr. Current Intelligence," p. 57.

23. On the copy of the Lehman Report released under CREST, there is a handwritten notation on the title page: "Save for the Pearl Harbor hearings—if some, or any." Lehman Report, CREST, NARA.

24. Walter Elder, "John A. McCone: The Sixth Director of Central Intelligence," 1987, Box 1, CIA Miscellaneous Files, John F. Kennedy Assassination Records Collection, NARA, p. 38.

25. Kovar, "Mr. Current Intelligence," p. 57. The Lehman Report via the CREST system does not include any annexes.

26. Smith, *Unknown CIA*, p. 149.

27. Lehman Report, p. 12.

28. A routine U-2 overflight on August 29 had uncovered the first evidence of SA-2s being emplaced on Cuba, the same SAM that had downed Francis Gary Powers's aircraft in May 1960. Completely coincidentally, the growing threat to U-2 overflights of the

island was underscored by two distant incidents in early September. On August 30 an air force U-2 had violated Soviet airspace for nine minutes during an air-sampling mission, and on September 9, a U-2 manned by a Taiwan-based pilot was lost over mainland China. Pedlow and Welzenbach, *The CIA and the U-2 Program,* p. 201.

29. Holland, "Photo Gap," pp. 19–21.

30. Interview with Richard Lehman, April 14, 2003.

31. Portions of the Lehman Report are still closed, and the annexes are apparently unavailable, so it is not possible to state the precise details Lehman left out. One example of an omitted detail might be the fact that at 3 pm on September 10, McGeorge Bundy had rescinded approval of the one remaining September overflight, presumably to demonstrate the administration's seriousness about avoiding a U-2 incident over Cuba. DD/R Memo for the Record, "Cuban Overflights," September 10, 1962, CREST, NARA.

32. Scoville maintained that the most important objective of the October 14 U-2 mission was coverage of the so-called San Cristóbal trapezoid, whereas Lehman suggested overflying an advanced SAM site in western Cuba had actually been a higher priority. For his part, McCone insisted that it was "erroneous to give the impression [that] this flight went where it went because we suspected [offensive missiles] were there. This was simply not the case." These divergent perspectives reflect the struggle that occurred in early October over resuming more intrusive U-2 overflights. Scoville was apparently more familiar with how the U-2 requirements were specifically developed on the basis of human intelligence, while the DCI was closer to the rationales behind the necessary approvals at the highest levels, for example, within the Special Group Augmented and inside the Oval Office. See Memo, DDR to DCI, "Comments on Lehman Paper," November 7, 1962, and "Notes for Mr. Earman," December 17, 1962, both in CREST, NARA; and Holland, "Photo Gap," pp. 25–26.

33. Lehman Report, p. 29.

34. During the Kennedy administration the Special Group, an interagency subcommittee of the National Security Council, oversaw all covert activity, including U-2 surveillance; the Special Group Augmented dealt solely with Cuba.

35. "John S. Earman Jr., 60," *Washington Post,* April 11, 1974.

36. Wrote Earman, "On 21 November you [McCone] asked me to consider two additional conclusions for my report." Memorandum for DCI, "Inspector General's Report on Handling of Intelligence Information During the Cuban Arms Build-Up (Revised), dated 20 November 1962," November 26, 1962, CREST, NARA.

37. Ibid.

38. Ibid.

39. Ibid.

40. As with the Lehman Report, Scoville reviewed the IG post-mortem. "From all the information available to the DD/R, it is believed that the report of the Inspector General is factually accurate," Scoville wrote. Memorandum for Deputy Director of Central Intelligence, "Handling of Intelligence Information During the Cuban Arms Build-up," December 15, 1962, CREST, NARA.

41. Memorandum for Director of Central Intelligence, "Department of State's Objections to the Report on the Cuban Arms Build-up," March 12, 1963, CREST, NARA.

42. Simultaneously, the president asked McCone personally for the same type of report. Memorandum of the Record, "Meeting with PFIAB, 7 December 1962," December 10, 1962, CREST, NARA.

43. PFIAB was originally called the President's Board of Consultants on Foreign Intelligence Activities, and created by Eisenhower based upon a recommendation of the second Hoover Commission. *The President's Foreign Intelligence Advisory Board* (Washington, DC: Hale Foundation, 1981), p. 1.

44. Memorandum for Director of Central Intelligence, "Department of State's Objections to the Report on the Cuban Arms Build-up," March 12, 1963, CREST, NARA.

45. At the time, one of the ways the DCI coordinated the intelligence effort was through the machinery of the USIB, which consisted of representatives from all the intelligence agencies, for example, the deputy director of CIA (General Marshall Carter), who represented the CIA; the directors of INR (Roger Hilsman), DIA (Lieutenant General Joseph Carroll), NSA (Lieutenant General Gordon Blake); the intelligence director for the Joint Chiefs of Staff (Major General Richard Collins); the assistant director (Alan Belmont) of the Federal Bureau of Investigation (FBI); and the assistant general manager for administration (Harry Traynor) of the Atomic Energy Commission. The heads of Army, Navy, and Air Force intelligence (respectively, Major General Alva Fitch, Rear Admiral Vernon Lowrance, Major General Robert Breitweiser) also attended USIB meetings as observers. The USIB met weekly, sometimes more frequently, and among other things rendered advice on National Intelligence Objectives (NIOs) and the production of National Intelligence Estimates (NIEs), two of the DCI's most important responsibilities. Statement for the Record, Document 21b, Central Intelligence Agency, Vol. II, Box 9, National Security File, Presidential Papers, LBJL; Memorandum of the Record, "Meeting With PFIAB, 7 December 1962," 10 December 1962, CREST, NARA.

46. Memorandum for the Record, "DCI Meeting With PFIAB," 7 December 1962, CREST, NARA.

47. The other working group members (as chosen by their respective agencies) were William McAfee, director of the Coordination Staff of the State Department's INR; Samuel Halpern, executive officer of the CIA's Task Force W on Cuba, representing the DD/P; a representative from the DIA's Office of Estimates; the chief of the DIA's Current Intelligence Indications Center; the deputy chief of the NSA's Policy Division; and the CIA's deputy assistant director for Central Reference, representing the DD/I.

48. DD/R Memo, "Cuban Missile Crisis," November 13, 1962, CREST, NARA.

49. Memorandum for Deputy Director (Research), "Interagency Review of Intelligence Activities Relating to the Cuba Situation," November 26, 1962, CREST, NARA.

50. After the meeting, Reber had reportedly observed, "When men of such rank involve themselves in planning mission tracks, good intelligence officers just listen." Dino Brugioni, *Eyeball to Eyeball: The Inside Story of the Cuban Missile Crisis* (New York: Random House, 1990), p. 138.

51. Memorandum for Deputy Director (Research), "Interagency Review of Intelligence Activities Relating to the Cuba Situation," November 26, 1962, CREST, NARA.

52. Recounting the facts for the questionnaire was fraught with problems. The DIA's answers, for example, placed that agency at the forefront of the decision to overfly the San Cristóbal trapezoid, although the truth was a bit more complicated. DIA, "Use of Intelligence Product," undated, CREST, NARA, and Holland, "Photo Gap," p. 25.

53. Memorandum for Deputy Director (Research), "Interagency Review of Intelligence Activities Relating to the Cuba Situation," November 26, 1962, CREST, NARA.

54. The detailed memorandum about the pivotal September 10 meeting printed in the relevant *Foreign Relations* volume was prepared well after the fact, that is, on

February 28, 1963. Acting DCI Marshall Carter wrote only a one-paragraph summary about the unusual meeting, and the only other contemporaneous record was a September 11 memo by Thomas Parrott, the assistant to General Maxwell Taylor, who was then the president's military representative. See "Memorandum Prepared in the Central Intelligence Agency for the Executive Director," dated September 10, 1962 (but prepared February 28, 1963), U.S. Department of State, *Foreign Relations of the United States (FRUS), 1961–1963,* Volume X: *Cuba 1961–1962* (Washington, DC: U.S. Government Printing Office, 1997), pp. 1054–55, and Document 296, "Acting," September 10, 1962, *FRUS,* Vol. X, Microfiche Supplement. The Parrott memorandum was cited in the USIB Report, pp. 69–70. See also Memorandum for the Record, "Telephone Conversation With Mr. Tom Parrott on 10 September Concerning IDEALIST Operations Over Cuba," September 10, 1962, CREST, NARA, and Memorandum for the Director, "White House Meeting on 10 September 1962 on Cuban Overflights," March 1, 1963, in McAuliffe, ed., *CIA Documents,* pp. 61–62.

55. Once, during a USIB meeting on September 19, acting DCI Carter remonstrated about the attenuation of U-2 overflights. "We cannot put a stop to collection," Carter fumed. "Otherwise, the president would never know when the point of decision was reached." McAuliffe, ed., *CIA Documents,* p. 42. CIA officials' willingness (apart from McCone) to accede to policy makers on the overflight regime probably was a consequence of the general disfavor in which the Agency was held by the administration following the Bay of Pigs.

56. Roger Hilsman Oral History, August 14, 1970, John F. Kennedy Library (hereafter JFKL), p. 4.

57. Ibid., p. 15.

58. Referring to the highly secret PICL prepared daily by Richard Lehman, Hilsman observed, "In McCone's day they [CIA] didn't play honest with me in that they did get out sort of a private thing for the President, which they tried like hell to keep anybody from seeing who wasn't too important." Hilsman tried to develop a rival publication, called the "Intelligence Note," which was an INR document of 300 hundred words or less that he would disseminate within six hours of an overseas event. "He who gets the first interpretation out commands the field," noted Hilsman. The INR director was also rankled by the fact that he had no authority or say over covert activities presented to the 5412 Group; the Under Secretary of State represented the State Department in the Special Group. Finally, when McCone was appointed DCI, Hilsman was furious with Rusk for not consulting him beforehand, and the INR director was one of the administration officials who energetically opposed the nomination of an "alley fighter" who was "a very rich . . . very militant, anti-communist Republican." Ibid., pp. 8–9, 13, 15. Because of opposition from liberal New Frontiersmen like Hilsman, McCone received more negative votes in the Senate than any DCI nominee had ever received.

59. Interview with Harold Ford, July 2, 2005. In a manner not appreciated by DD/R Scoville, for example, Hilsman had tried to insert himself in the decision-making process that led to the September 10 decision regarding U-2 overflights. Memorandum for the Record, "Telephone Conversation With Mr. Tom Parrott on 10 September Concerning IDEALIST Operations Over Cuba," September 10, 1962, CREST, NARA.

60. U.S. Department of State, *FRUS, 1961–1963,* Volume XI: *Cuban Missile Crisis and Aftermath* (Washington, DC: U.S. Government Printing Office, 1996), Document 323, "Conversation Between General Carter and Roger Hilsman," October 16, 1962, *FRUS,* Vol. XI, Microfiche Supplement.

61. Ibid.

62. Hilsman Oral History, pp. 6, 16, JFKL. McCone's prescience, ironically, did not win him admission into the president's inner circle; in fact, his stock with the Kennedys declined. Holland, "Photo Gap," pp. 29–30.

63. Memorandum for Director of Central Intelligence, "Additional Inspector General Conclusions on Cuban Arms Build-up," November 28, 1962, CREST, NARA.

64. "Notes for Mr. Earman," December 17, 1963, CREST, NARA.

65. McCone added that the CIA "had been remiss in proposing something less than complete coverage," having been overly influenced by policy makers intent on avoiding a U-2 incident. Ibid.

66. On December 26 Hilsman had second thoughts about the language of the sixth draft after it was agreed upon by the USIB working group and steering committee. According to a memo from Marshall Carter to McCone, Hilsman called Carter "with about 25 proposed changes to the final draft report. Some have great merit and others are nitpicks. I explained to him . . . that we could keep rewording the thing for months and not satisfy everyone, that we must presume that the Killian Board is friendly . . . and that all of us had different views of varying intensity as to just what happened and why. He seemed mollified." Memorandum for the Director, Untitled, December 26, 1962, CREST, NARA.

67. The CIA did not follow Bundy's injunction, on the grounds that it was the "Director's report [to PFIAB] and not a report of the entire administration." After reading it, Bundy reported to Marshall Carter that he thought "it was a pretty adequate job . . . [although] there were a number of places where he [Bundy] might have phrased things differently." Ibid.

68. Roger Hilsman, *To Move a Nation: The Politics of Foreign Policy in the Administration of John F. Kennedy* (Garden City, NY: Doubleday, 1967). The book was controversial because "kiss 'n' tell" memoirs, which unilaterally revealed classified information, had not yet become commonplace.

69. Hilsman, *To Move a Nation,* p. 188.

70. Ibid., p. 187.

71. Ibid. It's instructive to compare *To Move a Nation* with Hilsman's later treatment of the same subject in *The Cuban Missile Crisis: The Struggle Over Policy* (Westport, CT: Praeger, 1996). When this later volume appeared, previously classified information about the September 10 decision had been made public, leaving Hilsman little choice but to change his account. In contrast to his 1967 characterization, in 1996 Hilsman wrote, "there is no evidence of any attempt by the policy makers to suppress information or to hamper intelligence-gathering activities, except for Dean Rusk's *suggestions* [emphasis added] that the U-2 make peripheral flights around Cuba and only for special reasons actually 'dip into' Cuban airspace. But his motive was mainly to avoid a diplomatic brouhaha that might prevent any further U-2 flights, as happened after Gary Powers was shot down. No request from the intelligence community." Hilsman, *Missile Crisis,* p. 55.

72. Hilsman, *To Move a Nation,* p. 196. As pointed out earlier, an exhaustive 1964 CIA study found that the missiles were subject to being detected by U-2 photo coverage any time after September 17–18, weeks before they were actually discovered. To bolster his unprovable assertion, Hilsman engaged in some legerdemain. The former INR director wrote that the SGA lifted the ban on flying over known SAM positions in western

Cuba on October 4, when in fact the Special Group and the president had not made this decision until October 9. By moving up the date, Hilsman made it appear as if the administration had acted with alacrity after receiving new human intelligence reports alleging the presence of large missiles in that region. In fact, even after these reports percolated to the top, the State Department had argued in early October against resuming U-2 flights over known SAM sites, and discovery of the SSMs was postponed by at least an additional five days. Holland, "Photo Gap," pp. 24–26.

73. Hilsman chided the intelligence community for missing other signs of the missile deployment, such as the fact that two Soviet freighters, the *Omsk* and the *Poltava*, had exceptionally large hatches and rode "high in the water" because they were carrying a bulky but relatively light load. "It is difficult to understand why the professional intelligence technicians down the line failed to see enough significance in these facts to bring them to the attention of the top levels." He also deceptively asserted a U-2 could have been dispatched sooner and guided over suspected sites if the CIA had had "a better network of traditional agents" in Cuba. The "intelligence community should have . . . turned their attention to the western end of the island some ten days to two weeks sooner than it did," thereby leaving the inference, for anyone who insisted there was a photo gap, that any delay was primarily the CIA's fault. Hilsman, *To Move a Nation*, pp. 186–87, 189, 191.

74. USIB Report, p. 74.

75. The language quoted is from what appears to be the sixth draft of the USIB Report, and uses the handwritten changes that were presumably incorporated in the seventh draft. The original language of the sixth draft stated, "[B]ut this delay was not critical, because photography obtained prior to about 17 October would not have been sufficient to warrant action or to solicit support from Western Hemisphere or NATO allies." Ibid, p. 89. Presumably the wording was changed because this formulation was at odds with the facts, that is, photo coverage from October 14 had been sufficient to "warrant action."

76. At a meeting of the National Security Council on October 22, Robert Kennedy raised the issue of the photo gap and, in effect, laid down what would be the administration's position. The fact that there had been a delay would be obfuscated, and attributed whenever possible to adverse weather. Indeed, the administration would misleadingly claim that it had *increased* the number of U-2 flights in September. The bottom line, as enunciated by the attorney general, was that "even if there had been U-2 flights, construction at the missile sites was not far enough along to have been detected by photography much earlier than October 14." "Minutes of the 507th Meeting of the National Security Council," October 22, 1962, *FRUS*, Vol. XI, p. 154, and Document 370, "Memorandum of Meeting of Executive Committee of the NSC," October 23, 1962, *FRUS*, Vol. XI, Microfiche Supplement.

77. Because the IG report is still classified, of course, this observation is somewhat speculative.

78. Introducing the element of exactly when the photographs might prove persuasive to NATO and Latin American allies—that is, nonexperts in the detection of SSM sites—was not a trivial matter. But it did not have a great bearing on the issue at hand either. The photos from October 14, which NPIC took as conclusive proof of offensive missile sites, were not the ones shared with U.S. allies. Photos taken days later, deemed to be more revealing to the untrained eye, were shared instead.

79. In light of what later came to be understood as an extensive "denial and deception" program by the Soviets, Earman's report, interestingly, observed that "any postmortem ... must take into account whether there was a planned Soviet deception program to help cover their activities. There is little hard evidence on this pro or con, and may never be unless there is a knowledgeable Soviet defector." USIB Report, p. 42, and James Hansen, "Soviet Deception in the Cuban Missile Crisis," *SII* 46 (2002).

80. USIB Report, p. 42.

81. In March 1963 the State Department would attempt to claim, despite Hilsman's participation at every stage, that the USIB post-mortem was not a "coordinated report" but McCone's "personal report," and tried to distance itself from the findings. U. Alexis Johnson, Memorandum for the Honorable John A. McCone, "U-2 Overflights of Cuba, 29 August through 14 October 1962," March 6, 1963; and Memorandum for Director of Central Intelligence, "Department of State's Objections to the Report on the Cuban Arms Build-up," March 12, 1963, both in CREST, NARA.

82. "McCone, Memorandum for the President, 28 February 1963," in McAuliffe, ed., *CIA Documents*, p. 373; Clark Clifford with Richard Holbrooke, *Counsel to the President* (New York: Random House, 1991), p. 357.

83. The USIB Report was formally called the "Report to the President's Foreign Intelligence Advisory Board ... by the Director of Central Intelligence," in deference to McCone's role as DCI and USIB chairman. But, as shown, the report more genuinely represented the coordinated view of USIB principals than McCone's individual view.

84. Clifford, *Counsel*, p. 353.

85. Ibid., p. 354.

86. George Kistiakowsky, *A Scientist at the White House: The Private Diary of President Eisenhower's Special Assistant for Science and Technology* (Cambridge: Harvard University Press, 1976), p. 21. In one widely publicized incident, McCone, a Caltech trustee, accused some Caltech scientists in 1956 of being taken in by Soviet propaganda when they came out in support of a nuclear test ban. Chalmers Roberts, "McCone Selection Criticized by Some," *Washington Post,* October 23, 1961.

87. Ibid.

88. According to RFK's oral history, Killian declared his vigorous opposition to McCone's appointment. "McCone had made a lot of enemies. [Killian] said he was going to put out a report against John McCone," Kennedy recalled in 1964. "I had to call him and had a long conversation with him.... We finally got it straightened out." Edwin Guthman and Jeffrey Shulman, eds., *Robert Kennedy in His Own Words: The Unpublished Recollections of the Kennedy Years* (New York: Bantam Press, 1988), pp. 253–54.

89. U.S. Senate, Select Committee to Study Governmental Operations with Respect to Intelligence Activities, 94th Congress, 1st Session, *Hearings: Covert Action,* December 4–5, 1975 (Washington, DC: U.S. Government Printing Office, 1976), pp. 50–51.

90. A member of the transition team in 1960, Clifford had already been given his pick of several Cabinet posts by the president-elect in 1960, but he preferred to profit handsomely from his connections to the first Democratic White House in eight years. As Kennedy quipped, Clifford wanted nothing for his services "except for the right to advertise the Clifford law firm on the back of the one-dollar bill." Robert Dallek, *An Unfinished Life: John F. Kennedy, 1917–1963* (Boston: Little, Brown, 2003), p. 306.

91. Clifford, *Counsel,* p. 354.

92. Letter, Clark Clifford to President Kennedy, October 25, 1961, with attachment, "Memorandum on Central Intelligence Agency," in Senate Select Committee, *Hearings: Covert Action,* pp. 139–43. Clifford's 1961 memo, interestingly, advocates that the new DCI operate like the recently created post of Director of National Intelligence (DNI).

93. "Clifford Named to Killian Post," *New York Times*, April 24, 1963. The other PFIAB members in 1962–63 were William Baker, then director of research at Bell Laboratories; Air Force Brigadier General (Retired) James Doolittle; Gordon Gray, a special assistant for national security during the Eisenhower administration; Dr. Edwin Land, an inventor and physicist; Dr. William Langer, a Harvard history professor; former ambassador Robert Murphy; and Frank Pace Jr., secretary of the Army during the Truman administration.

94. Clifford, *Counsel,* p. 354.

95. PFIAB was well aware of McCone's prediction. On September 28 the DCI had discussed Cuba with the panel at some length, and in the context of the charges being made by Senator Kenneth Keating (R-NY) and other congressional critics of the administration's policy. McCone told PFIAB members the same thing he had been telling everyone holding an official position: Although his own analysts disagreed, he believed the Soviets would eventually deploy SSMs in Cuba. Ibid., p. 357.

96. Ibid., p. 355.

97. Ibid., p. 357.

98. "Although the matter was delicate," wrote Clifford, "I felt it was our responsibility to bring our views to Kennedy's attention—especially since his critics were publicly charging him with a failure to act on their early warnings." Ibid.

99. Memorandum for the Record, "DCI Meeting With PFIAB, 7 December 1962," December 10, 1962, CREST, NARA. Access to the Lehman Report, in all likelihood, provided some of the basis for Clifford's early recognition that PFIAB was going to face a "dilemma."

100. Insofar as Helms was concerned, this piece of intelligence was the only "positive and productive" aspect of Operation MONGOOSE. Ted Shackley with Richard Finney, *Spymaster: My Life in the CIA* (Dulles, VA: Potomac Books, 2005), p. 63.

101. Memorandum for the Record, "DCI Meeting with PFIAB, 7 December 1962," December 10, 1962, CREST, NARA.

102. Ibid.

103. The honeymoon cables referred to the telegrams sent to and from McCone while he was vacationing on the French Riviera in September. The DCI had remarried in August, following the death in late 1961 of his first wife.

104. Ibid.

105. The exact moment when McCone learned about the attenuation of U-2 surveillance remains vague to this day. He certainly protested the lack of photo coverage once he returned from the French Riviera in late September. Holland, "Photo Gap," pp. 22–24.

106. Memorandum for the Record, "DCI Meeting with PFIAB, 7 December 1962," December 10, 1962, CREST, NARA.

107. Clifford, *Counsel,* p. 357.

108. Ibid.

109. There probably was a marked difference between having McCone in Washington and receiving McCone's cables from the French Riviera. Nonetheless, as Sherman Kent, chairman of the CIA's Board of National Estimates later observed, even if McCone

"had been in Washington and made a federal case of his intuitive guess, and had got[ten] the President's ear, McCone would have had opposing him (1) the members of USIB, and (2) most presidential advisors including the four most important ones—[former Ambassador Charles] Bohlen, [former Ambassador Llewelyn] Thompson, [former Ambassador George] Kennan, and [serving Ambassador] Foy [Kohler]." All four Kremlinologists were "honest and decent enough" to confirm for Kent in 1971 that they had agreed completely with the September SNIE. Jack Davis, "Sherman Kent's Final Thoughts on Analyst-Policymaker Relations," Sherman Kent Center for Intelligence Analysis, Occasional Papers: Volume 2, Number 3.

110. Clifford also found the September 19 SNIE "preposterous" because, at that exact moment, the DCI was "predicting the opposite." Clifford, *Counsel,* p. 358.

111. Ibid., p. 357.

112. Ibid., p. 358.

113. Though wide of the mark, the Republicans' charge reflected widespread confusion—aided and abetted by the administration—over why the missiles had been discovered belatedly. Holland, "Photo Gap," pp. 28–29.

114. Clifford, *Counsel,* p. 358.

115. Clifford, of course, denied that his position was primarily political. "[M]y major objective, expressed repeatedly in PFIAB meetings, was to strengthen the intelligence efforts in any future crises." Ibid.

116. President's Foreign Intelligence Advisory Board, "Memorandum for the President," December 28, 1962, CREST, NARA.

117. Memorandum for the Record, "Meeting With the President in Palm Beach, Florida," January 7, 1963, *FRUS,* Vol. XI, pp. 651–52.

118. Ibid., p. 651.

119. Ibid., p. 652; Kent, "A Crucial Estimate Relived," *SII* (Spring 1964).

120. Clifford, *Counsel,* p. 355.

121. Ibid. Notwithstanding Clifford's account, the cover page of the final PFIAB report, signed by Dr. Killian, expressed appreciation for the "cooperation and assistance which was freely and promptly given." "PFIAB Memorandum for the President, 4 February 1964," in McAuliffe, ed., *CIA Documents,* p. 361.

122. The meeting was secretly recorded by President Kennedy, but neither the recording nor a transcript of the PFIAB meeting is yet available. See http://www.jfkli brary.org/pres-recordings_available.html.

123. "PFIAB Memorandum for the President, 4 February 1963," in McAuliffe, ed., *CIA Documents,* p. 363.

124. Ibid., p. 364.

125. Ibid.

126. Ibid., p. 365. It may be that this was one of the points on which Clifford and McCone allegedly clashed regarding PFIAB's access to records.

127. Ibid., p. 364.

128. Ibid., p. 365.

129. Richard Helms with William Hood, *A Look Over My Shoulder: A Life in the Central Intelligence Agency* (New York: Random House, 2003), p. 212.

130. Diary Notes, February 21, 1963, CREST, NARA.

131. McCone, "Memorandum for the President, 28 February 1963," in McAuliffe, ed., *CIA Documents,* p. 373.

132. McCone was not going to have the Agency in this position ever again, at least under his watch. In late January he issued a directive ordering Agency personnel "to be very aggressive in taking the initiative to obtain permission for any and all types of intelligence operations to obtain required information for national security." Lyman Kirkpatrick, "Agency Policy on Dynamic Intelligence Operations," January 28, 1963, CREST, NARA.

133. McCone, "Memorandum for the President, 28 February 1963," in McAuliffe, ed., *CIA Documents,* p. 373.

134. Ibid., pp. 373–74.

135. Clifford, *Counsel,* p. 358.

136. Raymond Garthoff, "Documenting the Cuban Missile Crisis," *Diplomatic History* 24 (Spring 2000), p. 300.

137. As pointed out earlier, too, some scholars of the missile crisis, most notably Alexander George and Gil Merom, have been almost as critical.

138. Kennedy, *Own Words,* p. 254.

139. Ibid.

140. Some aspects of the PFIAB post-mortem were simply wrong. The report scored McCone (rather than "higher authority") for imposing the first limitation that "endangered the necessary flow of information" within the intelligence community. "PFIAB Memorandum for the President, 4 February 1963," in McAuliffe, ed., *CIA Documents,* pp. 367, 369; Holland, "Photo Gap," p. 19.

141. The PFIAB report ended with this observation: "Throughout our review, we have been mindful of public charges to the effect that during the period of the Soviet military build-up in Cuba, the U.S. intelligence process was in some manner manipulated for partisan political purposes. We find no evidence whatsoever to support such charges." "PFIAB Memorandum for the President, 4 February 1963," in McAuliffe, ed., *CIA Documents,* p. 371.

142. "Clifford Named to Killian Post," *New York Times,* April 24, 1963.

143. "Cloudy Intelligence," *New York Times,* April 29, 1963.

144. Ibid.

145. Right after the November 1964 election, while discussing possible new appointments, McGeorge Bundy would recall Clifford's PFIAB promotion during a conversation with President Johnson. When Clifford was appointed, Bundy observed, "the *[New York] Times* . . . wrote a very disagreeable editorial saying [we] had replaced a great statesman in Dr. Killian by a Washington fixer named Clifford. Of course, there never were two sillier remarks, because a) Killian was not a great statesman, and b) Clark was just what the doctor ordered, and [did a] judicious job for JFK." Given Bundy's role in the photo gap, he may well have been recalling Clifford's role in the PFIAB post-mortem. Telephone conversation among Bill Moyers, McGeorge Bundy, and Lyndon Johnson, 10:34 am, November 4, 1964, LBJL.

146. Ray Cline, *Secrets, Spies, and Scholars: Blueprint of the Essential CIA* (Washington, DC: Acropolis Books, 1976), p. 197.

147. U.S. Senate, Committee on Armed Services, Preparedness Investigating Subcommittee, *Investigation of the Preparedness Program: Interim Report on the Cuban Military Buildup* (Washington, DC: U.S. Government Printing Office, 1963), p. 8.

148. Richard Shryock, "The Intelligence Community Post-Mortem Program, 1973–1975," *SII* 21 (Fall 1977), p. 27.

THE INTELLIGENCE CYCLE

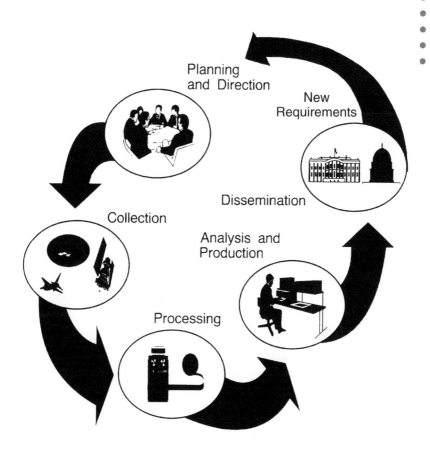

Planning and Direction

New Requirements

Collection

Dissemination

Analysis and Production

Processing

Adapted from *Factbook on Intelligence*, Office of Public Affairs, Central Intelligence Agency (October 1993), p. 14.

EXAMPLES OF AERIAL INTELLIGENCE COLLECTION "PLATFORMS" AND SMALLER COLLECTION DEVICES

A U.S. NAVY RECONNAISSANCE AIRCRAFT, THE EA-30, USED FOR GATHERING ELECTRONIC INTELLIGENCE

Photo courtesy of the CIA Office of Public Affairs, 2006.

THE GRAB II (GALACTIC RADIATION AND BACKGROUND) SATELLITE MODEL

Source: http://www.nsa.gov/museum/museu00027.cfm The GRAB II (Galactic Radiation And Background) satellite was the second Signals Intelligence satellite to be launched by the United States. The first GRAB satellite launched on June 22, 1960, followed the loss of the U-2 spy plane flown by Gary Powers in May. The successful launch of the GRAB II satellite occurred on June 29, 1961. It gathered radar pulses within a specific bandwidth from Soviet equipment. Based on the information NSA received, analysts determined that the Soviets had radars that supported the capability to destroy ballistic missiles. Photo courtesy of the CIA Office of Public Affairs, 2006.

A MINOX TLX CAMERA POPULAR WITH SPIES

Photo courtesy of the CIA Office of Public Affairs, 2006.

U.S. AMBASSADOR TO THE UNITED NATIONS, HENRY CABOT LODGE, JR., REVEALING THE SOVIET PLACEMENT OF AN ELECTRONIC LISTENING DEVICE IN A U.S. EMBASSY SEAL (MAY 26, 1960)

Photo courtesy of the CIA Office of Public Affairs, 2006.

EXAMPLES OF IMAGERY INTELLIGENCE FROM RECONNAISSANCE AIRCRAFT AND SURVEILLANCE SATELLITES

**TOMSK-7 REACTOR, RUSSIA; U-2 MISSION 4045,
21 AUGUST 1957**

Photo courtesy of the CIA Office of Public Affairs, 2006.

U2 PHOTO OF SOVIET MISSILE SITES
IN CUBA, 1962

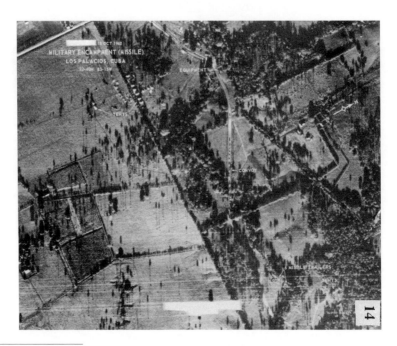

Photo courtesy of the CIA Office of Public Affairs, 2006.

CATEGORIES OF FINISHED INTELLIGENCE
AND THE MAJOR PRODUCTS

When information that has been reviewed and correlated with information from other sources, it is called "finished intelligence." The five primary categories of finished intelligence are:

1. *Current intelligence* addresses day-to-day events, seeking to apprise consumers of new developments and related background, to assess their significance, to warn of their near-term consequences, and to signal potentially dangerous situations in the near future. Current intelligence is presented in daily, weekly, and some monthly publications, and frequently in ad hoc written memorandums and oral briefings to senior officials.

2. *Estimative intelligence* deals with what might be or what might happen. Like all kinds of intelligence, estimative intelligence starts with the available facts, but then it migrates into the unknown, even the unknowable. The main roles of estimative intelligence are to help policymakers navigate the gaps between available facts by suggesting alternative patterns into which those facts might fit and to provide informed assessments of the range and likelihood of possible outcomes. Such intelligence is promulgated in forms ranging from oral briefings to videos, but the most common vehicles are printed documents, of which the IC's flagship is the National Intelligence Estimate.

3. *Warning intelligence* sounds an alarm or gives notice to policymakers. It connotes urgency and implies the potential need for policy action in response. Warning includes identifying or forecasting events that could cause the engagement of US military forces, or those that would have a sudden and deleterious effect on US foreign policy concerns (for example, coups, third-party wars, refugee situations). Warning analysis involves exploring alternative futures and low probability/high impact scenarios. The National Intelligence Officer (NIO) for Warning serves as the DCI's and the IC's principal adviser on warning. All

---

Source: *Intelligence: A Consumer Guide to Intelligence,* Office of Public Affairs, Central Intelligence Agency (Washington, DC, no date, but made available in the mid-1990s).

agencies and intelligence staffs have designated warning components, and some have specific warning responsibilities:

- NSA maintains the worldwide CRITIC system for the simultaneous alerting of US officials within minutes of situations that may affect US security.
- DIA manages the Defense Indications and Warning System (DIWS) to provide accurate and timely warning of developing threats to US and Allied military interests. Other members include the Combatant Commands, the military services, NSA, State Department/INR, the NIO for Warning, and a growing number of US Allies. DIWS disseminates warning information from DIA and other system members via briefings, weekly and quarterly warning products, and, on a priority basis, ad hoc bulletins.

4. *Research intelligence* is presented in monographs and in-depth studies by virtually all agencies. Research underpins both current and estimative intelligence; there are also two specialized subcategories of research intelligence:

- *Basic intelligence* consists primarily of the structured compilation of geographic, demographic, social, military, and political data on foreign countries. This material is presented in the form of maps, atlases, force summaries, handbooks, and, on occasion, sandtable models of terrain. The Directorate of Intelligence in CIA, NIMA, and the Directorate for Intelligence Production in DIA are major producers of this kind of material.
- *Intelligence for operational support* incorporates all types of intelligence production—current, estimative, warning, research, scientific and technical; it is tailored, focused, and rapidly produced for planners and operators. The top priority of DIA is to satisfy the intelligence needs of operational forces and their commanders. DIA also provides near-real-time intelligence to military forces in peacetime, crisis, contingency, and combat operations. To accomplish this, it operates the Joint Worldwide Intelligence Communication System (JWICS) and deploys National Intelligence Support Teams (NISTs) as needed, worldwide. The Associate Director of Central Intelligence for Military Support, via CIA's Office of Military Affairs, oversees deployment of CIA components of NISTs.

5. *Scientific and technical intelligence* includes information on technical developments and characteristics, performance, and capabilities of foreign technologies including weapon systems or subsystems. This information is derived from analysis of all-source data, including technical measurements. Generally, such technical analysis and reporting responds to specific national requirements derived from the weapons acquisition process, arms control negotiations, or military operations. It covers the entire spectrum of sciences, technologies, weapon systems, and integrated operations. This type of intelligence is provided to consumers via in-depth studies, detailed system handbooks, executive summaries, focused assessments and briefs, and automated databases.

SAMPLE NIES ON THE SOVIET UNION AND SNIES ON CUBA AND VIETNAM

NATIONAL INTELLIGENCE ESTIMATE NUMBER 11-6-55
(Supersedes SNIE 11-8-54)

PROBABLY INTELLIGENCE WARNING OF SOVIET ATTACK ON THE US THROUGH MID-1958

Submitted by the
DIRECTOR OF CENTRAL INTELLIGENCE

The following intelligence organizations participated in the preparation of this estimate: The Central Intelligence Agency and the intelligence organizations of the Departments of State, the Army, the Navy, the Air Force, The Joint Staff, the Atomic Energy Commission, and the National Security Agency.

Sources: The 1955 National Intelligence Estimate (NIE) on the Soviet Union, as well as the 1960 NIE on "Main Trends in Soviet Capabilities and Policies, 1960–1965," both stamped TOP SECRET originally, were declassified and released by the Historical Review Program, Central Intelligence Agency (Washington, DC: June 30, 1993; see Donald P. Steury, *Intentions and Capabilities: Estimates on Soviet Strategic Forces, 1950–1983,* CIA History Staff, Center for the Study of Intelligence, Washington, DC, 1993); the September 1962 Special National Intelligence Estimate (SNIE), written on the eve of the Cuban missile crisis and excerpted here, is from Mary S. McAuliffe, ed., CIA Documents on the Cuban Missile Crisis, CIA History Staff (October 1992), pp. 91–93; the SNIE on the situation in South Vietnam in October 1964, just two months after lawmakers approved the Gulf of Tonkin Resolution, and the NIE on "South Vietnam: Problems and Prospects," written in 1971, are both from the National Intelligence Council, Estimative Products on Vietnam, 1948–1975, NIC 2005–03 (April 2005), pp. 288–237, 575–593.

Concurred in by the
INTELLIGENCE ADVISORY COMMITTEE

On 1 July 1955. Concurring were the Special Assistant, Intelligence, Department of State; the Assistant Chief of Staff, G-2, Department of the Army; the Director of Naval Intelligence; the Director of Intelligence, USAF; the Deputy Director for Intelligence, The Joint Staff; and the Atomic Energy Commission Representative to the IAC. The Assistant to the Director, Federal Bureau of Investigation, abstained, the subject being outside of its jurisdiction.

CENTRAL INTELLIGENCE AGENCY DISSEMINATION NOTICE

1. This estimate was disseminated by the Central Intelligence Agency. This copy is for the information and use of the recipient indicated on the front cover and of persons under his jurisdiction on a need to know basis. Additional essential dissemination may be authorized by the following officials within their respective departments:

    a. Special Assistant to the Secretary for Intelligence, for the Department of State
    b. Assistant Chief of Staff, G-2, for the Department of the Army
    c. Director of Naval Intelligence, for the Department of the Navy
    d. Director of Intelligence, USAF, for the Department of the Air Force
    e. Deputy Director for Intelligence, Joint Staff, for the Joint Staff
    f. Director of Intelligence, AEC, for the Atomic Energy Commission
    g. Assistant to the Director, FBI, for the Federal Bureau of Investigation
    h. Assistant Director for Collection and Dissemination, CIA, for any other Department or Agency

2. This copy may be retained, or destroyed by burning in accordance with applicable security regulations, or returned to the Central Intelligence Agency by arrangement with the Office of Collection and Dissemination, CIA.

3. When an estimate is disseminated overseas, the overseas recipients may retain it for a period not in excess of one year. At the end of this period, the estimate should either be destroyed, returned to the forwarding agency, or permission should be requested of the forwarding agency to retain it in accordance with IAC-D-69/2, 22 June 1953.

This document has been approved for release through the HISTORICAL REVIEW PROGRAM or the Central Intelligence Agency

DISTRIBUTION:

White House
National Security Council
Department of State
Department of Defense
Foreign Operations Administration
Operations Coordinating Board
Atomic Energy Commission
Federal Bureau of Investigation

PROBABLE INTELLIGENCE WARNING OF SOVIET ATTACK ON THE US THROUGH MID-1958

THE PROBLEM

To estimate the probable degree of advance warning that could be provided by intelligence in the event of Soviet attacks on the United States and key US installations and forces overseas through mid-1958.[1]

INTRODUCTION—THE NATURE OF WARNING

When discussing the advance warning of Soviet attack which intelligence may be able to provide, it is necessary to define various possible kinds of warning:

1. Warning of the increased likelihood of war, probably resulting either from Soviet actions or Soviet reactions to Western actions, but not necessarily involving any direct military aspect;
2. Warning of increasing Soviet military readiness to attack, but without definitive evidence of intent to attack or of the time of attack;
3. Warning of clear intent to attack;
4. Warning of clear intent to attack at or about a particular time.

It seems improbable that stage 4, or possibly even stage 3, would be reached conclusively except in the event of high level penetration of the Soviet command, which today seems unlikely, or in case of some exceptional intelligence bonus or breakthrough. While intelligence might be able to say that the USSR would be fully prepared to attack within, say, 10 days, it would find it very difficult to say whether such preparations indicated a firm intent to attack, were primarily in anticipation of an expected US attack, were a deception maneuver, or were to prepare against any contingency. When we speak of degree of warning, therefore, it is important to bear in mind that both time and specificity are involved, and that the earlier the warning the less specific it is likely to be. This inverse relation between time and specificity is an inherent limitation of the warning function.

The fact that warning is likely to be in some degree imprecise or contingent also gives increased importance to other considerations affecting the warning function. Both the nature and degree of warning which can be obtained will always be dependent on many complex factors, some of them unique to any given set of circumstances. Warning will depend first of all on maximum alertness and a maximum scale of continuous effort by intelligence. These would probably be maintained only in a period of rising tension and might be reduced, even unwittingly, if the tension ceased to rise, if there were intermittent periods of apparently declining danger, or if intelligence had previously given false warnings. The effectiveness of warning also depends on the continued credibility of intelligence warnings to responsible officials, for warning as a process is complete only when it is acted upon. The warning process is thus affected by the whole context of events in which it operates, including psychological

---

[1] Since the Soviet attack on the US would be tantamount to general war, this estimate also deals with the over-all warning which the US would be likely to receive of Soviet initiation of general war. It does not consider the warning likely to be given by US or allied early-warning radar, nor the warning which could be obtained from a Soviet ultimatum, since such warning is outside the scope of the problem.

factors and even pure chance. It cannot be regarded as a mechanical process which it is possible for intelligence to set up once and for all and which thereafter operates automatically.

CONCLUSIONS

1. We believe that a Soviet initiation of general war by attacks on the US, its allies, or key overseas installations would almost certainly be preceded by heightened political tension. While such tension would in itself constitute warning that war was becoming more likely, the indications of Soviet preparations which would probably be obtained could be interpreted as evidence of preparations for defense or as part of a war of nerves. Therefore, Soviet behavior in a period of heightened political tension would not necessarily give specific warning of a Soviet intention to attack. Nevertheless, intelligence could probably give warning of the USSR's increasing war readiness and could probably chart the trend toward a period of maximum danger. *(Paras. 12–15, 18)*

2. It would also be possible for the Soviet leaders, after a period of prolonged tension in which they had brought both their political and military preparations to an advanced stage, to bring about an amelioration of the crisis atmosphere as a deception move. Such a move, while involving sacrifice of some advantages, would almost certainly be made if the Soviet leaders considered that a maximum degree of surprise was essential to their strategic plans. Allied intelligence, however, might still be able to detect the continuation of specific military preparations which would be particularly significant as evidence of a Soviet intention to achieve surprise in launching general war. *(Paras. 16–17)*

3. If the USSR chose to initiate war with full-scale land, naval, and air attacks after a period of mobilization, there would be numerous indications of military, as well as of economic and political measures necessary to prepare such attacks. We believe that US intelligence might be able to give a generalized degree of warning as long as four or possibly even six months prior to D-Day, and that the minimum period would not be less than 30 days. After D-30 the number of indications would probably be reduced due to Soviet security measures, although the latter would themselves provide warning. From D-10, and especially D-5, there would probably be certain indications of last-minute preparations, although processing and disseminating these on a timely basis would probably be difficult. As the time of attack drew near, indications of its approach would become increasingly specific. Based on observed Soviet military activities, warning could probably be given from a few hours to a few days in advance of the actual launching of the attack. *(Paras. 21–25)*

4. In order to gain some degree of surprise, the USSR might choose to initiate general war by attacks of less than full scale in Europe, the Middle East, or in the Far East directly or through the Chinese Communists, while simultaneously attacking the US and key overseas installations. The degree of prior Soviet preparations would vary greatly, depending on the location of the attack and the intensity and direction of the preceding political tensions. Even so, the minimum preparations which the USSR would have to take to put its forces in a state of readiness to attack, and to provide support after the attack began would probably require about 15 days. We believe that warning of the probability of attack could be given about one week in advance, but the period might vary from a few hours to as much as 10 days, depending on the seasonal pattern of Soviet military activity. *(Paras. 27–28)*

5. We have estimated in NIE 11-7-55 that by exercising its maximum capability the USSR could now launch about 950 bomber aircraft against the US in an initial attack. However, virtually all of these aircraft would be medium bomber types (BULLS and BADGERS); a few would be heavy bombers (BISONS and BEARS). The great bulk would

have to fly one-way missions. At present, Soviet preparatory activities for maximum scale attack would require at least several months, and probably considerably longer, and would probably become known to allied intelligence, especially if carried forward with great urgency. We believe that the indicators would probably assume a meaningful pattern in time for intelligence to give a generalized degree of warning 15–30 days prior to attack. US intelligence would also be likely to discover significant activities indicating the movement of the large numbers of aircraft to staging bases involved in such a maximum scale attack. We believe that intelligence could give specific advance warning of unusual and possibly threatening air activity on the order of 18–24 hours.[2] *(Paras. 35–38)*

6. We have estimated in NIE 11-7-55 that if the USSR attempted a surprise attack against the US in 1955, aircraft would probably be launched from 11 available staging bases in the Kola, Chukotski, and Kamchatka areas.[3] There is a lack of sufficient evidence to permit a firm assessment of the capabilities of the individual bases in these areas for staging bomber aircraft. However, we believe that by a major effort the USSR could launch some 450 aircraft on initial attack against the US. Preparations for such an attack would permit possible detection by allied intelligence and, if detected, would provide a generalized degree of warning of several days, and specific advance warning of unusual and possibly threatening air activity on the order of 18–24 hours. *(Para. 42)*

7. A reduced scale of attack, however, involving about 250 aircraft could be launched against the US and, accompanied by an extraordinary security effort, might be launched in 1955 with little or no specific advance warning to US intelligence. This estimate rests on the belief that the forward bases may now be capable of handling these aircraft or may become so without detectable preparations. (Para. *43)*

8. By 1958 the bases, training, and equipment of the Soviet Long-Range Air Force could, by a major effort, be advanced to a point where only minimum preparations would be required prior to a maximum attack which could then number about 1,100 bomber aircraft. Provided that such a major effort has been made, movements in and out of the forward staging bases may also become routine. The likelihood that these movements would be discovered would not be much less than at present, but the difficulty of assessing them as warning indicators would thus be very much greater. Moreover, by 1958, the increased speeds of jet bombers will reduce the time required for movement to staging bases and the probable increased handling capabilities at the bases will reduce time required for refueling and servicing. Consequently the specific advance warning of unusual and possibly threatening air activity which could be given, assuming that movement to the staging bases was discovered and correctly interpreted, would probably be on the order of 12–18 hours.[4] *(Para. 39)*

---

[2] Here and in paragraphs 6, 8, and 9 warning given in hours is defined as the elapsed time between the receipt of information (by a US command or agency having authority to alert US defenses) which indicates threat of a possible imminent Soviet air attack, and the time such an attack would reach the existing continental early warning line (1955) and the proposed (DEW) line (1958).

[3] For a full discussion of these forward bases, see NIE 11-7-55, "Soviet Gross Capabilities for Attacks on the US and Key Overseas Installations and Forces through 1 July 1958."

[4] The Director of Intelligence, USAF, believes that movement in and out of forward staging bases may become routine by 1958 if currently indicated efforts to improve the bases, training, and equipment of the Long-Range Air Force continue. He also believes it unlikely that such movement would be discovered and correctly interpreted before its value as warning had passed. Moreover, the increased capability of the Soviet Union to launch heavy bombers from interior bases will further degrade this source of warning information.

9. Both at present and in 1958, if the movement to staging bases was not discovered, warning could be obtained only if almost continuous reconnaissance of the staging areas was being maintained and aircraft were discovered after they had already reached these areas. However, reliance on this means alone might reduce the warning period to a few hours, or even virtually to zero, because of possible difficulties and delays in processing and interpreting the results of the reconnaissance. *(Para. 40)*

10. During the period of this estimate the USSR will have a progressively increasing capability for launching one-way attacks on the US from interior Soviet bases which would probably provide no specific advance warning to US intelligence.[5] Moreover, there are two other ways by which the USSR might by 1958 (and possibly somewhat before that year) launch an attack on the US in such a way that no specific warning would be likely before its actual launching:

a. Assuming that the USSR pressed ahead with development of its advance bases in the Chukotski, Kamchatka, and Kola areas, and with the general preparation of its Long-Range Air Force, "normal" flights of aircraft to and from these bases would almost certainly occur in increasing number as the development of the bases progressed. A pattern of activity would thus tend to be established. Under these circumstances, a considerable number of aircraft—roughly the number engaging in such "normal" activity—would almost certainly be able to take off from these bases (and those in the Leningrad area) for a surprise attack upon the US without any such unusual prior preparations or assembly as would particularly attract the attention of allied intelligence.

b. Assuming that the USSR acquires an inflight refueling capability (which it can do although there is no evidence at present that the Soviet Long-Range Air Force possesses such a capability) and develops it to the necessary degree, Soviet heavy bombers could also be launched on two-way missions from certain home bases without specific advance warning, and without staging at the advance bases.[6] *(Paras. 35, 45)*

11. If the USSR, concurrently with any of the scales of attack discussed above, undertook submarine operations against the US and key overseas installations, it would be necessary for the submarines so employed to proceed to wartime patrol stations shortly before the expected commencement of hostilities. The passage of these submarines might give up to two weeks warning of Soviet preparation for attack. If the USSR undertook concurrent raider operations with some of the major units of their surface fleet against allied lines of communication, the movement of these raiders might give up to 10 days warning of preparation for attack. *(Paras. 30–31)*

12. Soviet preparations to receive a retaliatory blow from allied air power could probably provide some indication of Soviet intent to attack. Minimum preparations would probably include the alerting of air defense forces and the civil defense organization, preparations of military units and installations for air defense, the dispatching of submarines accompanied by increased aerial reconnaissance to locate US carrier forces, and the evacuation of key personnel and possibly segments of population from potential target areas. If steps such as these were taken, they would probably provide a warning period of as much as a week to 10 days, and, taken in conjunction with other indicators, would

---

[5] For full discussion of Soviet long-range capabilities, see NIB 11-7-55, "Soviet Gross Capabilities for Attacks on the US and Key Overseas Installations and Forces through 1 July 1958."

[6] Only the BEAR (Turbo-prop), with its tentatively estimated characteristics, could reach all targets in the US. See NIE 11-7-55.

greatly increase the definiteness of any warning US intelligence might be able to give. We believe that in elementary prudence the USSR would be unwilling to forego preparation to receive a retaliatory blow; therefore, some important indicators of this type would probably be obtained. *(Para. 46)*

DISCUSSION

I. Warning From Soviet Behavior in Various Circumstances

13. The various possible circumstances in which the USSR might decide to attack the US and enter upon general war would have a considerable bearing on the degree of warning which might be obtained.

   a. There are three situations in which the USSR might deliberately decide to attack the US and key overseas installations, thus initiating general war. These situations would arise if the Soviet leaders came to believe: (1) that the USSR had acquired such military capabilities that it could be certain of success in a general war; (2) that the US and its allies were planning an attack on the USSR and that the USSR's only hope of survival lay in seizing the initiative; or (3) that an irreversible shift in the relative weight of military power was impending which would ultimately force the USSR to choose between certain defeat in war and sacrifice of its vital interests. We believe that the Soviet leaders are unlikely to come to any of these conclusions during the period of this estimate.

   b. There remains the possibility that general war might occur after a series of actions and counteractions in some local crisis which neither the USSR nor the Western Allies originally intended to lead to general war. If the USSR believed that the issues at stake were vital to its security or that the loss of prestige involved in backing down would be equally dangerous to Soviet power, and if it believed that the US would not yield, then the USSR might decide that general war was the unavoidable consequence of the crisis and that it should seize the initiative. We believe that if the USSR decides to launch general war in the period through mid-1958, the decision is most likely to come as the consequence of such a situation.[7]

14. *Likelihood of a Period of Tension.* In the situation described under *b.* above, a Soviet decision to attack the US would be preceded by a period of heightened tension. Moreover, even if the Soviet leaders reached any one of the three conclusions in *a.* above, they would probably do so because of an important shift in international alignments, or because of some equally open and marked alteration or impending alteration, of the relative weight of military power. Such developments would themselves be likely to produce heightened political tension. There are situations, however, in which a Soviet decision for war could be taken in the absence of political tension. For example, a Soviet decision motivated as under *a.* (1) above might be the result of some technical advance in Soviet military capabilities unknown to the Western Allies, or a Soviet decision motivated as under *a.* (3) above might be the result of some secret technical advance in Western military capabilities of which Soviet intelligence learned. We believe that such situations are unlikely to arise. Therefore, since an attack on the US, if it occurs, is most likely to

---

[7] The Soviet attitudes toward general war referred to in paragraph 13 are discussed more fully in NIE-3-55, "Soviet Capabilities and Probable Courses of Action Through 1960," dated 17 May 1955, Sections VI and VII.

arise from a series of actions and counteractions not originally intended to lead to general war (paragraph 13 *b*.), it would almost certainly be preceded by a period of heightened tension.

15. *Reliability of Political Indicators in a Period of Tension.* While the existence of a prior period of tension would in itself constitute warning that war was becoming more likely, it would also greatly increase the difficulty of obtaining from Soviet political behavior a specific warning of attack. Most of the political actions taken by the USSR during a period of war preparation might not differ greatly from those undertaken as routine in any period of heightened political tension. These actions might include: diplomatic approaches to some states designed to influence them toward abandonment of their alliances with the US; massive "peace" propaganda directed at the populations of Western states and intended to undermine the will to resist or to destroy confidence in the motives and intentions of governments; explicit threats against would-be aggressors; new proposals to ban nuclear weapons; instructions to Communist parties to ready themselves for their sabotage and subversion missions; intensified propaganda directed to the Bloc populations to prepare them psychologically for "resistance to aggression." All such actions, however, could be interpreted as defensively motivated or as part of a war of nerves. Thus while they might provide warning of the increased likelihood of general war, they would not provide specific warning of attack.

16. *Reliability of Military Indicators in a Period of Tension.* The existence of a period of heightened tension would also make more difficult the determination from Soviet military preparations of a specific intent to attack. If in such a period the USSR undertook various military preparations, it would probably be as difficult to distinguish offensive from defensive intent as in the case of indicators from Soviet political behavior. In a protracted situation of this sort intelligence probably could only give warning of the USSR's increasing war readiness and chart the trend toward the period of maximum danger, but not warn of a Soviet intention to attack. The USSR might be carrying out military preparations not in order to initiate war but in readiness for instant retaliation to a US attack which it feared might be impending.

17. *Possibility of Soviet Deception.* It would also be possible for the Soviet leaders, after a period of prolonged tension in which they had brought both their political and military preparations to an advanced stage, to bring about an amelioration of the crisis atmosphere as a deception move. They could offer concessions as a basis for new negotiations, and simulate reduction of some of their military preparations, or even actually reduce them. If they considered surprise essential to their plans and believed that they still could achieve some degree of surprise in their initial attack, this would be a likely course for the Soviet leaders to pursue. However, such a course would involve sacrifice of some advantages. An initial surprise assault aimed at Western retaliatory power might include air attacks on the territories of some states which the USSR might otherwise have hoped to neutralize politically. It would probably also involve the clear assumption of responsibility for initiating war by aggressive action, and thus might harden the will to resist in some Western countries. Nevertheless, the Soviet leaders would almost certainly accept these disadvantages and attempt deceptive political maneuvers if they considered that the maximum degree of surprise attainable was essential to their strategic plans.

18. Although a large degree of deception could be introduced into Soviet behavior, allied intelligence might still be able to detect the continuation of specific military preparations. Such indications could be interpreted as due to Soviet caution and mistrust, but they

would also point to the possibility of a deception maneuver and they would be particularly significant as evidence of a Soviet intention to achieve surprise in launching general war.

19. *Summary.* We believe, therefore, that Soviet behavior in a period of heightened tensions would not necessarily give warning of attack. It would probably establish that Soviet readiness for general war was increasing; it would also establish that the likelihood of war was increasing but would not necessarily indicate that general war was probable. It would also lead to heightened activity and sensitivity on the part of allied intelligence. However, neither a belligerent and unyielding attitude nor a defensive and conciliatory one would be a sure guide to Soviet intentions.

II. Alternative Scales of Soviet Attack

20. The probable, degree of warning that the West would receive of Soviet attack would depend in large part upon the type of attack initiated. Many courses of action are open to the Soviet planners in the event they should decide to initiate a general war. At one end of the spectrum would be a massive multifront Soviet attack on the US and allied states, undertaken after a period of intensive mobilization. Such a plan of attack would sacrifice strategic surprise in favor of maximum military preparation, although the USSR might still hope to achieve some degree of tactical surprise. At the other end of the spectrum would be a Soviet surprise attack, with no prior preparations of a nature that could be relied on to provide warning indicators. Such an attack would sacrifice weight for the advantages of surprise. This estimate does not attempt to forecast Soviet strategy or the probable scale of the initial attack. It only discusses the probable degree of warning which would be obtained if Soviet planners selected any one of the following alternatives for their initial attack:

a. Full-scale attack after a period of general mobilization;

b. Soviet campaign in Western Europe from existing deployments and simultaneous attacks on the US and key US overseas forces and installations;

c. Initial attacks only on the US and key US overseas forces and installations

(1) Maximum scale attack

(2) Surprise attack.

III. Warning of Full-Scale Soviet Attack

21. A full-scale attack employing all arms in strength at the outset of war would necessarily be preceded by a period of mobilization during which full war readiness, or a condition close to it, had been achieved. The range of activities necessary for such full mobilization of war potential in a highly industrialized state like the USSR is so extensive and involves so many measures affecting broad sections of the population that even a totalitarian government would find it impossible to conceal all of them. In the economic field, a complex redirection and intensification of productive effort would have to take place as materials, manpower, and facilities were transferred from consumption and investment goods industries to armament industries. These measures would probably be impossible without the use of public information media. In addition, manipulation of domestic opinion is so persistent a preoccupation of the Soviet government and its concern over popular morale under conditions of crisis is so intense that its vast propaganda

apparatus would certainly be openly committed to preparing the Soviet people to withstand the strains of general war.

22. In the military field itself, the induction of additional military classes, formation of new units and fleshing-out of existing units to full strength, intensified and more realistic training, redeployment of combat groups to forward areas, and a variety of logistic measures would hardly escape entirely the observation of Western intelligence. In particular, it would be difficult for the USSR to hide large-scale troop movements in East Germany or the other Satellites and forward deployment of its naval units. Withdrawal of a significant portion of civil aircraft from scheduled flights to augment the aircraft of the airborne forces or for other purposes might give additional warning of full-scale attack. At present numerous specific preparations for a full-scale air effort against the US would have to be made by the Soviet Long-Range Air Force, although by mid-1958 the extent and reliability of such indicators could be considerably reduced (see paragraph 37 below).

23. At present, if the USSR undertook to mobilize for a full-scale attack, US intelligence would probably receive numerous indications of large-scale Soviet mobilization during a period of about six months to about one month before D-Day, largely because the preparations likely to be undertaken during this period would be those least susceptible of concealment. However, if the decision to proceed to full mobilization came after a period of prolonged tension in which preparatory measures were initiated, or if by 1958 general Soviet war readiness should be substantially increased, then initial indicators might appear considerably later than six months prior to D-Day. In any event, from roughly D-30 to around D-10 days, we would be likely to get much less in the way of indications because the preparations in this period would be those which Soviet security is best equipped to conceal. Moreover, by about one month before D-Day the progressive tightening of Soviet security measures would probably have reached a high point. There would almost certainly be a reduction in information from sources within the Bloc; at the same time, however, the drying up of internal Bloc sources because of intensified security measures would in itself provide an indication of Soviet preparations. Then, in the period from D-10 and especially D-5 on, we could expect indications of last-minute preparations. At this time, however, there would be a serious problem of processing and disseminating such indications on a sufficiently timely basis.

24. We believe that allied intelligence would probably be able to sort the variety of indicators into a meaningful pattern at a relatively early stage of Soviet mobilization for a full-scale attack. US intelligence might become aware of this mobilization as long as four or possibly even six months prior to D-Day. The minimum period would probably not be less than 30 days. Even though intelligence was able to give only a generalized degree of warning, showing the progressive increase of Soviet war readiness, it would probably still be able to chart the trend of full-scale preparations, to anticipate their probable course to completion, and thus to designate the beginning of a period of maximum danger. It might even be able to identify features of Soviet full-scale mobilization which because of their uniqueness or extreme costliness could be interpreted specifically as evidence of an intention to attack.

25. As the time of attack drew near, indications of its possible approach would become increasingly specific. Based on observed Soviet military activities, warning could probably be given from a few hours to a few days in advance of the actual launching of the attack. This would be rendered very difficult, however, if Soviet forces, when their preparations for attack were known to be near completion, undertook air, naval, and

ground reconnaissance, or attempted major feints. These activities might provide evidence of Soviet intention to attack, but would aggravate the difficulty of determining the time of such attack. It might also be recognized that, in theory at least, the USSR could always refrain from or delay attacking even after preparations were complete. Hence the indications of military readiness, taken by themselves, would not necessarily provide conclusive evidence that attack was certain.

IV. Probable Degrees of Warning in the Event of Less Than Full-Scale Attack

26. If the USSR were to sacrifice weight for the advantages of surprise, it would be forced, depending upon the degree of surprise it sought, to accept certain major limitations: (a) no large-scale mobilization of additional units; (b) no large-scale redeployment of Soviet air, naval, or ground forces, especially to forward areas; and (c) no unusual movement of Soviet air, naval, or ground forces in such areas as would be likely to indicate the imminence of attack. However, even if the USSR attempted to achieve the utmost surprise in launching general war, it would still probably consider a minimum number of prior preparations a matter of necessity and elementary prudence. Therefore, at least some of the general preparations discussed in Section III above would almost certainly have to be undertaken. Some of these preparations would be detected by allied intelligence, but it probably would be very difficult to ascertain any such clear pattern of preparations as would be discernible in event of mobilization for full-scale attack. Again, the degree of readiness already achieved by Soviet forces would affect the number of indicators obtained and the general political situation would affect the intensity of US intelligence effort and the ability of intelligence to interpret correctly such indicators as it did obtain. Consequently, we believe it possible that these preparations would not lead to a warning of attack, especially if they were carried out over a long period of time and with careful concealment.

27. If the USSR decided to attack the US and key overseas installations without full prior mobilization for general war, and hence without full-scale attacks in other areas, two general alternatives would be open:

a. It could combine its attack against the US and key overseas installations with a surprise ground campaign in Europe, the Middle East, and in the Far East directly or through the Chinese Communists without prior reinforcement of its forces.[8]

b. It could undertake initially air, and possibly other forms of attack, against the US and key overseas installations, but delay its ground campaigns and discernible preparations for other military operations until after these initial attacks had been launched.

V. Soviet Campaign in Major Areas and Simultaneous Attacks on the US and Key Overseas Installations

28. If the USSR chose to initiate general war by an attack with the forces currently stationed in Europe, the Middle East, and the Far East, together with attacks on the US and key overseas installations, the degree of its over-all prior preparations would vary greatly,

---

[8] The USSR could of course strengthen this ground attack by some degree of prior reinforcement. For the purpose of this estimate, however, we take the above case as the limiting one: i.e., any prior reinforcement would tend to provide additional indicators and hence additional warning.

depending on the location of the attack and the intensity and duration of the preceding political tensions. If, as we think likely, there had been a long period of crisis, the USSR might have already achieved a considerable degree of military and economic mobilization for war, and its foreign and domestic political preparation might be well advanced. Moreover, during the period 1955–1958, measures may be taken ostensibly or actually in response to external developments, e.g., West German rearmament, which would greatly improve Soviet readiness for attack. Therefore, the indicators derived from such activities, though warning of the increased readiness for war and likelihood of war, would probably be of limited significance for warning of this type of attack. Even so, the minimum local preparations which the USSR would still have to take for an attack with forces in place would provide some degree of warning.

29. In Europe, for example, some time would be required to assemble major elements in forward positions, although this would vary seasonally. The longest period required would be between May and August when units are split between home stations and field training areas; a lesser period would be required between November and March when units are consolidated at home stations; the minimum period required would be in April when units are moving to training areas and in September–October when units are either engaged in large-scale maneuvers or are being moved back to home stations. Other minimum preparations would include the release from stocks of transport, munitions, and supplies in quantities well in excess of those used even on full-scale maneuvers. In addition, some two weeks before the attack it would probably be necessary to begin the movement of large numbers of locomotives and rolling stock from East Germany to the Soviet border in order to prepare for resupply and reinforcement operations to support and expand the offensive. Altogether, the USSR would probably be engaged in these preparations over a period of about 15 days and US intelligence would probably begin to acquire some indicators at an early stage, although varying with the season of the year. We believe that warning of the probability of attack could be given about one week in advance. However, in the absence of other indicators and with Soviet actions appearing to be part of a normal pattern, the warning could vary as follows:

a. from a few hours to a few days in April and in September–October;

b. from two to five days in November–March;

c. from five to 10 days in May–August.

30. If the USSR undertook concurrent submarine operations against the US and key overseas installations, it would be necessary for the submarines so employed to proceed to wartime patrol stations shortly before the expected commencement of hostilities. The passage of these submarines might give up to two weeks warning of Soviet preparation for attack.

31. If the USSR undertook concurrent raider operations with some of the major units of their surface fleet against allied lines of communication, it would be necessary for the units so employed to proceed to their assigned areas of operations shortly before the expected commencement of hostilities. The movement of these raiders might give up to 10 days warning of preparation for attack.

32. In addition, any unusual and unexplainable deviation from the normal operating pattern of the Soviet Bloc merchant marine could be a supporting indicator of Soviet preparations to attack.

33. The extent to which the preparations going on simultaneously for air attack on the US and key overseas installations and forces would tend to confirm and/or advance

the warning would depend somewhat upon the planned scale of these attacks, as discussed below.

VI. Initial Air Attacks on the US and Key US Overseas Forces and Installations

34. For the purposes of this estimate it is necessary to consider two types of air attack on the US and key overseas installations: (a) a maximum effort using as many aircraft as possible, and (b) an attack designed to achieve a high degree of surprise. The USSR could undertake these air attacks on the US and key overseas installations and forces simultaneously with a full-scale attack in Eurasia or with the less than full-scale attacks discussed in paragraphs 26–32. Alternatively, the USSR could initiate general war with such air attacks only, while delaying discernible preparations for other military operations in order to increase the likelihood of surprise against the US. In this case, the very disparity between preparations for long-range air operations and those for other general war campaigns could be a highly significant indicator of the probable nature of the initial Soviet attack.

35. *Maximum Air Attack.* We have estimated in NIE 11-7-55 that by exercising its maximum capability the USSR could now launch about 950 long-range aircraft against the US in an initial attack.[9] By mid-1958 the maximum number launched could be increased to about 1,100. However, we believe extensive prior preparations would be required, particularly in the early part of the period covered by this estimate. These would almost certainly include improving airfields, maintenance and fuel storage facilities in the Chukotski, Kamchatka, and Kola areas, bringing personnel and equipment to full strength in long-range air units, probably intensified training of air personnel, increased frequency of long-distance training missions, and raising levels of maintenance, and possibly training in inflight refueling techniques. The critical indicators would be those relating to increased levels of activity at staging bases in the Chukotski, Kamchatka, and Kola areas, since in 1958 as well as at present these bases would be essential to maximum attacks on the US. By 1958, however, the degree of Soviet dependence upon these forward areas, and thus their significance as a warning indicator, would decline if the USSR, as part of a maximum scale attack, chose to launch some or all of its heavy bombers directly from interior bases or either one- or two-way missions or combinations thereof. Except for the BEAR (turboprop), even Soviet heavy bombers employing inflight refueling would still require advanced bases for making two-way attacks on the most distant US targets.

36. At present, Soviet preparatory activities for maximum scale attack would require at least several months, and probably considerably longer, and would probably become known to allied intelligence, especially if carried forward with great urgency. We believe that the indicators associated with preparation of the advance bases, taken together with others pointing to the increased readiness of the Long-Range Air Force, would probably assume a meaningful pattern in time for intelligence to give a generalized degree of warning 15–30 days prior to attack. Nevertheless, this would be warning only of increased readiness and not of intent to attack.

---

[9] The great bulk of these aircraft would have to fly one-way missions, but the problem of *advance warning* by intelligence, as distinguished from *tactical warning* by early warning radar, would not be significantly different if the USSR, in order to permit two-way missions by more of the strike aircraft, chose to include some proportion of tankers, if available, in the total number of planes launched.

37. If such preparations proceeded gradually over the next few years, they would have even less significance for warning, since they could well be part of a normal build-up of the USSR's long-range air capability. Thus, by 1958, the bases, training, and equipment of the Soviet Long-Range Air Force could be advanced to a point where only minimum preparations would be required prior to an attack. There would then need to be little in the way of movement of personnel and equipment, logistic activity, or training flights which would depart from a normal pattern of activity. Under these circumstances, indicators of the preparations taking place in the Soviet Long-Range Air Force might be few, and warning would depend almost entirely on indicators received during the staging of aircraft.

38. At present, US intelligence would be likely to discover significant activities indicating the movement of the large numbers of aircraft to staging bases involved in a maximum scale attack. Considering also the amount of time that the aircraft would require to reach such bases, together with the time required for refueling and servicing at the bases, we believe that intelligence could give specific advance warning[10] of unusual and possibly threatening air activity on the order of 18–24 hours before the attacking aircraft reached the early warning radar screen. It would always be possible, of course, for such a movement to be a practice maneuver or a feint, and therefore warning of actual intent to attack could not be given with complete certainty.

39. Developments are taking place in the Soviet Long-Range Air Force which probably will decrease the possibility of detection, and increase the difficulty of interpreting indicators in terms of intent to attack. By 1958, movements in and out of forward staging bases may become routine, provided that during the interim a major effort had been undertaken to improve base facilities and training, logistics, and equipment of the Long-Range Air Force. The likelihood that these movements would be discovered would not be much less than at present, but the difficulty of assessing them as warning indicators would be very much greater. In addition, by 1958 the increased speeds of jet bombers will reduce the time required for movements to staging bases, and the probable increased handling capabilities at the bases will reduce time required for refueling and servicing. Consequently, the specific advance warning of unusual and possibly threatening air activity which could be given, assuming that movement to the staging bases was discovered and correctly interpreted, would probably be on the order of 12–18 hours.[11]

40. Both at present and in 1958, if the movement to staging bases was not discovered, warning could be obtained only if almost continuous reconnaissance of the staging areas was being maintained and aircraft were discovered after they had already reached these areas. However, reliance on this means alone might reduce the specific advance warning period to a few hours, or even virtually to zero, because of possible difficulties and delays in processing and interpreting the results of reconnaissance. Moreover, by 1958 the

---

[10] Here and in paragraphs 39, 40, 42, and 44 warning given in hour terms is defined as the elapsed time between the receipt of information by a US command or agency having authority to alert US defense which indicates an imminent threat of Soviet air attack, and the time such an attack would reach the existing continental early warning line (1955) and the proposed (DEW) line (1958).

[11] The Director of Intelligence, USAF, believes that movement in and out of forward staging bases may become routine by 1958 if currently indicated efforts to improve the bases, training, and equipment of the Long-Range Air Force continue. He also believes it unlikely that such movement would be discovered and correctly interpreted before its value as warning had passed. Moreover, the increased capability of the Soviet Union to launch heavy bombers from interior bases will further degrade this source of warning information.

probable growth in Soviet air defenses would make such reconnaissance considerably more difficult.

41. The additional preparations which would be necessary to attack US overseas installations would not increase the likelihood of specific advance warning.[12] In the event of a maximum scale attack, the long-range air arm would already be in a high state of readiness. The readying of the jet light bomber units which could also be used for attacks in Western Europe, the UK, and some parts of the Middle East and Far East could be accomplished without serious additional risk of detection unless very large numbers had to be deployed to forward bases. If guided missiles were employed, no warning of their use would be obtained, apart from the generalized warning which might have been derived from prior preparations for hostilities.

42. *Surprise Air Attack.* However much the Soviet planners desired to achieve surprise in their initial air attacks on the US and key overseas installations, they would still wish to achieve the optimum weight of attack consistent with surprise. We have estimated in NIE 11-7-55 that if the USSR attempted a surprise attack against the US in mid-1955, aircraft would probably be launched from the 11 available staging bases in the Kola, Chukotski, and Kamchatka areas. There is a lack of sufficient evidence to permit a firm assessment of the capabilities of the individual bases in these areas for staging bomber aircraft. However, we believe by a major effort the USSR could launch some 450 aircraft on initial attacks against the US. Preparations for such an attack would permit possible detection by allied intelligence and, if detected, would provide a generalized degree of warning of several days, and specific advance warning of unusual and possibly threatening air activity on the order of 18–24 hours.

43. A reduced scale of attack, however, involving about 250 aircraft could be launched against the US, and accompanied by an extraordinary security effort, might be launched in mid-1955 *with little or no specific advance warning to US intelligence.* This estimate rests on the belief that the forward bases may now be capable of handling these aircraft or may become so without detectable preparations.

44. As estimated in paragraphs 37 and 38, by 1958 the USSR could, provided forward base construction, training, and equipment of the Soviet Long-Range Air Force were sufficiently developed, launch its maximum air attack of about 1,100 aircraft against the US under such conditions that the period of specific advance warning of unusual and possibly threatening air activity would probably be on the order of 12–18 hours, and might be considerably less if the movement to staging bases was not discovered. Thus in 1958 the maximum Soviet air attack, provided no other warning of Soviet intent to go to war had been received, could achieve a high degree of surprise.

45. During the period of this estimate the USSR will have a progressively increasing capability of launching one-way attacks on the US from interior Soviet bases which would

---

[12] Although variations in the relative priority as to timing and weight of attack between the US and overseas installations would not affect the *advance warning* obtained by intelligence, they would be of great significance for the *tactical warning* derived from radar due to the varying times at which aircraft bound for targets at different distances would be picked up. For example, if the USSR chose to make attacks on overseas installations before launching attacks on the US itself, those attacks would alert the continental US defense system, although the overseas installations might obtain only radar warning of the attack. They would probably have been alerted, to some extent, however, by generalized warning derived from general preparations for hostilities.

probably provide no specific advance warning to US intelligence.[13] Moreover, there are two other ways in which the USSR might by 1958 (and possibly somewhat before that year) launch an attack on the US in such a way that no specific warning would be likely before its actual launching:

a. Assuming that the USSR pressed ahead with development of its advance bases in the Chukotski, Kamchatka, and Kola areas, and with the general preparation of its Long-Range Air Force, "normal" flights of aircraft to and from these bases would almost certainly occur in increasing number as the development of the bases progressed. A pattern of activity would tend to be established. Under these circumstances, a considerable number of aircraft—roughly the number engaging in such "normal" activity—would almost certainly be able to take off from these bases (and from those in the Leningrad area) for a surprise attack upon the US without any such unusual prior preparations or assembly as would particularly attract the attention of allied intelligence.

b. Assuming that the USSR acquires an inflight refueling capability (which it can do although there is no evidence at present that the Soviet Long-Range Air Force possesses such a capability) and develops it to the necessary degree, Soviet heavy bombers could also be launched on two-way missions from certain home bases without specific advance warning, and without staging at the advance bases.[14]

VII. WARNING FROM SOVIET PREPARATIONS TO RECEIVE RETALIATORY ATTACKS

46. An important element not included in the foregoing examination is that of Soviet defensive preparations to receive a retaliatory blow from allied power. Minimum preparations would probably include the alerting of air defense forces and the civil defense organization, preparations of military units and installations for air defense, the dispatching of submarines accompanied by increased aerial reconnaissance to locate US carrier forces, and the evacuation of key personnel and possibly segments of population from potential target areas. If steps such as these were not taken, they would constitute serious limitations on the USSR's ability to withstand a retaliatory blow. If they were taken, they would probably provide a warning period of as much as a week to 10 days, and, taken in conjunction with other indicators, would greatly increase the definiteness of any warning US intelligence might be able to give. The risk which the USSR would be willing to accept as a result of neglecting some or all of this type of defensive preparation would depend in part on the degree of success which the Soviet leaders expected their own initial attack to achieve. We believe that in elementary prudence they would be unwilling to forego preparation to receive a retaliatory blow; therefore, some important indicators of this type would probably be obtained.

---

[13] For full discussion of Soviet long-range capabilities, see NIE 11-7-55.

[14] Only the BEAR (Turbo-prop), with its tentatively estimated characteristics, could reach all targets in the US. See NIE 11-7-55.

NIE 11-4-60 MAIN TRENDS IN SOVIET CAPABILITIES AND POLICIES, 1960–1965

THE PROBLEM

To review significant developments affecting the USSR's internal political situation, economic, scientific, and military programs, relations with other Bloc states, and foreign policy, and to estimate probable Soviet policies and actions over about the next five years.

SUMMARY OF THE ESTIMATE

1. The attempt to forecast developments within the USSR and in Soviet power and policy for five years ahead is subject to some very severe limitations. Our estimative reach in many of the detailed matters discussed in the body of this Estimate is frankly acknowledged to fall well short of such a period. In respect of matters where we have actually made five-year estimates the degree of certainty falls off markedly for the later years. In the summary paragraphs which follow we are dealing with the broader trends which will determine the nature and magnitude of the challenge which the USSR will present to US security in the years ahead. These we believe are predictable in the main, although their particular manifestations clearly depend upon unknown and imponderable factors, or even upon purely fortuitous developments.

THE PRESENT SOVIET OUTLOOK

2. One of the principal factors which will shape future developments is the outlook of the Soviet leaders themselves. There are two essential aspects of this. One is the Soviet leaders' belief, derived from the Marxist-Leninist ideology which continues to dominate their thinking, that their society and the non-Communist world are locked in an irreconcilable struggle which must continue until their system comes to dominate the world. There is no evidence at present to indicate that the Soviets will come to accept a world system which assumes the genuine coexistence of states and ideologies. For so brief a period as five years, Soviet behavior and policy will surely be marked by fundamental hostility toward the West, and especially toward the US as the principal obstacle to the fulfillment of Soviet aims.

3. A second essential feature of the Soviet outlook in the current period is its high confidence in the growth of the USSR's power and influence. Looking back to the weak and perilous position in which the new Communist regime found itself in 1917, remembering all the internal and external trials it has survived, and considering its growth in relative economic and military power over the last 20 years, the Soviet leaders are encouraged in their doctrinaire expectations about communism's inevitable triumph. That it was a Communist rocket which first ventured into space symbolizes for them that they are marching in the vanguard of history. They think they see a response to their doctrines and influence in the revolutionary turmoils of Asia, Africa, and Latin America. They expect to associate the peoples emerging from colonialism and backwardness with their own cause, mobilizing them against an ever more constricted world position of the Western states. The relative internal stability of the latter at present they see as only a transient phase.

4. While hostility toward the West and confidence in the eventual outcome of the world struggle will inspire Soviet behavior in the period ahead, we do not believe that the result will be policies of recklessness. The Soviet leaders recognize that Western resources remain great, and that the struggle for Communist power in the uncommitted world will be prolonged. They are particularly conscious of the hazards of nuclear war. Moreover, they have numerous problems of their own within the Communist Bloc which may move them to caution. Their policies will be marked by a persistent activism and opportunism, but also by what they consider to be a due measure of caution. More important, however, than the Soviet outlook and aims, especially since these offer little hope for accommodation and genuine peace, are the strengths and resources which the Soviets will be able to bring to the pursuit of their aims.

The Soviet Power Base

ECONOMIC ASPECT

5. Perhaps the most firmly based of our estimates are those which relate to the growth of Soviet economic power. The Soviet economy has the resources and plant as well as the planning and directing mechanisms to insure steady fulfillment of most of the goals in industrial expansion which the leadership sets. The industrial targets of the Seven-Year Plan (1959–1965), providing for 8.6 percent annual increase in industrial output, will almost certainly be met ahead of schedule. We estimate that by 1965 total investment will reach about one-third of gross national product (GNP), as compared with the present US rate of about one-fifth of GNP. Only in agriculture, which is burdened by a heritage of errors and neglect, will the regime fall well short of its goals, but even here we estimate that output will increase by about 3 to 4 percent per year. The GNP of the USSR in 1959 was somewhat less than half that of the US; it is growing about twice as fast and by 1965 will probably be somewhat more than half of US GNP.

6. GNP is a rough measurement, however. More important in terms of world power competition are the uses to which economic resources are put. The USSR maintains a defense effort judged to be of about the same magnitude as that of the US. The dollar value of Soviet investment in industry in 1959 exceeded the highest US figure, achieved in 1957. For purposes related to national power—defense, science, foreign economic and political operations—the Soviets are increasingly in a position to assign resources freely and without agonizing self-denials. That they are able to provide the resources for national power on a scale equivalent to the US is due to the virtually absolute command which the leadership has over the disposal of resources. It will continue to give the highest priority to purposes related to national power in order to "overtake and surpass" the US. The Soviet regime has bought economic growth and military strength at the expense of the living standards of the Soviet people. But its resources are now great enough so that it feels able to provide for improved living standards also. The consumption level remains low but we estimate that per capita increases will occur over the next five years at the respectable rate of four percent annually. The Soviet challenge in the economic field will be increasingly formidable, not because the USSR has any chance of overtaking the US standard or style of living, but becomes Soviet resources for the competition in power are already great and will continue to grow rapidly.

MILITARY ASPECT

7. As indicated, military power has one of the first claims upon Soviet resources. Our estimates on the development of Soviet military power until 1965 are far less certain than those on the Soviet economy. This is partly due to unpredictable developments during a period of rapid change in military technology. It is due more to gaps in certain kinds of critical information about Soviet military programs. Although in recent years the Soviets have released fuller economic data than previously, on essential matters in the military field they continue to maintain a policy of extreme secrecy, which they evidently view as a major military asset in itself.

8. The most significant development in the military field during the period of this estimate will be the USSR's emergence from strategic inequality, primarily through the buildup of an ICBM force, and also through development of its defense systems against nuclear attack. The overcoming of an inferiority under which the Soviets have operated throughout the postwar period is already having a profound effect on Soviet attitudes and policy. It inspires the confidence remarked upon above, has emboldened the Soviets to challenge the West on a vital issue like Berlin, and has led them to engage the West in other areas around the world formerly conceded to be beyond the reach of Soviet power.

9. The Soviet leaders will not be content with the gains in military power they have made. They will seek, by intensive research and development through the years ahead, as well as by equipping their forces with advanced weapons as these become available, to acquire an advantage over the West. If they succeed, they will press their advantage ruthlessly, though still within what they would consider to be the limits of tolerable risk to their own rule and system. It seems quite clear that in their present view both sides are deterred from the deliberate initiation of general war as a rational course of action. Moreover, with the weapons systems now on hand or likely to be available during the next few years, the Soviets probably do not count on acquiring an advantage so decisive as to permit them to launch general war under conditions which would not gravely menace their regime. Nevertheless, they are building their nuclear striking power with vigor, and we believe that they will build a substantial missile force. What we can learn of Soviet ideas suggests that their long-range striking capability is thought of primarily in terms of deterrence, and of employment for a heavy blow should the Soviets finally conclude that deterrence had failed, rather than in terms of the deliberate initiation of general war.[1] The Soviet missile force will also constitute an important means of political pressure, even though it is never used in actual combat.

10. In order to deal more effectively with the continuing bomber threat the Soviets are incorporating a large number of surface-to-air missiles into their air defense. They are now also doing large-scale research and development on antimissile systems in the hope of obtaining an advantage in this critical aspect of the future weapons balance. By the period 1963-1966 they will probably begin to deploy such a system, though its effectiveness is

---

[1] The Assistant Chief of Staff, Intelligence, USAF, believes that the evidence of offensive missile and bomber production and deployment shows a definite intent by the Soviet rulers to achieve a clear military superiority at the earliest practicable date. He feels we are entering a very critical twenty-four month period in which the USSR may well sense it has the advantage. The Soviet leaders may press that advantage and offer the US the choice of war or of backing down on an issue heretofore considered red vital to our national interests.

uncertain. Soviet research and development effort will probably also focus on the new threat presented by Polaris.

11. Partly as a result of the increased security the Soviets feel they have gained from their development of a variety of offensive and defensive missiles, they have announced a major personnel reduction in their forces, from about 3.6 to about 2.5 million men by the end of 1961. Barring a serious deterioration in the international situation, we believe the cut will be substantially carried out. We believe that tactical aviation has already been cut by one-half and naval aviation by two-thirds, the latter primarily through elimination of the fighter arm. However, the main weight of the cut will fall on the very large ground forces. Even with the reduction, the Soviets will still have substantial field ground forces: we estimate nearly 1.5 million men organized in 65 divisions averaging two-thirds strength and some 60 cadre divisions at about one-fourth strength. The submarine force will become even more than it is today the primary component of the Soviet Navy, and will include nuclear and missile-carrying types suitable for strategic attack.

12. In sum, the USSR will continue to develop formidable military strength despite the personnel reduction. The Soviet military posture is designed primarily, we believe, to deter general war but also to fight such a war if necessary.[2] Equally, it is intended to bolster the USSR's power position and thereby to promote its general policies. Soviet capabilities for limited war in areas close to Bloc borders are obviously great, but for conflict in more distant areas they are comparatively slight. We do not believe that the USSR intends as a matter of policy to conduct limited war at remote ranges. However, we do not exclude that, with their current tendency to political involvement in remoter areas, the Soviets may seek to develop a greater capacity for intervening militarily, even if only to establish a military presence, in such areas. A really effective ability to do this would presumably depend heavily upon acquisition of base rights and facilities under friendly political arrangements.

SCIENTIFIC ASPECT

13. The Soviets obviously understand that science has become one of the key fronts in the world struggle, not only because of its relations to military capability but also because it is a major element in great power prestige. The scale of their effort, thanks to the heavy investment they made in training scientists in past years, is probably now roughly on a par with that of the US, at least in some fields of the basic sciences and in critical areas related to weapons technology. Presumably the scope of Soviet scientific activity will broaden as needs in these first priority areas are met. The quality of Soviet scientific work in many fields is now such that achievements conferring great prestige are as likely to occur in the USSR as in any other country.

POLITICAL ASPECTS

14. It is in estimating the political aspect of future developments within the Soviet Bloc that the greatest imponderables intrude. The political system within the USSR itself is stable, and it will almost certainly retain its totalitarian features. The regime will not be openly challenged by the Soviet people, who, even though many of them view it with

---

[2] The Assistant Chief of Staff, Intelligence, USAF, believes the Soviets seek a clear military superiority. See his footnote to paragraph 9.

apathy and ideological disillusionment, are in general hopeful for improvement in the conditions of their life and patriotically moved by the USSR's achievements and its position of world power. If there is change in the Soviet political system it will come from the higher levels of the party and government. In the relatively small group which constitutes the real governing class there are some signs of a desire for more regular participation in policy making, and for more reliance in policy execution on professional expertise instead of party agitational methods. While Khrushchev has avoided or been obliged to avoid the arbitrariness of Stalin, among those who surround him there are probably some who would like to move still further away from the domination of one man in the system. Given Khrushchev's age and state of health he may not survive as the dominating leader throughout the next five years. His successor at the head of the Soviet Government and party may be more restricted in the personal power he wields, but in any totalitarian system political developments are likely to depend heavily on the qualities and style which individual personalities bring to the exercise of great and arbitrary power.

15. In the area of political developments within the Communist Bloc it is the evolution of relations among the Bloc states which raises the greatest uncertainties at present. In general, the states of Eastern Europe have gained in economic strength and political stability in recent years, despite the continuing alienation and resentment of large parts of their populations. There seems little doubt that, with the more flexible and indirect methods of control the USSR has been employing since 1956–1957, it will be able to maintain a generally effective hegemony. However, China has raised a fundamental challenge to Soviet leadership of the Bloc. Even if some way is found to resolve the issues posed by China's desire to pursue a more militant policy toward the West, it raises the serious question as to whether the long-term unity of the Bloc under Soviet leadership can be maintained. We believe that there is a trend away from monolithic unity, and that in the long run, if China is to remain within the Bloc, a looser relationship is bound to develop. The future course of Sino-Soviet relations will obviously have profound consequences for the nature of the challenge which communism poses for the Free World. The West may be faced either with new dangers or new opportunities, or both.[3]

Soviet Policies Toward the Non-Communist World

16. The general Soviet strategy for carrying on the world struggle in the present phase rests on two propositions. The first is that general nuclear war must be avoided because the costs in physical damage and social disintegration would be intolerable. The second is that the world position and power of the "imperialist" states can be undermined by a persistent and aggressive campaign waged by methods short of war—political struggle, economic and scientific competition, subversion. Political struggle takes the form of a constant agitation designed to capture and organize in broad mass movements the sentiments which focus on the great issues of the current period—peace, disarmament,

---

[3] The Assistant Chief of Staff for Intelligence, Department of the Army, and the Director for Intelligence, Joint Staff, believe that, in spite of Sino-Soviet frictions, the USSR and Communist China will continue to be firmly allied against the West and will render one another mutual support whenever an important interest of one or the other is threatened by the non-Communist world.

anticolonialism, social justice, economic development. By manipulating these issues and by dramatizing the growth of Soviet power, the Soviets are also trying to align the governments of the underdeveloped and uncommitted states with the Bloc, and against the West. The Soviet leaders hope that the result will be a progressive isolation and loss of influence for the Western powers, divisions among them, and a decline in their ability to deal effectively with threats to their interests. This is what the Soviets mean by "peaceful coexistence"—a strategy to defeat the West without war.

17. This is not a strategy which aims immediately at the revolutionary seizure of power by Communist parties and the setting up of Communist regimes. The Soviets know that there are few countries where the Communists are strong enough to undertake such action, and where they themselves could count upon being able to deter intervention by non-Communist forces. The "peaceful coexistence" strategy is aimed mainly at gradually eliminating Western and building up Soviet influence around the world. The Soviets naturally expect that conditions will thereby be created which are favorable to the growth of Communist movements and which will sooner or later permit the latter to acquire state power peacefully, or by revolutionary action if necessary. Even though overt seizure of power is not now the main aim of the Soviet strategy, over a five-year period situations might arise where the gains from such action would seem important enough to the Soviets so that they would be willing to depart from their present general line.

18. The general line of Soviet policy estimated in the two preceding paragraphs falls within a range which excludes, on the one hand, the deliberate assumption of serious risks of general war, and on the other, abandonment of active struggle against the West. Within these limits we believe that the Soviet leaders will display both militancy and conciliation, at various times and in various proportions as seems to them most profitable. However, the Chinese challenge to Soviet authority involves basic questions of foreign policy, and brings severe pressure to bear on Soviet policy decisions. In trying to adjust to Chinese pressures, the Soviets may go farther in the direction of militancy and risk-taking than they otherwise would. On the other hand, if the Soviets should conclude that the Chinese were pushing them towards unacceptable dangers, they might move as a matter of temporary expediency toward a greater degree of stabilization in their relations with the West than they would otherwise consider, though without altering their long-term aim of establishing Communism throughout the world.[4]

19. As a general rule, we believe that the Soviets would consider that the initiation of limited war with Soviet or even Bloc forces entailed unacceptably high risks and political liabilities. However, it cannot be excluded that situations will appear in which they would conclude that some prize was great enough, and the military and political risks acceptable enough, to justify resort to such action. The Soviets are aware, however, that any limited war carries a danger of expanding into general war. We believe, therefore, that their attitude toward the involvement of Soviet or Bloc forces in local and limited war will be a very cautious one, and will be governed by their estimate of the risks and advantages, both

---

[4] The Assistant Chief of Staff, Intelligence, USAF, agrees that the Chinese challenge to Soviet authority will, undoubtedly, have its effect on Soviet policy toward the non-Communist world; however, he believes that the relationship of Soviet military power vis-a-vis the US is the essential determinant. Further, as expressed in his footnote to paragraph 9, he believes that should the Soviets feel that they have achieved a clear military superiority, they are likely to adopt policies involving serious risks of general war.

political and military, in each situation. Even so, there is always a possibility that they may miscalculate risks.

20. Negotiations with the Western Powers over outstanding issues are conceived by the Soviets as one of the modes of waging the struggle of "peaceful coexistence." They hope that the pressures which they attempt to build up against the West will result in concessions at the negotiating table. Intervals of more accommodating behavior and appeals for relaxed tensions are intended to encourage the making of such concessions. We expect this alternation of pressure and accommodation to be the regular pattern of Soviet behavior with respect to negotiation in the years ahead. Since the U-2 incident in May 1960 the Soviets have adopted a hostile and aggressive attitude which has made effective negotiation impossible. We believe that within the next six months or so the Soviets are likely to moderate this attitude and to attempt to get negotiations started again. It is also possible, however, that on the Berlin issue, where negotiation has so far failed to get them results, they will resort to intensified pressure and threats in an attempt to force the West into high-level negotiations under more unfavorable conditions.

21. We do not believe that the Soviets have a five-year plan for foreign policy in the sense that they set themselves particular goals to accomplish within a set time. Their policy is marked rather by an extraordinary opportunism, and in recent years by rapidity of response and vigor in execution. Over the next five years they probably look for new developments favorable to their interests to occur in a number of areas, but more especially in Africa, Latin America, Japan, Indonesia, and Iran. They probably intend to give particular attention to establishing a diplomatic and economic presence in Africa, to stimulating and exploiting movements on the Castro model in Latin America, and to encouraging the growth of a radical anti-American mass movement in Japan. Above all, however, they intend to build up their base of power within the Bloc itself, in the belief that during the next several years they can considerably improve their relative power position vis-a-vis the West. They believe that if they do so, more opportunities for Communist expansion, and more readily exploitable ones, will open up for them.

NIE 11-4-63 SOVIET MILITARY CAPABILITIES AND POLICIES, 1962–1967

DISCUSSION

I. Soviet Military Policy

A. Basic Views on War and Military Policy

1. The Soviets see military power as serving two basic purposes: defense of their system and support for its expansion. Thus, one of the most important objectives of Soviet military policy is to deter general war while the USSR prosecutes its foreign policies by means short of actual hostilities involving Soviet forces. Military power is constantly brought into play in direct support of these policies, through the threats which give force to Soviet political demands, through the stress on growing power which is intended to gain respect for the Soviet state and its Communist system, and through the military aid and support rendered to allies, friendly but neutral regimes, and anti-Western movements.

2. The Soviet leaders realize that their deterrent must be credible in the sense that it rests upon powerful military forces. Moreover, they recognize that deterrence may fail in some key confrontation in which, despite their best efforts to retain control over risks, either they or their opponents come to feel that vital interests are under challenge. Against this contingency they wish to have a combination of offensive and defensive capabilities which will enable them to seize the initiative if possible, to survive enemy nuclear attack, and to go on to prosecute the war.

3. The Soviets evidently believe that the present overall military relationship, in which each side can exert a strong deterrent upon the other, will probably continue for some time to come. The Soviets are vigorously pursuing programs of research and development in advanced weapons, hoping if possible to create a strategic balance favorable to them. It is possible that some future technological breakthrough or advance would persuade them that they had acquired a decisive advantage which permitted them to take a different view of the risks of general war. We do not believe, however, that the Soviets base their military planning or their general policy upon the expectation that they will be able to achieve, within the foreseeable future, a military posture which would make rational the deliberate initiation of general war or conscious acceptance of grave risks of such a war.

4. A number of Soviet statements in recent years have expressed the view that limited war involving the major nuclear powers would inevitably escalate into general war. While such statements are intended in part to deter the West from local use of force, this official view also reflects a genuine Soviet fear of the consequences of becoming directly engaged in limited war involving Soviet and US forces. This probably also extends to involvement of Soviet forces with certain Allied forces in highly critical areas, notably Western forces in the European area. Nevertheless, they might employ their own forces to achieve local gains in some area adjacent to Bloc territory if they judged that the West, either because it was deterred by Soviet nuclear power or for some other reason, would not make an effective military response. They would probably employ Soviet forces as necessary if some Western military action on the periphery of the Bloc threatened the integrity of the Bloc itself. Should the USSR become directly involved in a limited war with US or Allied forces, we believe that the Soviets would not necessarily expand it immediately into general war, but that they would probably employ only that force which

they thought necessary to achieve their local objectives. They would also seek to prevent escalation by political means.

5. Recent Soviet military writings call for professional study of the problems of nonnuclear combat, which could lead to some modification of the official view on limited war. However, we believe that the attention now being devoted to this problem is primarily responsive to indications of US interest in building NATO's capabilities for nonnuclear combat. In our view, it does not reflect any new Soviet conclusion that the USSR can now launch such wars without great dangers of subsequent escalation.

6. The USSR has regularly recognized the importance of the "war of national liberation," in which pro-Soviet or anti-Western forces challenge colonial or pro-Western regimes in a primarily internal conflict. In practice, Soviet behavior has followed neither the course of full support to all these wars, as Soviet propaganda often alleges, nor the course alleged by Khrushchev's Chinese critics, who claim that he withholds support entirely because of exaggerated fears that such a conflict might spark a general war. The USSR has rendered active assistance in some cases, such as Laos and Yemen, and little or none in others, such as Algeria and Angola, depending upon such practical factors as accessibility, the risk of defeat, and the attitude of other powers involved.

7. The USSR has also shown a recent willingness to provide some non-Bloc recipients of its military aid with more advanced equipment than heretofore. In some cases, notably Cuba and Indonesia, Soviet personnel have been employed to man this equipment, and are training indigenous specialists to operate it. This represents a significant departure from previous Soviet practice, which may be extended to other areas in the future.

8. As new and favorable opportunities arise, the Soviets will continue to offer these various kinds of assistance, and they may do this more frequently and aggressively in the future if their efforts to expand Soviet influence by political and economic means encounter continued frustration. We believe, however, that the Soviets will remain chary of any great commitment of prestige to the support of belligerents over whom they do not exercise substantial control or in circumstances in which they feel that winning is unlikely, and they will seek to avoid risk of widened hostilities which might result from "wars of national liberation." In particular, we believe that the Soviets will be very reluctant to commit their own forces openly in conflicts where they would risk a direct confrontation with US forces.

B. SOVIET MILITARY POLICYMAKING

9. The application of these basic attitudes to particular situations and to the allocation of resources does, of course, pose serious policy problems. A number of additional factors have long affected the character of Soviet military policy. Geography and the traditions bound up with historical experience have inclined the Soviets toward a military preoccupation with Western Europe and a stress on large-scale ground combat. The capabilities and structure of US and other opposing forces influence directly both the size and shape of Soviet forces and exert a general upward pressure upon requirements in all fields. Perhaps most important is the technological and economic base of the nation, which constantly offers prospects for more effective weapons but also determines the extent to which these opportunities can be exploited without too great a sacrifice in other programs.

10. These factors, pointing in many contradictory directions, do not make for easy or unanimous decisions. Indeed, we have clear evidence of disagreement, compromise, and

even reversal in the formulation of military policy in the last three years. This process of policymaking in the USSR appears in large part to involve the same problems familiar to US decision-makers. In addition, however, certain special features stand out. Fully informed Soviet military discussion, for example, seems to involve a smaller circle than in the US. Beyond the political leadership, some military officers, and a limited number of scientists and engineers, we know of no body of civilian advisers or publicists in the USSR comparable to the social scientists involved in the evolution of US military thinking. This is in part due to the great Soviet emphasis on security, which has the additional effect of reducing the flow of information within the officer corps. As a result, the Soviet military appear to experience special difficulty in adjusting their doctrine and concepts to the rapid changes characteristic of the postwar period. The continuing major influence of World War II commanders and the vivid memories of the Soviet experience in that war also contribute to a resistance to new concepts which is evident in professional discourse.

11. Military programs have become more complex and expensive, and the professional recommendations of the military leadership on military problems have a greater impact on economic and foreign policy decisions. Furthermore, the political climate which has developed under Khrushchev is one which permits continuing discussion on a variety of problems, and the military leaders have used this opportunity to expound their views. With military and economic debates proceeding simultaneously and in close dependence on each other, it seems likely that the arguments of the marshals have been supported by those political leaders who did not wish to permit programs for consumer goods to impinge upon allocations to heavy industry.

12. We do not believe that the military aspires to an independent political role within the political system, and if it were to, party traditions and controls appear strong enough to defeat any efforts in this direction. But if, as we expect, the military and economic choices facing the USSR become more acute, the senior officers will probably find themselves more deeply involved in matters of general policy.

C. THE RECENT COURSE OF MILITARY POLICY

13. The most important viewpoints in the controversy over military policy of the last few years have been those represented by Khrushchev and a few military theorists, on the one hand, and the majority of the senior military leaders, on the other. Three major differences have distinguished Khrushchev's approach to defense policy from that of the military leaders. First, Khrushchev is heavily concerned with the political uses of military power, whereas the professional responsibilities of the marshals require them to look in the first instance to actual war-fighting capabilities. Second, Khrushchev has asserted that a general war is almost certain to be short, with victory decided in the strategic nuclear exchange and with conventional arms, particularly theater forces, playing a quite secondary role. Most military leaders, on the other hand, appear to believe that general war would probably, but not certainly, be short but that, in any event, its conduct would require high force levels for most of the traditional service arms, including a multimillion man army. Third, Khrushchev is far more concerned than the marshals to keep military expenditures in check in order to meet what he regards as pressing needs in the civilian economy.

14. All these considerations were involved in the reorganization of the armed forces which Khrushchev inaugurated in January 1960. The essence of his plan was to place main

reliance on nuclear missile forces and, on this basis, to reduce military manpower substantially and to accelerate the retirement of older weapons. This, he asserted, was the force structure best suited both to deter war and to fight one if necessary; moreover, it would release men and money for the civilian economy.

15. From Khrushchev himself we know that this plan and its strategic justification were accepted only reluctantly by the military leadership. A controversial discussion ensued, encouraged by the regime, in which high officers debated, polemicized, and explored the military implications of modern warfare in a far more systematic fashion than previously. Several schools of thought became apparent, but a predominant view soon emerged which accepted the likelihood that the initial phase of a general war would be decisive, but went on to argue that even a relatively short war would require large forces of all types capable of defeating comparable enemy forces, overrunning base areas, and occupying territory in Eurasia. This discussion also focused attention on the enormous difficulties of mounting major military operations after receiving the full weight of a Western first strike, and the resulting importance, if in the Soviet view war became imminent and unavoidable, of seizing the strategic initiative by a pre-emptive attack.

16. At present, official military doctrine holds that a general war will inevitably involve the massive use of nuclear weapons, will begin with a strategic exchange, and will develop almost simultaneously along fronts of engagement as well. Strategic missile forces will play the primary role. The course and outcome of the war may well be decided in its initial phase by strategic nuclear weapons. However, the Soviets hold that such a conflict will not necessarily be short, and envisage the possibility of a long war involving protracted operations in Eurasia. Therefore, while current doctrine emphasizes a military policy of building strategic attack and defense capabilities, it supports as well the maintenance of large theater and naval forces, for use both in the initial and the possible subsequent phases of a general war.

17. We believe that debate continues in the USSR, not only over subsidiary propositions, but perhaps over some of the central tenets of this doctrine. The course of the debate was heavily influenced by external events in 1960–1961 which, intruding upon the discussion, undermined some of Khrushchev's contentions and permitted the military to retrieve some concepts which he had discarded. Thus the U-2 affair cast doubt on the adequacy of Soviet air defenses, on the efficacy of Soviet security, and on the wisdom of Khrushchev's efforts to relax tensions in relations with the US. In the following year, the US took decisions to step up both its strategic attack and general purpose forces. In Vienna, Khrushchev determined that the US did not regard the relationship of military power as requiring it to make major concessions on the Berlin question. All these developments called into question the adequacy of the Soviet military posture, both for supporting foreign policy and for conducting general war if necessary. In these circumstances, Khrushchev made such demonstrative military moves as the public suspension of the manpower reductions and the resumption of nuclear tests.

18. At about the same time, another burden was laid on Soviet military policy-making. For some months, US public disclosures had hinted that Soviet ICBM strength might be much smaller than had previously been believed. Beginning in the fall of 1961, the US began to assert this conclusion with great conviction, and to assert more strongly that the US was the strategic superior of the Soviet Union. From US statements and behavior, the Soviets could almost certainly judge that their security had been penetrated in an important way, probably one which, by permitting the US to locate Soviet targets,

had a tangible effect upon the military balance. Their fears that no major Western concessions on Berlin would be forthcoming must have been strengthened. And the image of Soviet superiority, which they had heavily exploited to document their claims of the inevitable triumph of their system, was badly damaged.

19. It was against this background that the USSR took its decision to deploy strategic missiles to Cuba. This move involved a host of policy considerations and judgments which are not yet fully clear. In its military terms, however, it appears to have been a response to the question of how to create new opportunities for Soviet foreign policy by improving the strategic position of the USSR vis-a-vis the US, at some acceptable cost and at some early date. Even deployment at the levels detected promised a significant increase in first-strike capabilities for general nuclear war, and the Soviets may have intended to follow this up by establishing a larger missile force as well as a submarine base.

20. Khrushchev, however, probably considered its main impact to be psychological. At one level, the deployment and its acceptance by the US was intended to demonstrate Soviet might and US inability to contain it, thereby reversing the tendency of world opinion to regard the West as strategically superior. At another, however, it was intended to increase the deterrence laid upon the US in cold war confrontations. Khrushchev evidently felt that, despite all the military problems involved in making effective strategic use of Cuba in wartime, the deployment would have a powerful impact on US opinion which would reduce resistance to his political demands, in the first instance those concerning Berlin.

D. PROBLEMS OF FUTURE MILITARY POLICY

21. The Cuban adventure and its outcome both highlighted and heightened the dilemma of the Soviet leaders. Both the deployment and its reversal constituted a tacit public admission that the USSR was in a position of strategic inferiority. Among its other results, the Cuban fiasco has almost certainly thrown the Soviets back onto a further re-evaluation of their strategic posture.

22. Programs already under way will largely govern the size and composition of Soviet strategic forces through about mid-1964, but new decisions taken this year could significantly affect force levels thereafter. We are unlikely to learn directly of such decisions. Moreover, the physical activities which might reveal their nature will probably not be apparent for another year or more. In considering future Soviet force levels, it is therefore necessary to explore the various alternatives now open to the USSR.

23. Confronted with the continuing buildup of US forces for intercontinental attack programmed for the next few years, Soviet planners may be considering a wide range of alternatives. At one extreme would be an attempt to achieve such a clear superiority over the US in strategic offensive weapons that they would have a high assurance of destroying US nuclear striking forces prior to launch. At the other extreme would be the acceptance of continued strategic inferiority, perhaps coupled with genuine efforts to reach agreement with the West on arms control.

24. The first of these extreme alternatives is probably now regarded as unattainable. Thousands of Soviet missiles would be required to give the Soviet leaders a high assurance of destroying even the fixed bases of US nuclear forces programmed for the mid-1960's. We do not believe that the Soviet leaders would be prepared to impose a strain of this magnitude upon the Soviet economy. In addition, the Soviets would almost certainly

expect the US to detect such an effort, and thereupon to step up its own program so as to raise Soviet requirements still higher. Moreover, US warning capabilities, fast reaction times, and mobile forces (airborne bombers and missile submarines) already have reduced Soviet capabilities, against US retaliatory forces. We believe that the Soviets will continue to estimate that, throughout the period of this estimate, the US will retain retaliatory capabilities which could not be eliminated by such striking forces as the USSR could acquire.

25. The second of these extreme alternatives might be considered by the Soviet leaders. Even if current strategic weapons programs were allowed to level off after 1964, the Soviets would possess a powerful deterrent force. Moreover, they might hope to reduce US superiority by means of disarmament agreements. But the main appeal of this alternative would be economic; resources would in time be made available to reverse the current slowdown in economic growth. However, we have seen as yet no persuasive indications that the USSR is prepared to move very far in this direction. The Cuban venture has indicated that, at least to date, the Soviet leaders are far from willing to accept a position of strategic inferiority.

26. Between these extreme alternatives, we believe that the Soviets have almost certainly considered an effort to attain rough parity with the US in intercontinental weapon systems. Soviet military leaders almost certainly have urged enlarged and improved forces of ICBMs and missile submarines. However, a major Soviet effort to attain parity in the near term would require either a substantial increase in the Soviet military budget or sharp cuts in other types of forces. Moreover, the Soviets would almost certainly reason that the US would detect an effort of such magnitude, and that they could have no assurance of winning the intensified race which would ensue. Our evidence does not indicate that the Soviets are attempting to match the US in numbers of weapons for intercontinental attack; we believe, however, that they will attempt to offset US superiority by other means.

27. Soviet statements and military writings suggest that the Soviet leaders see in technological achievements the means by which they may improve their total strategic position relative to that of the US. This consideration may lie behind the testing of very high-yield weapons, the claimed development of a global missile, the high priority given to the antimissile program, and the Soviet interest in military space programs. By such means, the Soviets may attempt to attain rough parity or even superiority in the total strategic context, although they remain numerically inferior in delivery vehicles. Hardened ICBMs and submerged-launch submarine missiles will contribute to Soviet strategic capabilities. In addition, over the next few years the ICBM force will probably come to include new large missiles, armed with very high-yield warheads or capable of global ranges. Moreover, the USSR is almost certainly investigating the feasibility of space systems for military support and offensive and defensive weapons.

28. In defense against strategic attack, the major new element is the antimissile program, where deployment of one system has already begun at one location, and research and development toward a more advanced capability is continuing. The Soviets may see a possible solution to their strategic confrontation with the US in a combination of antimissile defense plus very effective though numerically inferior intercontinental striking forces. The technical difficulties as well as the great expense of any extensive antimissile deployment will be restraining influences. Nevertheless, we believe that deployment of antimissile defenses may be the largest new Soviet military program in the period of this estimate.

29. Although we believe that Soviet military policy is most likely to continue along current lines, we cannot exclude the possibility of new departures in military policy, perhaps resulting in major changes in the composition of the Soviet military establishment and in the relative emphasis given to forces designed to accomplish the major military missions. Drastic cuts in the theater field forces remain a possibility; while Khrushchev's proposals for manpower reductions have been shelved for the present, economic pressures and developments in military technology almost certainly will cause this subject to be reconsidered. It is also possible that the increasing involvement of the USSR in the more remote areas of the world will lead to the development of new capabilities for distant, limited military action. In this connection, the Soviets may attempt to acquire base and logistical support rights in key non-Bloc countries, but we have no evidence that the USSR has raised this question with these countries.[1]

30. In general, Soviet military policy will continue to be shaped, not only by a variety of strategic, historical, technical, economic and political factors, but also by differing views about the relative importance of these factors, and shifting compromises among these views. As a result, we believe that the numerous aspects of this policy will not always be wholly consistent with each other, and that force structure and future programming will reflect neither a fully-integrated strategic doctrine nor a firm timetable for achieving specified force levels. In any case, we do not believe that the Soviets conceive of existing weapons systems as the answer to their military problem or that they have fixed and inflexible plans for their force structure in the period five to 10 years from now. They have debated and revised some of their ideas, and they will probably do so again. They have made scientific military research and the development of new weapons matters of high urgency, and they have a demonstrated capability to concentrate human and material resources on priority objectives. If they develop new concepts or new weapons which give promise of military and political advantage, they will seek to add them rapidly to their arsenal and to gain maximum benefit from them. Thus, during the next five years, we expect the Soviets to be working on even more advanced weapons with which they may hope to enhance their capabilities at a later date.[2]

II. SOVIET HIGH COMMAND STRUCTURE

31. We believe that during the past two or three years the Soviet military high command structure has been modified to speed the process of initiating or responding to strategic nuclear attack. The growth of nuclear and missile forces on both sides has almost certainly persuaded the Soviets to establish the command and control channels necessary for the swift initiation of military operations upon the decision of the political leadership.

32. We have information, some of it from classified documents and some from public statements, about both a Supreme Military Council and a Supreme High Command. Khrushchev is chairman of the Council and Supreme High Commander. The Council, a body of high-level party, government, and military officials, has existed since before

---

[1] For a discussion of the limitations imposed on such Soviet overtures by the receptivity of other countries, see NIE 10-63, "Bloc Economic and Military Assistance Programs," dated 10 January 1963.

[2] With reference to paragraphs 23–30, see the Assistant Chief of Staff, Intelligence, USAF, footnote to Conclusion E.

World War II to provide a forum for discussion and decision on major issues of military policy. The Supreme High Command directed military operations during World War II with Stalin at its head, but was disbanded thereafter. Such information as we have suggests that steps have been taken in recent years to designate membership in the Supreme High Command and to develop procedures to permit the quick assumption by this body of top level control of military operations under Khrushchev should events so dictate.

33. Adjustments in the structure of the Soviet high command have apparently been closely related to the growth of the USSR's strategic defense and long-range missile forces. A new rocket command was established in 1960 and designated a main component of the Soviet armed forces. This change followed by about five years the elevation of the Soviet air defense component to similar status. At present, there are five major force components administered by main directorates or equivalent headquarters within the Ministry of Defense: ground, naval, air, air defense, and rocket.

34. Highly centralized civilian control over the Soviet military establishment is exercised through the Council of Ministers, which includes the Minister of Defense. The Minister is assisted by the unified General Staff of the armed forces, which formulates the overall military program and would probably constitute the principal headquarters element of the Supreme High Command in time of war. Party and government leaders reportedly participate regularly in the deliberations of the Supreme Military Council. Additional channels for exercising party control over the military include the Main Political Directorate of the armed forces and the numerous party officials who are assigned to all levels of the military establishment.

35. The flow of operational orders from the Minister of Defense to the Soviet armed forces follows no rigid or consistent pattern. Commanders in Chief of the Strategic Rocket Forces, Long Range Aviation, the Air Defense Forces, and the Navy are believed to have direct operational control over the forces assigned to them. On the other hand, ground force components are operationally controlled by the commanders of the Military Districts and the Groups of Forces. The Commander in Chief of the Air Force similarly has no direct operational control over air components. The operations of other than Long Range Aviation air elements are controlled by the commands or forces to which they are assigned, i.e., commanders of Groups of Forces, Military Districts, Air Defense Districts, Fleets, and Airborne Forces.

NIE 11-4-64 MAIN TRENDS IN SOVIET
MILITARY POLICY

West remained unfavorable. The economic strain of the arms competition loomed as costly as ever. There is evidence of considerable hesitation and re-evaluation in Soviet policy since the failure of the Cuban missile venture, although since about mid-1963, a number of developments have occurred which suggest the general direction Khrushchev proposes to follow. In the economic sphere, short-term plans for 1964–1965 have been revised in order to shift resources, notably to the chemical industry. Consistent with this has been a change in foreign policy tactics, beginning with the test ban, in an effort to relax East-West tensions. The attempt to create a more favorable international climate, in turn, has allowed Khrushchev to secure reductions in the overt defense budget as well as to propose some reductions in military manpower. The sum total of these various steps in related fields suggests that Khrushchev has settled on a general line of policy to contain the arms race, if only in a limited way, and to reduce some of its burden on the Soviet economy.

19. In strategic terms, this line of policy suggests a recognition of the necessity to accept the general balance of power which emerged in the Cuban crisis. Presently, and for some time to come, the Soviet strategic forces will be numerically inferior to those of the US and more vulnerable to attack. The Soviet leaders must recognize, therefore, that the US would enjoy a considerable advantage should it strike first, and that the relative invulnerability, the fast reaction time, and the mobility of US strategic power make a Soviet first strike completely irrational. Nevertheless, in assessing the military balance, the Soviets are confident that they possess a credible deterrent based on both their massive capabilities to devastate Eurasia and their growing intercontinental striking power. Thus, the Soviets see the present situation as one in which both sides are deterred from deliberately initiating general war or from knowingly initiating courses of action which would involve grave risk of such a war.

II. Factors Affecting Future Soviet Military Policy

20. Soviet decisions as to force structure and military programs over the next several years are likely to be made in the context of a situation in which, although the US enjoys a clear strategic advantage, a condition of rough mutual deterrence exists. The Soviets will seek to improve their strategic capabilities *vis-a-vis* the US, however, policy decisions will be influenced by the continuing strain on economic resources, and the pressure arising from competition with the US in scientific and technological developments with military applications. Such decisions will be greatly influenced also by the Soviet estimate of the political situation, the opportunities which it affords, and the contribution which military power can make to the realization of these opportunities.

SPECIAL
NATIONAL INTELLIGENCE ESTIMATE
NUMBER 85-3-62
THE MILITARY BUILDUP IN CUBA
19 SEPTEMBER 1962

THE PROBLEM

To assess the strategic and political significance of the recent military buildup in Cuba and of the possible future development of additional military capabilities there.

CONCLUSIONS

A. We believe that the USSR values its position in Cuba primarily for the political advantages to be derived from it, and consequently that the main purpose of the present military buildup in Cuba is to strengthen the Communist regime there against what the Cubans and the Soviets conceive to be a danger that the US may attempt by one means or another to overthrow it. The Soviets evidently hope to deter any such attempt by enhancing Castro's defensive capabilities and by threatening Soviet military retaliation. At the same time, they evidently recognize that the development of an offensive military base in Cuba might provoke US military intervention and thus defeat their present purpose. *(Paras. 1–11)*

B. In terms of military significance, the current Soviet deliveries are substantially improving air defense and coastal defense capabilities in Cuba. Their political significance is that, in conjunction with the Soviet statement of 11 September, they are likely to be regarded as ensuring the continuation of the Castro regime in power, with consequent discouragement to the opposition at home and in exile. The threat inherent in these developments is that, to the extent that the Castro regime thereby gains a sense of security at home, it will be emboldened to become more aggressive in fomenting revolutionary activity in Latin America. *(Paras. 18–21)*

C. As the buildup continues, the USSR may be tempted to establish in Cuba other weapons represented to be defensive in purpose, but of a more "offensive" character: e.g., light bombers, submarines, and additional types of short-range surface-to-surface missiles (SSMs). A decision to provide such weapons will continue to depend heavily on the Soviet estimate as to whether they could be introduced without provoking a US military reaction. *(Paras. 22–28)*

D. The USSR could derive considerable military advantage from the establishment of Soviet medium and intermediate range ballistic missiles in Cuba, or from the establishment of a Soviet submarine base there. As between these two, the establishment of a submarine base would be the more likely. Either development, however, would be incompatible with Soviet practice to date and with Soviet policy as we presently estimate it. *It would indicate a far greater willingness to increase the level of risk in US-Soviet relations than the USSR has displayed thus far, and consequently would have important policy implications with respect to other areas and other problems in East-West relations. (Paras. 29–33)*

E. The Latin American reaction will be to the evidence of an increased Soviet commitment to Cuba, rather than to the technical implications of the military buildup. Many Latin Americans will fear and resent a Soviet military intrusion into the Hemisphere, but will regard the problem as one to be met by the US and not their responsibility.

We estimate the chances are better now than they were at Punta del Este to obtain the necessary two-thirds OAS majority for sanctions and other steps short of direct military action aimed at Cuba. If it became clear that the USSR was establishing an "offensive" base in Cuba, most Latin American governments would expect the US to eliminate it, by whatever means were necessary, but many of them would still seek to avoid direct involvement. *(Paras. 34–37)*

SPECIAL NATIONAL INTELLIGENCE ESTIMATE
53-2-64
1 OCTOBER 1964
THE SITUATION IN SOUTH VIETNAM

NOTE: This is an estimate as approved by the United States Intelligence Board.
No further distribution will be made.

Submitted by the
DIRECTOR OF CENTRAL INTELLIGENCE

Concurred in by the
UNITED STATES INTELLIGENCE BOARD

As indicated overleaf
1 October 1964

CENTRAL INTELLIGENCE AGENCY

1 October 1964

SUBJECT: SNIE 53-2-64: THE SITUATION IN SOUTH VIETNAM

THE PROBLEM

To examine the situation as it has developed since early September, and to assess its implications for the US.

CONCLUSIONS

A. Since our estimate of 8 September 1964* the situation in South Vietnam has continued to deteriorate. A coup by disgruntled South Vietnam military figures could occur at anytime. In any case, we believe that the conditions favor a further decay of GVN will and effectiveness. The likely pattern of this decay will be increasing defeatism, paralysis of leadership, friction with Americans, exploration of possible lines of political accommodation with the other side, and a general petering out of the war effort. It is possible that the civilian government promised for the end of October could improve GVN esprit and effectiveness, but on the basis of present indications, this is unlikely.

B. We do not believe that the Viet Cong will make any early effort to seize power by force of arms; indeed, we doubt that they have the capability for such a takeover. They will continue to exploit and encourage the trend toward anarchy, looking for the emergence of a neutralist coalition government which they can dominate.

---

* SNIE 53-64, "Chances for a Stable Government in South Vietnam," dated 8 September 1964.

DISCUSSION

THE GVN

1. *Continued Political Deterioration.* Political conditions in South Vietnam have continued to deteriorate since our estimate of early September.† Despite efforts by Prime Minister Nguyen Khanh to stabilize the situation, he has been faced with an attempted coup, rioting and demonstrations in the northern provinces, a massive labor strike in Saigon, and an armed revolt by Montagnard elements among the Special Forces. Khanh's authority, already weakened by the Buddhist-student crisis in August, has been further diminished, and the degree of his support within the military establishment is increasingly in question. Most of the non-Communist power elements appear to be marking time, pending their assessment of the civilian government which Khanh has promised will be formed by the end of October.

2. *The Picture in Saigon.* South Vietnam is almost leaderless at the present time. General Khanh has retained his position by making concessions to various interest groups— political, religious, students, military, and labor—which have pressed their demands upon him. In turn, these groups still seem bent on pursuing self interest and factional quarrels almost to the point of anarchy. A lack of sense of purpose and an absence of direction from above have seriously affected morale and created passiveness and apathy within the civil law enforcement agencies. Government ministries in. Saigon are close to a standstill, with only the most routine operations going on. Cabinet ministers, as well as second-level bureaucrats, freely express their pessimism, and even though US and GVN officials arc again meeting on pacification and other joint planning, these meetings are not being followed by action from the Vietnamese side.

3. *GVN Military Morale and Effectiveness.* The continuing disarray of the Saigon government, power struggles within the military leadership, and the activities of self-seeking politicians and religious leaders have adversely affected morale within the military establishment. However, the existing level of effectiveness of combat operations does not seem to have been seriously affected as yet. Nevertheless, continuing political instability would almost certainly aggravate such longstanding deficiencies in the Vietnamese military effort as inadequate motivation, initiative, and aggressiveness. A continuing lack of firm direction, and further squabbling among senior officers in particular, could depress the morale of the troops and junior officers to the critical point. Although the GVN armed forces have long had a high rate of desertion by individuals, there have been no important unit desertions or defections. If military morale continues to decline, however, desertion and defections within both the military and paramilitary services may occur on a larger scale, perhaps even by organized units.

4. *Signs of Defeatism in GVN Leadership.* High-ranking ARVN officers have confessed to US officers deep discouragement at the lack of leadership and direction. The J-3 of the Joint General Staff has indicated that he feels little reason even to discuss further pacification planning; various high-ranking field commanders have expressed similar pessimism; and General Khanh himself has shown signs of being overwhelmed by his responsibilities.

5. *The Situation in the Countryside.* The near paralysis of government initiative in Saigon appears to be spreading rapidly to outlying areas. Although the southern areas still

---

†SNIE 53-64 "Chances for a Stable Government in South Vietnam," dated 8 September 1964.

appear relatively unaffected by the crises of the past several weeks, governmental authority has declined seriously in the northern coastal provinces where provincial and police officials are apparently receiving little guidance from Saigon. In such urban centers as Hue, Danang, Qui Nhon, and Nha Trang, Vietnamese commanders have repeatedly failed to intervene in civil disturbances and rioting on the grounds they lacked precise orders; in some instances, actual authority has passed by default to extremist "vigilante" groups, such as the "People's Salvation (or Revolutionary) Council" (PRC). The nature of the provincial bureaucracy is such that it can rock along for considerable time, carrying out existing programs despite political deterioration in Saigon. Nevertheless, continued confusion and inaction in Saigon, or another coup, could rapidly produce a critical deterioration in government in the countryside. A slippage in morale and in programs among provincial administrations, at least in the central provinces, has already begun.

6. *The Peoples Revolutionary Council (PRC).* The PRC has established local councils in many coastal cities and may seek to form a chapter in Saigon, where two PRC leaders have recently been named to the new 17-men High National Council. The aims of the PRC are not clear, but the local councils seem vulnerable to Viet Cong penetration, and the fact that they have assumed government powers in some provincial cities tends to undermine Saigon's control and to damage the morale of civil servants.

7. *The Montagnard Problem.* The Rhade revolt of 20 September and the continuing possibility of further and more general uprisings by the Montagnards pose an immediate and very serious problem for the GVN. The Montagnards have a violent dislike for and distrust of the lowland Vietnamese, and have sought autonomy for years. The Vietnamese on their part look down on the Montagnards; until recently, the GVN has usually acted in a manner which has widened rather than lessened the breach between the two. The problem has been further compounded by constant and rather intensive Viet Cong political and psychological agitation among the Montagnards, playing on their aspirations and their dislike of the ethnic Vietnamese. Resentment over the killing of some 70 Vietnamese by tribesmen during their revolt will make it extremely difficult for the GVN to offer settlement terms acceptable to the Montagnards. Thus, there will probably be continuing disorders in the Highland areas, diminishing cooperation with the GVN, and increasing Viet Cong influence.

8. *Offsetting Considerations.* Although the signs of deterioration are many and clear, there are offsetting considerations that reduce the likelihood of sudden collapse and afford some very slim hope that the trend can be arrested. The Vietnamese people have a long record of resilience in the face of adversity; the ability of the peasants and even of urban elements to continue normal patterns of life despite political disorder makes for some degree of basic stability. The routine functions of government still work fairly normally; business does go on; and the streets are not places of constant terror. Discouragement over the absence of leadership and the progress of the war has not yet led to calls for ending the fighting. Few if any of the many groups now seeking to enlarge their powers regard an accommodation with the Communists as consistent with their interests. Finally, the military instrumentalities of pacification still exist and retain significant capabilities.

9. *Tensions in US-GVN Relations.* In the last month or so, there has been a disturbing increase in anti-American sentiment at various levels of Vietnamese society. Recent demonstrations in Hue, Da Nang, Qui Nhom, and Nha Trang have had definite anti-American overtones. These were probably attributable in part to Viet Cong agitation and incitement, but in some measure they seem also to have reflected a genuine irritation at the Americans

for various reasons having no direct connection with Viet Cong activity. For its part, the Buddhist leadership, whether anti-Communist or not, is imbued with intense nationalism which has at times manifested itself in opposition to US policies and actions. Suspicion of US motives and concern over US involvement in internal policy is growing among the top echelons of the GVN, and, most importantly, on the part of Khanh himself.

10. *GVN Contacts with the Communists.* The principal GVN leaders have not to our knowledge been in recent contact with the Communists, but there has been at least one instance of informal contact between a lesser governmental official and members of the "National Liberation Front," which is a creation of Hanoi. Moreover, there are numerous potential channels of communication between the present GVN leadership and the DRV authorities, and these could very likely be used without US knowledge.

11. *Coup Possibilities.* Although no definite coup plans are known to be afoot at the moment, we believe that further coup attempts are likely, given the ambitions, discouragement, and bitterness prevalent among certain key South Vietnamese military and civilian figures—and the comparative ease of mounting a coup attempt in the present deteriorating scene.

12. *Alternatives to Present GVN Leadership.* Present plans call for the establishment of a new, broadly based, and predominantly civilian government by the end of October. Such a government might do better than the present one, but the odds are against its having the cohesion and effectiveness necessary to arrest the current decline. No visible alternative seems any more promising. Indeed, we cannot presently see any likely source of real leadership; no Magsaysay has yet appeared. None of the military personalities and factions seems capable of commanding a sufficiently broad spectrum of support. Of nonmilitary figures, the Buddhist leader Tri Quang is the strongest political personality and has demonstrated talents for leadership and organization. But he apparently desires to avoid such responsibility, and a Tri Quang government would face strong opposition from militant Catholics, some of the military, and certain other groups. Not least, it would be a difficult government for the US to work with, and some of its major policies would almost certainly not be consonant with US interests.

THE VIET CONG

13. *Viet Cong Policy.* There are numerous signs that Viet Cong agents have played a role in helping sustain the level of civil disorder which has recently prevailed in the cities of South Vietnam; they have also affected the tone and direction taken by some recent protest demonstrations. Their hand was evident in the recent riots in the capital of Binh Dinh Province, and they may have already penetrated the PRC. Viet Cong propaganda throughout September has increasingly called upon the people to take advantage of the government's confusion by pressing on all fronts. This capitalizing on unrest is an old policy; what is new is the rich opportunity presented by the collapsing of GVN authority. The Viet Cong have apparently decided that heightened efforts on their part will reduce the country to near anarchy and the government to impotence, bringing an early victory in the form of a negotiated truce and a "neutralist" government dominated by their National Liberation Front. Although these heightened efforts may include some battalion-sized, or larger attacks, we do not believe that the Viet Cong are trying to force a military decision at this stage. Rather, they will continue stressing small-scale terrorist activity aimed at furthering the breakdown of administration and the decline of faith in the government.

14. *Viet Cong Capabilities in the Cities.* Viet Cong strength in the cities has almost certainly increased substantially in recent months. We base this conclusion on our general reading of the present situation rather than on specific knowledge of current Viet Cong assets. In the closing days of the Diem regime, Vietnamese police and security agencies had a fairly good reading on the nature and extent of the Viet Cong apparatus in the capital area, and it did not constitute a serious threat at that time. Immediately following the November 1963 coup, however, Colonel Tran Ba Thanh became Deputy Director of National Police. There are strong grounds for believing that Thanh may be a Communist agent; in any event he released some key Viet Cong prisoners, destroyed Viet Cong dossiers in police archives, and placed at least one known Viet Cong agent in a key position within the police structure. Although Thanh was ousted when Khanh seized power, the Saigon police and security services have not recovered their anti-Communist capabilities. The fact that Communist agitation still remains under careful cover, however, suggests that the Viet Cong intend still to husband these assets and not risk them in a premature takeover attempt.

NATIONAL INTELLIGENCE ESTIMATE 53-71
29 APRIL 1971
SOUTH VIETNAM: PROBLEMS AND PROSPECTS

NOTE

The US military presence in South Vietnam will be reduced to about 185,000 by the end of 1971 and even further by the end of 1972. But it is assumed in this paper that a US military support effort will be maintained beyond 1972 along with substantial amounts of US economic assistance. As the US disengages militarily, however, the noncommunist forces in South Vietnam will face the test of dealing with a variety of challenges largely on their own. This Estimate assesses the major problems which will confront the Saigon government in the future as the US reduces its presence and which, depending on how they are met, will largely determine South Vietnam's prospects through the mid-1970s.

CONCLUSIONS

A. The outlook in South Vietnam for the remainder of 1971 is reasonably good. The past three years have produced a more stable political situation, a marked improvement in security conditions, and considerable progress in Vietnamization. Meanwhile, communist problems in supporting the insurgency have mounted. Though communist military strength remains substantial, particularly in the northerly provinces, most of the available evidence suggests that—for the next six months or so—they will continue to rely essentially on the basically conservative tactics observed over the past year. While occasional spurts of larger scale military activity seem almost certain, particularly in the north, any such activity in South Vietnam would probably be limited in area and duration.

B. On the political front, the odds in the presidential election of October 1971 appear to favor a Thieu victory. His re-election would, of course, constitute a mandate for continuing to oppose the communists along present lines. But even the election of the more equivocal "Big" Minh would not necessarily lead to any major shift in Saigon's approach to the struggle, if only because the South Vietnamese military would compel Minh to be extremely circumspect in any dealings with the communists. As for Hanoi, the defeat of Thieu would provide a tempting opportunity to feel out South Vietnamese sentiment on continuing the war.

C. Prospects for 1972 are less clear. The approaching US election period, coupled with continued drawdowns of US troop strength in South Vietnam, make it probable that Hanoi will elect to step up its military activity by early 1972. We do not envisage an effort to duplicate in scale or intensity the 1968 Tet offensive. We would expect a general increase in the level of communist activity with sharp focus on a few selected areas, most likely the northern provinces and highland region of South Vietnam. The aim of this strategy would be to score tactical victories likely to impact adversely on the South Vietnamese and US will to persist in the struggle—specifically, to discredit the Vietnamization program and to encourage sentiment in the US for complete disengagement from the war. There are practical limits, however, to what the communists could accomplish militarily next year in South Vietnam, and we do not believe that they will be able to reverse the military balance there.

D. At the same time, there seems little doubt that the communists will continue to maintain an active military and political challenge to the GVN well beyond 1972. The question in their mind is how and at what level the campaign should be prosecuted. Much would depend on Hanoi's view of the remaining US presence and commitment to Saigon, and on what balance Hanoi struck in its willingness to continue investing resources in the struggle. There are risks and practical difficulties in any course which Hanoi might contemplate: an effort to exploit the drawdown of US forces by a return to large-scale military action; to continue a course not unlike that of the past two years; or to pursue a purely guerrilla struggle at a much lower level. In any case, as it views developments in Laos and Cambodia, Hanoi may well calculate that it can maintain forces on South Vietnamese borders as long as necessary to sap Saigon's will to continue the struggle.

E. In attempting to cope with the communist military threat, South Vietnamese forces will probably require substantial US support for many years. ARVN lacks the logistical system and technological and managerial skills required to maintain and support a modern fighting force. There are also serious personnel problems, including a shortage of qualified leaders and a propensity for enlisted ranks to desert. Problems of leadership and morale are even more severe in the territorial forces and village militia, key elements in the campaign to control the countryside.

F. A major element in Hanoi's ability to stay the course in South Vietnam is the apparent durability of the communist party apparatus there. The apparatus has been hurt, severely in some areas, but relatively few high-level communist cadres have been eliminated as a result of direct GVN action against them. The communists have been able to maintain a viable organization, and this is likely to continue to be the case for the foreseeable future.

G. In addition to the threat posed by the communists, the GVN will have to cope with internal problems. These include meeting the increased demands of a society in the process of change. A greatly enlarged urban slum population has been created and is a target for radical agitation, while the rural populace looks increasingly to the government to meet its growing needs. In the economic sphere, the GVN simply will not be able to satisfy the demands of this "revolution of rising expectations" from its own resources. The political impact of the changing South Vietnamese society is less easily defined. But the regime is likely to find itself faced with rising nationalism, often manifested as anti-Americanism. In the future, there is also likely to be a shift toward a more traditional Vietnamese pattern of a centralized executive authority, although the major elements of the present constitutional system are likely to be retained. Such a system might result in a more efficient government, but the regime might also rely increasingly on its coercive powers, thereby leading to instability and risking political disintegration.

H. Over the longer term, a critical factor in South Vietnam's survival will be the will of the South Vietnamese as a people and as a nation to sustain the struggle against the communists. As Vietnamization proceeds, the South Vietnamese will have to cope with the communists and face the country's problems largely on their own. Developments thus far suggest that they are responding reasonably well to the challenge. But there is no way to determine how tenacious they will be a few years hence when the US is much further along the road to disengagement.

I. Thus, it is impossible at this time to offer a clear-cut estimate about South Vietnam's prospects through the mid-1970s. There are many formidable problems and no solid assurances over this period of time. In our view, the problems facing the GVN, the uncertainties in South Vietnam about the magnitude, nature, and duration of future US support, doubts concerning the South Vietnamese will to persist, the resiliency of the communist apparatus in South Vietnam, and North Vietnam's demonstrated ability and willingness to pay the price of perseverance are such that the longer term survival of the GVN is by no means yet assured.

DISCUSSION

I. THE PRESENT SITUATION

1. Over the past three years, South Vietnam has made substantial progress. The performance of the army (ARVN) has improved steadily; it has assumed the bulk of the ground fighting responsibility without any appreciable decline in territorial security. Indeed, in this period, the Government of South Vietnam (GVN) has extended its control, or at least its access, to most of the country's territory and almost all of its population. As a result, people's confidence in the government has increased, particularly in the rural areas.

2. A more stable political situation has also evolved in South Vietnam. Political participation has broadened greatly, and all major groups have at least a piece of the action—if not in the executive branch, then in the legislature or at the local level. The regime apparently values the aura of legitimacy that accrues from operating on a constitutional basis, and most political elements, including the key military leaders, show no disposition to challenge the government frontally. To most groups, the gains to be derived from working within the system appear to outweigh the costs and risks of efforts to overturn it. In addition, the government's administrative structure has improved, making possible a more vigorous and effective attack on the country's problems. Overall, there is considerable forward momentum in South Vietnam today, and an air of cautious optimism permeates many sectors of the population.

3. As for the Vietnamese communists, during the past year their military/political position in the countryside has been further eroded, considerably in some areas, and their forces have continued to suffer substantial casualties despite lower levels of combat activity. Captured documents continue to reflect difficulties in the communist effort to strengthen the party's control apparatus. Nor has Hanoi been able to achieve decisive results on the political front. Despite surges in antiwar sentiment in the US, the administration has been able to pursue Vietnamization at a deliberate pace, thus dimming any hopes that Hanoi may have had of winning concessions from the US in the near term. The turn of events in Cambodia and southern Laos has compounded communist problems in South Vietnam, requiring Hanoi to divert energy and manpower toward reconstituting and expanding logistical routes. The loss of sanctuaries and the widened area of conflict have particularly complicated the communist situation in South Vietnam. Hanoi also has problems on the home front, where economic reconstruction and development continue to be subordinated to the requirements of the war. Morale problems have resulted as manpower losses in the South have increasingly been brought home to the North Vietnamese populace.

4. But the war is far from over. Despite their difficulties, the communists retain important military capabilities throughout Indochina. As their recent performance in southern Laos demonstrates, they can still fight hard when they choose to do so. Meanwhile, the tightly disciplined communist party organization in South Vietnam gives them considerable flexibility in adapting to changing conditions. Finally, as the US withdraws, existing weaknesses in South Vietnamese government and society will tend to surface, requiring increased attention in Saigon to basic problems affecting internal stability and national development.

II. GVN Problems and Prospects Through 1971

A. POLITICAL PROBLEMS—THE OCTOBER ELECTION

5. As the next order of business, the South Vietnamese must settle the question of national leadership for the next several years. This process will come to a head in the presidential election now scheduled for October 1971.[1] The election will test public acceptance of Thieu's stewardship and, to some degree, the strength of the system of government now prevailing in South Vietnam.

6. The Thieu government's image with the electorate is at best gray. Inability to bring peace, the military's large role in government, corruption, economic problems, and the GVN's extensive dependence on US support all will cost Thieu votes. Even so, Thieu seems to be the front runner at this time. He has, first of all, tremendous assets at his disposal. Thieu can utilize available governmental and military personnel and funds to propagandize for his candidacy and to get out the vote. His control of the massive governmental administrative and security apparatus and his personal support within the military establishment probably assure him a large number of votes from these sectors. Finally, he has worked hard in recent years to broaden his appeal to the rural population; the land reform program and the improved security conditions in the countryside should serve to bolster his standing among the peasantry.

7. *Thieu's Opposition.* Thieu's major opponent currently appears to be Duong Van ("Big") Minh, though he may ultimately decide not to run. Minh's appeal has never been tested at the polls, but he is a national figure and appears to have a favorable image throughout much of the country. And despite his ineffective performance during his three months as Chief of State (1963–1964), Minh apparently retains some support within military and administrative establishments. The An Quang Buddhists, despite certain reservations, are also likely to throw their considerable influence behind his candidacy. Although he is neither a "peacenik" nor anti-American, Minh would probably pull a substantial proportion of the pro-peace and anti-US vote. More important, Minh should also gain the bulk of the anti-administration protest vote. Finally, Minh might be the recipient of whatever votes the communists could deliver, though there are no indications that they believe Minh would wittingly serve communist ends.

8. Minh so far has stuck to platitudes about national unity under his leadership; his stand on major issues has been vague. He blames Thieu for inflation in South Vietnam, but has not indicated how he would handle the problem. He has identified himself more or less with groups espousing peace sentiments, but he has not come forth with any specific proposals for settlement of the war. He seems to believe that he could outmaneuver the communists and has adopted a less bellicose stand than Thieu against their participation in the political process, but he has ruled out the possibility of a coalition arrangement. He has been in contact with most major political elements in South Vietnam, but has made no firm commitments to any. Many people, including some of his supporters, have reservations as to whether Minh will run and whether he could provide adequate leadership, especially in the period when the US is withdrawing from South Vietnam.

---

[1] Elections for the Lower House will take place in August. Although these elections may provide clues to the way the political winds are blowing in South Vietnam, they are more likely to reflect local issues and personalities.

9. Vice President Nguyen Cao Ky is also a potential candidate. Although he has not officially declared himself in the race, he is casting about for political support and is increasingly vocal in his criticism of Thieu and his policies. Ky, however, does not appear to have a major power base or a large popular following and would appear to have little chance of winning the election. Thus, it is possible that his current maneuvering is designed to enhance his bargaining power and that he will not actually run. But if he does, Ky's candidacy will be a complicating factor in the election. He would probably cut into Thieu's support among the military; since he seems to be trying to project a somewhat "dovish" image, Ky could also draw some support away from Minh.

10. *The Communist Role in the Election.* The communists would certainly like to see Thieu defeated or at least to discredit the election results in South Vietnam. It is doubtful, however, that they have the capability to do very much either to influence the election's outcome or to disrupt the voting process on a countrywide basis. Their past performance in this area has been weak, and captured documents suggest that their shortcomings have not yet been overcome. Thus, while the communists would attempt to exploit any anti-regime demonstration that occurred, it is doubtful that they could spark significant demonstrations on their own. Beyond this, Hanoi might surface a "peace" initiative during the campaign in an effort to complicate Thieu's position.

11. But in general Hanoi seems to assume that Thieu will be re-elected and is already denouncing the elections as a fraud. Even if Minh won, the communists probably would not view his victory as portending a decisive shift in the political climate in their favor. Communist hopes in the event of a Minh victory would probably rest more on an expectation that the GVN would be more inefficient and unstable under his leadership than on a belief that he would be conciliatory. They might feel out Minh's intentions, however, by adopting a less bellicose attitude toward the new government and perhaps by showing a somewhat greater interest in talking with Minh.

12. *Election Prospects.* Uncertainties as to trends in the overall military situation over the next few months complicate an election forecast. If, on top of Lam Son 719, the communists maintain a considerable show of military strength over the next few months, Thieu's election prospects might be affected adversely. On the other hand, a generally low level of communist military action during this period could enhance the regime's claims to progress in the military and security fields, and increase Thieu's support in the election.

13. Another factor in the election campaign will be the South Vietnamese perception of the US posture. Paramount in the minds of many South Vietnamese is the question of whether the election results would significantly affect the level of US support. Most South Vietnamese believe that the US favors Thieu staying in office, and this may incline many voters to opt for him in hopes of ensuring continued US support. Aware of such sentiment, Minh has gone to some lengths to urge a policy of "neutrality" for the US in the election, stating that unless the US demonstrates that it favors no particular candidate, he may not even run since Thieu would be sure to win. In any event, if the South Vietnamese public came to believe that the US was truly neutral or favored someone other than Thieu, his chances of election would probably decline.

14. All things considered, however, Thieu appears to stand a better than even chance of winning the election. His control of the governmental apparatus and the financial resources at his disposal are advantages difficult to overcome. This knowledge should encourage discretion on his part and reduce the possibility of blatantly underhanded election tactics by the regime. For their part, despite a desire to unseat Thieu, most of the

noncommunist opposition elements would probably be loath to risk undermining the present system by disruptive actions.

15. If Thieu is re-elected, it will be an obvious mandate for continuing along present lines. But Minh also might not depart significantly from existing policies. He would face the same problems with basically the same assets as Thieu; and, ultimately, he would have to rely on the military as the major prop of his regime. There would be a chance of erosion in governmental effectiveness under Minh as he attempted to put his stamp on the administration, mainly because this would almost certainly entail a shake-up in personnel assigned to key programs. Minh's policies toward the communists, however, would be the key factor in his hold on power once elected. If he began to assume what the military deemed an overly accommodating posture toward the communists, they would probably warn him to desist; a coup would be possible.

16. Previous elections under the Thieu regime have appeared to be relatively honest. But the stakes are higher than ever before. The country's future is likely to be determined by developments during the next four years, a period in which the South Vietnamese will have to demonstrate that they can fend largely for themselves as the US progressively disengages from Indochina. This could increase the regime's nervousness about the Minh candidacy. Ky's appearance on the ballot would increase the uncertainty in Thieu's camp. The regime might conclude that a relatively honest election was too risky and be tempted to rig the voting. If they did so in a blatant manner, it could inflame the political opposition and special interest groups, and the regime might find itself faced with demonstrations and rioting, especially in the cities. Such developments obviously would lessen the prospects for national cohesion over the longer term.

B. ECONOMIC PROBLEMS

17. With the help of large infusions of US economic assistance, the South Vietnamese economy has responded relatively well to years of war and military mobilization. Per capita consumption has remained approximately stable, and there has been no serious decline in domestic production despite the massive dislocation of the labor force. In addition, as a result of military construction activities, South Vietnam now possesses a well-developed transportation network and air and port facilities. In the past few years, the agricultural sector has benefited from technological advances, and a revolutionary land reform program has gotten underway.

18. Nevertheless, there are still serious shortcomings in the South Vietnamese economy. It is far from being self-sustaining; large-scale US assistance provides the basic underpinning for the economy and will have to do so for years to come. And GVN economic policies have perforce largely been concerned with the short-term military and political consequences of the war, and have slighted the more basic aspects of economic development.

19. Over the short term, the major problem continues to be the threat of inflation.[2] Although the regime's recent economic reforms contributed to a substantial slowdown in the pace of inflation, it is a persistent and serious problem. At its heart is the massive

[2] The increase in prices ranged from 30 percent to 55 percent each year from 1965 through 1969 and amounted to 30 percent in 1970. Since July 1970, however, there has been almost no increase in basic prices.

spending by the Vietnamese and US Governments for war-related purposes. As a result, effective demand has tended to exceed the available supply of goods and services. Only by recourse to a program of massive imports, financed almost totally by the US, has the GVN been able to keep inflation from skyrocketing.[3] The availability of imported consumer goods has improved the GVN's image at home, but at the same time it has conditioned the population to expect relative abundance in the midst of war. In short, consumer demand has become rather sophisticated, while the GVN's economic base and practices, despite some improvements, have not.

20. The US troop withdrawal program will tend to complicate the effort to find solutions to the GVN's economic problems. Large numbers of South Vietnamese workers are being released by US forces and their contractors. Providing additional jobs in the civilian economy would require increases in production and imports, which in turn would require increased foreign aid. Meanwhile, the reduction in US military expenditures is reducing the GVN's supply of dollars, and hence its own resources for purchasing imports and stimulating economic growth.

21. *Short-Term Economic Prospects.* Income distribution will continue to be an important issue in South Vietnam. In recent years, farmers have had a significant increase in real income, but the political will to tax the farmer directly does not seem to exist. Within the urban areas, workers in the private sector have done reasonably well despite some erosion of real income. On the other hand, the civil service and military are much worse off than several years ago despite a recent wage increase, and their unhappiness could create problems for the government in addition to making any systematic attack on corruption vastly more difficult. Despite this, the GVN probably will not attempt to redistribute income significantly through another government pay hike or by other means in this election year.

22. Grievances growing out of the maldistribution of income may cause political difficulties for Thieu in the months ahead, but are not likely to pose a critical threat to the GVN's viability during 1971. The worst of the regime's other economic problems will continue to be alleviated by large-scale US assistance. Labor dislocations caused by US withdrawals will create some localized problems, but these are not likely to be critical.

C. MILITARY PROBLEMS—COMMUNIST STRATEGY AND UNITED STATES' WITHDRAWALS

23. *Communist Military Action in the Near Term.* The communists retain significant military capabilities in various parts of South Vietnam, particularly in the northerly provinces. But in southern South Vietnam, these capabilities are severely limited relative to the period 1967–1969 as a result of the loss of the Sihanoukville supply route, disruption and attrition of the communist support structure in South Vietnam itself, continued air interdiction, and allied cross-border operations in Cambodia and Laos. The communists recognize their weaknesses in South Vietnam and over the past year have been trying to

---

[3] From an annual average of $334 million during 1963–1965, imports of goods rose to an average of $725 million during 1966–1969. On the other hand, exports declined rapidly because of reduced production of the country's two major export commodities—rice and rubber. In 1969, exports amounted to only 4 percent of imports; data for 1970 are not available.

repair the situation. Heavy emphasis has been given to beefing up the infrastructure, increasing the number of "legal" communist cadres who can operate in GVN-controlled areas, and subverting the South Vietnamese military and security forces. In the meantime, the communists have relied largely on small unit actions, terror tactics, and sabotage in an effort to conserve forces in anticipation of a prolonged struggle.

24. Most of the available evidence suggests that, for the next six months or so, the communists will continue with these same basic tactics to husband manpower and resources and to rebuild their position in the countryside. Nevertheless, occasional spurts of communist military activity will occur and there may be some military pyrotechnics prior to the South Vietnamese presidential election. But the present pattern of communist action in most of the country, the state of readiness of their forces in South Vietnam, the restrictions imposed by their logistic support capability, and the evidence drawn from captured documents, clandestine reports, and interrogation of communist prisoners and ralliers all suggest that any heightened military activity in South Vietnam over the next several months will be limited in area and duration.

25. *Impact of US Withdrawals.* South Vietnamese forces are being spread more thinly with each succeeding US withdrawal, and despite the weaknesses of communist forces, there will probably be some deterioration in local security during 1971. The combat effectiveness of ARVN may also suffer somewhat as US artillery and helicopter support is diminished. But for the next several months at least, no critical problems are likely to develop. So far, the psychological impact of the withdrawals has been limited; most South Vietnamese have by now adjusted mentally to the fact that the US will continue to scale down its military involvement in Vietnam. Even though demonstrated ARVN shortcomings may raise doubts in South Vietnam about ARVN's ability to fill the gap over the longer term as the US disengages from Indochina, such doubts are unlikely to result in any serious deterioration in the morale of ARVN or the general public during 1971.

III. Major Problems Over the Longer Term

A. THE NATURE OF THE COMMUNIST THREAT

26. *Prospects for 1972.* Hanoi's approach to the war in 1972 will be conditioned by certain basic elements in the situation such as continued US withdrawals, improvements in the pacification situation and in the capabilities of South Vietnam's military forces, and communist determination to gain control of South Vietnam. Certain recent developments, particularly allied operations in Laos and Cambodia, will also have some effect. On the one hand, the communists suffered heavy casualties in these operations, lost and expended significant quantities of supplies, and had their supply lines disrupted; and this is likely to impose restrictions on the scale of military action possible during the early stages of the 1971–1972 dry season. Beyond this, allied action or the threat of action in Laos and Cambodia will impose a continuing burden on Hanoi to protect and maintain the Laos supply route.

27. On the other hand, having weathered the recent ARVN cross-border operations in southern Laos, Hanoi probably feels somewhat more confident that it can wait out the withdrawal of US forces and stay the course in Indochina. Hanoi's view is probably tempered by the realization that communist forces suffered very heavy casualties in Lam Son 719 and benefited from terrain which favored the defense, as well as from superior numbers in place on the ground. The operation did not provide any solutions to the many

problems the communists face in South Vietnam. But from Hanoi's point of view, its forces contained a threat to its vital supply lines, and avoided a critical setback to the 1970–1971 supply effort. Hanoi probably calculates that ARVN, on its own, would have great difficulty in mounting further cross-border operations of this magnitude once the US is largely out of the picture.

28. Given this outlook, Hanoi might opt in 1972 for a continuation of its basically low-profile military approach in South Vietnam. In the meantime, the communists would pursue their efforts to prepare the logistical and organizational base necessary for either a long drawn-out struggle or a return to large-unit action once US forces were no longer an important factor in the war.

29. But there are other considerations which could lead Hanoi to attempt a step-up in military activity in 1972. For example, if communist fortunes took a sharp turn for the worse in the months ahead, Hanoi might hope to reverse the trend by increasing its attacks against ARVN and other government security forces during the 1971–1972 dry season campaign. Such a decision on Hanoi's part could also come later in 1972 if Hanoi at that time were convinced that the US was determined to maintain an effective residual presence in South Vietnam for an extended period.

30. Regardless of the course of the war, Hanoi's leaders might see considerable advantage in a show of military muscle prior to the US election, intended to demonstrate that Vietnamization was not working and to fan antiwar sentiment in the US. In their view, the effort could help generate increased domestic pressure on the US Administration to disengage completely from the war or, failing this, it might affect the election outcome itself. They might also calculate that the backlash in South Vietnam from negative US reactions to adverse battlefield developments would work to communist advantage by sharpening US-South Vietnamese differences.

31. On balance, we believe that Hanoi will find the arguments for some step-up in its military activity in South Vietnam persuasive. But this would be likely to differ from Hanoi's present strategy more in degree than in kind. Thus, we would not envisage an effort by Hanoi to duplicate in scale or intensity the 1968 Tet offensive. Instead, we would expect a general increase in the level of communist activity with sharp focus on a few selected areas, most likely the northern provinces and highland region of South Vietnam. The thrust of this strategy would be to attempt, with greater determination than in recent years, to score tactical victories aimed at impacting adversely on the South Vietnamese and US will to persist in the struggle.

32. Whether or not the communists initiate such increased activity, we do not believe that they will be able to reverse the military balance in South Vietnam in 1972. Continuing communist difficulties will impose limits on how much they can accomplish, and continued allied pressures during the remainder of 1971 and pre-emptive operations in the 1971–1972 dry season could forestall communist preparations for extensive military operations. But the communists are unlikely to be frustrated at every turn; there are too many vulnerabilities in the South Vietnamese situation. For example, the adverse psychological impact in South Vietnam of increased communist military activity could be considerable, particularly if it led—or were thought by the South Vietnamese to be leading—to a weakening of US resolve. And even if—in a purely military sense—the odds seem to favor the South Vietnamese being able to contain the communist effort in 1972, the GVN will still be faced with a communist military and political organization retaining significant strength and potential.

33. *Beyond 1972.* At this point in time, there seems little doubt that the communists will continue to maintain an active challenge to the GVN well beyond 1972. Despite continued concern over the Sino-Soviet dispute, Hanoi probably assumes that it will continue to receive military and economic assistance from both Moscow and Peking as long as necessary. For its part, Hanoi has committed enormous manpower and material resources and has suffered staggering losses in attempting to gain control of South Vietnam. And while there have been shifts in strategy, Hanoi's will to persist has shown little indication of flagging. The war has been going on for over a generation—it has become a way of life for the communists and a part of their ethos. Any leader in Hanoi who advocated giving up the struggle would risk losing his position. Indeed, the present communist leadership might find it difficult to contemplate any course other than continuation of the struggle even if it meant throwing away additional resources in a basically fruitless effort. The question in their minds is not whether to continue the struggle, but how and at what level it should be pursued.

34. The "how" and "at what level" may be as difficult for Hanoi to decide as it is for us to estimate at this stage. Much would depend on how Hanoi viewed the remaining US presence and commitment to Saigon, on the strength and morale of ARVN at that time, and on what balance Hanoi struck in its willingness to continue investing resources in the struggle. There are risks and practical difficulties in any course which Hanoi might contemplate.

35. Assuming that ARVN and the territorial forces maintain or improve their capabilities over the next year or so, any communist effort in the period beyond 1972 to return to large-scale military action in South Vietnam would involve heavy manpower commitments and other strenuous demands on a North Vietnamese population already weary from the cumulative effects of the war. It would also require, as a precondition, the maintenance of secure logistic routes to the South and the rebuilding of an infrastructure in South Vietnam capable of supporting the operations of main force units in the countryside. And, of course, a large-scale military effort might fail and put at risk the ability of Hanoi to rebuild its forces once again.

36. To do too little also involves serious risk. There is no way to be sure what the impact of a long, drawn-out, low-level struggle would be on communist cadres and lower level elements in South Vietnam. Many of them might in time abandon the effort, rendering the communists unable to present a credible challenge to local security in South Vietnam. In North Vietnam, the communists might also face a decline in popular commitment to the struggle. In a sense, the war is an "old man's" war, and whether the younger generation in the North shares the same unswerving dedication to the reunification of Vietnam as their elders cannot be determined.

37. The communists may conclude that their circumstances at home and in the South leave them little choice but to pursue a middle course, one not unlike that of the past two years. This would mean that the GVN would be faced with a continuing threat from some main force units, particularly in Military Regions (MRs) I and II, and a generalized local security threat posed by highly self-sufficient guerrillas, sappers, and terrorists throughout the country. And the political, psychological, and subversive struggle would go on at all levels of society.

38. Hanoi can also hope that developments in Laos and Cambodia will further communist objectives in South Vietnam in the years ahead. The communist position in both countries, particularly Laos, is stronger than in South Vietnam. In Laos, Hanoi

probably calculates that Vang Pao's Meo guerrillas are fading as an effective fighting force; this, coupled with the possibility that the US air role in Laos may be reduced, could lead Hanoi to foresee the end of any effective indigenous resistance in Laos to communist aims. In Cambodia, on the basis of performance, the communists probably foresee little threat to their established positions from Phnom Penh's fighting forces. Thus, Hanoi probably believes that its prospects over the longer term of being able to hold the key logistical routes extending through the Laotian Panhandle and northeastern Cambodia into South Vietnam are good. And it may calculate that even a moderate level of activity in South Vietnam coupled with the permanent threat posed by communist control of the border areas would in time sap the South Vietnamese will to continue the struggle. At a minimum, Hanoi would expect this situation to impose heavy additional burdens on South Vietnamese forces, both in protecting the country's long border and in doing the work of indigenous anticommunist forces in southern Laos and Cambodia, all the while filling in for departing US forces in South Vietnam.

B. GVN CAPABILITIES TO DEAL WITH THE COMMUNIST THREAT

39. *Military and Security Forces.* As the US scales down its involvement in the war, the South Vietnamese military forces will be required to assume increasing responsibilities in the struggle against the communists. Given in political requirement to provide security to the population throughout large portions of the countryside, the GVN will be forced to maintain a large military establishment to check communist activity. Progress has been made in preparing the South Vietnamese forces for the time when they are more or less on their own, but it will be years before the South Vietnamese can be self-sufficient in the military field.

40. For example, although the South Vietnamese have a significant capability for in-country air support, plans are only in the embryonic stage to provide them with a capability to mount air interdiction efforts against the communist logistical network in southern Laos. Further, ARVN has come to rely on helicopter support, and current plans call for a major reduction in the number of helicopters to remain in South Vietnam as US forces depart. Despite substantial improvements, the GVN's logistical system is not yet capable of meeting the large military establishment's needs without relying heavily on US assistance. Similarly, it will be many years before the South Vietnamese military acquires the requisite technological and managerial skills to handle the complexities of maintaining and supporting a modern fighting force.

41. The availability of technical and logistical assistance will be especially vital to the maintenance of ARVN's fighting effectiveness. ARVN has become increasingly dependent on the availability of such complex equipment as helicopters, advanced communications and fire-control equipment, and electronic monitors and sensors. The use of such equipment has given the South Vietnamese considerable advantages in combating the communists. But without substantial US assistance in maintenance, much of the modern equipment would probably deteriorate over time. ARVN might find it difficult to change its tactics and to fight without all of its technically sophisticated paraphernalia. The South Vietnamese will look to the US to continue to provide—and to assist in maintaining—the types of equipment presently available.

42. The persistence of certain basic shortcomings within the South Vietnamese military establishment is likely to impede military progress over the longer run. Despite

improvements, there is little prospect that the military leadership will lose its elitist cast; high-level promotions are likely to continue to be based more on social class and personal loyalties than on military competence. Life for the common soldier will continue to be hard, and separation from families will be frequent. Military pay and allowances at all ranks, already very low, probably will not keep up with the pace of inflation. Under these conditions, military desertions are likely to continue at a fairly high rate.

43. Problems of leadership, morale, and material support are even more severe in the territorial security forces (Regional Forces and Popular Forces—RF/PF) and in the People's Self Defense Force (PSDF) than in the regular military branches. This is so even though these forces are now performing well in many parts of South Vietnam and deserve much of the credit for the improvement in local security. As the US withdraws, ARVN will have to assume the full burden of the main force war, leaving local security even more fully in the hands of the territorial forces and the PSDF. The critical importance of these forces appears to be understood at the highest levels of government, and they are receiving better training and equipment. But a considerable part of the pressure to improve the local units has come from the US. Only with a continued push from the highest national levels will the territorial security forces be assured the equipment and support needed to assume increased responsibilities. Without this support, the GVN's position in the countryside would probably suffer gradual deterioration.

44. Corruption could also continue to impair the military effectiveness of the GVN in the future. Many, possibly most, of the upper echelons of the military establishment engage in some form of corruption; in some cases, the abuses are flagrant and common knowledge. Such excesses tend to lower morale within the ranks and may contribute to the poorly paid, lower level soldier's lack of commitment and tendency to desert. The abundance of US goods has contributed to the growth of corruption and to the improper diversion of military goods and supplies. As the US scales down its effort, such diversions could leave some units short of needed supplies and vulnerable to communist attack.

45. A final critical factor in considering the GVN's military and security forces is that of will. There are no precise guidelines with which to measure the will of the South Vietnamese fighting man. To the extent that they have positive motivation, the RF, PF, and PSDF probably are fighting more from a desire to protect family and village than from any commitment to the Saigon government or aversion to communism. Within the ARVN, many senior officers and noncoms appear ideologically opposed to the communists. Moreover, while most soldiers would like to see the war come to an end, they would certainly prefer that South Vietnam remain non-communist. In general, however, the commitment of ARVN to the struggle rests more on the force of discipline and being caught up in the system than any other factor.

46. *The Attack on the Communist Apparatus.* The GVN's ability to eliminate the communist party structure is questionable. The communist apparatus has been hurt, severely in some areas, but most of the damage stems from the expanded GVN military presence in the countryside and from attrition resulting from the fighting. GVN programs against the communist apparatus have had limited success; relatively few high-level communist cadres have been eliminated as a result of direct GVN action. Moreover, much of the impetus in the GVN's effort has come from US involvement in the programs. As the US reduces its role in these programs, the GVN is unlikely to take up all the slack, and the effort against the communist apparatus would be likely to decline in effectiveness.

47. The South Vietnamese police forces are ill-equipped to take on the task of rooting out the communist apparatus; their operating procedures are inclined to be erratic, and their motivation appears low. The communists have penetrated the regime's security and police forces, and there is a widespread reluctance among the people to turn in communist cadres to the authorities. Many, perhaps most, South Vietnamese have connections, often family ties, with someone in the communist apparatus. Furthermore, the GVN's detention and judicial systems are lax; when apprehended, communists often go free because of slipshod procedures or the venality of GVN officials. As a consequence, the communists have been able to maintain a viable organization despite the GVN's counterefforts, and this is likely to continue to be the case for the foreseeable future.

C. POLITICAL TRENDS

48. The GVN's political cohesion will be subject to increased stress over the next few years as the US presence with its stabilizing influence declines. Frictions between the executive and the legislative branches are likely to sharpen. Though political groups will expect to participate increasingly in the politics of the nation, there is little prospect for the development of truly nationally-based political parties. It is more likely that the political groupings will continue to reflect various parochial and regional interests. The politics of South Vietnam are likely to remain basically divisive in nature much as in the past. Though these conditions may complicate the development of a cohesive political system, they need not necessarily lead to political instability.

49. In the future, there is likely to be a further shift toward a more traditional Vietnamese pattern: a centralized executive authority which nonetheless permits a considerable degree of popular participation and responsibility at the village level. The major elements of the present, foreign-inspired constitutional system, however, are likely to be retained. Continued dependence on US aid and support will provide one incentive to retain them. Additionally, the constitution tends to bestow an aura of legitimacy on whoever holds the presidency. At the same time, many groups of South Vietnamese have come to view the system as something of a barrier against extreme abuses of executive power.

50. The stronger central control envisaged for South Vietnam might well result in more efficient government; if so, it would probably be acceptable to the majority of the South Vietnamese even if democratic niceties were honored more in form than in substance. But the danger in strong central control, especially if popular political participation were severely restricted, is that it could lead to extremes in coercion, increasing grievances against the system and leading organized groups to take their complaints into the streets. The organization and skills necessary to make authoritarian controls effective have not existed in South Vietnam, and in the event of mounting popular opposition, the risk of a breakdown in public order would be high.

51. In any case, as the US phases down in South Vietnam—particularly if the communist military threat increases—the political role of the military is likely to become more open and active. Though hardly a monolith, it seems apparent that the military will remain the ultimate arbiter of power in South Vietnam; not only is it the only truly nationally organized group, but it contains most of the country's competent administrators. Moreover, as any GVN president will recognize, the government will be more secure with heavy military participation than with the generals relegated to the position of disgruntled

observers or plotters. The withdrawal of US forces, however, will remove some of the inhibitions to extra-legal action by the military. If the problems confronting the GVN became particularly critical or if the generals feared that political leaders were about to make a dangerously soft settlement with the communists, they would be likely to attempt a coup. Before making such a move, however, the military leadership would probably attempt to correct such tendencies by exerting influence within the system.

52. Over the longer term, the GVN will have to face the problems of both developing and coping with nationalism. Nationalism is hardly a new emotion for the Vietnamese; in past centuries, nationalism—bordering on xenophobia—has provided strong cement for the nation in its struggle against foreign invaders. It was the ability of Ho Chi Minh to harness this force that provided the major impetus for the communist movement in the struggle for independence against the French. But the GVN has not and probably cannot, over the next few years at least, develop a sense of South Vietnamese nationalism that could be used effectively in the struggle with the North.

53. The traditional sense of Vietnamese nationalism with its xenophobic overtones, however, is alive and growing in the GVN. This is likely to pose problems for US-GVN relations. For the last decade the South Vietnamese have been forced to rely on the US for survival. Many South Vietnamese have found this dependence humiliating, and there is little doubt that a reservoir of anti-American sentiment exists in South Vietnam. Recent demonstrations, sparked by offenses—real and alleged—against South Vietnamese by US military personnel, have illustrated the volatility of the issue.

54. In the future, many issues will be given an anti-American twist by oppositionists anxious to tag the leadership as puppets of the US. Sensitive to such charges, the GVN will try to demonstrate its independence of Washington. Indeed, the government in many cases will find it convenient to shunt the blame for its own shortcomings onto the US, further feeding anti-American sentiment in the South. In short, the US is likely to be placed more frequently in the role of the villain and charged with being insensitive to the needs and interests of South Vietnam.

D. THE CHANGING SOUTH VIETNAMESE SOCIETY

55. Over the longer term, the government in Saigon will be called upon to contend with other new tensions and anxieties which have developed in South Vietnamese society. Since the fall of the Diem regime, South Vietnam has been undergoing a revolutionary transformation—unanticipated, virtually unreported, and largely without guidance or objectives. Years of gradual adjustment to the stresses of war have led to vast alterations in social organization: the displacement of large populations, the disruption and often the destruction of traditional village life, the breakdown and partial replacement of the traditional class system, and the chaotic growth of urban centers.

56. Striking changes in Vietnamese society are taking place in the countryside. In much of the country, Viet Cong and GVN-sponsored land reforms have tended to undermine the power of traditional provincial elites. Radio, television, the Honda, and other manifestations of modernization are altering the small farmer's way of life; the adoption of even a modest amount of modern farming technology is changing his role and expectations. He sees his prosperity linked to free access to GVN-controlled markets. Moreover, after years of GVN neglect, sometimes benign but often not, the Thieu government has begun to woo the villager. In addition to land reform, local leadership and village

autonomy are being emphasized, and there have been promises of large investments in agricultural development.

57. The political implications of these processes cannot be defined with confidence. The rural Vietnamese are not only exceedingly weary of war and political turmoil, but also considerably more sophisticated about national developments. Thus, although the villager resents GVN corruption and abuses of power, there is reason to believe that he is also more resistant to communist blandishments. If the GVN is moderately successful in meeting rural demands for more effective administrative and economic services, and demonstrates greater overall concern with their personal well-being, it may in time alleviate many of the adversities which the farmers have suffered over the past decade and prevent the countryside from serving as the seedbed for yet another cycle of guerrilla activity.

58. While roughly 60 percent of South Vietnam's population still lives in the countryside, there has been an unprecedented influx into the country's towns and cities. Originally caused by rural insecurity, the migration was accelerated by a belief that economic opportunities were greater in the cities. Though any improvements in security and economic conditions in the countryside—and prospective GVN programs—will draw some back to their home areas, problems of rapid urban growth will not dissipate. Those who remain in the towns will still be crowded into slums, detached from their traditional communal ties, and exposed to various forms of agitation. Underemployment will be a problem, particularly as US labor needs diminish. Over time, city dwellers—especially frustrated middle class elements and veterans—could become considerably more receptive to radical appeals if the government is unable to meet their demands.

59. These changes in city and country will strain the government's relatively limited funds and expertise. The GVN's efforts to meet its "revolution of rising expectations" will also be impeded by a cumbersome administrative apparatus and widespread corruption. Even with the best of intentions, the GVN simply will not be able with its own internal resources to generate the jobs and capital needed to satisfy the level of economic demand (goods, services, and technology) already reached. While the Vietnamese are basically ambitious and hard working, industrialization can come only slowly. And it will be some time before they can export large quantities of agricultural products; in particular, the rubber industry, will take years to recover its former vigor. Moreover, prospects are not good for substantial foreign investment or large-scale economic assistance so long as the conflict with the communists remains unresolved.[4]

E. THE "X" FACTOR: THE QUESTION OF WILL

60. All of the political, military, and economic factors discussed above will be important in terms of South Vietnam's future prospects. Nonetheless, an examination of these elements does not provide any certain answer to the key issue: the will of the South Vietnamese as a people and as a nation to sustain the struggle against the communists. There are times when "will" can be measured with a fair degree of confidence. By the spring of 1965, for example, it was clear that the South Vietnamese had lost the will to persist; only the large-scale intervention of US combat troops saved South Vietnam from a communist takeover. At Tet 1968, on the other hand, it became clear that ARVN—as well

---

[4] Japan and a few European countries have shown some interest in aiding or investing in South Vietnam, but to nothing like the extent that will be required.

as some significant portion of the population—had developed a sufficient sense of commitment to offer vigorous resistance to the communist offensive. Since that time, this sense of commitment seems to have developed further.

61. The problem remains, however, of determining the extent to which the growth in commitment in South Vietnam derives from and is dependent on a continued US presence. For the past five or six years, the Americans have always been present or readily available with their manpower, materiel, and money to assist with military and economic problems. As Vietnamization proceeds, this will no longer be as true. Vietnamization is already bringing home to the South Vietnamese leaders that the time is fast approaching when they will have to cope with the communists and face the country's problems largely on their own. Developments thus far suggest that they are responding reasonably well to the challenge. But there is no way to determine how tenacious they will be a few years hence when the US is much further along the road to disengagement.

62. Thus, it is impossible at this time to offer a clear-cut estimate about South Vietnam's prospects through the mid-1970s. There are many formidable problems and no solid assurances over this period of time. In our view, the problems facing the GVN, the uncertainties in South Vietnam about the magnitude, nature, and duration of future US support, doubts concerning the South Vietnamese will to persist, the resiliency of the communist apparatus in South Vietnam, and North Vietnam's demonstrated ability and willingness to pay the price of perseverance are such that the longer term survival of the GVN is by no means yet assured.

SAMPLES AND EXTRACTS FROM THE
PRESIDENT'S DAILY BRIEF

Note from the Editor: The *PDB is* the most exclusive and prestigious intelligence product, disseminated only to the president and anywhere from a half-dozen to a dozen senior national security officials (the number has varied from administration to administration). It arrives at the offices of these individuals early in morning and consists of as few as two or three pages or as long as thirty pages or more, depending on the extent of noteworthy news from the day before. In recent years, the *PDB* has been printed on slick paper in four colors, with charts, photographs, and lively prose, all in an effort to keep the reader's attention in a world of multiple information sources. While a member of the Aspin-Brown Commission staff, the editor reviewed multiple copies of the *PDB* on behalf of the Commission to determine the extent to which it "added value" over the *New York Times,* the *Wall Street Journal,* and other public media outlets. The results showed that the document was useful, especially on questions of terrorism, the military capabilities of nations around the world, and events and conditions in closed societies, although the public newspapers and magazines often outperformed the *PDB* in some domains, such as contemporary European politics.

Ten declassified (once top-secret) *PDB*s are presented in this appendix, all from the administration of President Lyndon Baines Johnson. They are followed by two extracts from *PDB*s (also once top-secret), one from the Clinton administration and another from the second Bush administration.

Source: The Johnson administration *PDB*s are from the National Security Archive, George Washington University, Washington, DC; the Clinton administration extract is from the Kean Commission, *The 9/11 Report,* The National Commission on Terrorist Attacks Upon the United States (2004), pp. 128–129; and the Bush extract is also from *The 9/11 Report,* pp. 261–262, with a facsimile of the original document on the National Security Archive Website. The Johnson administration documents were declassified and approved for release in 1993, and the two other extracts in 2004.

THE PRESIDENT'S DAILY BRIEF

1. *President's Daily Brief, 7 August 1965 (4 pp.), declassified 15 July 1993*
   Source: Lyndon Baines Johnson Library (Austin, Texas), National Security File, Intelligence Briefings File, obtained by Dr. William Burr.
2. *President's Daily Brief, 13 May 1967, (1 p. excerpt), declassified 14 May 1993*
3. *President's Daily Brief, 16 May 1967 (2 pp. excerpt), declassified 14 May 1993*
4. *President's Daily Brief, 27 May 1967 (1 p. excerpt), declassified 14 May 1993*
5. *President's Daily Brief, 5 June 1967 (3 pp. with "Late Items"), declassified 14 May 1993* Compare to FRUS version which omits Nigeria at http://www.state.gov/r/pa/ho/frus/johnsonlb/xix/28058.htm
6. *President's Daily Brief, 6 June 1967 (1 p. excerpt), declassified 14 May 1993*
7. *President's Daily Brief, 7 June 1967 (1 p. excerpt), declassified 14 May 1993*
8. *President's Daily Brief, 8 June 1967 (2 pp. excerpt), first page declassified 14 May 1993, "Late Item" page declassified 6 November 1985*
9. *President's Daily Brief, 9 June 1967 (3 pp.), first two pages declassified 14 May 1993, "Late Item" page declassified 6 November 1985*
   Source for the above 1967 PDB excerpts: Lyndon Baines Johnson Library (Austin, Texas), National Security Council History, Middle East Crisis, Appendix A, obtained by Dr. William Burr.
10. *President's Daily Brief, 1 April 1968 (5 pp.), declassified 21 December 1989*
    Source: Lyndon Baines Johnson Library (Austin, Texas), National Security File, Intelligence Briefings File, obtained by Dr. William Burr.

CENTRAL INTELLIGENCE AGENCY
THE PRESIDENT'S DAILY BRIEF
7 AUGUST 1965

1. Vietnam   A Soviet cargo ship, the Polotsk, [a still-classified section missing here] is en route to Haiphong, The ship unloaded military cargo in Indonesia; there is no evidence it is carrying such cargo now.

2. South Vietnam   There has been no significant change in the situation at Duc Co in Pleiku Province, where South Vietnamese airborne troops are trying to eliminate Viet Cong harassment of a government paramilitary camp.

3. Communist China   The loss of two Chinese Nationalist patrol craft on 5 August in an encounter with Chinese Communist naval vessels off the mainland coast at the southern end of the Taiwan Strait appears so far to be an isolated incident. Before contact with them was lost, one of the Chinese Nationalist vessels reported sinking three "targets," but there is no confirmation. There is no sign of any other significant Communist military reaction to what seems to have been a Nationalist incursion into Communist-controlled waters. (See map)

4. Indonesia   [still-classified section here] Sukarno collapsed three days ago and was still in bed yesterday.

Despite Sukarno's long-standing kidney ailment, for which he delays proper treatment, he has seemed quite chipper lately. [Classified section.] [A] team of Chinese

COMMUNIST CHINA

Communist doctors has been scheduled to visit Djakarta and there is some suspicion that another acupuncture treatment may be involved. [Classified section.]

[A]lthough Sukarno may only have the flu, background political maneuvering may already have begun against the possibility it is more serious.

5. Greece   The King continues to talk with political leaders. The last word [still-classified section] was that he would delay until Monday announcing his next choice for the premiership, even though he may make his decision today.

The Communist press is playing up a fabricated document purporting to link the US with a tragic explosion last November at a Communist-sponsored celebration. This is an obvious effort to discredit pro-US elements during this period of crisis.

6. Dominican Republic   The Organization of American States team continues its talks with leaders from both sides. It may publicize its proposals Monday in hopes of building up popular support for them.

There is a report that extremists among the rebels are attempting to recruit youths from the countryside for indoctrination and the military training they have been conducting in their Santo Domingo stronghold.

3. Vietnam   The North Vietnamese seem to want a war of attrition in the two provinces just south of the Demilitarized Zone.

In a CIA assessment completed this week, we have wrung out the available evidence and we conclude that the enemy is not trying to "liberate" these provinces now. Instead, we feel, the Communists hope to create the illusion of "a war no one can win."

Attacks will be aimed at spreading US forces thin and keeping them under constant pressure without offering the opportunity for a clear-cut allied victory. We believe up to five enemy divisions may now be involved along the zone and in the mountain redoubts to the south.

4. Soviet Union   The Soviets are increasing their military presence in Mongolia and they may be about to station a few combat units there. The British ambassador to Ulan Bator says that Russian air force troops are arriving by rail and that many Russian field grade officers have been seen in the capital since March. One Soviet motor pool there has doubled in size since late April.

5. Israel   The Israelis continue to threaten the Syrians with retaliation for recent Syrian-supported terrorist incidents. Prime Minister Eshkol has warned publicly that "if there is no other way out," Israel will be forced to take "appropriate means of action" to punish Syria.

New trouble with Jordan is another real possibility. On Monday, the Israelis plan to stage a military parade—perhaps with heavy weapons—in Jerusalem. This would be a clear violation of the armistice of 1949; a nasty incident in the divided city may result.

3. Laos   Supplies brought to the North Vietnam–Laos border during late March and April are continuing to filter into Laos toward the Plaine des Jarres. [Still-classified section.] [I]nside Laos report that about 36 trucks a day—the highest rate in recent months—moved west along the route between 6 and 10 May. We still believe that this is a stock-piling operation in anticipation of the rainy season.

4. South Arabia   Last week the cabinet in London formally endorsed the decision to unload Britain's South Arabian protectorates next January. The British hope they can give independence to a government with some base of support among the diverse peoples there. This will be difficult and the British will probably accept almost any kind of regime they can get. British troops are to leave as quickly as possible after independence.

A naval force is to be stationed nearby for six months [still-classified material] but there will be no British guarantee against internal subversion—or against a deterioration into political chaos. The whole nasty problem may well end up in the lap of the United Nations.

5. Egypt Nasir is going all out to show that his mutual security pact with Syria is something which the Israelis should take very seriously. Large troop contingents were seen moving through Cairo yesterday and there are other signs of a wide-scale mobilization.

Nasir must be hoping desperately that there will be no need for him to fight the Israelis. He probably feels, however, that his prestige in the Arab world would nose-dive if he stood idly by while Israel mauled Syria again.

6. Egypt—[Still classified.]

7. Dominican Republic Juan Bosch is still in Spain, leading the life of a rather embittered philosopher while his party back home carries on the wars. The latest party move has been to call again for a broad "anti-Trujillo front" to resist the Balaguer government.

So far, the only groups to respond positively to this idea have been extremists of the left. This response has put pressure on party leaders to go ahead with some kind of opposition "front"—even though this would surely produce a further exodus of the more moderate members.

President Balaguer continues on a hard-nosed course as he tries to restore public confidence in the wake of the upsurge of political terrorism. In the process, he is becoming more and more dependent on his conservative and right-wing supporters.

8. Ecuador President Arosemena is faced with a new upsurge of violence. Several people were killed and many wounded late last week before police and troops were able to suppress crowds of workers and students demonstrating their support for striking railwaymen. Further violence is feared and there is talk of more strikes to come.

DAILY BRIEF
27 MAY 1967

1. Arab States–Israel (As of 5:45 AM EDT) No challenge to the blockade appears likely today and there have been no new military developments overnight.

A tanker is due at Eilat about 31 May, but may be diverted as was a sister ship yesterday. A cargo vessel may enter the Gulf on 30 or 31 May.

U Thant may propose that all nations temporarily hold up strategic cargoes (including oil) normally shipped through the Gulf. [Still-classified section.] [A] two-week hiatus on strategic shipping was one of two proposals made by the UN Secretary General during his visit to Cairo. The second proposition was that he send a permanent and personal representative to the Middle East. The Egyptians bought both proposals, [still-classified section].

Moscow is still dodging a definitive position on the blockade. [Still-classified section.] remarked that the Arabs will have a difficult time defending the blockade from the international point of view. [Still-classified section.]

DAILY BRIEF
5 JUNE 1967

1. Arab States Israel Hostilities began early this morning. Both sides report heavy Israel fighting in the air and between armored forces along the Israeli border with Egypt.

Israeli planes raided airfields in Cairo and other areas beginning at about 8:00 AM local time (2:00 AM Washington time).

Cairo has just been informed that at least five of its airfields in Sinai and the Canal area have suddenly become "unserviceable." Israel's war plans had put high priority on quick action against the Egyptian Air Force because of the threat to its own more vulnerable airfields and vital centers.

Reports are still fragmentary, but the signs point to this as an Israeli initiative. Over the weekend it became apparent that Israeli leaders were becoming increasingly convinced that time was running against them. The new Israeli cabinet was meeting late yesterday with Ambassador Harmel present, and reconvened early today.

Cairo radio is calling on Egypt's Arab allies to attack Israel. [Still-classified section.]

2. Libya   The big US Wheelus base is becoming more and more exposed to nationalist pressures as the Arab war fever sweeps over this desert kingdom. Cairo is going all out to intensify the pressures, and responsible Libyans are worried; they see no way they can convincingly refute the propaganda that the base is being used to support the Israelis.

The Libyan foreign minister has been in Cairo this weekend, and Wheelus surely must have been discussed during his talk with Nasir.

3. Soviet Union   [Still classified.]

4. Nigeria   Both sides are preparing for war. Leaders of the breakaway republic in the East have evidence leading them to expect federal troops to attack today. The orderly evacuation of US dependents from the East began yesterday and is to continue today.

The federal government was strengthened over the weekend with the formation of an executive council with civilian representation. The leading political chieftain of the West was included. This has, at least for a time, reduced the danger of Western secession, which would surely have produced serious violence.

LATE ITEMS

Libya   The US Embassy in Benghazi flashed word at 4:30 AM EDT that it was being attacked by a large mob. It is burning its papers.

Syria   Damascus radio announces that Syrian planes are bombing Israeli cities and that "we have joined the battle."

DAILY BRIEF
6 JUNE 1967

1. Arab States–Israel   Cairo may be preparing to launch a campaign urging strikes against US interests in the Arab world. Both Egyptian and Syrian domestic broadcasts this morning called on the "Arab masses" to destroy all US and "imperialist" interests in the "Arab homeland." Last night Cairo radio claimed it had proof of US and British participation in the "aggression."

Demonstrations have now taken place against US embassies and installations all over the Arab world.

Arab oil-producing countries, meeting in Baghdad, say they will stop selling oil to any country which takes part in or supports Israel in the fighting. Baghdad radio said this morning that the pumping of Iraqi oil has been stopped "because of US and UK attitudes."

In the fighting, Israel has gained an early and perhaps overwhelming victory in the air, but the progress of the war on the ground is unclear. If Israeli claims regarding damage to Arab combat aircraft are valid, they have destroyed the entire Jordanian inventory of 21, two thirds of the Syrian inventory of 69, and 250 of some 430 Egyptian planes.

Arab counterclaims of 158 Israeli planes destroyed seem grossly exaggerated, but actual losses to the Israeli force of about 270 aircraft are not known.

Firm information on ground action remains sparse. The Israelis claim they have captured the "outer positions" of Kuntilla in southeastern Sinai and reached the outskirts of al-Arish in northern Sinai.

In Jordan, King Husayn said this morning that Israel is pushing ahead in a "punitive fashion." He ended with a plea that the US intercede.

DAILY BRIEF
7 JUNE 1967

1. Arab States–Israel (As of 5:30 AM EDT)   At this point, the shooting continues despite the UN ceasefire resolution. Early this morning Israeli planes were hammering Jordanian positions outside Jerusalem. There also was some firing in the city last night.

The Israelis appear to-hold substantial portions of the' Sinai Peninsula, and Cairo is ordering the Egyptian force at Sharm ash-Shaykh on the Straits of Tiran to withdraw. In fact, there are strong indicat'ions that the Egyptians may be withdrawing most, if not all, of their forces from the Sinai.

Although the Soviets are airlifting in some spare parts for Egyptian tanks and aircraft, there are no indications of any major Soviet military moves. [Still-classified section.]

In last night's Security Council meeting, Federenko demanded withdrawal of forces after a ceasefire, but this performance seems intended to put the best face possible on the retreat. [Still-classified section.]

The US Embassy in Cairo was not set on fire as reported in this morning's *Washington Post*.

DAILY BRIEF
8 JUNE 1967

1. Arab States–Israel (As of 5:00 AM EDT)   The UN's ceasefire order is being disregarded. Egypt has officially announced it will not comply, and Nasir has personally so informed most other Arab governments. The Israelis may have broken their ceasefire agreement with Jordan.

Early this morning the Jordanian prime minister told our embassy that Israeli tanks were moving into northwestern Jordan. The ultimate aim of such a movement might be to attack Syria. The embassy also says fighting on the Israeli-Jordanian front picked up during the night. [Still-classified section.]

On the Sinai Peninsula, the Israelis have apparently accomplished most of their military objectives. Yesterday the Israelis approached the Suez Canal so rapidly that they probably cut off the major portion of the retreating Egyptians.

Embassy Cairo believes that public realization of the Arab defeat has generated strong feeling against Nasir, and foreign diplomats in Cairo consider the Egyptians are in a state of panic over the military debacle. [Still-classified section.] Senior Iraqi officials in New York are said to believe Nasir is desperate and might do almost anything to maintain his position.

Mobs in Dhahran, Saudi Arabia, have damaged US installations, and our consulate in Aleppo has been attacked and burned. As the extent of the defeat sinks into the Arab countries, danger to US citizens still there may increase. Refugees from the fighting in Jordan's West Bank are already streaming into Amman, where they could cause disorder directed at Americans.

LATE ITEM

Arab States–Israel (As of 5:30 AM EDT)   The Israelis have just announced (according to the press) that Egyptian armored forces have counterattacked "in force" in an effort to fight their way out of the Sinai Peninsula. This could refer to Egyptian troops trapped in the rapid Israeli advance.

DAILY BRIEF
9 JUNE 1967

1. Arab States–Israel   The ceasefire was observed on all fronts during the night. Further Israeli action is still possible against Iraqi forces in Jordan, however, since Baghdad has yet to accept the ceasefire.

The Israeli commander in Sinai reported that his forces were camping on the banks of the Suez Canal and the Red Sea.

Tel Aviv is beginning to discuss the terms it hopes to achieve in a permanent settlement with the Arab states. These include the establishment of an autonomous province of Jordan on the West Bank in which all Arab refugees could hopefully be settled.

The Israelis also intend to insist on the demilitarization of the Gaza strip and the Sinai border, guaranteed access to the Gulf of Aqaba, and an as yet undefined "new status" for a unified Jerusalem. The latter would guarantee people of all religions access to the holy places.

As for the Arab side, attention is now turning to what can be salvaged in post-ceasefire negotiations. Nasir, after earlier proposing an Arab summit as a means of preserving Arab unity, is now proposing the publication of a ten-point joint resolution to be signed by all Arab chiefs of state. The proposed statement trots out all of Nasir's propaganda attacks on the US and other "colonialist forces supporting Israel." On balance, it looks like a rather feeble effort to save face.

Signs are growing that Egypt's defeat has badly damaged Nasir's prestige in the Arab world. He will have trouble getting many other chiefs of state to adhere to his "joint resolution."

2. Arab States   Arab resentment against the West continues to threaten US facilities. Libya appears to be a particularly dangerous spot at the moment.

3. Soviet Union   The Soviets are finding it hard to conceal their shock over the rapid Egyptian military collapse. A Soviet [still-classified section] could not understand "how our intelligence could have been so wrong." He asked despairingly, "How could we have gotten into such a mess?" Comments from other Soviets, while more restrained, reflect a similar state of mind.

4. Brazil   President Costa e Silva is still sidestepping the difficult economic decisions necessary to support the country's vital stabilization program. Anxious to avoid offending any pressure group, he is drifting into policies that could undermine much of the good work begun under Castello Branco.

5. Panama   President Robles is trying to keep student agitators off balance until the Canal treaties come up for ratification. This is the reason for unusually harsh sentences handed out to a number of extremist-led students who engaged in a minor ruckus on Tuesday. The bigger, Moscow-oriented student organization at the university is lying low for now, however, and saving its, ammunition for the treaty issue.

LATE ITEM

Arab States–Israel   Israeli spokesmen told the press this morning that Egyptian troops had launched an attack on Israeli troops near the Canal, thus violating the ceasefire.

THE PRESIDENT'S DAILY BRIEF
1 APRIL 1968

1. North Vietnam   [Still-classified material here] Hanoi reports the Vietnamese Communists are organizing a broad offensive to take place in South Vietnam this summer. [More classified material.] Hanoi expects the offensive to set the stage for a settlement on Communist terms and that the US will accept an "armistice" by early next year. [Classified material] report that a special mobilization of manpower is under way in North Vietnam to provide large numbers of new forces for the South.

* * *

What appear to be eight more infiltration groups were discovered [classified] over the weekend, raising the number of units en route through central North Vietnam in March [classified] More than 17,000 troops could be involved.

2. South Vietnam   Vice President Ky, chief of the Joint General Staff Vien, and at least three of the four corps commanders plan to submit their resignations en masse unless Thieu resolves certain doubts and agrees to consult them closely on policy, according to [classified]. These doubts include rumors that Thieu is embarking on wholesale personnel changes which would revive the influence of the southern Dai Viet party at the expense of the military hierarchy.

The commanders are already disturbed by Thieu's recent provincial appointments which they see as a substitution of Thieu's followers for their own protégés or as creating unrest among province chiefs and military officers in general.

3. Panama   The Supreme Court will reconvene today to decide on the constitutionality of the Assembly's impeachment of Robles. No matter how the court rules, the situation is likely to deteriorate further.

The people around Arnulfo Arias are now working on more legal moves against the government, and are also keeping pressure on Robles and the National Guard through demonstrations and disorders. If the court invalidates the impeachment, Arias and company are prepared to impeach the court.

Pro-Arias demonstrators plan to be in the streets "to create an atmosphere of tension" while the court is deliberating. Influential families on both sides are becoming more and more convinced that a takeover by the guard is the only solution.

4. Brazil   Extremists have taken over the leadership of a major student demonstration planned for today in Rio. Large antigovernment demonstrations already have been held in most key Brazilian cities since the police killed a youth in Rio on Thursday.

The student leaders [classified] plan to focus on the "repressive military dictatorship," but the US will also be a target. There is widespread sympathy for the students' cause.

There is already some evidence of military dissatisfaction with the government's failure to crack down on the students. If students and police clash again, military pressure on the government will probably build quickly.

5. Cyprus   Prospects for talks between representatives of the Greek and Turkish communities are better now than at any time since the outbreak of violence in late 1963. Preliminary contacts between the two groups have been aided by the steady decrease in tension since last November. Much distrust remains, however, and no easy solution to the basic problems is in sight.

6. Egypt   Nasir, in a speech to the nation on Saturday, outlined a "program of action" to bring about political reform. We doubt that it will amount to much.

[PRESIDENT'S DAILY BRIEF]

The following is the text of an item from the Presidential Daily Brief received by President William J. Clinton on December 4, 1998. Redacted material is indicated in brackets.

SUBJECT: Bin Ladin Preparing to Hijack US Aircraft and Other Attacks

1. Reporting [—] suggests Bin Ladin and his allies are preparing for attacks in the US, including an aircraft hijacking to obtain the release of Shaykh 'Umar 'Abd al-Rahman, Ramzi Yousef, and Muhammad Sadiq 'Awda. One source quoted a senior member of the Gama'at al-Islamiyya (IG) saying that, as of late October, the IG had completed planning for an operation in the US on behalf of Bin Ladin, but that the operation was on hold. A senior Bin Ladin operative from Saudi Arabia was to visit IG counterparts in the US soon thereafter to discuss options—perhaps including an aircraft hijacking.

- IG leader Islambuli in late September was planning to hijack a US airliner during the "next couple of weeks" to free 'Abd al-Rahman and the other prisoners, according to what may be a different source.
- The same source late last month said that Bin Ladin might implement plans to hijack US aircraft before the beginning of Ramadan on 20 December and that two members of the operational team had evaded security checks during a recent trial run at an unidentified New York airport. [—]

2. Some members of the Bin Ladin network have received hijack training, according to various sources, but no group directly tied to Bin Ladin's al-Qa'ida organization has ever carried out an aircraft hijacking. Bin Ladin could be weighing other types of operations against US aircraft. According to [—] the IG in October obtained SA-7 missiles

and intended to move them from Yemen into Saudi Arabia to shoot down an Egyptian plane or, if unsuccessful, a US military or civilian aircraft.

- A [—] in October told us that unspecified "extremist elements" in Yemen had acquired SA-7s. [—]

3. [—] indicate the Bin Ladin organization or its allies are moving closer to implementing anti-US attacks at unspecified locations, but we do not know whether they are related to attacks on aircraft. A Bin Ladin associate in Sudan late last month told a colleague in Kandahar that he had shipped a group of containers to Afghanistan. Bin Ladin associates also talked about the movement of containers to Afghanistan before the East Africa bombings.

- In other [—] Bin Ladin associates last month discussed picking up a package in Malaysia. One told his colleague in Malaysia that "they" were in the "ninth month [of pregnancy]."
- An alleged Bin Ladin supporter in Yemen late last month remarked to his mother that he planned to work in "commerce" from abroad and said his impending "marriage," which would take place soon, would be a "surprise." "Commerce" and "marriage" often are codewords for terrorist attacks. [—]

FOR THE PRESIDENT ONLY
6 AUGUST 2001
BIN LADIN DETERMINED TO STRIKE IN US

Clandestine, foreign government, and media reports indicate Bin Ladin since 1997 has wanted to conduct terrorist attacks in the US. Bin Ladin implied in US television interviews in 1997 and 1998 that his followers would follow the example of World Trade Center bomber Ramzi Yousef and "bring the lighting to America."

After US missile strikes on his base in Afghanistan in 1998, Bin Ladin told followers he wanted to retaliate in Washington, according to a [—] service.

An Egyptian Islamic Jihad (EIJ) operative told an [—] service at the same time that Bin Ladin was planning to exploit the operative's access to the US to mount a terrorist strike.

The millennium plotting in Canada in 1999 may have been part of Bin Ladin's first serious attempt to implement a terrorist strike in the US. Convicted plotter Ahmed Ressam has told the FBI that he conceived the idea to attack Los Angeles International Airport himself, but that Bin Ladin lieutenant Abu Zubaydah encouraged him and helped facilitate the operation. Ressam also said that in 1998 Abu Zubaydah was planning his own US attack.

Ressam says Bin Ladin was aware of the Los Angeles operation.

Although Bin Ladin has not succeeded, his attacks against the US Embassies in Kenya and Tanzania in 1998 demonstrate that he prepares operations years in advance and is not deterred by setbacks. Bin Ladin associates surveilled our Embassies in Nairobi and Dar es Salaam as early as 1993, and some members of the Nairobi cell planning the bombings were arrested and deported in 1997.

Al-Qa'ida members—including some who are US citizens—have resided in or traveled to the US for years, and the group apparently maintains a support structure that could aid attacks. Two al-Qa'ida members found guilty in the conspiracy to bomb our Embassies in East Africa were US citizens, and a senior EIJ member lived in California in the mid-1990s.

A clandestine source said in 1998 that a Bin Ladin cell in New York was recruiting Muslim-American youth for attacks.

We have not been able to corroborate some of the more sensational threat reporting, such as that from a [—] service in 1998 saying that Bin Ladin wanted to hijack a US aircraft to gain the release of "Blind Shaykh" 'Umar 'Abd al-Rahman and other US-held extremists.

Nevertheless, FBI information since that time indicates patterns of suspicious activity in this country consistent with preparations for hijackings or other types of attacks, including recent surveillance of federal buildings in New York.

The FBI is conducting approximately 70 full field investigations throughout the US that it considers Bin Ladin-related. CIA and the FBI are investigating a call to our Embassy in the UAE in May saying that a group of Bin Ladin supporters was in the US planning attacks with explosives.

HOUSE PERMANENT SELECT COMMITTEE ON INTELLIGENCE CRITIQUE OF HUMINT, 2004

AREAS OF SPECIAL INTEREST

In the following several pages, the Committee highlights areas of concern that it believes must be addressed with a high priority by the Director of Central Intelligence, (DCI) as the leader of the Intelligence Community, if intelligence sufficient to protect our national security is to be obtained and provided to policy makers. The Committee places particular emphasis on issues that impact the Intelligence Community as a whole or that involve several various programs.

GLOBAL HUMAN INTELLIGENCE COLLECTION

All is not well in the world of clandestine human intelligence collection (HUMINT). The DCI himself has stated that five more years will be needed to build a viable HUMINT capability. The Committee, in the strongest possible terms, asserts that the Directorate of Operations (DO) needs fixing. For too long the CIA has been ignoring its core mission activities. There is a dysfunctional denial of any need for corrective action. The CIA must collect against all types of targets needed to gain the insights into plans and intentions of our adversaries, be they terrorist, political, economic, military, in nature. Countering the threat from terrorism is, of course, and should be, at the top of CIA's list of collection priorities, but the Central Intelligence Agency must continue to be much more than just the "Central Counterterrorism Agency" if America is to be truly secure, prosperous, and free.

The Committee has placed in the classified annex of this intelligence authorization its comprehensive analysis of what specifically is not right with the way the Directorate of

Source: Excerpt from "Intelligence Authorization Act for Fiscal Year 2005," *Report 108-558,* Permanent Select Committee on Intelligence (the Goss Committee), U.S. House of Representatives, 108th Cong., 2d Sess. (June 21, 2004), pp. 23–27.

Operations is being and has been managed. The Committee also assesses that the consequences of continued CIA mismanagement of the HUMINT mission are significant. Replete throughout this analysis, which includes specific recommendations for corrective action, are footnoted references to similar criticisms made by this Committee in the classified annexes of past intelligence authorization bills stretching back well before the 9/11 terrorist attacks. So, this is not new territory for the Committee. CIA has officially registered its strong objection to the Committee's exhaustively researched conclusions, which were reached over the course of years of close oversight and informed by hundreds of meetings and continuous dialogue with experienced CIA field operatives and Headquarters officials. That none of it could be made unclassified is unfortunate.

The Committee respects the authority of the DCI to make classification decisions and will, of course, abide by his ruling in this matter. After years of trying to convince, suggest, urge, entice, cajole, and pressure CIA to make wide-reaching changes to the way it conducts its HUMINT mission, however, CIA, in the Committee's view, continues down a road leading over a proverbial cliff. The damage to the HUMINT mission through its misallocation and redirection of resources, poor prioritization of objectives, micromanagement of field operations, and a continued political aversion to operational risk is, in the Committee's judgment, significant and could likely be long-lasting. Immediate and far-reaching changes can still reverse some of the worst factors eroding its capabilities, however. If the CIA continues to ignore the experience of many of its best, brightest, and most experienced officers, and continues to equate criticism from within and without—especially from its oversight committees—as commentary unworthy even of consideration, no matter how constructive, informed, and well-meaning that criticism may be, they do so at their peril. The DO will become nothing more than a stilted bureaucracy incapable of even the slightest bit of success. The nimble, flexible, core-mission oriented enterprise the DO once was, is becoming just a fleeting memory. With each passing day, it becomes harder to resurrect. The Committee highlights, with concern, the fact that it only took a year or two in the mid-1990's to decimate the capabilities of the CIA, that we are now in the 8th year of rebuild, and still we are more than 5 years away from being healthy. This is tragic. It should never happen again.

The Committee believes that the DO's difficulties are manifest in the discussion on Iraq's WMD. The analysts have taken a significant amount of criticism on the issue. It is imperative to point out, however, that the analysts do not collect the information they analyze. They simply take what is available and reach educated assessments. It is incumbent on the DO and other areas of the IC collection community to gather the information that will present a more complete picture. There was an insufficiency of the right amount of information available on this topic for the analysts. The U.S. cannot afford to be in such a position.

THE STATE OF THE CIA'S
DIRECTORATE OF INTELLIGENCE (DI)

In the aftermath of the terrorist attacks on the United States on September 11, 2001, the CIA's Directorate of Intelligence has experienced dramatic personnel shifts and a rapid increase in the demand for both its analysts and work product. The DI, much like the CIA's clandestine arm, the Directorate of Operations, suffered from disinvestments resulting from the so-called "peace dividend" of the 1990's. It was not until the World Trade Center and Pentagon were struck that senior DI management began to realize just how desperate the need is for an expanded and experienced analytic cadre.

DI analysts have earned a reputation in the Intelligence Community for being highly educated, well trained, motivated, and capable of handling demanding and fast moving assignments. As a result, with the expansion of the terrorist mission, DI analysts are in demand across the Intelligence Community, and in line with the CIA's "can-do" attitude has committed significant numbers of DI analysts to other organizations and posts. The CIA's analytic cadre, much like its covert counterpart in the DO, toil quietly, without significant praise, seldom ever to tell of success publicly, but sharply criticized for the least inaccuracy. The Committee notes the hard-working and dedicated rank-and-file professionals that provide the link between collection and truth and add value to raw data for policymakers.

The Committee notes four developments that, if not adequately addressed in the near-term, will work together to seriously undermine and degrade the relevance of the DI and its critically important products at a time when they are needed most by consumers. The first factor—the unsustainable surges in DI personnel to cover crisis issues without adequate back-filling—may be the easiest of the four problems to address. Aggressive new hiring is helping to mitigate this problem, but in the interim, overall DI expertise is declining, as new analysts need substantial training and on-the-job learning of their accounts. While there may be a strong temptation to surge these analysts to meet new crisis needs, it is important that this not be done prematurely or so haphazardly that it creates more problems than it seeks to solve. DI analysts must be allowed to develop true expertise. The DI must not be permitted to become an organization of generalists. Longer assignments on specific countries, regions, or issues—once discouraged by DI management concerned about analytic "clientitis"—should be strongly encouraged. This is, in the Committee's view, a major way to reverse permanently the trend towards widening global analytic gaps. Analytic depth can be more about skills than about numbers of bodies.

The second major DI problem area concerns the culture of analytic risk aversion, begun long before 9/11, but fostered through the continued perception on the part of the rank-and-file that senior DI managers do not want risk taking—however calculated, caveated, and warranted—and that they will not stand by an analyst who has made the wrong prediction. With some exceptions, the DI has become more focused on coordinated judgments that are often so caveated that they are of little use to consumers who are searching for some form of clarity in the very gray world of finished intelligence reporting. While clarity will not always be possible, analysts should be encouraged to be more forward leaning and to push the analytic envelope whenever possible, lest consumers turn more and more—as they have in recent years—to uncorroborated single-source HUMINT or SIGINT reports to inform their decisions. Creating an environment of some stability for analysts to develop adequate expertise will be an essential part of breaking the DI's risk averse culture, lest risk-taking become a reckless rather than calculated process.

The Committee recognizes that the DI is suffering from the difficult combination of vastly increasing requirements and too few bodies to service them. Strong DI leadership, however, with a demonstrated commitment to calculated risk-taking and to the true expertise building that must come with it, would begin to bridge the gap between where DI personnel numbers are now and the time when adequate help arrives. With the CIA's analysis on Iraq being widely criticized, DI leaders simply cannot afford to sit on their heels. If analysts decided to give up on risk-taking entirely, the national security interests of the country will suffer. This cannot be permitted to happen.

The third major problem area was also clearly evident to the Committee as a problem in the years before 9/11 and appeared in the form of criticial classified report language in past intelligence authorizations. This is the continuing overemphasis by senior DI managers on current intelligence reporting instead of on the longer-term, predictive, strategic intelligence forecasting that was once the strength of the DI and the staple of the DI's avid consumer base. The explosion of all form of open-source reporting, combined with technology for transmitting news across the globe in near-real time makes it nearly impossible for DI analysts to keep up. Instead of "chasing CNN," as the Committee has observed in the past, the DI should be devoting much more of its resources to doing the kind of all-source, in-depth analysis that cannot, and is not, being done elsewhere in government or through media outlets. The DI will always have to leave some capability in place to make sure that its judgments about overnight developments in the world's hot spots are rapidly provided to consumers each day via tried and tested means, such as daily publications, spot reports, and briefings, for example. But, analysts have complained for years, and the Committee has heard the message loud and clear, that the preference of senior DI managers for current intelligence and opportunities to brief such product to high-level consumers far outstripped the DI's capacity to be useful. More importantly, such DI priorities damaged the DI's base of expertise by squandering scarce analytic resources that could be put to better use helping the more sophisticated line-consumers understand better what was behind the facade of the daily or hourly news reports. The crisis atmosphere post-9/11 has indeed generated more interest in rapid analytic judgments to address fast-moving situations, but the DI needs to play to its strengths and fill a badly needed function of giving the consumer a much higher degree of education than the "sound-bite" analysis currently being emphasized. These are the types of priorities to be set by the DI's top manager. The Committee continues to disagree with the rationale for the continuing trend towards current intelligence at the expense of nearly every other form of the discipline.

Finally, the Committee remains concerned that senior DI managers still do not have the ability to drive collection priorities, despite past Committee exhortations about the urgency of fixing this problem, and the CIA's own stated goals. A number of analytic judgments on Iraq have so far been found to be inconsistent with the facts on the ground. While intelligence analysis seldom, if ever, provides a 100 percent accurate picture, deficiencies were largely the result of years of inadequate or insufficient HUMINT collection, and extensive and ingrained denial and deception tactics that defeated technical collection efforts. Analysts had little actual ground truth with which to work. The Committee now finds the DO overly focused on a few priority targets, leaving analysts once again reliant on the media and other mostly open or insufficiently validated sources of information with which to make its key judgments. Given the recent performance on Iraq, the Committee believes that senior DI management should play a stronger role in determining collection priorities and advocating the need for global coverage.

SENATE SELECT COMMITTEE ON INTELLIGENCE REPORT ON IRAQI WMD INTELLIGENCE, 2004

I. INTRODUCTION

(U) In June 2003, the Senate Select Committee on Intelligence began a formal review of U.S. intelligence into the existence of Iraq's weapons of mass destruction (WMD) programs, Iraq's ties to terrorist groups, Saddam Hussein's threat to stability and security in the region, and his violations of human rights including the actual use of weapons of mass destruction against his own people, as a part of the Committee's continuing oversight of the intelligence activities of the United States.

(U) Committee staff had, for the previous several months, already been examining aspects of intelligence activities regarding Iraq, including the Intelligence Community's (IC's) intelligence support to the United Nations Monitoring, Verification, and Inspection Commission (UNMOVIC) weapons inspections in Iraq and the IC's analysis and collection of reporting related to the alleged Niger-Iraq uranium deal. On June 20, 2003, however, Senator Pat Roberts, Chairman, and Senator John D. Rockefeller IV, Vice Chairman, of the Senate Select Committee on Intelligence released a press statement announcing their joint commitment to continue the Committee's thorough review of U.S. intelligence. Chairman Roberts and Vice Chairman Rockefeller said the Committee would examine:

- the quantity and quality of U.S. intelligence on Iraqi weapons of mass destruction programs, ties to terrorist groups, Saddam Hussein's threat to stability and security in the region, and his repression of his own people;
- the objectivity, reasonableness, independence, and accuracy of the judgments reached by the Intelligence Community;

Source: Excerpt from *Report on the U.S. Intelligence Community's Prewar Intelligence Assessments on Iraq* (the Roberts Report), Senate Select Committee on Intelligence (the Roberts Committee), U.S. Senate, 108th Cong., 2d Sess. (July 7, 2004), pp. 1–35.

- whether those judgments were properly disseminated to policymakers in the executive branch and Congress;
- whether any influence was brought to bear on anyone to shape their analysis to support policy objectives; and
- other issues we mutually identify in the course of the Committee's review.

With the exception of the question of accuracy, all of the foregoing are addressed in this report.

(U) On February 12, 2004, the Committee unanimously agreed to refine the terms of reference of the Committee's inquiry. In addition to the matters set forth in the joint release of the Chairman and Vice Chairman on June 20, 2003, the Committee agreed to examine additional issues in two phases. Issues annotated as phase one have been addressed in this report. Issues annotated as phase two are currently under review by the Committee. The additional issues are:

- the collection of intelligence on Iraq from the end of the Gulf War to the commencement of Operation Iraqi Freedom (phase I);
- whether public statements, reports, and testimony regarding Iraq by U.S. Government officials made between the Gulf War period and the commencement of Operation Iraqi Freedom were substantiated by intelligence information (phase II);
- the postwar findings about Iraq's weapons of mass destruction and weapons programs and links to terrorism and how they compare with prewar assessments (phase II);
- prewar intelligence assessments about postwar Iraq (phase II);
- any intelligence activities relating to Iraq conducted by the Policy Counterterrorism Evaluation Group (PCTEG) and the Office of Special Plans within the Office of the Under Secretary of Defense for Policy (phase I and II); and
- the use by the Intelligence Community of information provided by the Iraqi National Congress (INC) (phase I and II).

(U) In early June 2003, the IC provided the Committee with nineteen volumes (approximately 15,000 pages) of intelligence assessments and source reporting underlying the IC's assessments of Iraq's WMD programs, ties to terrorist groups, threat to stability and security in the region, and repression of its own people. Committee staff began immediately to read and analyze every report provided to determine how intelligence analysts reached their conclusions and whether any assessments were not supported by the intelligence provided to the Committee. In late August and early September 2003, Committee staff requested additional intelligence to support IC assessments which Committee staff had judged were not supported by the intelligence that had been previously provided.

(U) The Committee began to receive this additional supporting intelligence in October 2003. In late October 2003, Committee staff requested that the IC provide any intelligence, which had not already been provided, that contradicted the IC's analyses regarding Iraq. For example, Committee staff requested intelligence that showed Iraq had not reconstituted its nuclear program, had not renewed production of chemical agents, and had abandoned an offensive biological weapons program. In early November 2003, the IC wrote to the Committee that it was working to provide the contradictory intelligence requested by Committee staff. In the same letter, the IC said it had uncovered an additional six volumes of intelligence material that supported the IC's assessments on Iraq's WMD programs. These materials were also reviewed by Committee staff. The IC provided the contradictory intelligence information in late November. During the twelve months of the Committee's review, Committee staff submitted almost 100 requests for supplemental intelligence information, received over 30,000 pages of documents in response to those requests, and reviewed and analyzed each document provided. The Committee's request to review Presidential Daily Briefs (PDBs) relevant only to Iraq's weapons of mass destruction capabilities and links to terrorists was denied by the White House. Without examining these documents, the Committee is unable to determine fully whether Intelligence Community judgments were properly disseminated to policymakers in the executive branch, one of the tasks outlined for review.

(U) Committee staff interviewed more than 200 individuals including intelligence analysts and senior officials with the Central Intelligence Agency (CIA), Defense Intelligence Agency, Department of Defense, Department of Energy, Department of State, National Ground Intelligence Center, the Air Force, and the Federal Bureau of Investigation. Staff also interviewed former intelligence analysts, National Intelligence Officers, operations officers, collection managers, signals intelligence collectors, imagery analysts, nuclear experts with the International Atomic Energy Agency, Ambassadors, former United Nations inspectors, Department of Defense weapons experts, State Department officials, and National Security Council staff members.

(U) The Committee held four preliminary hearings on aspects of U.S. intelligence on Iraq: the Iraq-Niger connection, the CIA and State Department Inspectors General report on the review of the Iraq-Niger issue, the history and continuity of weapons of mass destruction assessments pertaining to Iraq, and Iraq prewar intelligence.

(U) These efforts have enabled the Committee to develop a full understanding of the quantity and quality of intelligence reporting on Iraq's WMD programs, Iraq's ties to terrorist groups, Saddam Hussein's threat to stability and security in the region, and his violations of human rights including the actual use of weapons of mass destruction against his own people. The Committee has also gained an understanding of how intelligence analysts throughout the IC used that intelligence to develop their assessments on these issues, how those assessments were disseminated to policymakers, whether those assessments were reasonable, objective, independent of political consideration, and whether any influence was brought to bear to shape their analysis to support policy objectives.

A. UNDERSTANDING INTELLIGENCE ANALYSIS

(U) Over a period of one year, Committee staff, many of whom are former intelligence analysts, reviewed over a decade of Intelligence Community (IC) assessments and the intelligence that underlay them. In all cases our staff endeavored, to the greatest extent possible, to disregard post-war discoveries concerning Iraq until after completing the analysis of the prewar intelligence material in order to replicate the same analytical environment IC analysts experienced prior to the war. The Committee's review surfaced strengths and weaknesses throughout the intelligence process. These are identified in the Report's findings and conclusions.

(U) Intelligence analysis is not a perfect science and we should not expect perfection from our IC analysts. It is entirely possible for an analyst to perform meticulous and skillful analysis and be completely wrong. Likewise, it is also possible to perform careless and unskilled analysis and be completely right. While intelligence collection is not an analytical function, it is the foundation upon which all good analysis is built. Problems with collection priorities and management will be discussed in detail throughout the report.

(U) The Committee, therefore, believes that it is important to understand the role of analysts and how they learn and apply their craft. With that background, the Committee hopes the reader can fully appreciate the content of this report.

1. Developing Professional Intelligence Analysts

(U) In order to give context to the Committee's review of the Intelligence Community's (IC) prewar analyses, Committee staff spoke with senior CIA officers at the Sherman Kent School for Intelligence Analysis at the CIA. The CIA relies on the Kent School to teach new analysts the trade craft of analysis. Committee staff members also drew on their own experiences working in the IC's analytic community.

(U) Kent School officials provided a briefing, slides, and a copy of the school's brochure to explain the school's approach and how analytic trade craft is presented to new CIA analysts. The training also address how the Directorate of Intelligence (DI) views the analytic process and the DI's structure.

(U) The CIA's Directorate of Intelligence requires its new analysts to complete a training program called the Career Analyst Program, or CAP. The CAP includes eleven weeks of classroom instruction and a five week interim assignment. The participants receive two weeks of training on analysis, three weeks on DI writing and one week each on briefing, teamwork, and the business of intelligence. (These are the core analytic trade craft areas.) The CAP also devotes time to task-force exercises and visits to U.S. military commands and other agencies to help the students develop a broader perspective on the role of intelligence analysis in policymaking. For the interim assignment, analysts consult with their "home offices" to choose an assignment that is relevant to the account they will cover as a DI analyst. They can work in other intelligence agencies, a policy office or in a law enforcement agency for their interim assignment.

(U) According to the school's brochure, "The CAP emphasizes the Directorate's goal: to produce analysis that is rigorous, well-reasoned, and appropriately caveated. The analytic thinking courses' focus on questioning key assumptions and considering possible explanations and outcomes. Analysts learn to be aware of psychological, cultural, and informational factors that affect their analytic judgments." Kent School officials stated that this training involves a very hands-on approach and many small exercises that help the analysts learn by doing. Instructors give the students a number of short classroom assignments, many of which are done in groups. Students receive extensive feedback from the instructors.

(U) The same is true for the development of the analysts' writing skills. The long brochure states, "DI writing style emphasizes the bottom line up front, precise and concise language, and a clear articulation of our judgments and our confidence in them." The analysts practice writing each of the types of products that the DI produces including situation reports and short and long papers. They also participate in a final four-day course on writing for the President and senior policymakers. The Kent School officials stated that many of these assignments use case studies, such as the attack on Pearl Harbor, the Cuban Missile Crisis, the bombing of Khobar Towers, the break-up of Yugoslavia and the September 11 attacks.

(U) Kent School officials outlined the key analytic goals as:

- providing timely, credible, and relevant intelligence analysis for the consumer;
- warning and identifying opportunities;
- maintaining analytic integrity and objectivity; and
- using all source intelligence.

They also described the analytic process as 1) dealing with facts and assertions, 2) testing assumptions and logic, 3) developing findings, 4) interpreting information, 5) developing scenarios (to include both high probability/low impact and low probability/high impact), 6) determining indicators, and 7) discussing options to determine opportunities, identifying vulnerabilities and revealing potential outcomes.

(U) By using case studies and providing the CAP participants with the intelligence cables used by analysts to build their assessments, the instructors are able to help the new analysts develop their ability to weigh information and become accustomed to the format of the reporting and source descriptions. They also learn to task collectors, structure data for presentations, and recognize indicators of activities. They also learn to recognize the strengths and weaknesses of the various "INTs"—human intelligence (HUMINT), signals intelligence (SIGINT), imagery intelligence (IMINT), and measurement and signature intelligence (MASINT).

(U) The Kent School also incorporates a module which alerts new analysts to the pitfalls of assumptions and biases in their own analysis and in the work of others. Recognizing one's own bias is extremely difficult, however. Therefore, it is critical to develop a workforce of analysts that are comfortable questioning each other. While it is stressed in the initial training provided by the CAP, it appears to be the lesson that analysts neglect first.

(U) In her February 11, 2004 address to the Directorate of Intelligence, the Deputy Director for Intelligence (DDI) stated:

> I want to focus on the danger of inherited assumptions. That may be the single most important aspect of our trade craft that needs to be examined. That is something I speak about to every new CAP class: How do we ensure that we are not passing along assumptions that haven't been sufficiently questioned or examined?

2. An Analyst's Daily Taskings

(U) In terms of day-to-day work, intelligence analysts review raw reporting, draft assessments, and disseminate those assessments to policy makers. Each written assessment may be drafted by one or several analysts who have reviewed raw reporting over a period of time. Intelligence collected by the CIA, Defense Intelligence Agency (DIA), National Security Agency (NSA), National Geospatial-Intelligence Agency (NGA) and in some cases, State Department diplomatic reporting, is reviewed daily by intelligence analysts using computer software that searches the various agencies' databases and produces a daily electronic read file for each analyst that is specific to their area of responsibility. In many instances, analysts from regional and functional offices, which cover issues that span across regions, such as terrorism, drug trafficking, and humanitarian issues, will read the same material and draw conclusions relative to their interests and responsibilities.

(U) Each IC agency that has an all-source analysis capability or responsibility will have one or more analysts reviewing intelligence reporting on the same issues. In an ideal situation, these analysts will be in regular contact over secure communications to discuss new information, to share ideas and to brainstorm about how the information can be presented to policymakers to best satisfy their requirements, however, this exchange does not always occur. The analysts are responsible for sifting through large amounts of information and drawing connections or reaching conclusions about the implications of the information at their disposal. Depending on the product, the analysis may be coordinated with other IC members, but in many instances, each agency produces its own finished products which are subject to review and editing by its own internal management.

3. THE FINISHED PRODUCT

(U) Analysts create their products for intelligence consumers, including policy makers and warfighters, to name two of many. While DIA products are generally intended for the Secretary of Defense, CIA products for the White House, and the State Department's Bureau Intelligence & Research products for the Secretary of State, most products are available to policy makers at each of these agencies regardless of the author's organization. The vast majority of intelligence products are available to the Congress as well.

(U) It is important to note that in many cases the manager responsible for approving the final product may not, and often does not, review the raw intelligence upon which the assessment is based. Kent School officials who have worked as branch chiefs or division managers stated, however, that products are reviewed more carefully when the drafter is a relatively new analyst. When the drafter is a more senior, well-established analyst, the product will often be edited, but not substantively reviewed before it goes up the chain to the policymaker. If the intelligence product was not coordinated with other intelligence agencies, it is entirely possible that one analyst's views may be presented to high-level officials including the President of the United States without having been reviewed by other analysts with the same depth of knowledge. This is a dynamic we found on a number of occasions in the course of this review.

B. WEAPONS OF MASS DESTRUCTION CAPABILITIES

(U) The Weapons of Mass Destruction (WMD) related sections of the report recount the Committee's efforts to evaluate the quantity and quality of the intelligence underlying prewar assessments. Each section contains its own set of conclusions. There is also a separate section on the issue of objectivity which addresses whether analysts were pressured to reach specific conclusions to support a particular policy objective. This report does not address the question of accuracy regarding WMD. When the Iraq Survey Group (ISG) completes its work in Iraq, we will then be able to evaluate to the maximum extent possible the accuracy of the IC's judgments prior to the war.

(U) The Committee focused its evaluation of the Intelligence Community's WMD analysis primarily on the October 2002 National Intelligence Estimate (NIE): *Iraq's Continuing Programs for Weapons of Mass Destruction.* This document was selected for several reasons:

- First, according to the National Intelligence Council (NIC) and the Director of Central Intelligence (DCI), National Intelligence Estimates (NIE) are the IC's most authoritative written judgments concerning national security issues. The process by which the IC produces NIEs—including the one on Iraqi WMD—has been honed over nearly 30 years. According to the Central Intelligence Agency's (CIA) webpage, it is designed to provide policymakers in both the executive and legislative branches with the "best, unvarnished, and unbiased information—regardless of whether analytic judgments conform to U.S. policy."

- Second, the 2002 NIE addressed all of Iraq's WMD programs and was a co-ordinated community judgment in which all agency views were represented and dissenting opinions were noted.
- Third, the 2002 NIE was comprehensive, encompassing more than ten years of source reporting and analysis. The intelligence documentation provided to the Committee to support the assessments in the 2002 NIE also included the documents which were the basis for the previous decade of analytical products on Iraq's WMD programs.
- Fourth, the 2002 NIE presented some new IC assessments, some of which shifted in significant ways from previous judgments regarding Iraq's WMD programs.
- Finally, the 2002 NIE was requested by Senate Select Committee on Intelligence (SSCI) Members so that policymakers could benefit from the IC's coordinated judgment on Iraq's WMD programs while they debated authorizing military action against Iraq.

(U) Since June 2003, Committee staff has worked through a decade of intelligence assessments on Iraqi WMD programs and the intelligence source reporting used by IC analysts to make those assessments—over 20,000 pages of documents. Committee staff interviewed over 160 people, including intelligence analysts from every agency involved in preparing WMD assessments on Iraq, ambassadors, operations officers, collection managers, nuclear experts with the International Atomic Energy Agency (IAEA), former United Nations (UN) inspectors, Department of Defense (DoD) weapons experts, State Department officials, and National Security Council (NSC) staff members.

(U) These efforts have enabled Committee staff to develop a full understanding of the body of intelligence on Iraq's WMD capabilities and an understanding of how intelligence analysts throughout the IC used that body of intelligence reporting to develop their assessments, particularly those in the 2002 NIE on *Iraq's Continuing Programs for Weapons of Mass Destruction.*

1. WHAT IS AN NIE?

(U) A National Intelligence Estimate is the IC's most authoritative written judgment concerning a specific national security issue. The Estimates are intended to provide policymakers in both the executive and legislative branches with the best, unvarnished, and unbiased information—regardless of whether analytic judgments conform to any particular policy objective.

(U) A 2003 NIC paper on the NIE process stated that an NIE is "...the most authoritative written means by which the Director of Central Intelligence conveys to the President and other senior leaders the judgments of the entire Intelligence Community regarding national security issues." Sherman Kent,[1] a former Chairman of the Board of

---

[1] *Sherman Kent and the Board of National Estimates: Collected Essays,* (Http://www.odci.gov/csi/ books/shermankent/inst.html). From 1952 to 1967, Sherman Kent was the Chairman of the Board of National Estimates, which would later become the National Intelligence Council.

National Estimates, described the purpose and importance of NIEs in an essay in 1976, which noted that the NIE

> ...was and is the Director's estimate, and its findings are his. Although many experts from perhaps all intelligence components of the community participated in the production of the papers in the NIE series, and although the intelligence chiefs themselves formally passed on the final text, they could not bend its findings to suit their own judgments contrary to the will of the DCI. They could try to win him to their sides by full and free discussions, but they could not outvote him and force him to join them, nor could they make him dissent from them...they could of their own accord concur with his findings or, not being able to, they could dissent and make their alternative views known in footnotes to his text.

(U) NIEs and the formal process by which they are produced, were established in the 1950s. An NIE can be requested by a variety of individuals, including members of the executive branch, members of Congress, and military commanders. After an NIE has been requested and authorized, the next step is the preparation of a document which has come to be called the Terms of Reference (TOR). According to a 1994 NIC paper describing NIE drafting guidelines, the TOR is an outline of the "issues and key questions to be covered in the Estimate." Sherman Kent describes the TOR as a "statement of precisely what was wanted."

(U) An officer of the NIC, typically the National Intelligence Officer (NIO) with responsibility for the substantive issue being examined in the NIE, is given responsibility for managing the NIE from its initial drafting, through the coordination process with the national intelligence agencies, to final approval. The officer presiding over the drafting of the NIE can draw on the staff of the NIC as well as the national intelligence agencies to write the draft.

(U) The 1994 NIE drafting guidelines state that an NIE can be drafted by an IC analyst, a member of the NIC staff, a deputy NIO, or an outside expert. After the draft has been reviewed within the NIC staff, it is then sent to the national intelligence agencies where each agency's appropriate subject matter experts review the draft and prepare their comments. Agency comments are then carried forward to the first interagency coordination session. At this and any successive coordination sessions, the goal is to produce a draft that, without unnecessary hedging or ambiguity, reflects the collective judgment of the IC. In the event any of the agency representatives find a part of the NIE with which they do not concur, they are free to argue their case before their colleagues in order to sway them. If they fail to convince their colleagues, they are free to draft a dissenting footnote. Once the agency representatives arrive at a consensus paper, with or without footnotes, this final draft is usually submitted to IC peers and to a panel of IC experts for their review. A summary of the outside experts' views is included in the NIE. The NIC front office reviews the final draft prior to forwarding it to the National Foreign Intelligence Board (NFIB) principals for their approval. The NFIB is composed of senior representatives of the IC organizations involved in the collection, processing and analysis of intelligence[2] and is

---

[2] The members of the NFIB are the DCI; Deputy Director of Central Intelligence (DDCI); Associate Director of Central Intelligence for Military Support; Assistant Secretary for Intelligence and Research (INR), Department of State; Deputy Director for Intelligence (DDI), Central Intelligence Agency (CIA); Director, Defense Intelligence Agency (DIA); Director, National Security Agency (NSA); Director, National Geospatial-Intelligence Agency (NGA); Executive Assistant Director, Federal Bureau of Investigation (FBI); Director, Office of Intelligence, Department of Energy (DOE); Special Assistant to the Secretary of the Treasury; Chairman, National Intelligence Council.

chaired by the DCI. The senior representatives of the military intelligence services may also attend as members of the NFIB when matters under their purview are considered and may attend other NFIB sessions as observers. The NFIB typically approves the NIE the same day it is presented.

(U) The 1994 NIE drafting guidelines described three rough time frames for the production of an NIE: a "fast track" of two to three weeks, a "normal track" of four to eight weeks, and a "long track" of two months or more. The Vice Chairman of the NIC told Committee staff that an NIE prepared within 60 days would be considered very fast, and that typically NIE's take three to six months. Sherman Kent noted in his essay that prior to 1976, NIE's had historically taken up to six to eight months to produce, but under conditions of urgency the time line has been considerably shortened. For example, during the Suez crisis of 1956, the Soviets sent a threatening note to Britain and France, who, along with the Israelis, had begun an attack on Egypt. The acting DCI convened the heads of the national intelligence agencies to develop an NIE to provide the IC's appraisal of Soviet intentions. There were no TORs and a draft was produced in about 30 minutes. The draft was immediately presented to the heads of the IC, who discussed and cleared the NIE within a few hours. The NIOs told Committee staff that ideally they would like about three months to produce an NIE.

2. The 2002 NIE on Iraq's Continuing Programs for Weapons of Mass Destruction

(U) In an unclassified letter dated September 9, 2002, Senator Richard Durbin, a member of the SSCI, wrote to the DCI expressing concern that the IC had not drafted an NIE on the status of Iraq's WMD program, and requested that the DCI "direct the production" of such an NIE—expressing the belief that "policymakers in both the executive branch and the Congress will benefit from the production of a coordinated, consensus document produced by all relevant components of the Intelligence Community" on this topic. Senator Durbin also requested that the DCI "produce an unclassified summary of this NIE" so "the American public can better understand this important issue."

(U) On September 10, 2002, Senator Bob Graham, then SSCI Chairman, sent a second letter to the DCI requesting the production of an NIE "on the status of Iraq's programs to develop weapons of mass destruction and delivery systems, the status of the Iraqi military forces, including their readiness and willingness to fight, the effects a U.S.-led attack on Iraq would have on its neighbors, and Saddam Hussein's likely response to a U.S. military campaign designed to effect regime change in Iraq."

(U) On September 13, 2002, Senator Diane Feinstein, a member of the SSCI, wrote to President Bush to request his assistance in ensuring that the DCI prepare, on an immediate basis, an NIE "assessing the nature, magnitude and immediacy of the threat posed to the United States by Iraq." Senator Feinstein added, "there has not been a formal rigorous Intelligence Community assessment, such as a National Intelligence Estimate, addressing the issues relating to Iraq, and I deeply believe that such an estimate is vital to Congressional decision making, and most specifically, any resolution which may come before the Senate."

(U) On September 17, 2002, Senator Carl Levin, a member of the SSCI and then Chairman of the Senate Armed Services Committee, wrote to the DCI stating that it was "imperative" for the IC to prepare an NIE on Iraq "including the central question of the current state of Iraq's weapons of mass destruction programs." Senator Levin asked that the NIE address a number of issues including Iraq's WMD holdings, development facilities, acquisition activities, denial and deception activities, deployment, doctrine for employment, means of delivery, the likelihood that Saddam Hussein would use WMD against the U.S., our allies, or our interests, the likelihood that Iraq would comply with UN resolutions; and Iraq's terrorist activities.

(U) By the morning of September 12, 2002, the NIO for Strategic and Nuclear Programs had received official guidance from the DCI to begin work on the NIE. The work of assembling and coordinating the NIE was divided primarily between four NIO's: the NIO for Strategic and Nuclear Programs was responsible for the nuclear and ballistic missile portions as well as overall management of the entire NIE, the NIO for Conventional Military Issues was responsible for the chemical warfare (CW) and unmanned aerial vehicle (UAV) portions, and the NIO for Science and Technology was responsible for the biological weapons (BW) portion. The NIO for Near East South Asia (NESA) was also involved in issues regarding regional reactions, interfacing with the NIO for Conventional Military Issues on the doctrine issues, and some terrorism issues, specifically whether Iraq might use terrorists to deliver WMD.

(U) Because of the short time period to prepare the NIE, the NIOs began by drawing language from existing agency and interagency papers. The NIO for Strategic and Nuclear Programs disseminated a draft to the IC agencies for review on September 23, 2002 and held an all-day coordination meeting with IC analysts on September 25, 2002. The NIO for Strategic and Nuclear Programs disseminated a second draft which incorporated the analysts' changes and comments on September 26, 2002. Due to the compressed schedule of this NIE, the NIC did not submit the draft for peer review or to a panel of outside experts. The Vice Chairman of the NIC told Committee staff that because preparation for this NIE involved four NIOs, there was a "virtual peer review," and said that he did not believe that outside experts would have had substantially different views from the NIE, noting that "I think all you could have called in is an amen chorus on this thing, because there was nobody out there with different views." The NIE was approved by a meeting of the full NFIB on October 1, 2002 and printed that day.

(U) The scope note of the NIE said that it "was requested by the Director of Central Intelligence to address the status of and outlook for Iraq's weapons of mass destruction programs" and built on the work and judgments of twelve previous IC products. The NIE contained four sections on specific WMD programs including:

1) Saddam's Pursuit of Nuclear Weapons;
2) Chemical Warfare Program—Rebuilt and Expanding;
3) Biological Warfare Program—Larger Than Before; and
4) Delivery Systems—Iraq Increasing Its Options.

(U) Committee staff examined each of these sections in detail, including the intelligence source reporting underlying the assessments. Committee staff also reviewed previous IC products and assessments from individual IC agencies that discussed Iraq's WMD programs to understand the progression of analysis from the time United Nations inspectors left Iraq in December 1998 until just before the war with Iraq in 2003. The nuclear, biological, chemical and delivery sections of this report discuss the assessments made in those products and the intelligence source reporting the IC analysts used to make their judgments.

3. OVERALL CONCLUSIONS—WEAPONS OF MASS DESTRUCTION

(U) **Conclusion 1. Most of the major key judgments in the Intelligence Community's October 2002 National Intelligence Estimate (NIE),** *Iraq's Continuing Programs for Weapons of Mass Destruction,* **either overstated, or were not supported by, the underlying intelligence reporting. A series of failures, particularly in analytic trade craft, led to the mischaracterization of the intelligence.**

(U) The major key judgments in the NIE, particularly that Iraq "is reconstituting its nuclear program," "has chemical and biological weapons," was developing an unmanned aerial vehicle (UAV) "probably intended to deliver biological warfare agents," and that "all key aspects—research & development (R&D), production, and weaponization—of Iraq's offensive biological weapons (BW) program are active and that most elements are larger and more advanced than they were before the Gulf War," either overstated, or were not supported by, the underlying intelligence reporting provided to the Committee. The assessments regarding Iraq's continued development of prohibited ballistic missiles were reasonable and did accurately describe the underlying intelligence.

(U) The assessment that Iraq "is reconstituting its nuclear program" was not supported by the intelligence provided to the Committee. The intelligence reporting did show that Iraq was procuring dual-use equipment that had potential nuclear applications, but all of the equipment had conventional military or industrial applications. In addition, none of the intelligence reporting indicated that the equipment was being procured for suspect nuclear facilities. Intelligence reporting also showed that former Iraqi nuclear scientists continued to work at former nuclear facilities and organizations, but the reporting did not show that this cadre of nuclear personnel had recently been regrouped or enhanced as stated in the NIE, nor did it suggest that they were engaged in work related to a nuclear weapons program.

(U) The statement in the key judgments of the NIE that "Baghdad has chemical and biological weapons" overstated both what was known and what intelligence analysts judged about Iraq's chemical and biological weapons holdings. The intelligence reporting did support the conclusion that chemical and biological weapons were within Iraq's technological capability, that Iraq was trying to procure dual-use materials that could have been used to produce these weapons, and that uncertainties existed about whether Iraq had fully destroyed its pre-Gulf War stocks of weapons and precursors. Iraq's efforts to deceive and evade United Nations weapons inspectors and its inability or unwillingness to fully account for pre-Gulf War chemical and biological weapons and precursors could have led analysts to the reasonable conclusion that Iraq may have retained those materials, but intelligence analysts did not have enough information to state with certainty that Iraq "has" these weapons.

([still classified]) Similarly, the assessment that "all key aspects—R&D, production, and weaponization—of Iraq's offensive BW program are active and that most elements are larger and more advanced than they were before the Gulf War" was not supported by the underlying intelligence provided to the Committee. Intelligence showed that Iraq was renovating or expanding facilities that had been associated with Iraq's past BW program and was engaged in research that had BW applications, but few reports suggested specifically that the activity was related to BW. Intelligence reports did indicate that Iraq may have had a mobile biological weapons program, but most of the reporting was from a single human intelligence (HUMINT) source to whom the Intelligence Community (IC) never had direct access. It was reasonable for intelligence analysts to be concerned about the potential weapons applications of Iraq's dual use activities and capabilities. The intelligence reporting did not substantiate an assessment that all aspects of Iraq's BW program "are" larger and more advanced than before the Gulf War, however.

([still classified]) The key judgment in the NIE that Iraq was developing a UAV "probably intended to deliver biological warfare agents" also overstated what the intelligence reporting indicated about the mission of Iraq's small UAVs. Numerous intelligence reports confirmed that Iraq was developing a small UAV program [still-classified section missing here], but none of the reports provided to the Committee said that Iraq intended to use the small UAVs to deliver chemical or biological weapons. The Air Force footnote, which stated that biological weapons delivery was a possible mission for the small UAVs, though other missions were more likely, more accurately reflected the body of intelligence reporting.

(U) The failure of the IC to accurately analyze and describe the intelligence in the NIE was the result of a combination of systemic weaknesses, primarily in analytic trade craft, compounded by a lack of information sharing, poor management, and inadequate intelligence collection. Many of these weaknesses, which are described in detail below, have not yet been fully addressed, despite having been identified previously by other inquiry panels, including the *Joint Inquiry into Intelligence Community Activities Before and After the Terrorist Attacks of September 11, 2002* (2002), *The Intelligence Community's Performance on the Indian Nuclear Tests* (The Jeremiah Report, 1998), and the *Report of the Commission to Assess the Ballistic Missile Threat to the United States* (The Rumsfeld Commission, 1998). The Committee found no evidence that the IC's mischaracterization or exaggeration of the intelligence on Iraq's weapons of mass destruction (WMD) capabilities was the result of political pressure.

(U) **Conclusion 2. The Intelligence Community did not accurately or adequately explain to policymakers the uncertainties behind the judgments in the October 2002 National Intelligence Estimate.**

(U) One of the key failures in analytic trade craft of the National Intelligence Estimate (NIE) was the failure of the Intelligence Community (IC) to explain the details of the reporting and the uncertainties of both the reliability of some key sources and of intelligence judgments. Intelligence analysts are not only charged with interpreting and assessing the intelligence reporting, but with clearly conveying to policymakers the difference between what intelligence analysts know, what they don't know, what they think, and to make sure that policymakers understand the difference. This articulation of the IC's responsibility to policymakers is widely attributed to Colin Powell when he was serving as the Chairman of the Joint Chiefs of Staff, but the effective communication of judgments has been accepted as a primary analytic function for decades. For example, in 1964, Sherman Kent, considered the founder of intelligence analysis as a profession, wrote about the importance of using appropriate words of estimative probability to "set forth the community's findings in such a way as to make clear to the reader what is certain knowledge and what is reasoned judgment, and within this large realm of judgment what varying degrees of certitude lie behind each key statement."[3]

---

[3] *Sherman Kent and the Board of National Estimates: Collected Essays,* (Http://www.odci.gov/csi/books/shermankent/inst.html). From 1952 to 1967, Sherman Kent was the Chairman of the Board of National Estimates, which would later become the National Intelligence Council.

(U) At the time the IC drafted and coordinated the NIE on Iraq's weapons of mass destruction (WMD) programs in September 2002, most of what intelligence analysts actually "knew" about Iraq's weapons programs pre-dated the 1991 Gulf War, leaving them with very little direct knowledge about the current state of those programs. Analysts knew that Iraq had active nuclear, chemical, biological, and delivery programs before 1991, and had previously lied to, and was still not forthcoming with, UN weapons inspectors about those programs. The analysts also knew that the United Nations was not satisfied with Iraq's efforts to account for its destruction of all of its pre-Gulf War weapons, precursors, and equipment. Additionally, the analysts knew that Iraq was trying to import dual-use materials and equipment and had rebuilt or was continuing to use facilities that had been associated with Iraq's pre-Gulf War weapons programs, and knew that WMD were likely within Iraq's technological capabilities.

(U) The IC did not know whether Iraq had retained its pre-Gulf War weapons, whether Iraq was intending to use those dual-use materials and facilities for weapons or for legitimate purposes, or even if Iraq's attempts to obtain many of the dual-use goods it had been trying to procure were successful. The IC thought that Iraq had retained its pre-Gulf War weapons and that Iraq was using dual-use materials and facilities to manufacture weapons. While this was a reasonable assessment, considering Iraq's past behavior, statements in the 2002 NIE that Iraq "has chemical and biological weapons," "Iraq has maintained its chemical weapons effort," and "is reconstituting its nuclear weapons program," did not accurately portray the uncertainty of the information. The NIE failed in that it portrayed what intelligence analysts thought and assessed as what they knew and failed to explain the large gaps in the information on which the assessments were based.

([still classified]) In the cases in the NIE where the IC did express uncertainty about its assessments concerning Iraq's WMD capabilities, those explanations suggested, in some cases, that Iraq's capabilities were even greater than the NIE judged. For example, the key judgments of the NIE said "we judge that we are seeing only a portion of Iraq's WMD efforts, owing to Baghdad's vigorous denial and deception efforts. Revelations after the Gulf War starkly demonstrate the extensive efforts undertaken by Iraq to deny information." [Still-classified section here.] While this did explain that key information on Iraq's programs was lacking, it suggested that Iraq's weapons programs were probably bigger and more advanced than the IC had judged and did not explain that [classified section here] analysts did not have enough information to determine whether Iraq was hiding activity or whether Iraq's weapons programs may have been dormant.

(U) Accurately and clearly describing the gaps in intelligence knowledge is not only important for policymakers to fully understand the basis for and gaps in analytic assessments, but is essential for policymakers in both the executive and legislative branches to make informed decisions about how and where to allocate Intelligence Community resources to fill those gaps.

(U) **Conclusion 3. The Intelligence Community (IC) suffered from a collective presumption that Iraq had an active and growing weapons of mass destruction (WMD) program. This "group think" dynamic led Intelligence Community analysts, collectors and managers to both interpret ambiguous evidence as conclusively indicative of a WMD program as well as ignore or minimize evidence that Iraq did not have active and expanding weapons of mass destruction programs. This presumption was so strong that formalized IC mechanisms established to challenge assumptions and group think were not utilized.**

(U) The Intelligence Community (IC) has long struggled with the need for analysts to overcome analytic biases, that is, to resist the tendency to see what they would expect to see in the intelligence reporting. In the case of Iraq's weapons of mass destruction (WMD) capabilities, the Committee found that intelligence analysts, in many cases, based their analysis more on their expectations than on an objective evaluation of the information in the intelligence reporting. Analysts expected to see evidence that Iraq had retained prohibited weapons and that Iraq would resume prohibited WMD activities once United Nations' (UN) inspections ended. This bias that pervaded both the IC's analytic and collection communities represents "group think," a term coined by psychologist Irving Janis in the 1970's to describe a process in which a group can make bad or irrational decisions as each member of the group attempts to conform their opinions to what they believe to be the consensus of the group. IC personnel involved in the Iraq WMD issue demonstrated several aspects of group think: examining few alternatives, selective gathering of information, pressure to conform within the group or withhold criticism, and collective rationalization.

(U) The roots of the IC's bias stretch back to Iraq's pre-1991 efforts to build WMD and its efforts to hide those programs. The fact that Iraq had repeatedly lied about its pre-1991 WMD programs, its continued deceptive behavior, and its failure to fully cooperate with UN inspectors left the IC with a predisposition to believe the Iraqis were continuing to lie about their WMD efforts. This was compounded by the fact that Iraq's pre-1991 progress on its nuclear weapons program had surprised the IC. The role this knowledge played in analysts' thinking is evident in the 2002 National Intelligence Estimate's (NIE) introduction which said, "revelations after the Gulf War starkly demonstrate the extensive efforts undertaken by Iraq to deny information. The revelations also underscore the extent to which limited information fostered underestimates by the Intelligence Community of Saddam's capabilities at that time." This bias was likely further reinforced by the IC's failure to detect the September 11th terrorist plot and the criticism that the Community had not done all it could to "connect the dots."

(U) The IC had long assessed that Iraq maintained its ambitions to obtain WMD, and would seek to resume full WMD efforts once UN sanctions and inspections ended. Accordingly, after UN inspectors left Iraq in 1998, IC analysts began to look for evidence that Iraq was expanding WMD programs. Analysts interpreted ambiguous data as indicative of the active and expanded WMD effort they expected to see. The presumption that Iraq would take advantage of the departure of inspectors to restart its WMD efforts essentially became a hypothesis in search of evidence.

([still classified]) The IC's bias was compounded by the fact that prior to 1998, the IC had become heavily dependent on UN information on the state of Iraq's WMD programs. When the IC lost this important information, analysts were forced to rely on less reliable and less detailed sources. For example, [still-classified section here] reporting during UN inspections often described the [still classified]. These reports provided IC analysts with much of the insight [still classified]. Intelligence reporting after inspectors departed relied on less direct sources of information such as satellite imagery of activity at suspect facilities, fragmentary and ambiguous reports of Iraqi dual-use procurement efforts, and reporting of suspicious or prohibited activity from human sources who were no longer in the country. These indirect sources left the IC with few ways to determine the exact nature of suspicious Iraqi activity. The expectation, however, that Iraq would take advantage of the departure of inspectors to resume and expand its WMD programs led analysts to downplay or ignore the increased uncertainty that came with these less detailed and less reliable sources.

([still classified]) The Committee found that the IC had a tendency to accept information which supported the presumption that Iraq had active and expanded WMD programs more readily than information which contradicted it. This was evident in analysts' assessments of Iraq's attempts to procure dual-use materials and activities at dual-use facilities. Dual-use materials and facilities are those which could be used in a WMD program, but which also have conventional military or legitimate civilian applications. The IC properly noted the potential threat embodied in these dual-use capabilities, should they be turned toward WMD purposes, and did an effective job of analyzing [classified section] Iraq's attempts to purchase dual-use equipment and materials to show how they could advance Iraq's WMD capability. But, the IC fell short by accepting most reporting of dual-use material imports or capabilities as intended for WMD programs. Information that contradicted the IC's presumption that Iraq had WMD programs, such as indications in the intelligence reporting that the dual-use materials were intended for conventional or civilian programs, was often ignored. The IC's bias that Iraq had active WMD programs led analysts to presume, in the absence of evidence, that if Iraq could do something to advance its WMD capabilities, it would.

([still classified]) Another example of the IC's tendency to reject information that contradicted the presumption that Iraq had active and expanded WMD programs was the return of UN inspectors to Iraq in November 2002. [Classified section.] When these inspections did not find evidence of active Iraqi WMD programs and, in fact, even refuted some aspects of the IC's nuclear and biological assessments, many analysts did not regard this information as significant. For example, the 2002 NIE cited [classified section] Iraq's Amiriyah Serum and Vaccine institute as [still classified] reasons the IC believed the facility was a "fixed dual-use BW agent production" facility. When UN inspectors visited Amiriyah after their return to Iraq in November 2002, however, they did not find any evidence of BW work at the facility [classified section]. Analysts discounted the UN's findings as the result of the inspectors relative inexperience in the face of Iraqi denial and deception. Similarly, when International Atomic Energy Agency (IAEA) inspectors returned to Iraq in late 2002, one of their key lines of work was to investigate Iraq's claims that aluminum tubes it was trying to procure were intended for artillery rockets. The IAEA found that Iraq's claims that the aluminum tubes were intended for artillery rockets was completely consistent with the evidence on the ground in Iraq. The Central Intelligence Agency (CIA) responded to the IAEA's analysis by producing intelligence reports which rejected the IAEA's conclusions. Without giving many details of the IAEA's findings, CIA's analysis suggested that the IAEA was being fooled by Iraq, and reiterated CIA's assessment that the tubes were to be used in uranium centrifuges.

(U) Intelligence analysts' presumption that all dual-use activity was intended for WMD programs recurs throughout the 2002 NIE. Analysts believed that the fact that Iraq often attempted to obtain dual-use materials surreptitiously, through front companies and other illicit means in violation of UN sanctions, indicated that Iraq intended to use those materials for WMD. Analysts argued that Iraq would have no reason to hide itself as the end user of these materials if they were intended for legitimate purposes. However, analysts ignored the fact that Iraq typically used front companies and evaded UN sanctions for imports of purely legitimate goods. Analysts who monitored Iraq's compliance with the Oil for Food Program noted several reasons that Iraq wanted to avoid legitimate channels for imports including 1) the UN often denied materials needed for legitimate purposes because the materials had WMD applications, 2) using the UN's bureaucratic process was more cumbersome and time consuming than using illicit channels, and 3) transactions using front companies were less transparent, making corruption and profit taking easier for Iraqi managers and officials.

(U) Likewise, analysts were predisposed to identify as suspect any activity by scientists and officials involved in Iraq's pre-1991 WMD programs. While the IC should not have ignored the activity of these people, IC analysts failed to fully consider the possibility that Iraq, having spent significant national resources developing their capabilities, might have been seeking non-WMD purposes to fully employ the idle expertise left over from closed WMD programs.

([still classified]) The presumption that Iraq had active WMD programs affected intelligence collectors as well. None of the guidance given to human intelligence collectors suggested that collection be focused on determining *whether* Iraq had WMD. Instead, the requirements assumed that Iraq had WMD, and focused on uncovering those activities and collecting against the extent of Iraq's WMD production and the locations of hidden stocks of weapons. A former manager in the CIA's Iraq WMD Task Force also told Committee staff that, in retrospect, he believes that the CIA tended to discount human intelligence (HUMINT) sources that denied the existence of Iraqi WMD programs as just repeating the Iraqi party line. In fact, numerous interviews with intelligence analysts and documents provided to the Committee indicate that analysts and collectors assumed that sources who denied the existence or continuation of WMD programs and stocks were either lying or not knowledgeable about Iraq's programs, while those sources who reported ongoing WMD activities were seen as having provided valuable information.

([still classified]) The presumption that Iraq had active WMD programs was so strong that formalized IC mechanisms established to challenge assumptions and "group think," such as "red teams," "devil's advocacy," and other types of alternative or competitive analysis, were not utilized. The Committee found no evidence that IC analysts, collectors, or managers made any effort to question the fundamental assumptions that Iraq had active and expanded WMD programs, nor did they give serious consideration to other possible explanations for Iraq's failure to satisfy its WMD accounting discrepancies, other than that it was hiding and preserving WMD. The fact that no one in the IC saw a need for such tools is indicative of the strength of the bias that Iraq had active and expanded WMD programs. The Committee does not regard the [still-classified section] analysis on Iraq's aluminum tubes performed by CIA contractors as an attempt to challenge assumptions, but rather as an example of the collective rationalization that is indicative of "group think." The contractors were only provided with information by CIA, did not question agencies about their analysis, were not briefed by other agencies about their analysis, and performed their analysis of a complex intelligence issue in only one day.

(U) The IC's failure to find unambiguous intelligence reporting of Iraqi WMD activities should have encouraged analysts to question their presumption that Iraq had WMD. Instead, analysts rationalized the lack of evidence as the result of "vigorous" Iraqi denial and deception (D&D) efforts to hide the WMD programs that analysts were certain existed. The 2002 NIE's introduction stated that "we judge that we are only seeing a portion of Iraq's WMD efforts owing to Baghdad's vigorous D&D efforts." The intelligence provided to the Committee showed that Iraq was making efforts to hide some activity, but the reporting was not clear about what activity was being hidden or why it was being hidden.

Although the IC lacked unambiguous reporting of either active WMD programs or a vigorous D&D effort to hide WMD programs, the assumptions that Iraq was engaged in both were tied together into a self-reinforcing premise that explained away the lack of strong evidence of either.

(U) **Conclusion 4. In a few significant instances, the analysis in the National Intelligence Estimate suffers from a "layering" effect whereby assessments were built based on previous judgments without carrying forward the uncertainties of the underlying judgments.**

(U) The Committee defines "layering" as the process of building an intelligence assessment primarily using previous judgments without substantial new intelligence reporting. While this process is a legitimate and often useful analytic tool in making logical connections between intelligence reports and in understanding complex analytic problems, the process can lose its legitimacy when the cumulative uncertainties of the underlying assessments are not factored into or conveyed through the new assessments.

(U) In discussions with the Committee about his experience running the Iraq Survey Group, Dr. David Kay suggested that the IC's mind set before Operation Iraqi Freedom concerning Iraq's weapons of mass destruction (WMD) programs was a train that seemed "to always be going in the same direction." The IC drew on very few pieces of new evidence to reach large conclusions in which new pieces of evidence would accrete to the previous conclusion and pieces that did not fit tended to be thrown aside.

(U) One example of this layering effect occurred in the IC's analysis of Iraq's chemical weapons program. The NIE assessed that Iraq had renewed production of chemical weapons agents and stockpiled as much as 500 metric tons of chemical agent, much of it added in the last year. These assessments were largely based on another assessment, that Iraq may have been engaged in chemical weapons transshipment activity in the spring of 2002. This assessment was largely based on yet another assessment, that the presence of a specific tanker truck was a possible indicator that chemical or biological weapons related activities were occurring. The IC did not make it clear in its latter assessments that its judgments were based on layer upon layer of previous analytic judgments. This gave the reader of the NIE the impression that Iraq's chemical weapons program was advancing and growing, but did not convey that the assessment was based on very little direct or credible intelligence reporting.

([still classified]) Similarly, the IC based its judgment that "all key aspects—research & development (R&D), production, and weaponization—of Iraq's offensive biological weapons (BW) program are active and that most elements are larger and more advanced than they were before the Gulf War" primarily on its assessment that Iraq had mobile biological production vans. While this assessment was based on direct intelligence that indicated Iraq had mobile biological production units, the reporting was largely from a single source to whom the Intelligence Community did not have direct access. The Committee believes that the IC's expectation that Iraq would move to mobile biological weapons production, focused their attention on reporting that supported that contention and led them to disregard information that contradicted it. This exemplifies Dr. Kay's concerns that the IC made large new conclusions based on only a few pieces of new evidence that were joined to previous conclusions and that pieces that did not fulfill its expectations tended to be thrown aside.

(U) These are just two, of many, examples of this layering effect the Committee found in the IC's analysis of Iraq's weapons of mass destruction programs. The Committee recognizes the importance of analysts' ability to perform this type of analytic extrapolation, particularly in trying to "connect the dots" of sometimes seemingly disparate pieces of intelligence. Incorporating and accurately explaining the cumulative underlying uncertainties inherent in that process is equally important, however.

(U) **Conclusion 5. In each instance where the Committee found an analytic or collection failure, it resulted in part from a failure of Intelligence Community managers throughout their leadership chains to adequately supervise the work of their analysts and collectors. They did not encourage analysts to challenge their assumptions, fully consider alternative arguments, accurately characterize the intelligence reporting, or counsel analysts who lost their objectivity.**

(U) This report describes a variety of serious analytical and collection failures in the Intelligence Community's (IC) work on Iraq's weapons of mass destruction programs. While not in any way diminishing the responsibility of the analysts and collectors that were directly involved, the Committee believes that blame for these failures can not be laid at their feet alone. In each instance, the analysts' and collectors' chains of command in their respective agencies, from immediate supervisors up to the National Intelligence Council and the Director of Central Intelligence, all share responsibility for not encouraging analysts to challenge their assumptions, fully consider alternative arguments or accurately characterize the intelligence reporting. They failed to adequately question and challenge analysts about their assessments, and, most importantly, to recognize when analysts had lost their objectivity and take corrective action. It seems likely that these failures of management and leadership resulted at least in part as a result of the fact that the Intelligence Community's chain of command shared with its analysts and collectors the same "group think" presumption that Iraq had active and expanded weapons of mass destruction programs.

(U) **Conclusion 6. The Committee found significant short-comings in almost every aspect of the Intelligence Community's human intelligence collection efforts against Iraq's weapons of mass destruction activities, in particular that the Community had no sources collecting against weapons of mass destruction in Iraq after 1998. Most, if not all, of these problems stem from a broken corporate culture and poor management, and will not be solved by additional funding and personnel.**

(U) The Committee's review into the prewar intelligence concerning Iraq's weapons of mass destruction programs has entailed an unprecedented outside examination of a broad range of the Intelligence Community's (IC) human intelligence (HUMINT) operations. The Committee found significant short-comings in almost every aspect of these operations.

([still classified]) From 1991 to 1998, the IC relied too heavily on United Nations (UN) inspectors to collect information about Iraq's weapons of mass destruction programs and did not develop a sufficient unilateral HUMINT collection effort targeting Iraq to supplement UN-collected information and to take its place upon the departure of the UN inspectors. While the UN inspection process provided a valuable source of information, the IC should have used the time when inspectors were in Iraq to plan for the possibility that inspectors would leave and to develop sources who could continue to report after inspectors left.

([still classified]) Because the United States lacked an official presence inside Iraq, the Intelligence Community depended too heavily on defectors and foreign government services to obtain HUMINT information on Iraq's weapons of mass destruction activities.

While these sources had the potential to provide some valuable information, they had a limited ability to provide the kind of detailed intelligence about current Iraqi weapons of mass destruction efforts sought by U.S. policymakers. Moreover, because the Intelligence Community did not have direct access to many of these sources, their credibility was difficult to assess and was often left to the foreign government services to judge. Intelligence Community HUMINT efforts against a closed society like Iraq prior to Operation Iraqi Freedom were hobbled by the Intelligence Community's dependence on having an official U.S. presence in-country to mount clandestine HUMINT collection efforts.

(U) When UN inspectors departed Iraq, the placement of HUMINT agents and the development of unilateral sources inside Iraq were not top priorities for the Intelligence Community. The Intelligence Community did not have a single HUMINT source collecting against Iraq's weapons of mass destruction programs in Iraq after 1998. The Intelligence Community appears to have decided that the difficulty and risks inherent in developing sources or inserting operations officers into Iraq outweighed the potential benefits. The Committee found no evidence that a lack of resources significantly prevented the Intelligence Community from developing sources or inserting operations officers into Iraq.

([still classified]) [Still-classified section.] When Committee staff asked why the CIA had not considered placing a CIA officer in Iraq years before Operation Iraqi Freedom to investigate Iraq's weapons of mass destruction programs, a CIA officer said, "because it's very hard to sustain ... it takes a rare officer who can go in ... and survive scrutiny [still classified] for along time." The Committee agrees that such operations are difficult and dangerous, but they should be within the norm of the CIA's activities and capabilities. Senior CIA officials have repeatedly told the Committee that a significant increase in funding and personnel will be required to enable to the CIA to penetrate difficult HUMINT targets similar to prewar Iraq. The Committee believes, however, that if an officer willing and able to take such an assignment really is "rare" at the CIA, the problem is less a question of resources than a need for dramatic changes in a risk averse corporate culture.

(U) Problems with the Intelligence Community's HUMINT efforts were also evident in the Intelligence Community's handling of Iraq's alleged efforts to acquire uranium from Niger. The Committee does not fault the CIA for exploiting the access enjoyed by the spouse of a CIA employee traveling to Niger. The Committee believes, however, that it is unfortunate, considering the significant resources available to the CIA, that this was the only option available. Given the nature of rapidly evolving global threats such as terrorism and the proliferation of weapons and weapons technology, the Intelligence Community must develop means to quickly respond to fleeting collection opportunities outside the Community's established operating areas. The Committee also found other problems with the Intelligence Community's follow-up on the Iraq-Niger uranium issue, including a half-hearted investigation of the reported storage of uranium in a warehouse in Benin, and a failure, to this day, to call a telephone number, provided by the Navy, of an individual who claimed to have information about Iraq's alleged efforts to acquire uranium from Niger.

([still classified]) The Committee also found that the Defense HUMINT Service (DHS) demonstrated serious lapses in its handling of the HUMINT source code named CURVE BALL, who was the principle source behind the Intelligence Community's assessments that Iraq had a mobile biological weapons program. The DHS had primary responsibility for handling the Intelligence Community's interaction with the [still-classified section] debriefers that were handling CURVE BALL, but the DHS officers that were involved in CURVE BALL's case limited themselves to a largely administrative role, translating and passing along reports [lengthy still-classified section here] analysts do not have the benefit of the regular interaction with sources or, in this case, CURVE BALL's debriefers, that could have allowed them to make judgments about the reliability of source reporting.

(U) Another significant problem found by the Committee is the fact that the CIA continues to excessively compartment sensitive HUMINT reporting and fails to share important information about HUMINT reporting and sources with Intelligence Community analysts who have a need to know. In the years before Operation Iraqi Freedom, the CIA protected its Iraq weapons of mass destruction sources so well that some of the information they provided was kept from the majority of analysts with a legitimate need to know. The biological weapons and delivery sections of this report discuss at length the CIA's failure to share important information about source reporting on Iraq's alleged mobile biological weapons program and unmanned aerial vehicle (UAV) program that left analysts and policymakers with an incomplete and, at times, misleading picture of these issues.

(U) The process by which the Intelligence Community calculates the benefits and risks of sharing sensitive human intelligence is skewed too heavily toward withholding information. This issue has been raised repeatedly with the Intelligence Community, particularly after the lack of information sharing was found to have played a key role in the intelligence failures of 9/11. The Committee believes that the Intelligence Community must reconsider whether the risks of expanding access to *cleared* analysts are truly greater than the risks of keeping information so tightly compartmented that the analysts who need it to make informed judgments are kept in the dark.

(U) **Conclusion 7. The Central Intelligence Agency (CIA), in several significant instances, abused its unique position in the Intelligence Community, particularly in terms of information sharing, to the detriment of the Intelligence Community's prewar analysis concerning Iraq's weapons of mass destruction programs.**

(U) The Intelligence Community is not a level playing field when it comes to the competition of ideas in intelligence analysis. The Director of Central Intelligence's (DC's) responsibility, established by the National Security Act of 1947, to coordinate the nation's intelligence activities and correlate, evaluate, and disseminate intelligence that affects national security, provides the CIA with a unique position in the Intelligence Community. The fact that the DCI is the head of the CIA and head of the Intelligence Community, the principal intelligence advisor to the President, and is responsible for protecting intelligence sources and methods, provides the CIA with unique access to policymakers and unique control of intelligence reporting. This arrangement was intended to coordinate the disparate elements of the Intelligence Community in order to provide the most accurate and objective analysis to policymakers. The Committee found that in practice, however, in the case of the Intelligence Community's analysis of Iraq's weapons of mass destruction programs, this arrangement actually undermined the provision of accurate and objective analysis by hampering intelligence sharing and allowing CIA analysts to control the presentation of information to policymakers, and exclude analysis from other agencies.

(U) The Committee found in a number of cases that significant reportable intelligence was sequestered in CIA Directorate of Operations (DO) cables, distribution of sensitive intelligence reports was excessively restricted, and CIA analysts were often provided with "sensitive" information that was not made available to analysts who worked the same issues at other all-source analysis agencies. These restrictions, in several cases, kept information from analysts that was essential to their ability to make fully informed judgments. Analysts cannot be expected to formulate and present their best analysis to policymakers while having only partial knowledge of an issue.

([still-classified]) For example, important information concerning the reliability of two of the main sources on Iraq's alleged mobile biological weapons program was not available to most Iraq biological weapons analysts outside the CIA. Some analysts at other agencies were aware of some of the credibility concerns about the sources, but the CIA's DO did not disseminate cables throughout the Intelligence Community that would have provided this information to all Iraq biological weapons analysts. [Still-classified section here.]

([still classified]) The CIA also failed to share important information about Iraq's UAV software procurement efforts with other intelligence analysts. The CIA did share sensitive information that indicated Iraq [still-classified section here] was trying to obtain mapping software that could only be used for mapping in the U.S. This suggested to many analysts that Iraq may have been intending to use the software to target the U.S. The CIA failed to pass on additional information, until well after the coordination and publication of the National Intelligence Estimate (NIE). [Still-classified section here.] This information was essential for analysts to make fully informed judgments about Iraq's intentions to target the U.S.

(U) In some cases CIA analysts were not open to fully considering information and opinions from other intelligence analysts or creating a level playing field in which outside analysts fully participated in meetings or analytic efforts. This problem was particularly evident in the case of the CIA's analysis of Iraq's procurement of aluminum tubes during which the Committee believes the agency lost objectivity and in several cases took action that improperly excluded useful expertise from the intelligence debate. For example, the CIA performed testing of the tubes without inviting experts from the Department of Energy (DOE) to participate. A CIA analyst told Committee staff that the DOE was not invited "because we funded it. It was our testing. We were trying to prove some things that we wanted to prove with the testing. It wasn't a joint effort." The Committee believes that such an effort should never have been intended to prove what the CIA wanted to prove, but should have been a Community effort to get to the truth about Iraq's intended use for the tubes. By excluding DOE analysts, the Intelligence Community's nuclear experts, the CIA was not able to take advantage of their potentially valuable analytic insights. In another instance, an independent Department of Defense (DOD) rocket expert told the Committee that he did not think the CIA analysts came to him for an objective opinion, but were trying "to encourage us to come up with [the] answer" that the tubes were not intended to be used for a rocket program.

(U) The Committee also found that while the DCI was supposed to function as both the head of the CIA and the head of the Intelligence Community, in many instances he only acted as head of the CIA. For example, the DCI told the Committee that he was not aware that there were dissenting opinions within the Intelligence Community on whether Iraq intended use the aluminum tubes for a nuclear program until the NIE was drafted in September 2002, despite the fact that intelligence agencies had been fervently debating the issue since the spring of 2001. While the DCI, as the President's principal intelligence advisor, should provide policymakers, in particular the President, with the best analysis available from throughout the Intelligence Community, the DCI told Committee staff that he does not even expect to learn of dissenting opinions "until the issue gets joined" through interagency coordination of an NIE. This means that contentious debate about significant national security issues can go on at the analytic level for months, or years, without the DCI or senior policymakers being informed of any opinions other than those of CIA analysts. In addition, the Presidential Daily Briefs (PDBs) are prepared by CIA analysts and are presented by CIA briefers who may or may not include an explanation of alternative views from other intelligence agencies. Other Intelligence Community agencies essentially must rely on the analysts who disagree with their positions to accurately convey their analysis to the nation's most senior policymakers.

(U) These factors worked together to allow CIA analysts and officials to provide the agency's intelligence analysis to senior policymakers without having to explain dissenting views or defend their analysis from potential challenges from other Intelligence Community agencies. The Committee believes that policymakers at all levels of government and in both the executive and legislative branches would benefit from understanding the full range of analytic opinions directly from the agencies who hold those views, or from truly impartial representatives of the entire Intelligence Community.

C. IRAQ'S TIES TO TERRORISM

(U) The terrorism related sections of the report recount the Committee's efforts to evaluate the quantity and quality of the intelligence underlying prewar assessments. Each section contains it own set of conclusions. There is also a separate section on the issue of objectivity and whether analysts were pressured to reach specific conclusions to support a particular policy objective. Unlike the WMD sections of the report, in some instances, the issue of accuracy has been addressed as post-war reporting has become available.

(U) Because there was no National Intelligence Estimate specifically focused on Iraq's ties to terrorism, the Committee focused its work primarily the January 2003 Intelligence Report entitled *Iraqi Support for Terrorism*. This intelligence assessment was drafted by the Director of Central Intelligence's (DCI) Counterterrorist Center (CTC). (The CTC includes analysts from across the Intelligence Community.) *Iraqi Support for Terrorism* was first published for a limited executive audience in September 2002 under the same title. There were a few changes made to the January 2003 version of the document including the addition of new information that had been collected following the September publication. The Committee chose to evaluate it as the IC's most comprehensive product on the subject because the January 2003 paper was the most current version and was disseminated to a much wider audience.

(U) To complete this section of the report, the Committee's staff interviewed a total of sixty-two individuals and reviewed more than 1,000 documents provided by the Central Intelligence Agency (CIA), the Defense Intelligence Agency (DIA), the State Department's Bureau of Intelligence and Research (INR), and the Federal Bureau of Investigation (FBI). To gain an in-depth understanding of the Intelligence Community (IC) and CTC collection posture, Committee staff received a briefing from the Assistant Director of Central Intelligence for Collection (ADCI/C) and met with two former heads of the DCI's Counterterrorist Center (CTC). Committee staff interviewed analysts from the CTC, DIA, and FBI who were responsible for assessing Iraq's links to al-Qaida. Committee staff also met with National Security Agency (NSA) employees who collected and analyzed signals intelligence (SIGINT) related to Iraq's links to terrorism. To address analytical objectivity and allegations concerning the politicization of the intelligence process, Committee staff received a briefing from the CIA Ombudsman for Politicization and interviewed IC analysts who interacted with, *inter alia,* personnel from the Office of the Under Secretary of Defense for Policy (OUSDP).

(U) In addition to reviewing activities specifically relating to Iraq's links to terrorism, the Committee staff participated in a briefing to the Committee by the Under Secretary of Defense for Policy and in a Committee hearing with the former Special Advisor to the DCI on Iraq's Weapons of Mass Destruction. On each occasion, the Committee raised the issue of Iraq's links to terrorism.

(U) Intelligence from the 1960s and 1970s first established the link between Iraq and terrorism, resulting in Iraq's inclusion in the State Department's 1979 list of State Sponsors of Terrorism. The State Department removed Iraq from the list in 1982.[4] Iraq returned to the list in 1990 based upon intelligence information linking the regime to acts of terrorism conducted by the Iraqi Intelligence Service (IIS) and its support for Palestinian terrorists. The first intelligence reports suggesting links between Iraq and al-Qaida emerged in the mid-1990s. The IC continues to receive reporting on these links from detainees and document exploitation.

(U) While the nature of the intelligence reporting produced or obtained by the IC has not changed dramatically in the past decade, there has been a significant shift in the way IC analysts evaluate reporting regarding terrorism, particularly in the aftermath of the September 11 attacks. CIA officials interviewed by Committee staff indicated that, following the terrorist attacks of September 11, 2001, the trade craft of terrorism analysis shifted and analysts now feel obligated to make more conclusive assessments regardless of the quality of the available intelligence. In this new analytic environment analysts cannot set aside intelligence reports because the information does not fit within the context of their prior knowledge or because the report has not been corroborated. The CIA Deputy Director for Intelligence (DDI), describing the unique nature of terrorism analysis, said, "... terrorism analysis is just fundamentally different on some issues." She commented further that:

> Sometimes it is the walk-in who has the best information about the impending attack. What we teach people in trade craft is that you want to get a report. It's preferable that that report come from a fully-vetted source whose information is from a long-established reporting record, has direct access and you've been able to corroborate it somehow. That's what you would ideally like and that's what you ideally teach analysts to look for. But with terrorism you can't dismiss the walk-in.

The Deputy Director of the CTC's Office of Terrorism Analysis noted that this is the most difficult issue he has encountered in his eighteen years of intelligence analysis. He also stated that:

> On the other hand, I would also say that we've encouraged and developed a sense of trade craft specifically on terrorism that says push the envelope because the implications are so high and because we have to acknowledge up front that, unlike in some other cases, some other lines of analysis, that we have to accept that often our information is going to be fragmentary and, if we wait too long to reach conclusions, we might make a mistake.

---

[4] The 1982 State Department publication *Patterns of Global Terrorism* explained Iraq's removal from the list of State Sponsors of Terrorism in the following manner: "The Iraqi Government has reduced support to non-Palestinian groups, thereby moving closer to the policies of its moderate Arab neighbors."

(U) The focus of the Committee's terrorism review, *Iraqi Support for Terrorism,* addressed four main issues:

- terrorist activities conducted by the IIS;
- Iraqi support for terrorist activities conducted by regional terrorist groups;
- Iraqi contacts with al-Qaida; and,
- potential Iraqi use of terrorism in the event of a war with the United States.

(U) Committee staff evaluated each of these and other issues including the intelligence source reporting underlying the assessments. The terrorism related sections of this report discuss the assessments and the intelligence reporting in detail.

1. OVERALL CONCLUSIONS—TERRORISM

(U) **Conclusion 8. Intelligence Community analysts lack a consistent post-September 11 approach to analyzing and reporting on terrorist threats.**

(U) Though analysts have been wrong on major issues in the past, no previous intelligence failure has been so costly as the September 11 attacks. As the Deputy Director of Intelligence (DDT) explained during an interview with Committee staff, terrorist threat analysts now use a different type of trade craft than generally employed by political, leadership or regional analysts. Threat analysts are encouraged to "push the envelope" and look at various possible threat scenarios that can be drawn from limited and often fragmentary information. As a result, analysts can no longer dismiss a threat as incredible because they cannot corroborate it. They cannot dismiss what may appear to be the rantings of a walk-in until additional vetting shows those stories to be fabricated.

(U) To compensate for the fragmentary nature of the reporting on Iraq's potential links to al-Qaida, Intelligence Community (IC) analysts included as much detail as they could about the nature of the sources and went to great lengths to describe their analytic approach to the problem. For example, where information was limited to a single or untested source or to a foreign government service, a source description was provided. As discussed in more detail in the body of this report, a "Scope Note" was incorporated in each product to describe the analytic approach the drafters had taken to address the issue. In *Iraq and al-Qaida: Interpreting a Murky Relationship,* the Scope Note explained that the authors had purposefully taken an aggressive approach to interpreting the available data. In both the September 2002 and January 2003 versions of *Iraqi Support for Terrorism,* the Scope Note did not describe an analytic approach, but rather it highlighted the gaps in information and described the analysts' understanding of the Iraq–al-Qaida relationship as "evolving."

(U) Though the Committee understands the need for different analytical approaches and expressions of competing viewpoints, the IC should have considered that their readership would not necessarily understand the nuance between the first "purposely aggressive" approach and a return, in *Iraqi Support for Terrorism,* to a more traditional analysis of the reporting concerning Iraq's links to al-Qaida. A consistent approach in both assessments which carefully explained the intelligence reports and then provided a spectrum of possible conclusions would have been more useful and would have assisted policymakers in their public characterizations of the intelligence.

(U) **Conclusion 9. Source protection policies within the Intelligence Community direct or encourage reports officers to exclude relevant detail about the nature of**

their sources. As a result, analysts community-wide are unable to make fully in-formed judgments about the information they receive, relying instead on nonspecific source lines to reach their assessments. Moreover, relevant operational data is nearly always withheld from analysts, putting them at a further analytical disadvantage.

(U) A significant portion of the intelligence reporting that was used to evaluate whether Iraq's interactions with al-Qaida operatives constituted a relationship was stripped of details prior to being made available to analysts community-wide. Source information and operational detail was provided only to Central Intelligence Agency (CIA) analysts. This lack of information sharing limited the level of discussion and debate that should have taken place across the Community on this critical issue. While in the case of Iraq's links to terrorism, the final analysis has proven, thus far, to have been accurate and not affected by a lack of relevant source or operational detail, we cannot rely on this system in the future. Until changes are made concerning how and when source information is made available to analysts, we run the risk of missing critical data that might provide early warning.

(U) The absence of source and operational detail affects not only analysts, but policymakers as well. The Committee found that policymakers took an active role by personally examining individual intelligence reports for themselves. If this trend continues, it is even more important that such relevant detail be provided.

([still-classified]) **Conclusion 10. The Intelligence Community relies too heavily on foreign government services and third party reporting, thereby increasing the potential for manipulation of U.S. policy by foreign interests.**

([still-classified]) Due to the lack of unilateral sources on Iraq's links to terrorist groups like al-Qaida [still-classified section here], the Intelligence Community (IC) relied too heavily on foreign government service reporting and sources to whom it did not have direct access to determine the relationship between Iraq and [still-classified] terrorist groups. While much of this reporting was credible, the IC left itself open to possible manipulation by foreign governments and other parties interested in influencing U.S. policy. The Intelligence Community's collectors must develop and recruit unilateral sources with direct access to terrorist groups to confirm, complement or confront foreign government service reporting on these critical targets.

(U) **Conclusion 11. Several of the allegations of pressure on Intelligence Community (IC) analysts involved repeated questioning. The Committee believes that IC analysts should expect difficult and repeated questions regarding threat information. Just as the post 9/11 environment lowered the Intelligence Community's reporting threshold, it has also affected the intensity with which policymakers will review and question threat information.**

(U) A number of the individuals interviewed by the Committee in conducting its review stated that Administration officials questioned analysts repeatedly on the potential for cooperation between Saddam Hussein's regime and al-Qaida. Though these allegations appeared repeatedly in the press and in other public reporting on the lead-up to the war, no analyst questioned by the Committee stated that the questions were unreasonable, or that they were encouraged by the questioning to alter their conclusions regarding Iraq's links to al-Qaida.

(U) In some cases, those interviewed stated that the questions had forced them to go back and review the intelligence reporting, and that during this exercise they came across information they had overlooked in initial readings. The Committee found that this process—the policymakers probing questions—actually improved the Central Intelligence

Agency's (CIA) products. The review revealed that the CIA analysts who prepared *Iraqi Support for Terrorism* made careful, measured assessments which did not overstate or mischaracterize the intelligence reporting upon which it was based.

(U) The Committee also found that CIA analysts are trained to expect questions from policymakers, and to tailor their analysis into a product that is useful to them. In an Occasional Paper on improving CIA analytic performance, written by a Research Fellow at the Sherman Kent Center, the fellow states:

> If the mission of intelligence analysis is to inform policymaking—to help the U.S. government anticipate threats and seize opportunities—then customization of analysis is the essence of the professional practice, not a defilement of it (i.e., politicization). **In effect there is no such thing as an unprofessional policymaker question for intelligence to address so long as the answer reflects professional analytic trade craft (e.g., tough-minded weighing of evidence and open-minded consideration of alternatives).** (Emphasis added)

(U) The same Research Fellow commented on strategic warning stating, "Key to the warning challenge is that the substantive uncertainty surrounding threats to U.S. interests requires analysts, and policymakers, to make judgments that are inherently vulnerable to error." This vulnerability has never been so apparent as in the failure to detect and deter the attacks on September 11, 2001. While analysts cannot dismiss a threat because at first glance it seems unreasonable or it cannot be corroborated by other credible reporting, policymakers have the ultimate responsibility for making decisions based on this same fragmentary, inconclusive reporting. If policymakers did not respond to analysts' caveated judgments with pointed, probing questions, and did not require them to produce the most complete assessments possible, they would not be doing their jobs.

GLOSSARY

ACCM	Alternative or Compensatory Control Measure
AFIO	Association of Former Intelligence Officers
AG	Attorney General
Aman	Agaf ha-Modi'in (Israeli military intelligence)
ANC	African National Congress
BDA	Battle Damage Assessment
BfV	Bundesamt für Verfassungsschutz (German equivalent of the FBI)
BMD	Ballistic Missile Defense
BND	Bundesnachrichtendienst (German foreign intelligence service)
BSO	Black September Organization
BW	Biological Weapons
CA	Covert Action
CAS	Covert Action Staff (CIA)
CBW	Chemical/Biological Warfare
CCP	Consolidated Cryptographic Program
CDA	Congressionally Directed Action
CE	Counterespionage
CHAOS	Code name for CIA illegal domestic spying
CI	Counterintelligence
CIA	Central Intelligence Agency
CIFA	Counterintelligence Field Activity
CIG	Central Intelligence Group
CMS	Community Management Staff
CNC	Crime and Narcotics Center (CIA)

COINTELPRO	FBI Counterintelligence Program
COMINT	Communications Intelligence
Corona	Codename for first U.S. spy satellite system
COS	Chief of Station (CIA)
COSPO	Community Open Source Program Office
CPA	Covert Political Action
CPSU	Communist Party of the Soviet Union
CSI	Committee on Intelligence Services (Britain)
CT	Counterterrorism
CTC	Counterterrorism Center (CIA)
CW	Chemical Weapons
D & D	Denial and Deception
DARP	Defense Airborne Reconnaissance Program
DAS	Deputy Assistant Secretary
DBA	Dominant Battlefield Awareness
DC	Deputies Committee (NSC)
DCD	Domestic Contact Division (CIA)
DCI	Director of Central Intelligence
D/CIA	Director of Central Intelligence Agency
DDA	Deputy Director of Administration (CIA)
DDCI	Deputy Director for Central Intelligence (DDCI)
DD/CIA	Deputy Director, Central Intelligence Agency
DDO	Deputy Director for Operations (CIA)
DDP	Deputy Director for Plans (CIA)
DDS&T	Deputy Director for Science and Technology (CIA)
DEA	Drug Enforcement Administration
DGSE	Directorie Génerale de la Sécurité Extérieure (French intelligence service)
DHS	Department of Homeland Security
DI	Directorate of Intelligence (CIA)
DIA	Defense Intelligence Agency
DIA/Humint	Defense Humint Service
DINSUM	*Defense Intelligence Summary*
DNI	Director of National Intelligence
DO	Directorate of Operations
DoD	Department of Defense
DOD	Domestic Operations Division (CIA)
DOE	Department of Energy
DOJ	Department of Justice
DOT	Department of Treasury
DOS	Department of State
DP	Directorate of Plans (CIA)
DST	Directoire de Surveillance Territoire (France)
ECHR	European Convention of Human Rights

ELINT	Electronic Intelligence
ENIGMA	Code machine used by the Germans during World War II
EO	Executive Order
EOP	Executive Office of the President
ETF	Environmental Task Force (CIA)
FARC	Fuerzas Armadas Revolucionarias in Colombia
FBI	Federal Bureau of Investigation
FBIS	Foreign Broadcast Information Service
FISA	Foreign Intelligence Surveillance Act (1978)
FNLA	National Front for the Liberation of Angola
FOIA	Freedom of Information Act
FRD	Foreign Resources Division (CIA)
FSB	Federal'naya Sluzba Besnopasnoti (Federal Security Service, Russia)
GAO	General Accountability Office (Congress)
GCHQ	Government Communications Headquarters (the British NSA)
GEO	Geosynchronous Orbit
GEOINT	Geospatial Intelligence
GRU	Soviet Military Intelligence
GSG	German Counterterrorism Service
HEO	High Elliptical Orbit
HPSCI	House Permanent Select Committee on Intelligence
HUAC	House Un-American Activities Committee
HUMINT	Human Intelligence (assets)
I & W	Indicators and Warning
IAEA	International Atomic Energy Agency
IAF	Israel Air Force
IC	Intelligence Community
ICS	Intelligence Community Staff
IDF	Israeli Defense Force
IG	Inspector General
IMINT	Imagery Intelligence (photographs)
INR	Bureau of Intelligence and Research (Department of State)
INTELINK	An intelligence community computer information system
INTs	Collection disciplines (IMINT, SIGINT, OSINT, HUMINT, MASINT)
IOB	Intelligence Oversight Board (White House)
ISA	Israeli Security Agency
ISC	Intelligence and Security Committee (U.K.)
ISI	Inter-Services Intelligence (Pakistani intelligence agency)
IT	Information Technology
JCAE	Joint Committee on Atomic Energy
JCS	Joint Chiefs of Staff
JIC	Joint Intelligence Committee (U.K.)

JSOC	Joint Special Operations Command
JSTARS	Joint Surveillance Target Attack Radar Systems
KGB	Soviet Secret Police
KH	Keyhole (satellite)
LTTE	Tamil Tigers of Tamil Elam
MAGIC	Allied code-breaking operations against the Japanese in the World War II
MASINT	Measurement and Signatures Intelligence
MI5	Security Service (U.K.)
MI6	Secret Intelligence Service (U.K.)
MON	Memoranda of Notification
MONGOOSE	Code name for CIA covert actions against Fidel Castro of Cuba (1961–62)
Mossad	Israeli Intelligence Service
MPLA	Popular Movement for the Liberation of Angola
NAACP	National Association for the Advancement of Colored People
NBC	Nuclear, Biological, and Chemical (Weapons)
NCS	National Clandestine Service
NCIC	National Counterintelligence Center
NCTC	National Counterterrorism Center
NED	National Endowment for Democracy
NFIB	National Foreign Intelligence Board
NFIC	National Foreign Intelligence Council
NFIP	National Foreign Intelligence Program
NGA	National Geospatial-Intelligence Agency
NGO	Nongovernmental organization
NIA	National Intelligence Authority
NIC	National Intelligence Council
NID	*National Intelligence Daily*
NIE	National Intelligence Estimate
NIO	National Intelligence Officer
NOC	Nonofficial Cover
NPIC	National Photographic Interpretation Center
NRO	National Reconnaissance Office
NSA	National Security Agency
NSC	National Security Council (White House)
NSCID	National Security Council Intelligence Directive
NTM	National Technical Means
OB	Order of Battle
OC	Official Cover
ODNI	Office of the Director of National Intelligence
OMB	Office of Management and Budget
ONI	Office of Naval Intelligence

OPC	Office of Policy Coordination
OSD	Office of the Secretary of Defense
OSINT	Open-Source Intelligence
OSS	Office of Strategic Services
P & E	Processing and Exploitation
PDB	*President's Daily Brief*
PFIAB	President's Foreign Intelligence Advisory Board (White House)
PFLP	Popular Front for the Liberation of Palestine
PIJ	Palestinian Islamic Jihad
PLO	Palestine Liberation Organization
PM	Paramilitary
PRO	Public Record Office (U.K.)
RADINT	Radar Intelligence
RFE	Radio Free Europe
RL	Radio Liberty
SA	Special Activities Division (DO/CIA)
SAS	Special Air Service (U.K.)
SBS	Special Boat Service (U.K.)
SDO	Support to Diplomatic Operations
SHAMROCK	Code name for illegal NSA interception of cables
SIG	Senior Interagency Group
SIGINT	Signals Intelligence
SIS	Secret Intelligence Service (U.K., also known as MI6)
SISDE	Italian Intelligence Service
SMO	Support to Military Operations
SMS	Secretary's *Morning Summary* (Department of State)
SNIE	Special National Intelligence Estimate
SO	Special Operations (CIA)
SOCOM	Special Operations Command (Department of Defense)
SOE	Special Operations Executive (U.K.)
SOG	Special Operations Group (DO/CIA)
SOVA	Office of Soviet Analysis (CIA)
SSCI	Senate Select Committee on Intelligence
SVR	Russian Foreign Intelligence Service
TECHINT	Technical Intelligence
TELINT	Telemetery Intelligence
TIARA	Tactical Intelligence and Related Activities
TPED	Tasking, Processing, Exploitation, and Dissemination
UAV	Unmanned Aerial Vehicle (drone)
ULTRA	Code name for the Allied operation that deciphered the German ENIGMA code in World War II
UN	United Nations
UNITA	National Union for the Total Independence of Angola

UNSCOM	United Nations Special Commission
USIB	United States Intelligence Board
USTR	United States Trade Representative
VCI	Viet Cong Infrastructure
VENONA	Code name for SIGINT intercepts against Soviet spying in America
VOA	Voice of America
VX	A deadly nerve agent used in chemical weapons
WMD	Weapons of mass destruction

INDEX

ABOUT THE EDITOR AND CONTRIBUTORS

EDITOR

Loch K. Johnson is Regents Professor of Public and International Affairs at the University of Georgia and author of several books and over 100 articles on U.S. intelligence and national security. His books include *The Making of International Agreements* (1984); *A Season of Inquiry* (1985); *Through the Straits of Armageddon* (1987, coedited with Paul Diehl); *Decisions of the Highest Order* (1988, coedited with Karl F. Inderfurth); *America's Secret Power* (1989); *Runoff Elections in the United States* (1993, coauthored with Charles S. Bullock III); *America as a World Power* (1995); *Secret Agencies* (1996); *Bombs, Bugs, Drugs, and Thugs* (2000); *Fateful Decisions* (2004, coedited with Karl F. Inderfurth); *Strategic Intelligence* (2004, coedited with James J. Wirtz); *Who's Watching the Spies?* (2005, coauthored with Hans Born and Ian Leigh); *American Foreign Policy* (2005, coauthored with Daniel Papp and John Endicott); and *Seven Sins of American Foreign* Policy (2007). He has served as special assistant to the chair of the Senate Select Committee on Intelligence (1975–76), staff director of the House Subcommittee on Intelligence Oversight (1977–79), and special assistant to the chair of the Aspin-Brown Commission on Intelligence (1995–96). In 1969–70, he was an American Political Science Association Congressional Fellow. He has served as secretary of the American Political Science Association and President of the International Studies Association, South. Born in New Zealand and educated at the University of California, Johnson has taught at the University of Georgia since 1979, winning its Meigs Professorship for meritorious teaching and its Owens Award for outstanding accomplishments in the field of social science research. In 2000, he led the founding of the School of Public and

International Affairs at the University of Georgia. He is the senior editor of the international journal *Intelligence and National Security*.

CONTRIBUTORS

Matthew M. Aid is Managing Director in the Washington, DC, office of Citigate Global Intelligence and Security and coeditor of *Secrets of Signals Intelligence During the Cold War and Beyond* (2001).

James E. Baker sits on the U.S. Court of Appeals for the Armed Forces. He previously served as Special Assistant to the President and Legal Adviser to the National Security Council and as Deputy Legal Adviser to the NSC. He has also served as Counsel to the President's Foreign Intelligence Advisory Board, an attorney at the Department of State, a legislative aide to Senator Daniel Patrick Moynihan, and as a Marine Corps infantry officer. He is the coauthor with Michael Reisman of *Regulating Covert Action* (Yale University Press, 1992).

David M. Barrett is Associate Professor of Political Science at Villanova University and author of *Congress and the CIA* (Kansas, 2005).

Hans Born is a senior fellow in democratic governance of the security sector at the Geneva Centre for Democratic Control of the Armed Forces (DCAF). He is an external member of the crisis management and security policy faculty of the Federal Institute of Technology and a guest lecturer on governing nuclear weapons at the UN Disarmament Fellowship Programme. He has written, co-authored, and co-edited various books on international relations and security policy, including the Inter-Parliamentary Union Handbook on *Parliamentary Oversight of the Security Sector: Principles, Mechanisms and Practices* (Geneva: IPU/DCAF, 2003, translated in 30 languages); *Making Intelligence Accountable: Legal Standards and Best Practice for Oversight of Intelligence Agencies* (Oslo: Publishing House of the Parliament of Norway, 2005, translated in 10 languages); *Who is Watching the Spies? Establishing Intelligence Agency Accountability* (Dulles, VA: Potomac Publishers, 2005); *Civil-Military Relations in Europe: Learning from Crisis and Institutional Change* (London: Routledge, 2006); and *The Double Democratic Deficit: Parliamentary Accountability and the Use of Force under International Auspices* (London: Ashgate Publishers: Aldershot).

A. Denis Clift is President of the Department of Defense Joint Military Intelligence College. He was born in New York City and educated at Friends Seminary, Phillips Exeter Academy (1954), Stanford University (B.A., 1958), and the London School of Economics and Political Science (M.Sc., 1967). He began a career of public service as a naval officer in the Eisenhower and Kennedy administrations and has served in military and civilian capacities in ten administrations, including thirteen successive years in the Executive Office of the President and the White House. From 1971–76, he served on the National Security

Council staff. From 1974–76, he was head of President Ford's National Security Council staff for the Soviet Union and Eastern and Western Europe. From 1977–81, he was Assistant for National Security Affairs to the Vice President. From 1991–94, he was Chief of Staff, Defense Intelligence Agency. From 1963–66, he was the editor of the U.S. Naval Institute *Proceedings*. His published fiction and nonfiction include the novel *A Death in Geneva* (Ballantine Books, Random House), *Our World in Antarctica* (Rand McNally), *With Presidents to the Summit* (George Mason University Press), and *Clift Notes: Intelligence and the Nation's Security* (JMIC Writing Center Press).

William J. Daugherty holds a doctorate in government from the Claremont Graduate School and is Associate Professor of government at Armstrong Atlantic State University in Savannah, Georgia. A retired senior officer in the CIA, he is also the author of *In the Shadow of the Ayatollah: A CIA Hostage in Iran* (Annapolis, 2001) and *Executive Secrets: Covert Action and the Presidency* (Kentucky, 2004).

Jack Davis served in the CIA from 1956 to 1990 as analyst, manager, and teacher of analysts. He now is an independent contractor with the Agency, specializing in analytic methodology. He is a frequent contributor to the journal *Studies in Intelligence*.

Stuart Farson is Lecturer, Political Science Department, Simon Fraser University, Vancouver/Surrey, Canada. He is a former Secretary-Treasurer of the Canadian Association for Security and Intelligence Studies, and served as Director of Research for the Special Committee of the House Commons (Canada) on the Review of the Canadian Security Intelligence Service Act and the Security Offences Act. He has numerous articles on security, intelligence, and policing issues and is the coeditor of *Security and Intelligence in a Changing World* (with David Stafford and Wesley K. Wark, Cass, 1991).

Timothy Gibbs is a final-year doctoral student in history at Robinson College, Cambridge University, and a member of the Cambridge University Intelligence Seminar. He is also a former Visiting Scholar at the University of Georgia. His doctoral dissertation, titled *British and American Intelligence and the Atom Spies*, was submitted in the summer of 2006 and was supervised by Professor Christopher Andrew.

Peter Gill is Reader in Politics and Security, Liverpool John Moores University, Liverpool, United Kingdom. He is coauthor of *Introduction to Politics* (1988, 2nd ed.) and *Intelligence in an Insecure World* (2006). He is currently researching the control and oversight of domestic security in intelligence agencies.

Harold M. Greenberg graduated with a B.A. in history from Yale University in 2005. At Yale, he participated in the Studies in Grand Strategy program, and he has recently published research on CIA covert action in the 1950s. He now works as a legislative aide in the U.S. House of Representatives.

Daniel S. Gressang IV is Professor at the Joint Military Intelligence College (JMIC) in Washington, DC, and serves concurrently as the National Security Agency/National Cryptologic School of Liaison to JMIC. He has researched, written, and lectured extensively on terrorism and counterinsurgency. His research focuses primarily on the application of complex adaptive systems perspectives to understanding the dynamics of terror and other forms of unconventional warfare. In 2004, he was designated Intelligence Community Officer by the Director of Central Intelligence.

Glenn Hastedt received his doctorate in political science from Indiana University. Until recently he was Professor and Chair of the Political Science Department at James Madison University. He is now chair of the Justice Studies Department there. Among his publications is *American Foreign Policy: Past, Present, Future*, 6th ed. (Prentice Hall).

John Hollister Hedley, during more than thirty years at CIA, edited the *President's Daily Brief*, briefed the *PDB* at the White House, served as Managing Editor of the *National Intelligence Daily*, and was Chairman of the CIA's Publications Review Board. Now retired, Hedley has taught intelligence at Georgetown University and serves as a consultant to the National Intelligence Council and the Center for the Study of Intelligence.

Michael Herman served from 1952 to 1987 in Britain's Government Communications Headquarters, with secondments to the Cabinet Office and the Ministry of Defence. Since retirement he has written extensively on intelligence matters, with official clearance. He has had academic affiliations with Nuffield and St. Antony's Colleges in Oxford and is Founder Director of the Oxford Intelligence Group and Honorary Departmental Fellow at Aberystwyth University. In 2005 he received the degree of Honorary D.Litt from Nottingham University. He is a leading British intelligence scholar and author of *Intelligence Power in Peace and War* (Cambridge, 2001).

Frederick P. Hitz is Lecturer (Diplomat in Residence) in Public and International Affairs, Woodrow Wilson School, Princeton University.

Max M. Holland is the author of *The Kennedy Assassination Tapes* (Knopf, 2004).

Arthur S. Hulnick is Associate Professor of International Relations at Boston University. He is a veteran of thirty-five years of intelligence service, including seven years in Air Force Intelligence and twenty-eight years in the CIA. He is author of *Fixing the Spy Machine* (Praeger, 1999) and *Keeping Us Safe* (Praeger, 2004).

Rhodri Jeffreys-Jones is Professor of American History at the University of Edinburgh. The author of several books on intelligence history, he is currently completing a study of the FBI.

Ephraim Kahana is Professor of Political Science and faculty member in the Western Galilee College, Acre, Israel. He teaches courses on international relations, national security and intelligence, and foreign policy in the National Security Program in the University of Haifa. Kahana has written numerous papers on intelligence and foreign policy. His most recent book is the *Historical Dictionary of Israeli Intelligence* (2006).

Patrick Radden Keefe is a graduate of the School of Law at Yale University and is presently a Fellow with the Century Foundation in New York City. He is the author of *Chatter: Uncovering the Echelon Surveillance Network and the Secret World of Global Eavesdropping* (Random House, 2006), and has published essays in *The New York Review of Books*, *The New York Times Magazine*, the *New York Times*, the *Boston Globe*, the *Yale Journal of International Law*, *Legal Affairs*, *Slate*, and *Wired*. He has been a Marshall Scholar and a 2003 fellow at the Dorothy and Lewis B. Cullman Center for Scholars and Writers at the New York Public Library.

Jennifer D. Kibbe is Assistant Professor of Government at Franklin and Marshall College. Between 2002 and 2004, she was a postdoctoral fellow at the Brookings Institution. Her research interests include U.S. foreign policy, intelligence and covert action, presidential decision making, and political psychology. She has published work on U.S. policy in Iraq and the Middle East, and the military's involvement in covert actions.

Katharina von Knop is a doctoral candidate in Political Science at Leopold-Franzens University in Innsbruck, Austria, specializing in counter- and antiterrorism, and coeditor with Heinrich Neisser and Martin van Creveld of *Countering Modern Terrorism: History, Current Issues, and Future Threats* (2005).

Lawrence J. Lamanna is a doctoral candidate in the School of Public and International Affairs at the University of Georgia. He holds an M.A. from Yale University and a B.A. from the University of Notre Dame.

Ian Leigh is Professor of Law and Codirector of the Human Rights Centre at the University of Durham. He lives in Durham, England.

Kristin M. Lord is Associate Dean at George Washington University's Elliott School of International Affairs. In 2005–2006, she was a Council on Foreign Relations International Affairs Fellow and Special Adviser to the Under Secretary of State for Democracy and Global Affairs. Lord is the author of *The Perils and Promise of Global Transparency: Why the Information Revolution May Not Lead to Security Democracy or Peace* (SUNY Press, 2006); coeditor, with Bernard I. Finel, of *Power and Conflict in the Age of Transparency* (Palgrave Macmillan, 2000); and the author of numerous book chapters, articles, and papers on international politics and security. Lord received her doctorate in government from Georgetown University.

Minh A. Luong is Assistant Director of International Security Studies at Yale University, where he teaches in the Department of History. He also serves as adjunct Assistant Professor of Public Policy at the Taubman Center at Brown University.

Cynthia M. Nolan earned a doctorate at American University in the School of International Service, researching intelligence oversight. She is a former officer in the Directorate of Operations in the CIA and has published in the *International Journal of Intelligence and Counterintelligence*.

Kevin A. O'Brien is a former research associate with the Canadian Institute of Strategic Studies and is currently a senior analyst for RAND Europe.

Mark Phythian is Professor of International Security and Director of the History and Governance Research Institute at the University of Wolverhampton, United Kingdom. He is the author of *Intelligence in an Insecure World* (2006, with Peter Gill), *The Politics of British Arms Sales Since 1964* (2000), and *Arming Iraq* (1997), as well as numerous journal articles on intelligence and security issues.

Harry Howe Ransom is Professor Emeritus of Political Science at Vanderbilt University. He has a B.A. from Vanderbilt and an M.A. and Ph.D. from Princeton University. He was a Congressional Fellow of the American Political Science Association and a Fellow of the Woodrow Wilson International Center for Scholars. He taught at Princeton, Vassar College, Michigan State University, Harvard University, and the University of Leeds. His books include *Central Intelligence and National Security* (1958), *Can American Democracy Survive Cold War?* (1963), and *The Intelligence Establishment* (1970).

Jeffrey T. Richelson is Senior Fellow with the National Security Archive in Washington, DC, and author of *The Wizards of Langley*, *The U.S. Intelligence Community*, *A Century of Spies*, and *America's Eyes in Space*, as well as numerous articles on intelligence activities. He received his doctorate in political science from the University of Rochester and has taught at the University of Texas, Austin, and the American University, Washington, DC. He lives in Los Angeles.

Jerel A. Rosati is Professor of Political Science and International Studies at the University of South Carolina since 1982. His area of specialization is the theory and practice of foreign policy, focusing on the U.S. policy-making process, decision-making theory, and the political psychological study of human cognition. He is the author and editor of five books and over forty articles and chapters. He has received numerous outstanding teaching awards. He has been Visiting Professor at Somalia National University in Mogadishu and Visiting Scholar at China's Foreign Affairs College in Beijing. He also has been a Research Associate in the Foreign Affairs and National Defense Division of the Library of Congress's Congressional Research Service, President of the International

Studies Association's Foreign Policy Analysis Section, and President of the Southern region of the International Studies Association.

Richard L. Russell is Professor of national security studies at the National Defense University. He is also an adjunct associate professor in the Security Studies Program and research associate in the Institute for the Study of Diplomacy at Georgetown University. He previously served as a CIA political-military analyst. Russell is the author of *Weapons Proliferation and War in the Greater Middle East: Strategic Contest* (2005).

Frederick A. O. Schwarz Jr. received an A.B. from Harvard University and J.D. from Harvard Law School, where he was an editor of the *Law Review*. After a year's clerkship with Hon. J. Edward Lumbard, U.S. Court of Appeals for the Second Circuit, he worked one year for the Nigerian government as Assistant Commissioner for Law Revision under a Ford Foundation grant. He joined the New York City law firm of Cravath, Swaine and Moore in 1963 and was elected a partner in 1969. From 1975 through mid-1976, he served as Chief Counsel to the Senate Select Committee to Study Government Operations with Respect to Intelligence Activities (the Church Committee); from 1982–89, he served as Corporation Counsel and head of the Law Department of the City of New York. In 1989, he chaired the New York City Charter Revision Commission.

James M. Scott is Professor and Chair of the Department of Political Science at Oklahoma State University. His areas of specialization include foreign policy analysis and international relations, with particular emphasis on U.S. foreign policy making and the domestic sources of foreign policy. He is author or editor of four books, over forty articles, book chapters, review essays, and other publications. He has been President of the Foreign Policy Analysis section and President of the Midwest region of the International Studies Association, where he has also served as conference organizer for both sections and has been a two-time winner of the Klingberg Award for Outstanding Faculty Paper at the ISA Midwest Annual Meeting. Since 1996, he has received over two dozen awards from students and peers for his outstanding teaching and research, including his institution's highest awards for scholarship in 2000 and 2001. Since 2005, he has been Director of the Democracy and World Politics Summer Research Program, a National Science Foundation Research Experience for Undergraduates.

Len Scott is Professor of International Politics at the University of Wales, Aberystwyth, where he is Director of the Centre for Intelligence and International Security Studies. Among his recent publications are *Understanding Intelligence in the Twenty-First Century: Journeys in Shadows* (2004, coedited with Peter Jackson) and *Planning Armageddon: Britain, the United States and the Command of Nuclear Forces, 1943–1964* (2000, coedited with Stephen Twigge).

Katherine A. S. Sibley is Professor and Chair of the History Department at St. Joseph's University. She is currently working on a biography of Florence Kling

Harding, titled *America's First Feminist First Lady*. Sibley's work will revise the typical portrait of Mrs. Harding as manipulative, unhappy wife, casting new light on her public and private life. In 2004, Sibley published *Red Spies in America: Stolen Secrets and the Dawn of the Cold War* with the University Press of Kansas. She is also the author of *The Cold War* (1998) and *Loans and Legitimacy: The Evolution of Soviet-American Relations, 1919–1933* (1996). Her work has appeared in journals including *American Communist History*, *Peace and Change*, and *Diplomatic History*, and she also serves as book review editor for *Intelligence and National Security*. She is a three-term Commonwealth Speaker for the Pennsylvania Humanities Council.

Jennifer Sims is Director of Intelligence Studies and Visiting Professor in the Security Studies Program at Georgetown University's Edmund A. Walsh School of Foreign Service. She also consults for the U.S. government and private sector on homeland security and intelligence related matters. Prior to this, Sims was Research Professor at Johns Hopkins University's Nitze School of Advanced International Studies in Washington, DC (Fall 2001–Summer 2003). She has served as defense and foreign policy adviser to Senator John Danforth (1990–94), a professional staff member of the Senate Select Committee on Intelligence (1991–94), Deputy Assistant Secretary of State for Intelligence Coordination (1994–98), and as the Department of State's first Coordinator for Intelligence Resources and Planning in the office of the Under Secretary for Management. In 1998 Sims was awarded the U.S. Intelligence Community's Distinguished Service Medal. She received her B.A. degree from Oberlin College and her M.A. and Ph.D. in national security studies from Johns Hopkins University in 1978 and 1985, respectively. She is the author of a number of books and articles on intelligence and arms control. The most recent of these include "Foreign Intelligence Liaison: Devils, Deals and Details," *International Journal of Intelligence and Counterintelligence Affairs* (Summer 2006); *Transforming US Intelligence,* coedited with Burton Gerber (Georgetown University Press, 2005); "Transforming U.S. Espionage: A Contrarian's Approach," *Georgetown Journal of International Affairs* (Winter/Spring 2005); "Domestic Factors in Arms Control: The U.S. Case," in Jeffrey A Larson (ed.), *Arms Control: Cooperative Security in a Changing Environment* (Lynne Rienner, 2002); "What Is Intelligence? Information for Decision-Makers," in Roy Godson, Ernest R. May, and Gary Schmitt, *U.S. Intelligence at the Crossroads* (Brassey's, 1995); "The Cambridge Approach Reconsidered," *Daedalus* 120 (Winter 1991); and *Icarus Restrained: An Intellectual History of American Arms Control* (Westview Press, 1990).

Robert David Steele is CEO of OSS.Net, an international open source intelligence provider. As the son of an oilman, a Marine Corps infantry officer, and a clandestine intelligence case officer for the CIA, he has spent over twenty years abroad in Asia and Central and South America. As a civilian intelligence officer he spent three back-to-back tours overseas, including one tour as one of the first officers assigned full-time to terrorism, and three headquarters tours in offensive counterintelligence, advanced information technology, and satellite program management. He resigned from the CIA in 1988 to be the senior civilian founder of the Marine Corps Intelligence Command. He resigned from the Marines in 1993. He is the author of three works on intelligence, as well as the editor of a book on peacekeeping intelligence. He has earned graduate degrees in international relations and public administration, is a graduate of the Naval War College, and has a certificate in Intelligence Policy. He is also a graduate of the Marine Corps Command and Staff Course and of the CIA's Mid-Career Course 101.

John D. Stempel is Senior Professor of International Relations at the University of Kentucky's Patterson School of Diplomacy and International Commerce, where he was Associate Director (1988–93) and Director (1993–2003). He came to the University of Kentucky following a 24-year career in the U.S. Foreign Service. There he focused on political and economic affairs, with overseas assignments in Africa (Guinea, Burundi, Zambia), Iran, and India, concluding with three years as U.S. Consul General in Madras. His Middle East service (1975–79) in Tehran provided the material for his book *Inside the Iranian Revolution*. His subsequent academic writings have focused on religion and diplomacy, intelligence and diplomacy, and American views of negotiation. His Washington assignments featured duty for both the State and Defense Departments, including a two-year tour as Director of the State Department's Crisis Center. He has taught at George Washington and American Universities, plus two years as Diplomat in Residence at the U.S. Naval Academy, Annapolis. Stemple is a member of the New York Council on Foreign Relations and is listed in *Who's Who in the World* and *Who's Who in America*. He holds an A.B. degree from Princeton University and M.A. and Ph.D. degrees from the University of California at Berkeley.

Stan A. Taylor is an Emeritus Professor of Political Science at Brigham Young University in Provo, Utah. He has taught in England, Wales, and New Zealand and in 2006 was a visiting professor at the University of Otago in Dunedin, New Zealand. He is founder of the David M. Kennedy Center for International Studies at Brigham Young University. He writes frequently on intelligence, national security, and U.S. foreign policy.

Athan Theoharis is Professor of History at Marquette University whose research has focused on government secrecy, Cold War politics, and the history of the FBI. He is the author, coauthor, and editor of eighteen books, including *The FBI and American Democracy* (2004), *Chasing Spies* (2002), *A Culture of Secrecy* (1998), and *The FBI: A Comprehensive Reference Guide* (1998). He has received numerous awards, including the American Bar Association's Gavel Award and selection as a fellow by the Wisconsin Academy of Arts, Sciences, and Letters.

Gregory F. Treverton is senior analyst at the RAND Corporation. Earlier, he directed RAND's Intelligence Policy Center and its International Security and Defense Policy Center, and he is Associate Dean of the Pardee RAND Graduate School. His recent work has examined at terrorism, intelligence, and law enforcement, with a special interest in new forms of public-private partnership. He has served in government for the first Senate Select Committee on Intelligence, handling Europe for the National Security Council, and most recently as vice chair of the National Intelligence Council, overseeing the writing of America's National Intelligence Estimates. He holds an A.B. *summa cum laude* from Princeton University, a master's in public policy, and Ph.D. in economics and politics from Harvard University. His latest books are *Reshaping National Intelligence for an Age of Information* (Cambridge University Press, 2001), and *New Challenges, New Tools for Defense Decisionmaking* (edited, RAND, 2003).

Michael A. Turner is a political scientist who has taught international relations and national security matters in San Diego, California, for the past twelve years. Before that, he spent over fifteen years in various positions within the CIA. Turner is the author of *Why Secret Intelligence Fails* (2005; 2006) and the *Historical Dictionary of United States Intelligence* (2006).

Michael Warner serves as Historian for the Office of the Director of National Intelligence.

Nigel West is a military historian specializing in security and intelligence topics. He is the European editor of the *World Intelligence Review* and is on the faculty at the Center for Counterintelligence and Security Studies in Washington, DC. He is the author of more than two dozen works of nonfiction and recently edited *Guy Liddell Diaries*.

Reg Whitaker is Distinguished Research Professor Emeritus, York University, and Adjunct Professor of Political Science, University of Victoria, Canada. He has written extensively on Canadian and international security and intelligence issues.

James J. Wirtz is Professor in the Department of National Security Affairs at the Naval Postgraduate School, Monterey, California. He is Section Chair of the Intelligence Studies Section of the International Studies Association and President of the International Security and Arms Control Section of the American Political Science Association. Wirtz is the series editor for *Initiatives in Strategic Studies: Issues and Policies*, published by Palgrave Macmillan.

Amy B. Zegart is Associate Professor of Public Policy at the University of California, Los Angeles. A specialist on national and homeland security, she has served on the National Security Council staff, as a foreign policy advisor to the Bush-Cheney 2000 presidential campaign, and as a consultant to California state and local homeland security agencies. She has published articles in leading academic journals, including *International Security* and *Political Science Quarterly*, and is the author of *Flawed by Design: The Origins of the CIA, JCS, and NSC* (Stanford, 1999). She received her Ph.D. in political science from Stanford, where she studied under Condoleezza Rice, and an A.B. in East Asian Studies from Harvard University.